Peasant Intellectuals

Steven Feierman

PEASANT INTELLECTUALS

Anthropology and History
in Tanzania

The University of Wisconsin Press

The University of Wisconsin Press
2537 Daniels Street
Madison, Wisconsin 53718

3 Henrietta Street
London WC2E 8LU, England

8   7   6   5   4

Printed in the United States of America

Maps by The University of Wisconsin–Madison
Cartographic Laboratory

Library of Congress Cataloging-in-Publication Data
Feierman, Steven, 1940–
    Peasant intellectuals: anthropology and history in Tanzania/
Steven Feierman.
352 pp.   cm.
    Includes bibliographical references and index.
    1. Lushoto District (Tanzania) – Politics and government.
2. Peasantry – Tanzania – Lushoto District – Politics and government.
3. Shambala (African people) – Politics and government.
4. Shambala (African people) – Kings and rulers – Folklore.
5. Shambala (African people) – Rites and ceremonies.   6. Rainmaking rites – Tanzania – Lushoto District.   7. Shambala language –
Political aspects – Tanzania – Lushoto District.   I. Title.
DT450.49.L87F85   1990
967.8'22 – dc20
ISBN 0-299-12520-3   90-50086
ISBN 0-299-12524-6 (pbk.)   CIP

For Joshua and Jessica

Contents

Maps

Acknowledgments

This book grew out of an earlier manuscript, now abandoned, on concepts of sovereignty in the precolonial Shambaa kingdom. The book has been written over the past few years in time snatched from other projects and from family and friends. It relies on oral field materials collected as early as 1966 and as late as December 1988, and so a proper set of acknowledgments would recognize everyone who has been important in my life and work over the past twenty-five years. That is impossible, but some debts cannot pass unacknowledged.

I owe a profound debt to the many people who have given me their help and friendship in Shambaai. The list of people interviewed is given at the end of this book. A few special friends have helped make the mountains into my home, especially Leo Hassani, Martin Msumari, the late Hatibu Hassani, the late Shechonge Kishasha, the late Ali Shechonge, Mzee Kazushwe, and Joshua Mtunguja. Everyone in Shambaai will find something to disagree with in this book, and so I must emphasize that the opinions expressed are entirely my own.

The same disclaimer applies to my friends and colleagues in Dar es Salaam who provided a warm and supportive environment in which to work, and also an example of scholarly commitment. Fred and Theresa Kaijage have been supportive at many points, along with Geoffrey, Milembe, Stella, Mkurasi, and Karumuna. The book is a contribution to the more general history of the Pangani Valley region, a subject on which I have worked with Isaria Kimambo for many years. Kapepwa Tambila helped to provide a friendly but intellectually challenging environment in the Department of History. I am grateful to Abdul Sheriff, Ruth Besha, and Joseph Mbele for friendship and for stimulating criticism of my ideas. The late May Balisidya commented on parts of the argument and provided an example of how life should be lived.

The early research set out to answer questions put to me by Rodney Needham, the supervisor of my D.Phil. thesis and an important influence on my thought. My understanding of historical issues at that time was shaped by Terence Ranger and John Iliffe, who were then in Dar es Salaam, and whose recent works have continued to inform me. Iliffe's *A Modern History of Tanganyika* established a basic framework of knowledge which made my own job much easier.

Jean Comaroff commented critically on the entire manuscript. Sandra Barnes, Lee Cassanelli, Nancy Farriss, Steve Stern, and Florencia Mallon all commented on parts of the manuscript. Marcia Wright helped during a period of writing in New York. David Henige helped with library resources.

Philip Curtin provided help and encouragement at several points along the way. Dorothee Janetzke, Magdalena Hauner, and Mark Trewartha, all in very different ways, have been important friends during the period of writing. My students at the University of Wisconsin and at the University of Florida read and commented on parts of this manuscript and its predecessors. I owe them a debt of gratitude.

Work on this book continued alongside a number of projects that were supported by the Social Science Research Council, the Fulbright-Hays program, the National Science Foundation, the University of Wisconsin Graduate School, and the University of Florida.

This book would never have been completed without the warm support of close friends and family. My debt to Allen Isaacman can never be repaid. Barbara Hanrahan has been both a good friend and an excellent editor. Stanley and Barbara Trapido helped at an important time. I have learned from long discussions on many issues with Gerda Lerner. Jeanette Sheinman, Martin Feierman, and Joanne Feierman were always there when I needed them. My children Jessica and Joshua have been patient and understanding. They also commented on parts of the manuscript. Finally, I would like to thank Virginia Boyd, whose presence has made the process of writing far pleasanter than it would otherwise have been.

Peasant Intellectuals

Introduction

       This book is a history of peasant political discourse and of the peasant intellectuals who create and transmit it. When peasants organize political movements, or when they reflect on collective experience, they speak about how politics can be ordered to bring life rather than death, to bring prosperity rather than hunger, and to bring justice rather than inequity. The means for achieving these are defined by peasants themselves. It is peasants who draw upon a rich variety of past forms of political language; it is peasants who create new political discourse.

       The description of peasants as active cultural creators unfolds, with seeming paradox, alongside the demonstration that central terms in peasant discourse have endured for over a century. Long-term continuity and active creation are in fact compatible. Even when forms of discourse are inherited from the past, the peasant must make an active decision to say that they are meaningful at this moment, to select a particular form of disccourse as opposed to other possible forms, and to shape the inherited language anew to explain current problems.

       Historians, with increasing frequency since the 1960s, have studied long-term durations and also the coexistence of shorter and longer historical durations (Braudel 1980). Events in the short term are the sort reported in the daily newspaper: a fire, a political speech, a railway crash. Alongside these are historical regularities of longer duration. The cyclical rise and fall of prices continues for ten, or twenty, or fifty years. Other regularities continue for much longer periods. In Europe, the dominance of transport by water and ships and the location of growth points on the coastal fringes continued for centuries. The emphasis on long-term durations has been useful in directing historians' attention away from short-term fluctuations in the fortunes of political leaders and towards stable patterns of regional economy, but it can lead also to the mystification of cultural continuities — to a sense that the continuity of a cultural form is unexceptional and expected, that it is passively accepted by the people who use it. When people select a particular form of discourse, when they shape a political argument in a particular way, this is by no means a passive act. The social analysis of peasant discourse in this book will show that long-term continuities in political language are the outcome of radical social change and of struggle within peasant society.

Each stream of discourse has its own coherence, its expressive quality, and its capacity to shape experience. Discourse cannot be seen as a mere reflection of the social order or a reflection of the distribution of power. The forms of discourse survive because they are used by living peasant intellectuals. Discourse does not float independently above the play of social forces, nor is it a mere instrument of social forces.

To say that patterned discourse is continuously created is to mediate the opposition between structure and change, synchrony and diachrony, subject and object, cultural elements in a frozen relationship with one another and unpatterned social action. Each moment of new action is patterned; each bit of patterned discourse continuously undergoes transformation. This approach — seeing pattern in each new action and innovation in the repetition of ancient patterns — has by now been adopted by a generation of social theorists, the most prominent among them Anthony Giddens (1979), who writes of "ruled-governed creativity," and Pierre Bourdieu (1977) who discusses "regulated improvisations."

The overall direction of change in discourse cannot be explained as growing out of thousands of random acts of regulated improvisation. Not all regulated improvisations are created equal; not all have an equal weight in shaping the language that will be in general use in the future. To explain the direction of change it is necessary to introduce power into the equation and explore the relationship between the character of domination by ruling groups and the evolution of discourse. The purpose of studying the social position of intellectuals, as we shall see below, is to understand those individuals within peasant society who are best able to shape discourse, their position within the framework of domination, and the relationship between their position and their political language.

Within African peasant society, analyzing the links between domination and peasant culture opens up a difficult problem of the scale — the extent in space — of the things being studied. Local cultural forms (the rituals or narratives of a particular place) deserve to be given special weight, yet the framework of domination can never be understood within narrow boundaries. Most African languages are quite local in their distribution, spread over a much narrower area than a single colonial territory or a single national state. However, if we begin from the assumption that peasant discourse is local and the organization of power national, then change can be shaped in only one direction: the powerful colonial or national state shapes the fragile and helpless local culture, which at best succeeds in fighting a rear guard defensive battle. The contrasting impressions of national power and local helplessness are less the products of the data and more the consequences of an analytic framework which looks at language locally and power nationally.

Impressions of peasants as passively receiving external ideologies, or at best as reacting to external initiatives, are widely distributed in academic writings. The picture of peasant culture as inert is equally common. The corrective cannot be found in image making. We must systematically shift the angle of vision, changing the analytic approach. This is the goal of the present work, which sees peasant intellectuals at the nexus between domination and public discourse. Peasant intellectuals (defined fully at a later point in this chapter) are characterized not by their thought but by their social position, which is directive, or organizational, or educative. Peasant intellectuals, defined socially in this way, mediate the relationship between domination and discourse, between the active creation of political language and long-term continuity, and also between local society and the wider world. Making intellectuals the focus of analysis shifts the point from which peasant culture is viewed. At the present moment, however, we must apprehend the context for the discussion of peasant intellectuals. The ethnographic question at the core of this work needs to be set out; it concerns the social history of peasant discourse in northeastern Tanzania.

A Problem in Historical Ethnography

The central contradiction in historical ethnography emerged during field research between 1966 and 1968 among peasants in northeastern Tanzania, in areas which had been part of the precolonial Shambaa kingdom. The contradiction, as it seemed then, was between a continuity which had lasted for over a century in the central propositions of peasant political debate, and fundamental change over the same period in the actual practice of politics. The contrast between rocklike stability in conceptions alongside radical change in practice seemed to defy descriptive interpretation.

I began to learn about peasant politics in the early stages of research. In mid-1966, when I first arrived in Shambaai, Tanzania had been independent for less than five years. Before that, the British had governed through local chiefs, who collected taxes and were paid a salary; tribute had no legal role in this system. Chiefship itself had been abolished soon after independence. Nevertheless, it quickly became clear that peasants in many parts of the West Usambara mountains (the area which I am calling Shambaai) were offering cows, labor, and quantities of food as tribute to chiefs who had inherited their positions from pre-colonial rulers. The tribute came most visibly at times when the rainy season was expected to start.

When I first observed a cow being taken to a chief in 1966, I discussed the reasons with my companion, who explained that the chief had powerful medicines for making rain, that someone with pretensions towards taking his place as rainmaker was holding up the rain in order to erode the old chief's popular support, and that it was important for the people to demonstrate their loyalty to the chief so that he would continue to make rain despite the efforts of the unnamed competitor.

In subsequent rainy seasons, after I had become fluent in the Shambaa language, it became clear that the relationship between chiefship and rain was a subject of obsessive interest. Near the old royal capital, in 1967 and 1968, I lived next to a small house made of clay over a framework of branches, indistinguishable from any other peasant house on the outside, in which a friend sold tea and homemade fried cakes. Many local men would stop on their way home from the fields in the early evening, and I often joined them there. I did not direct or elicit these conversations; they were not interviews. They turned, many dozens of times, to the subject of rainmakers and to measures which were necessary to "heal the land."

Through all these conversations, there was uniform agreement on the central terms of discussion. People invariably argued that a centralization of power led to good rains and plentiful crops. *Nguvu* is the word for "power," and people debated about whether there was only one holder of power, or whether there was competition, known as *nguvu kwa nguvu*, "power against power." If the latter was the case, it meant that one rainmaker or the other was holding back the rain, either to erode his competitor's support, or because he felt that the local peasants were not adequately loyal to him.

Two terms which recurred over and over were *kubana shi* and *kuzifya shi:* "to harm the land" and "to heal the land." It was said that rainmakers harm the land when they compete with one another in a contest of *nguvu kwa nguvu*, "power against power." One knows that the land has been harmed when the sun shines down every day, leading to famine. "To heal the land" is to restore proper relations between subjects and their chief, or to resolve conflicts between chiefly competitors, so that the rains fall in their proper season and peasants win good harvests. Just as "power against power" harms the land, a centralization of power in the hands of a chief who can "cover over the land" (*-funika shi*), suppressing all competition, heals the land and brings prosperity. Drought is a sign that the land has been harmed, plentiful food a sign that it has been healed. The proposition that "power against power" harms the land is an unvarying one, as is its complement, that suppressing competition leads to satiety.

These propositions call into play a whole range of metaphors and emotionally charged images. The land harmed was like the sun, which shines down every day; the rains of a land healed like the moon, which comes with rhythmed regularity. Moon and sun, satiety and hunger, call forth associations also of femininity and masculinity. The rhythms of the rains and of the moon are like a woman's fertility, for she is fertile only at the appropriate time in her monthly cycle (her "moon," *ng'wezi*). A man is fertile every day; his fertility is more like the daily continued shining of the sun. People would speak of a feminine farming season, meaning a fertile one, as contrasted with the hunger of a masculine farming season. Healing the land and harming the land call forth a series of images of the rhythmed or continuous passage of time, the moon or the sun, masculine or feminine, with all of the images rooted in the individual and collective experience of hunger and of satiety.

We can see, then, that ethnographic observation in the 1960s made it clear that *kuzifya shi* and *kubana shi* and the associated propositions and metaphors were important in peasant political practice at that time. Historical traditions collected at the same time, combined with archival research, demonstrated that the configuration of conceptions, images, and figures of speech had been in active use a hundred years earlier. An awareness of this fact came through extended research on patterns of nineteenth-century politics: studies of competition at the level of the chiefs and, where possible, of the relationship between the precolonial state and local society. The historical reconstruction emerged from the critical comparison of a great many oral traditions drawn from multiple competing chiefly lines and of prominent lineages of commoner-peasants (Feierman 1974).

Healing and harming the land, which were central to the politics of the 1960s, had also been at the core of nineteenth-century politics, associated with a complex and fully articulated set of practices. The traditions defined two very different conditions of the kingdom, one centralized and the other decentralized, as defined in the language of power (*nguvu*). The centralized condition was remembered as a time when the land was fertile and the rains fell in their proper season, when cases were settled justly and peace reigned; the decentralized condition was remembered as a time of famine, warfare, and the unjust settlement of cases. Many of the actual words used in the 1960s language about healing the land had been in use, with similar meaning, a hundred years earlier. Certainly the metaphors comparing rain and famine to the feminine and the masculine, and to rhythmed as opposed to continuous time, had been in common use.

The most important determinant of the kingdom's condition, in the indigenous historical interpretation, was the set of kinship relations between the king and the ostensibly subordinate chiefs. When a new king came to power his ability to dominate the chiefs depended on whether they were his brothers and therefore his competitors, unlikely to subordinate themselves without a struggle; or nonroyals who could be pushed aside; or (best of all) junior relatives. Each king tried in the course of his reign to replace brothers with sons who would obey commands from the royal capital. A king who succeeded in doing this made the entire kingdom into a single *nguvu*: a territory with a single locus of sovereign power. In the reign of some kings, then, the land was visibly healed; in the reigns of others it was harmed.

The facts of nineteenth-century history appeared to confirm the validity of indigenous political theory. Kimweri ye Nyumbai, who ruled from about 1815 to 1862, did in fact replace most local chiefs with his children, of whom there were dozens. Once he had done this, his own rain medicines became the most important in the kingdom; the chiefs would ultimately depend on him to get their own patrimony of rain charms. In Kimweri's time, warfare was indeed far less common than it was to become in later reigns, when kings faced chiefs who were their brothers. During Kimweri's reign, commoners could appeal judicial decisions to the court of the king, who as father could overrule his sons, and tribute collection was more carefully controlled and less rapacious than it was later to become. Thus indigenous political theory has it, and the facts seem to confirm, that the kindom's centralized condition was more humane when seen from the point of view of its subjects than its decentralized condition. "Covering over the land," suppressing competition as Kimweri ye Nyumbai did, was preferable to *nguvu kwa nguvu*, "power against power."

Once again, it was not only the practice but many of the words and images which had been the same in the nineteenth century as they were to become in the twentieth: "power" (*nguvu*), "to cover over," the periodicity of the moon and of the rains, and the association between the king's masculinity and his power and between the king and the moon were all part of nineteenth-century cultural usage.

The central problem in historical ethnography, then, was this: from the time of Kimweri ye Nyumbai until the late 1960s, the central terms of peasant political language retained the strongest continuities, even though the character of the actual political forces changed many times. The changes were fundamental: in the late nineteenth century, warfare tore apart the kingdom, and many of the chiefs traded slaves to the clove plantations and dhows of the Indian Ocean. In 1895 the Germans hanged the king; later they destroyed the authority of the chiefs; local people were forced to work on European-owned farms and plantations. After the First World War the British took Tanganyika and restored the chiefs, now no longer sovereign but serving as minor colonial functionaries. In the 1950s the British did everything they could to draw African agriculture fully into the capitalist sphere. Many local people, in revolt against their king, joined proto-nationalist organizations, ultimately leading to the triumph of TANU (the Tanganyika African National Union), to national independence in 1961, to the removal of all chiefs, and to the introduction of a policy of democratic socialist self-reliance. Through all these changes, the symbols, conceptions, and metaphors of chiefship appear to have remained stable.

These facts — the facts of change in patterns of political action and in the distribution of power alongside stability in political language and symbols — seemed an anomolous case when seen from the point of view of general interpretations of the embeddedness of culture within social action, or of social action within culture.

Symbolic Classification: Structure and Contingency

The form in which the ethnographic problem was stated made its solution difficult, if not impossible. Those were the days before the movement of anthropology into the period which one observer has described as "post-binary bliss" (Parkin 1982: xiii, citing Sturrock). The opposition between political language and symbols on the one side and political action or the distribution of power on the other, carried a strong and misleading message about the nature of social reality: that political action could somehow be treated in a pure form separate from its cultural expression, that political discourse was not itself action, and that language and symbols could exist outside the daily flow of political practice.

The original research had in fact been inspired by a unitary holistic vision rather than a dualistic one; the binary definition of the problem emerged from the failure of the original unitary framework. The research had begun as a study of symbolic classification, on the assumption that a single set of categories in indigenous language would organize knowledge of both the social world and the natural order. Durkheim and Mauss (1963) had discussed categories which divided up the natural world (classifying directions, birds, animals) and at the same time defined and classified social groups. The question for me was whether the same could not be done for political action: *kuzifya shi* and *kubana shi* were terms which classified political action as well as the character of the rains at the same time.

It was difficult, however, to explain the fact that the forms of political action had changed drastically, while the words in which they were explained remained static. One way out was to see that the terms did not tightly classify types of rainfall and types of political action in clearly bounded sets; *kuzifya shi* and *kubana shi* were in part labels for loose sets of associations in a polythetic classification. Rodney Needham (1972, 1975), drawing on Wittgenstein, showed that many terms are not so much bounded definitions of perceived reality as assemblages of elements which bear a family resemblance to one another. This is a vague similarity of a kind that family members share; I have my father's nose and my mother's height, but these are not parts of a clearly definable set of family characteristics which one could apply predictably to still other family members. Similarly, *kuzifya shi* indicated a set of elements which bore a family resemblance to one another. The continuity in language was easier to explain if one pictured the classification as a loose polythetic one, based on family resemblances, rather than a precise definition of a particular class of reality.

Nevertheless, the terms of political discourse displayed a remarkable persistence, and it was a persistence in the propositions by which people explained political events, and not only continuity in a polythetic classification. Bloch, who explores the long-term continuity of a Malagasy ritual, argues that the more ritually formalized an utterance is, the less likely it is to express a proposition, since the capacity of language to express propositions depends on choice. Because ritualized language is repetitive and fixed, it cannot easily be adapted to match a particular ritual expression to a particular event (Bloch 1986:180–84). The loose fit between ritual and event makes it possible for rituals to endure over the long term, even while the social organization to which the ritual is tied changes radically. In the current case, however, the continuity was not in a particular ritual; it was in the key terms of variable propositional language. Bloch's explanation therefore does not apply.

The continuity in cultural terms made each event appear as "a unique actualization of a general phenomenon, a contingent realization of the cultural pattern" (Sahlins 1985:vii, citing Geertz). A synchronically defined set of relationships endured, it appeared, and found expression in innumerable contingent events. This is a position which ultimately had to be radically revised, one which depends on a binary opposition between the cultural pattern, which is deeply rooted, enduring, and necessary, and the particular events, which are contingent.

In Lévi-Straussian structuralism, explanations of long-term continuity are organized around the opposition between structure and event, necessity and contingency, the unconscious and the conscious. For Lévi-

Strauss the enduring relationships among terms in myth, in cosmology, and in ritual exist at an unconscious level. Historical change may shatter the conscious structures, while the unconscious ones remain intact. An example is traditional history of the Osage, in which the earliest ancestors were divided into two groups: one peaceful, vegetarian, associated with the left, the other warlike, carnivorous, associated with the right (Lévi-Strauss 1966:69–71). Circular Osage camps included seven clans of peace on the northern half and seven clans of war on the southern half. These then met a third group of warlike carrion eaters who joined them. The clans realigned themselves so as to keep a dualistic organization, with a warrior group of seven clans and a peaceful group of seven clans. Each of the three groups was originally composed of seven clans, for a total of twenty-one. But one warrior group reduced its clans to five and the other to two, so that the sum of the warrior clans did not exceed seven and the balanced relationship between the two groups was maintained. If this example is factually correct, the actual mechanism of historical continuity is easily identified. The organization of the circular camps was merely a contingent expression of a structural relationship between peace and war, vegetable foods and meat, north and south, left and right which found expression in many contexts in Osage life. Change of any one contingent expression, for example in the constitution of the clans, did not erase the wider classification, which was rooted in a number of contexts: in myth, in ritual, in the shape of the camp.

The opposition between *kuzifya shi* and *kubana shi* can be seen within this framework as merely a contingent expression of a more general structural relationship between ownership and the benevolent use of ritual power. Powerful medical substances cannot be used to heal unless they also have the capacity to kill. The most certain guarantee that the possessor of medicine will use his power on the side of life rather than death is to give him, as his own property, all that must be preserved. In the rite of sacrifice (*fika ya chekecheke*), members of the sacrificing lineage all left their house at a certain point and then reentered, explaining in a song that the house now belonged to the visiting healer, a dangerous practitioner. He would use his medicines to sustain the house because it had become his own. This relationship was turned upside down in the case of a witch, who was said to begin by killing "his own"—often his child. In the myth of the kingdom's origin, Mbegha, the founding king, changed from a destroyer of life to a preserver of life when he was given the kingdom, when it became his own (Feierman 1974). Similarly, the king who was given the tribute of the entire land as his own would use his medicines to heal the land.

One reason *kuzifya shi* and *kubana shi* survived is that these ideas about sovereignty were a limited expression of a more general relationship between ownership and the benevolent use of medicines. The same relationship was rooted, in everday life, in thousands of acts of healing. Even if chiefship declined, the structural relationship would continue to exist because its substratum in everyday life continued to exist. This is similar to Packard's explanation for the persistence, among the Bashu of Zaire, of the idea that chiefs are rainmakers. In his interpretation, ideas about Bashu chiefship endure because they are embedded within a larger Bashu cosmological scheme (1981:190).

Even if one were to accept a structuralist framework, and to explain *kuzifya shi* and *kubana shi* as contingent expressions of a structural relationship, the explanation of historical change would be inadequate, for it does not explain why some contingent expressions of the structural relationship disappear while others continue to thrive. Between the 1890s and the 1960s sacrifice became increasingly rare in Shambaai, yet the relationship between ownership and power survived in everyday healing and in healing the land. Why did one contingent expression of the structural relationship decline while others survived? Neither the notion of an unconscious structure underlying all the contingent contexts, nor the picture of the replication of a single set of conceptions in multiple concrete contexts offers a satisfactory understanding.

An analysis of healing the land based on the opposition between structure and contingency does not work because of a central theoretical gap which makes systematic historical analysis difficult or impossible. The gap can be seen in all the various forms in which structure and contingency are expressed: as *langue* and *parole*, synchrony and diachrony, or system and event. Giddens shows that the central weakness is the lack of a theory of the competent speaker or actor (1979:17). The difficulty can be seen most easily in Saussure's distinction between "language" (*langue*) and "speech" (*parole*), which is at the heart of Lévi-Strauss's thought (Saussure 1966). For Saussure, language is a social institution, one in which the relationship between word and object, signifier and signified, is arbitrary. Language is a self-contained system whose terms are defined according to difference: according to the demarcations between them. Different individuals write the letter *t* in different ways. What ultimately defines the letter is not its substance, but its difference from other letters. For Saussure the system of language is conventional, arbitrary, and defined by difference.

Language as a system exists independently of individually created speech acts, each of which is contingent. Each speaker, following the rules and definitions of language, creates unique acts of speech, unique utterances. Language as an arbitrary system is completely separate from speech, created voluntarily within the rules of the system. It is difficult therefore to explain how language changes. If each speaker adheres to the rules, then language will never change. If speakers depart from the rules, then they will not be understood by other members of the speech community. It is here that the competent speaker enters the picture, following the rules yet creating new forms at the same time. "'Rule-governed creativity' is not merely . . . the employment of fixed, given rules whereby new sentences are generated; it is at the same time the medium whereby those rules are reproduced and hence in principle modified" (Giddens 1979:18, emphasis deleted).

It was with the purpose of bridging the chasm between structure and event, equivalent to the chasm between *langue* and *parole*, that Marshall Sahlins redefined the term, *structure of the conjuncture*. By this he means "the practical realization of cultural categories in a historical context, as expressed in the interested action of the historic agents" (1985:xiv; see also 125, 125n., and 1981:33). Sahlins uses "historic agents" here as the equivalent of language's competent speakers. The historic agent can both continue and modify cultural categories. The difficult task in actual historical analysis is to create a method and a form of ethnographic description which can capture the cultural categories as both continuous and in transformation, and the actors as both creating new language and speaking inherited words, all at the same time.

We can now see why it was not possible to explain the continuities and discontinuities in Shambaa conceptions and ritual practices with reference to an enduring structure and contingent events. In order to explain why healing the land endured even though sacrifice (another expression of the same core conception) declined, we would need an approach to understanding the actual historical actors. It is not "society" which creates cultural continuities or discontinues practices. Individuals do this: individuals living within a particular historical context. The purpose of this book is to explore the relationship between the historical context in which peasants, as historical actors, found themselves and the way in which they created and recreated political discourse.

Dar es Salaam Historiography and New Facts in Shambaai: Decentering the Ethnographic Object

In the 1970s my own research assumptions about the extension of the ethnographic object in space and in time began to crumble; indeed easy assumptions about the existence of an object came into doubt. The original assumptions posited a political system with clear boundaries in time and space. The extension in space was limited by the boundaries of the precolonial Shambaa kingdom, with a core in the West Usambara mountains at the heart of the old kingdom and fringes of uncertain status beyond that core. The extension in time began at an uncertain time in the early days of the kingdom, and could be documented from the reign of Kimweri ye Nyumbai, who ruled for about forty-five years before his death in 1862. It continued to the completion of the first period of field research in 1968. The central question, as we have seen, was about the reasons for continuity in the relationship between chiefship and rain for the whole of that time period and within the specified boundaries.

The first challenge to these assumptions came from my colleagues-at-a-distance, the second generation of historians at the University of Dar es Salaam. In the 1960s the first generation had focused on African initiatives in creating political and social institutions and also initiatives in making economic advances. Colonial rule had tried to make Africans voiceless; the historians of an independent Tanzania would honor their voices.[1] This approach came under attack in the late 1960s and early 1970s. After the celebrations of independence had been absorbed, Tanzania had to cope with the fact that it was a very poor country in an increasingly difficult international economic environment, and that its fate was being shaped also by the outcome of the conflicts in Mozambique, Zimbabwe, and South Africa. Walter Rodney (1972:308) talked about "flag-independence" as a way of saying that the real liberation struggles were still to come. Historians criticized the earlier writings on African initiatives. They argued that initiatives taken by Africans in conformity with terms dictated by a worldwide economic system led to the creation of a dependent economy.[2]

Walter Rodney was the leader of the socialist historians in those years. He had arrived in Tanzania by the time of the Arusha Declaration in 1967 and stayed until 1974 (Shivji 1980). The Dar es Salaam historians did not, for the most part, theorize an articulation of modes of production. They explored the political economy of Tanzania in the nineteenth and twentieth centuries (especially the period after 1920) and its implications for local economic history.[3] It was impossible to deny, reading their works, that African society was profoundly transformed through its relationship to the colonial state and to the capitalist economy. Even the most static-looking local institutions were shown on closer examination to have been reshaped, radically, from within. Here is how Rodney put it in an essay published in 1983, after his death: "Social phenomena seemingly reminiscent of pre-colonial Africa acquired an entirely new meaning in a colonial context, and were more likely to be blocked in their development than reinforced by the onset of the money economy. The presentation of the modern as an enclave within the traditional all but overlooks the dynamic of interpenetration which made the colonial economy a new organic whole" (Rodney 1983:5). The interpenetration transformed political institutions; it was not narrowly economic. Chiefs in various parts of colonial Tanganyika enforced rules on coffee planting, recruited migrant labor, and employed their clients as laborers for cash cropping. Chiefship became something new in its new context.

The Dar es Salaam historians made it impossible to continue treating the spatial boundaries of the Shambaa kingdom as the boundaries of a political system. In the twentieth century the kingdom was an integral part of colonial Tanganyika; the kingdom could not be explained as a system on its own. In the nineteenth century the impact of the international economy had already been clear: the ivory trade transformed patterns of political action in the kingdom. I myself had demonstrated the importance of this transformation in 1970 in a history Ph.D. dissertation, but I continued to treat the Shambaa kingdom as a bounded political system in an anthropology D.Phil. thesis of 1972 because that is what anthropological discourse seemed to require.[4]

Destroying the spatial boundaries of the ethnographic object created more problems than it solved. It seemed impossible now to define boundaries for a new system. The culturally patterned politics associated with healing the land were localized within the old kingdom's boundaries. The kingdom had links with coastal traders and with Indian Ocean clove plantations in the nineteenth century. It was part of the colonial state and dependent on international commodity prices in the twentieth century. Where was the system? How was it possible to create any systematic explanation of the relationship between local culture and the larger fields of political and economic force?

Local culture itself began to disintegrate under this lens. Once the boundaries of the system were opened up, there seemed no reason to include Shambaa conceptions about healing the land while excluding the propositions taught in local schools in Shambaai about the nature of democracy or the history of the slave trade, and the ideas taught in the mosque or in church. Where did healing the land fit into this complicated and undefined set of forces and conceptions? On this, Dar es Salaam historiography was not helpful because it did not address questions about the local culture of the peasantry.

Alongside the spatial decentering came a temporal one; the continuity in time from the nineteenth century to the 1960s dissolved. I came to understand the temporal decentering during a return trip to Shambaai in 1979–80 for research on an unrelated topic. One day in 1980 I was sitting in a smoke-blackened room in the house of a friend in a mountain village. A respected old man entered and asked the men to contribute a shilling each to pay the rainmaker, because the rains had not fallen. Half the men paid; some made excuses and did not pay; one, a renowned healer, refused to pay. He said, "You go and tell him [that I haven't paid and so he ought] to stop the rain from falling on my farm." Suddenly it was clear that the unity of expressed opinion about healing the land had broken apart. Ideas about rain and fertility were in a period of ferment.

There had undoubtedly been debate in the 1960s also: discussions about the role of God as opposed to the role of the Kilindi in making rain; but these were speculative discussions which did not undermine the unity of accepted practice. Their significance is discussed in chapter 10. In the 1960s there appeared to be complete unanimity, in the realms of the great rainmakers, about the fact that those particular ex-chiefs could control the rains, and that the political relations between people and chiefs and government determined how rich the rains would be, and how fertile the land. At the later time, in 1980, many local people were openly discussing the problem of the "contempt" in which villagers held rainmakers. They acknowledged that fifteen years earlier no one had questioned the powers of rainmakers, and that now questioning was taking place. The problem was that as the old rainmakers died, the next generation of men who claimed to be rainmakers did not have the stature to take their place.

This change reinforced the point made by the Dar es Salaam historians that the local unit was not a self-contained system. The most likely explanation for the decline in acceptance of rainmakers was that it was a consequence of the government's removal of chiefs from office after independence. But if removal from office led to the decline in the cultural phenomena being studied, then the previous continuity in those phenomena must have had something to do with the fact that the British had placed chiefs in office and had tried to reinforce their prestige and authority. This was an unexpected outcome indeed: the British as responsible for continuities in precolonial African political language. It was unexpected because British administrators did not know or care about the terms of the language they were propagating, and local Africans did care, passionately.

Understanding that the British had played a role in continuing *kuzifya shi* and *kubana shi* challenged the central idea of continuity: the extension of the ethnographic object in time. The British began to govern Tanganyika only at the end of World War I. Before that, the Germans had ruled for a period, and they had destroyed the authority of chiefs, a brutal destruction compared with the gentle process in which the independence government asked chiefs to retire. It was distinctly possible that the German destruction of chiefship had led to a period of "contempt" for chiefs and their rain, much like the contempt of 1980. In this case, what seemed like a continuity over the long term was in fact something quite different: a set of terms of political language in use in the nineteenth century, reduced to marginality by the early twentieth century, revived again under the British, and challenged again after independence.

Michel Foucault, insisting that discourse must be "treated as and when it occurs," points to the fallacy of a secret origin: a time before which we can hear any words being spoken, but one at which the form of discourse must already have existed. It is "an ever-receding point," and one never to be intruded upon by "the irruption of a real event" (1976: 25). In the present case the fallacy was not one of a secret origin, but of a secret continuity through a middle period, the years of colonial rule. The presumption that terms which existed in the nineteenth century and in the 1960s must also have existed in the same form through the intervening years was not only a false presumption in fact, but it had the effect of placing the discourse beyond "the irruption of a real event."[5]

The hypothesis about colonial change therefore challenged more than just the facts of continuity: it undermined the fundamental way in which the ethnographic object was itself constituted. That object had been seen as an enduring cultural product with an existence reaching beyond the actions of any one individual or combination of individuals, and beyond the influence of events. *Kuzifya shi* and *kubana shi* had an existence of their own in the original framework, capable of imposing a shape on contingent events. But now it was clear that the terms had been the object of struggle: attacked by the Germans and supported by the British, with local people undoubtedly taking positions as the struggle unfolded. What had been lacking in the original framework was a place for the competent actor, the agent working to shape historical events. We have already seen that the lack of a theory of the competent speaker or actor was the central flaw in the Lévi-Straussian world defined according to an opposition between structure and contingency. It is no accident that the empirical materials would not fall into a comprehensible pattern until examined from the point of view of a general interpretation of the role of intellectuals as historical agents.

Intellectuals

Intellectuals are defined in this work by their place in the unfolding social process: they engage in socially recognized organizational, directive, educative, or expressive activities. Teachers, artists, political leaders, healers, and bureaucrats are all intellectuals within this definition of the term. The definition is derived, of course, from Gramsci, who explained that it is not possible to define intellectuals simply by the fact that they engage in intellectual activities, because these activities proceed within every social group. "In any physical work, even the most degraded and mechanical, there exists . . . a minimum of creative intellectual activity" (Gramsci 1971:8). All people are therefore intellectuals, but not all people have the social function of intellectuals, a function that is directive, organizational, or educative.[6] Intellectuals are not defined by the quality and content of their discourse (although these are of fundamental interest to us); they are defined by their place within the ensemble of social relations. Many anthropological researchers have come across nonliterate people who possess a brilliant, self-conscious, discursive understanding of knowledge within their own culture, and yet earn their livings doing what most people around them do and are not recognized as engaging in directive or educative activities. These people are not defined as intellectuals in the sense adopted here.

Who were the peasant intellectuals? These were men and women who earned their daily livelihood by farming. At normal times they might not have met Gramsci's test as to whether their professional activities were weighted towards "intellectual elaboration" rather than towards "muscular-nervous effort" (1971:9). At crucial historical moments, however, peasant leaders organized political movements of the greatest long-term significance, and in doing so elaborated new forms of discourse. At other times these leaders would have spent much of their time farming. Even in the periods of intense political activity, most spent some time farming. To call them peasant intellectuals defines their historical role at moments of leadership, moments of organization, and moments of direction. In this respect the analysis is not far from Gramsci's own, for he wrote about organic intellectuals who originated in the working class and who then became practical party organizers (see Femia 1981).

The analysis is very far from Gramsci's in other respects. He described the peasantry as incapable of elaborating or assimilating its own intellectuals (1971:6). In his view, only the working class, through its organic link to the Communist Party, is capable of leading the peasantry to challenge the hegemony of dominant groups.[7] This position is unacceptable on many counts, and it is necessary to place the disagreement in context in order to preserve the valuable core of the analysis of intellectuals.

Gramsci provided an answer to one of the central questions of twentieth-century Marxism: Why did the Western European working class not become revolutionary? Why did it not attack the roots of capitalist control?[8] His answer was that the capitalist order remains stable because the great masses of the population accept it as necessary and spontaneously consent to it. There is a substratum of agreement on the worth of basic institutions and on the distribution of social benefits. This deeply rooted ideological dominance, this concept of reality diffused throughout society, Gramsci called *hegemony*. Foucault discussed a concept of reality which permeates the individual's understanding of the world in much the same terms: "When I think of the mechanics of power, I think of its capillary form of existence, of the extent to which power seeps into the very grain of individuals, reaches right into their bodies, permeates their gestures, their posture, what they say, how they learn to live and work with other people."[9]

In Gramsci's view political dominance rests on coercion as well as consent. In moments of political or economic crisis, however, it would be possible for the working class to overthrow the coercive apparatus, were it not for the deep entrenchment of hegemonic consent. According to Gramsci, revolution could come only after a period in which the moral dominance of the established order is challenged. This long-term assault on the consensual bases of capitalism, a war of position, cannot be carried out, according to Gramsci's interpretation, by the working class alone. He explained that the proletariat can only win the war of position if it is led by the Communist Party, to which it is organically bound. The Communist Party, in Gramsci's view, is the collective intellectual of the proletariat (Femia 1981:133).

Gramsci was profoundly concerned with the need for the Party to be truly democratic — to integrate initiatives from below and orders from above and to create structures allowing popular participation. All care must be taken, in Gramsci's view, that the Party not degenerate into a rigid bureaucratic body. But in the end, centralized control must be maintained (Femia 1981: chap. 5).

The present book's modest history is about a small group of peasants in one part of Tanzania, but it leads one to reject Gramsci's position on several counts. It shows that peasants were capable of creating their own counter-discourse, and it leads one to question Gramsci's faith in a centralized party, indeed to reject centralism of any kind, whether of colonial governments or of one-party states. The heroic age of these peasants came during the 1950s. In that decade the peasant intellectuals of Shambaai struggled to create forms of discourse dissenting from the order of colonial society, dissenting from the hierarchies of local peasant society as it existed at the time, and from hierarchies as they had existed a hundred years earlier. They did not need the leadership of the working class or of a Communist Party to create a dissenting discourse. It was the energy of the peasantry, which emerged locally but then merged with a nationalist party, which made possible the end of colonial rule. Once national independence came, however, the independence party (TANU, the Tanganyika African National Union), now bureaucratized, emerged as the sole party in Tanzania's political life. The party tried to build institutions for popular participation: *ujamaa* villages, organized on principles of African socialism; ten-house cells; and party branches. But the party was, in the end, better at representing its own interests than those of the peasantry. Chapter 9 of this book describes the measures taken by the party to prevent political expression by peasant intellectuals and by other intellectuals within Tanzanian society. This happened even though TANU was not a truly centralized party. More freedom of thought and expression emerged in Tanzania than in many other states of Africa, Europe, and the Americas. Nevertheless, the absence of political alternatives cut off possibilities for groups other than the bureaucracy to work towards their own goals. The history of parties that practice democratic centralism leads one to the conclusion that Gramsci was naive about the possibility for democracy in a centralized party. Nevertheless his understanding of intellectuals remains a central contribution to the social understanding of culture.

Gramsci distinguished between organic and traditional intellectuals (Vacca 1982; Adamson 1980:143). "Every social group, coming into existence on the original terrain of an essential function in the world of economic production, creates with itself, organically, one or more strata of intellectuals which give it homogeneity and an awareness of its own function not only in the economic but also in the social and political fields" (Gramsci 1971:5). Industrial technicians and specialists in the capitalist legal system, for example, are created alongside capitalist entrepreneurs and are organically linked to them. We have already seen that the Communist Party, for Gramsci, is organically bound to the proletariat. The link between intellectuals and production is not always direct; it is mediated by the whole fabric of society and the whole complex of superstructures.

Alongside organic intellectuals, other groups of intellectuals exist who may at one time have been tied organically to groups with essential functions in the world of production, but who then survive the end of a historical epoch, and live on into a later period as traditional intellectuals. According to Gramsci ecclesiastics were at one time organically bound to the landed aristocracy, but continued to exist through periods of fundamental change in the organization of society. Traditional intellectuals develop an *esprit de corps,* and see themselves as "autonomous and independent of the dominant social group" (1971:7). New groups that are moving towards dominance usually try to draw in and make use of traditional intellectuals. In just this way the British of colonial Tanganyika drew in the Kilindi chiefs, who by then had become intellectuals, in the sense that they performed organizational work in the service of a dominant group. Because the traditional intellectuals see themselves as partially autonomous, they have some freedom of maneuver in allying with one power bloc or another, although they usually compromise with the dominant social group.

Gramsci saw the structure of European society as enormously complex, and in no way simply reducible to the organization of production. He expressed impatience with it for this reason; he saw its demographic composition as "irrational." European "civilisation" is characterized by the existence of numerous classes "with no essential function in the world of production . . . created by the 'richness' and 'complexity' of past history. This past history has left behind a heap of passive sedimentations produced by the phenomenon of the saturation and fossilisation of civil-service personnel and intellectuals, of clergy and landowners, piratical commerce and the professional . . . army" (1971:281). A history written in harmony with Gramsci's vision would need to account for all the passive sedimentations, the history of groups "with no essential function in the world of production." Yet changes in production and in dominance would remain core issues.

The great potential contribution of Gramsci's approach to the social history of discourse should be clear. In every case he focuses sharply on the links which tie intellectual practice to production and to power, yet his understanding is anything but mechanically reductionist. The relationship between the intellectual practice and production is mediated by the entire fabric of society. The various categories of intellectuals follow their own trajectories and choose their own paths within the historically conditioned range of possibilities.

Studying intellectuals in this way has great benefits for understanding the social uses of discourse. It is profitable, in exploring the web of discourse and power, to ask about the social position and tacit knowledge of the intellectuals who create or transmit a particular form of discourse, and then to understand that discourse within the full context of their interests and their life situations. To view the social position of the intellectuals within the larger society and in relation to production and power, to understand their discursive practice within this context, is a satisfying and potentially rigorous way of understanding power/knowledge.

Gramsci's interpretation of traditional intellectuals makes it possible to explore continuities in discourse without tying each moment in the formation of discourse mechanically to the immediate narrow interests of the intellectuals. The difficulty of relating discourse, in a relentless way, to interests and social position is, of course, that forms of discourse have their own coherences and continuities through time, even through periods of fundamental change in power over society and of fundamental change in the organization of production. The coherence of ecclesiastical discourse in Italy, or the coherence of discourse about healing or harming the land in Shambaai, survives through radical changes in the organization of production and power. At the same time, the significance of the discourse in social life changes along with the changing place of the intellectuals (whether Catholic ecclesiastics or Kilindi chiefs) through the periods of social upheaval. The social context of *kuzifya shi* and *kubana shi* is radically different in different periods. Early in the history of the kingdom, the Kilindi chiefs struggled to take over the rain medicines of predynastic fertility specialists, who then became intellectual organizers in the service of the chiefs. In the 1930s it was the Kilindi themselves who functioned in the mediating subordinate role of intellectuals, thus introducing into the heart of British rule the discourse on healing the land. The continuity of the discourse thus emerged out of a succession of acts by which dominant groups subordinated preexisting fertility specialists. The changing significance of the discourse is related to the shifting compromises and alliances between dominant groups and mediating intellectuals.

The Kilindi functioned, from the mid-1920s onward, in a framework established by the British, who were able to shape local African politics in three ways. Firstly, they made use of preexisting groups as intellectuals. They did this by appointing chiefs as local administrators, thus focusing peasant politics on local rather than territorial issues, and especially on dynastic issues. Secondly, they restricted the emergence of alternative categories of leading Africans. In particular, they tried to prevent the growth of a class of large African traders with interests stretching across local boundaries. The localizing influence of the chiefs and the suppression of large traders went with a policy of local agricultural self-sufficiency and short-term migrant labor. Thirdly, they elaborated a new set of intellectuals — clerks and minor functionaries who were educated by Christian missions and employed by the government.

The African politics of British Tanganyika therefore revolved around chiefs, literate functionaries, and peasants. In the crisis of the 1950s the peasantry fought to limit the power of the chiefs. They found allies in the nationalist party. This left an independent Tanzania in the 1960s with only two main centers of gravity: peasants and bureaucrats, with the latter working to establish their sole dominance. The bureaucrats continued the British policy of keeping trade out of the hands of African traders and keeping it in the hands of government-controlled agencies. In relation to the newly emerging working class, the bureaucrats continued the British policy of suppressing an independent labor movement. The new government continued and elaborated a policy of bureaucratic control over the day-to-day workings of peasant agriculture within an overall framework which continued to emphasize the production of export crops traded through state agencies, along with peasant self-sufficiency in food crops. Bureaucratic control over the peasantry, which had been called *indirect rule* under the British and the chiefs, now continued within the context of African socialism. We can see that the history of intellectuals in colonial Tanganyika is central to understanding the emergence of socialist Tanzania.

Within Shambaai (as in a number of Tanganyika's districts) the crisis of the 1950s, which led to independence, was provoked by an erosion-control scheme which threatened to undermine the fundamental bases of subsistence as understood by the peasantry. Chiefs, African functionaries, and African traders all understood that the government's policy was misguided, but only the peasants were capable of organizing open resistance. The chiefs depended on the British for their jobs and were therefore required to enforce the erosion-control rules. The few African bureaucrats who held responsible positions were required to live far from their home districts during their years of education and to be moved from district to district around the country while at work. They could not organize political movements with local roots and were prohibited from doing so in any event through most of this period.

In several chiefdoms in Shambaai a large peasant movement emerged to resist erosion-control measures. This happened mostly in territories where chiefs were reputed to be poor rainmakers. Peasants said that these chiefs were "harming the land," meaning that they could not protect its fertility by preventing erosion control or by making rain.

Most leaders of the peasant associations which had the greatest political impact were men who had some primary education, who in many cases had worked as government functionaries at a very low level, and who had returned to peasant farming. They were peasants who had participated in the world of the clerks. Because of their low level of education, and because they were not active in the world of government employment, they had greater autonomy than the chiefs or the better-educated bureaucrats. It was they who elaborated the discourse of the movements of peasant resistance.

Healing the land still occupied a central place within the peasant movements. But alongside it, the peasant intellectuals created new forms of political discourse. They debated the nature of *demokrasi.* Was it rule

by a council of elders? Was it a system in which only the best-educated
held jobs? Would all power be given to the lineages of nonroyals? Would
a peasant king sit on the throne? Should each man and woman be given
a vote in formal elections? And they debated the nature of *freedom* and
slavery. Was control by old men over young men incompatible with freedom? If a chief took a woman arbitrarily and by force, was that characteristic of a regime of slavery?

The peasant intellectuals were people who farmed the land but who,
in most cases, drew on some other experience besides farming: experience at trade, in the Christian or Islamic community, at work as petty
functionaries, or at work as minor servants in the courts of chiefs. The
peasantry was not an undifferentiated and homogeneous mass, drawing
on a single stream of discursive practice. A great many peasants were
completely rooted in the countryside, and at the same time had diverse
experiences beyond the peasant world. They had an important asset: unlike the large traders, unlike the chiefs, and unlike African bureaucrats
at the higher levels, they were capable of elaborating dissenting discourse
without losing valued occupations.

Sara Berry, who writes with great subtlety about rural differentiation
among Yoruba farmers of southwestern Nigeria, concludes that when the
career paths of farmers lead them to draw sustenance from non-farm
sources, or to accumulate capital, one can no longer call them peasants
(Berry 1985:4–5, 12). This raises the question of what is a "peasant," a
term widely debated in the literature. For purposes of the present analysis, peasants are farmers who produce a large part of what they consume,
have access to the use of land, coordinate their own labor with that of
close relatives, integrate their organization of farming labor with the organization of care-giving, domestic work, and biological reproduction,
and are involved in a wider economic system in which non-peasants also
play a role.[10] In Berry's interpretation, Yoruba who hold small plots of
cocoa do not produce the majority of their own food; they purchase much
of what they consume. They are therefore not peasants. Successful farmers as described by Berry do not acquire large farms as rich peasants would;
instead they diversify into non-farm enterprises. She argues that the characteristic issues which provoke resistance among Yoruba farmers are not
those of a peasantry. "State exploitation is resented because it constrains
farmers' ability to accumulate and diversify their activities, rather than
because it threatens to disrupt the stability and autonomy of village life"
(Berry 1985:4).

In the case of Shambaai, peasants produce the majority of food they
consume, but Berry's concern about the diversity of non-farm activities
is justified. The diversity of peasant activities, career paths, and inher-

ited streams of discourse is central, and it is the reason an interpretation based on the study of intellectuals is particularly revealing. Despite this diversity, it is appropriate to speak of Shambaa agriculturalists as peasants, so long as it is understood that this label gives us a set of questions to ask, and that it does not specify the answers. To call a set of people a peasantry opens up the exploration of the relationship between the rural population and dominant strata; it opens up questions about the existence of the household as a unit of production, reproduction, and consumption, and about the control of labor and of crops within that unit; and it opens up exploration of the diverse forms of political consciousness. It does not supply ready-made answers (Cooper 1981:34; Beinart and Bundy 1987:29–30).

The term "peasant" would have no use in historical description or analysis if it specified a static mode of subsistence and a static form of consciousness. Living people in real historical situations are inevitably in transition, caught in contradictions. The reconstituted peasantries of the Caribbean, for example, were in the process of movement from slave to peasant. Some peasants began life as slaves and then either deserted or ran away, or in some cases began farming on their own even while remaining slaves (Mintz 1979). For Mintz, who studies these reconstituted peasantries, it is not relevant to describe all their characteristics at one moment as slave-like and at another as ideal-typically peasant. Instead, the scholar must explore the dynamics of the particular historical process. Each society has its own history, its own class structure, land use pattern, and so on. One cannot therefore abstract a narrowly comparable peasantry from each of many divergent cases (Mintz 1979:221; 1974). The central question is about the direction of movement in each case — the pattern of change through time. In studying that direction, peasant intellectuals are central.

Most difficult of all, in our study of peasant intellectuals, is the problem of peasant women as intellectuals. Their large and sustained protests occupy a significant part of the present book's narrative, but the leaders had been systematically deprived of recording their names in the archival record. The women did not, for the most part, communicate with the government in writing because many fewer women than men attended school in Shambaai. The women did not have public standing: they were not taxpayers; at a time when the government required that political organizations win government registration, no one thought to ask peasant women to register their large and active organizations. Their invisibility won them some immunities, but at the cost of losing a part of their public voice.

The peasant intellectuals, women and men, led movements which de-

feated the chiefs, and which provided the driving force for winning national independence. Their discourse of democracy and technical competence was then shaped by the new government of the bureaucrats, one
in which the peasant intellectuals had little role. Nyerere himself, in 1961,
described going to district meetings where he would see, off to one side,
"a few chaps in torn green shirts wielding banners but looking somewhat
forlorn" (Pratt 1978:108). The chaps in torn green shirts were the peasant
intellectuals who had fought for and won the nation's independence. Peasant intellectuals lived on to resist the government of the bureaucrats just
as their predecessors had resisted the government of the colonialists.

The analysis of this book is cast in terms of intellectuals and their
discourse, not in terms of the nature of hegemony. Gramsci defined hegemony as "The 'spontaneous' consent given by the great masses of the
population to the general direction imposed on social life by the dominant fundamental group" (1971:12). The dominant group's interests are
accepted as universal ones. The achievement of hegemony is not a simple
process by which the dominant group imposes its own ideology on other
groups. According to Chantal Mouffe (1979b:193), interpreting Gramsci's
thought, the hegemonic ideology can make use of ideological elements
from diverse sources, even from the ideology of those who are dominated.
In this way American popular culture integrates many elements drawn
from the culture of African Americans. In Mouffe's interpretation the
dominant group provides the underlying principle that organizes and ar-
ticulates ideology drawn from diverse sources. When there is fundamental social change, when a new group rises toward hegemony, this does
not lead to the creation of a wholly new ideology; it leads to a rearticu-
lation of inherited ideological elements. Mouffe's interpretation disposes
of one of the most fundamental objections to the concept of hegemony —
that it is an impoverished mechanistic concept which interprets each particular ideological element as caused or imposed by a particular set of
class relations. Therborn expressed it well: "No theory of the feudal mode
of production can explain why Feudalism was accompanied in Europe
by Catholic Christianity and by Shintoism in Japan" (quoted in Bloch
1986:177). Mouffe argues that Gramsci was not so narrowly reductionist.
If I extrapolate her argument to the issue of feudal religions, I believe
she would say Gramsci understood that in each case inherited ideological
elements (Shinto in the one case, Catholic in the other) were articulated
within a framework which won consent for feudal domination. I would
argue, however, that it is important to focus on the history of intellectuals, not merely on the history of disembodied cultural elements. The
relationship between Catholicism and feudalism can only be understood
within the framework of a history of intellectuals in medieval Europe.

Gramsci did exactly this. He focused on the relationship between clerics and landed aristocrats, and on the church's struggle to prevent the emergence of two religions: one for the intellectuals and the other for the "simple souls." The process by which socially central ideas evolve is much more difficult to understand when the ideas are treated as objects, divorced from human agency.

Discursive Consciousness, Practical Consciousness, and the Intellectuals: Spatial Boundaries Reconsidered

The distinction between practical knowledge and discursive knowledge must occupy a central place in any attempt to understand peasant politics and peasant culture. It is important to know, when we examine a course of action pursued by peasants, whether they are acting only practically, on the basis of tacit knowledge, or whether they formulate the rationale for their action discursively—whether they can account for a plan of action in words. Accounting for the action discursively involves placing it in a context. When peasants lay down their tools, for example, they might situate their action by saying that it is a feast day, not suited for work, or they might say that a particular landowner or government official is cruel, or they might speak about the unfairness of a national pattern of trade, of labor, and of political control, or they might simply lay down tools without situating the action discursively. The same physical action has very different significance in relation to varying discourse. In the realm of expressive culture, also, the distinction between practical and discursive knowledge is a significant one. Is the creator of a myth capable of explaining its structure, its mode of operation, and the character of its stylistic devices, or does the creator simply tell the story?

Practice is explored fully in the work of Pierre Bourdieu, who argues that anthropology is undermined by the disjuncture between discourse and practice. Anthropologists learn about exotic society through indigenous discourse, even though practice is the authentic basis of social organization. Anthropologists find it easy to study the rules that local people list when explaining how their own society works. They find it easy also to make maps of categories by which local people classify the objects of their world. The map-making anthropologist appears as an omniscient observer, who sees society from outside and above, as though at a distance. This position leads anthropologists "to reduce all social relations to communicative relations and, more precisely, to decoding operations" (Bourdieu 1977:1). Informants' discursive accounts of rules are not descriptions of social reality, nor are they accounts that local informants

would give to one another. They are special creations meant only for anthropologists as outsiders. Discourse intended for an insider would not
state the general rules of social organization, but would instead discuss
specific cases.

The heart of Bourdieu's *Outline of a Theory of Practice* is his discussion of Kabyle marriage, in which discursive accounts of the rule or norm
— that men ought to marry parallel cousins within their own lineages —
do not explain behavior. The public rule is in the men's sphere; the actual
marriage strategies are often worked out by women. Issues such as the
wife's relations with her husband's mother may be central to the marriage decision in practice, but are not described in official discourse about
marriage. Within the men's sphere, unstated practical considerations
about lineage wealth may lead the negotiators to redefine the official ge-
nealogical relationship as closer or more distant. The practical knowledge used in marriage negotiations is never coherently stated; words are
found afterwards, in the officializing discourse of parallel-cousin marriage, to give the union standing with reference to the public norm.

Practice is central to the understanding of Kabyle society, yet unknow-
able to the anthropologist who studies only discursive rules. Practice is
not, for Bourdieu, an alternative set of rules — hidden or esoteric rules
known by the people themselves but hidden from anthropologists. The
material conditions of life and the facts of intimate socialization (the way
in which children learn the organization of interior space within a house,
for example) produce a homogenization of dispositions and interests,
leading people to improvise in regular ways. The generative principle of
regulated improvisations Bourdieu calls *habitus*. The definition of habitus
as a subjective but not individual system shows that even though extended
discussion in Bourdieu's book is devoted to Marcel Mauss, his central debt
is to Max Weber (Bourdieu 1977:64, 78, 86).

Practice is a central issue in recent anthropology. Sherry Ortner, in
an influential review of anthropological theory, characterizes the 1980s
as the decade of practice (1984:144). The literature is fascinating, with
two consistent and interrelated weaknesses: the first is that the major works
on the issue picture any change in practice and discourse as occurring
through thousands of individual but anonymous acts; this leaves us with
no way of identifying crucial innovations in practice or discourse — crucial
moments of change. The second is the absence of a clear link between
consciousness and power. The study of intellectuals provides a way of
addressing both these problems, as we will see after a brief mention of
some influential approaches to practice.

Ortner herself leaves discourse silent. All the action is in the realm of
practice. The problem then is how to explain change. She mentions the

general agreement among theorists in opposing a view of action that sees it as merely the execution of preexisting rules and norms. The alternative, she writes, is a romantic or heroic voluntarism, built on a false sense of the freedom and inventiveness of actors. In the end she rejects voluntarism and argues that anthropology needs to move back in the direction of social action as the enactment or execution of preexisting norms (1984:150). How then does change come about? For her answer, Ortner relies on Sahlins (1981): People in different social positions have different interests, without necessarily having radically different views of the world.

> Change comes about when traditional strategies, which assume traditional patterns of relations (e.g. between chiefs and commoners, or between men and women), are deployed in relation to novel phenomena (e.g. the arrival of Captain Cook in Hawaii) which do not respond to those strategies in traditional ways. This change of context, this refractoriness of the real world to traditional expectations, calls into question both the strategies of practice and the nature of relationships which they presuppose (Ortner 1984:155–56).

This approach has significant strengths. It allows for divergence of interests and of power among actors within a single society, and it demonstrates that the reproduction of practice may also be the mechanism of the transformation of practice. Yet there are also difficulties.

Sahlins's approach is based on the assumption that societies, each with its own historicity, have relatively clear boundaries—that they are "Islands of History." In an African context the whole weight of historical research since the 1960s has shown that important institutions and patterns of action stretched across the boundaries of linguistic/ethnic/cultural groups. Trade diasporas, religious brotherhoods, regional healing cults, the movement of individual households in search of farming land, and migration during famine all took place within spatial boundaries very different from the lines on any ethnic map. Religious brotherhoods had their own historicities, as did healing cults, descent groups, and royal dynasties. African society, even during the precolonial period, was not homogeneous. The heterogeneity of spatial boundaries for overlapping institutions and patterns of action led also to the coexistence of multiple historicities within any particular locality.

Sahlins sees practice and prescription, habitus and history, as the central emphases of whole societies or of strata within a society. The common people in Hawaiian society "are left without an historical appreciation of the main cultural categories. . . . For them, the culture is mostly 'lived'—in practice and as *habitus*" (1985:51). It is the kings who have history. Sahlins distinguishes between ideal-typical performative and pre-scriptive structures, characterized by a predominant emphasis on society as constituted by practice or on society as constituted by rules. Where the performative mode dominates, peoples "seem to make up the rules as they go along." In this mode "society seems sedimented, as if by an Invisible Hand, out of the pragmatic interests of its acting subjects" (1985: 26–27). But there are also societies in a prescriptive mode, "with bounded groups and compelling rules that do prescribe in advance much of the way people act and interact." In these societies nothing is new, "all is execution and repetition" (1985:xii, 28).

Maurice Bloch sees practical knowledge as adapted to "the immediate tasks to be performed in changing circumstances" (1986:187; 1977). Ritual knowledge, by contrast, is an autonomous system, imprecise in its reference to everyday circumstances. Practical knowledge therefore changes along with material changes in everyday life, whereas ritual is characterized by long-term continuity. Parkin (1984:349) and Fabian (1983:44) both reject Bloch's position as one which artificially compartmentalizes ritual and practical knowledge. These must be seen as merged in a unified practice. Comaroff also calls for a fusion of what she terms the "pragmatic and semantic [practical and discursive?] dimensions" of the communicative process (1985:5).

Bourdieu is single-minded in following the thread of practice and habitus rather than discourse, which almost never appears in *Outline of a Theory of Practice*. The rare appearance of discourse is a sign of the failure of practice. Written grammars of practice, originating within the society studied, simply make good the "misfirings" of practice. The mere fact that a discursive rationalization of practice exists leads to a speeding up of change (1977:20). The existence of discourse is both a sign that habitus no longer functions as it should, and an obstacle to the future maintenance of practice. Bourdieu quotes Sartre as saying that "Words wreck havoc when they find a name for what had up to then been lived namelessly" (1977:170).

Many of the difficult issues in defining the relationship between discursive consciousness and practical consciousness are resolved by Anthony Giddens. One central point seems obvious, but is not clearly understood by analysts who characterize whole societies or sets of activities as either discursive or practical. Discursive consciousness and practical consciousness exist side by side. Practical consciousness is embodied in what actors "know how to do." It is "tacit knowledge that is skilfully applied in the enactment of courses of conduct, but which the actor is not able to formulate discursively." Discourse is "what actors are able to 'talk about' and in what manner or guise they are able to talk about it" (Giddens 1979:57, 73). Within the domain of language, every bit of discourse is at the same time an instance of practical consciousness, for the speaker knows how to arrange words according to the rules of his or her language without being able to state discursively what those rules are.

Discourse and practice vary from one social position to another. Each person has a sphere of competent knowledge based on his or her everyday activity. A farmer, a priest, a chief, a trader, a casual laborer will all be competent in different spheres of knowledge. "The parameters of practical and discursive consciousness are bounded in specifiable ways, that connect with the 'situated' character of actors' activities, but are not reducible to it" (Giddens 1979:73).

The central unresolved question is about who invests a form of discourse or of practical activity with authority. Who authorizes it? Who succeeds in defining a set of issues or a course of action as the appropriate one, preempting the space of opposed utterances or alternative practice (Asad 1979:621)? Each person has a sphere of competent knowledge, but not all knowledge is equal in its weight within society, in its capacity to move people towards collective action, or to create authoritative discourse. The study of intellectuals is an attempt to examine the variation in discourse from one social position to another. The purpose of doing this is not to draw a map, a chart, to create yet another distant ethnographic object; it is to understand the contest in society over whose discourse is to become authoritative, whose practice will be accepted.[11]

Gramsci described the relationship between practical consciousness and discursive consciousness, and saw in the contradictions between them the possibility for an assault on hegemony. He did not use the terms *practical* and *discursive*, but he explained that ordinary individuals act in ways which contradict their own superficial moral affirmations. There is a tension between received interpretation and practical experience (Williams 1977:130). In Gramsci's interpretation:

> The active man-in-the-mass has a practical activity, but has no clear theoretical consciousness of this activity. . . . One might almost say that he has two theoretical consciousnesses (or one contradictory consciousness): one which is implicit in his activity and which truly unites him with all his fellow-workers in the practical transformation of reality; and one, superficially explicit or verbal, which he has inherited from the past and uncritically accepted. But this 'verbal' conception is not without consequences. It binds together a specific social group, it influences moral conduct and the direction of will, in a manner more or less powerful, but often powerful enough to produce a situation in which the contradictory character

of consciousness does not permit of any action, any decision or choice, and produces a condition of moral and political passivity (Translated in Femia 1975:33).

The practical activity that unites the "man-in-the-mass" with fellow workers is a whole range of activities of resistance: absenteeism, the laying down of tools, sabotaging the production process, spontaneous strikes, and so on. In Gramsci's view this spontaneous activity embodies a consciousness which rejects hegemonic values. But the same individual's discourse accepts, uncritically, the dominant values of society's ruling groups (Femia 1981:43). The contradiction, for Gramsci, is between the radicalism of practical consciousness and the conservatism of discursive consciousness. It is a contradiction which leads to passivity. In Gramsci's view it is necessary for the Communist Party, as the collective intellectual of the working class, to build on the radicalism of practical activity, and to shape along with it a radical discursive consciousness. Only when the discourse of the workers challenges hegemonic discourse is it possible to imagine fundamental change.

The valuable contribution here is the recognition that practical consciousness and discursive consciousness can coexist in a state of contradiction. It is clear, however, that no regular relationship exists that ties practical consciousness to rebellion or discursive consciousness to consent. Some workers are articulate in their discussions of the inhumanity of the workplace but are then entirely deferential to managers in practice. In the case reported in this book, there were peasant intellectuals who explained in eloquent discourse that Kilindi chiefs had no right to exercise authority over their subjects, and that chiefship was inherently unjust, but who then paid their respects to the rain chiefs or offered tribute labor. Their practice accepted the established order, while their discourse challenged it. There is no limit to the way contradictions can appear — contradictions between dissenting discourse and consenting practice, or the reverse, in addition to contradictions within practice and within discourse.[12]

The point is an important one, for the implication of Gramsci's position is that peasants are incapable of formulating a discursive critique of their situation and must therefore rely on leaders from outside the peasantry. The case described in this book shows that dissenting peasants discussed their situation with eloquence and penetration. They lost the final battle not because they accepted hegemonic discourse, but because the emerging bureaucrats (most of whom did not criticize the colonial government before it fell) were prepared to take over the instruments of government, and the peasant intellectuals were not. The men who ended up in office were the ones who could keep the flow of paperwork moving.

The question as posed by Gramsci about consciousness which accepts or challenges hegemony is somewhat different from the core question posed here, which is Who authorizes discourse and practice? The difference is an important one. To say that discourse is hegemonic tells us about its ultimate origin (with a ruling class) and its ultimate purpose (to support the established class order). The present analysis is more modest, less susceptible to a teleological interpretation, but equally interested in the relationship between discourse and power. We ask several questions: What is the nature of an inherited stream of discourse? What is the history of the intellectuals who use that discourse; what is their social position and what are their interests? Finally, what is the relationship of the intellectuals and their discourse to holders of power at a wider level? In the 1950s, for example, some peasants began to demand that local job-holders be educated and technically competent. What was the position of these peasant intellectuals? Where did they learn elements of this discourse? What were its internal coherences? How did these peasants reshape the inherited discourse? They used the discourse of technical competence to challenge the authority of chiefs, but it had the effect, at the same time, of asserting the authority of men with school education over illiterate peasants. In the 1960s, questions of technical competence became central in public discourse (to the point where the cognate of an *expert* is used commonly in Swahili and now in Shambaa). How did the bureaucrats come to power, and through what means did they make their discourse the official one? These questions can be given concrete answers which account for the character of discourse, its social context, and its uses within a field of power.

The method being proposed is to explore the history of divergent groups of intellectuals within peasant society, or closely attached to peasant society, and also to study streams of discourse and practice within their social contexts. It becomes possible to place discourse and the intellectuals within the framework of larger historical processes, to ask which group authorizes a particular stream of discourse at a particular time.

This approach has a significant advantage within current ethnographic usage: it allows us to situate habitus and discourse in a society without making the assumption that the whole of a society shares a single body of practice. A single local culture, superficially homogeneous, includes many streams of discourse, each located in the differentiated organization of intellectuals. The intellectuals can be understood, for their part, with reference to their social positions and their interests. Men who have held government jobs have learned the discourse and practice appropriate to office work and bureaucratic organization, even though these men now farm the land. Women who attend at births learn the appropriate bodies of discourse and practice. Members of the community of Islam become socialized within yet another tradition. Chiefs, healers, and lay evangelists have their own interests, their own discourse, their own practice. Yet all these members of local society live side by side, speak a common language, and share many basic assumptions. The groups of institutions are, however, linked to power — to the dominant forces of the wider society — in very different ways.[13]

Giddens writes about the need to mediate the opposition between structure and agency. If we study intellectuals and their discourse as they evolve in relation to power, it is possible to speak about the structure *of* agency. The agents are the historical actors, the intellectuals. When we study the practical interests and the consciousness of intellectuals, we move beyond the assumption that structure is form and agency is formlessness. If we understand the streams of discourse as related to the social positions and interests of the agents, then agency itself has a structure. Agency has a cultural structure — knowledge used by the particular groups of intellectuals — and it has a material structure related to the interests and alliances of the intellectuals themselves within the wider world of power and production.

Studying the history of intellectuals and of their consciousness is an attempt to contribute to a continuing enterprise, one described well by the Comaroffs:

> The anthropological concept of culture has been criticized for overstressing the implicit and categorical, for treating signs and symbols as if they were neutral and above history, and for ignoring their empowering and authoritative dimensions. On the other hand, Marxist theory has been taken to task for neglecting both the meaningful bases of consciousness and the expressive forms of ideology. The effort to draw together the two perspectives, and so to address the shortcomings of both, lies at the core of much theoretical debate (1987:205).

They go on to say that consciousness must be understood as an active process. The present work suggests that beyond this, consciousness can be located within a structured historical framework — structured through the historical continuities in particular varieties of discourse and practice, and structured according to the positions of the historical agents.

The study of intellectuals, of their discourse and practice, leaves us with a strategy for dealing with the dissolution of a spatially coherent ethnographic object — the end of the "tribe," the "ethnic group," the "ethnolinguistic community." The problem, as we saw, is that local society and the larger society merge and interpenetrate at many levels, to the point where we cannot say what is local and what is larger. Young men who saw themselves in terms that could best be translated as *tribesmen* or as *peasant farmers* actually earned much of their livelihood far from home, working on sisal plantations or in towns. The Christianity of Shambaa Lutherans shared many of its central terms with religion as practiced in Scandinavia or the American Middle West. Chiefs, who claimed to be quintessentially local, were actually employees of the colonial government, agents serving masters based in London and Dar es Salaam, under the supervision of the Trusteeship Council of the United Nations in New York. The British decision-makers planned the role of chiefs so as to harmonize with Tanganyika's economic role within the British Empire. Where were the boundaries of this society, of this culture? They were different in every different context of action and in every domain of discourse.

Local ethnic boundaries in Africa have always been a fiction, when taken in the classic ethnographic sense as marking off coherent, isolated islands of cultural practice, each with its own political structure. The growing understanding that this is so, the dissolution of the imagined societies, has presented a central challenge to scholars who describe African culture and society at the local level. The strategies for dealing with an unbounded local society are as numerous as the scholars, perhaps more numerous. It is possible to sketch only a few of them before returning to the implications of the present argument.

One strategy is simply to abandon local society as the unit of analysis altogether, even while continuing to analyze social action at a local level. This is possible if one describes institutions, or forms of discourse, which exist locally but are organized within a much larger spatial framework. Karen Fields defines the spatial limits for her study of Watchtower in colonial Northern Rhodesia as the limits of Watchtower's organization in the world. Indeed, Fields explains that she carried out field research at Kingdom Hall in Boston (1985:297). She is concerned also with the interaction between Watchtower and colonial control, and so the spatial organization of colonial rule provides a second set of boundaries, interacting with the first.

A second strategy is to focus on culturally embedded categories for understanding transformations that occur on a scale wider than any local society. A dramatic if somewhat uncontrolled example of this can be found, in relation to Latin America, in Michael Taussig's *The Devil and Commodity Fetishism in Latin America* (1980), which explores the indigenous construction of discourse and practice to interpret alienation in the mines and plantations as opposed to the primeval reciprocity of rural life. Even when the examples are local (as they often are in similar African studies), the opposed principles imply the existence of historical change in a wider world.

A third approach is relentlessly empiricist. It begins with the recognition that the local and the global interpenetrate in unpredictable ways, and simply follows the connections as and when they occur. This is John Peel's approach, written in reaction against the mechanical reasoning of studies on modes of production and on dependency. Marxist approaches, according to Peel, assume answers; they foreclose on issues which need to be kept open. They do not account for the central place of culture and of politics in twentieth century African history. "What is needed . . . ," Peel writes, "is a rounded, non-reductionist history of the transformation of social structures" (1983:12). This is what he provides, with accounts of the relationship between a Yoruba kingdom and the colonial state, of the role of cocoa production in changing occupational structures, and also of patterns of migration, careers, religious conversion, and party politics. Each particular empirically defined sphere of action is described in its appropriate spatial framework.

A final approach is a subtle and powerful one which bases its strategy on fundamental characteristics of life amongst the peasantry. Sara Berry studies patterns of economic differentiation among Yoruba farmers.[14] She finds that they are neither self-sufficient nor committed to remaining farmers. Differentiation among the farmers has more to do with farmers' differential links to the regional political economy than with differential access to rural land and agricultural capital. Relations of political patronage and access to the state are central to rural accumulation. If one wants to understand accumulation, mobility, and class formation in a Yoruba community, one needs to follow the relevant political and economic links wherever they lead. The wider world is not external to the local community; it is at the heart of the community's internal processes of differentiation.

In a similar way, the central changes in political practice and discourse in twentieth-century Shambaai owed their particular form to linkages between local society and the wider world. The linkages took their form in three ways. Firstly, intellectuals defined their communities of shared discourse and practice in ways which reached across spatial boundaries. A Lutheran lay evangelist in Shambaai was part of a community which included lay evangelists among the Zaramo (near Dar es Salaam), and at Tanga. Aspiring Muslim teachers similarly participated in a community, centered on the coast, whose spatial definition had nothing to do with the ethnic boundaries of Shambaai, nor with governmental boundaries. Government workers, school teachers, even local healers participated in communities with their own particular spatial boundaries. The particular traditions of discourse and practice were transmitted within these dispersed communities, which played a crucial role in the socialization of succeeding generations of intellectuals. Even chiefs, who owed their livelihoods to their mastery of Shambaa practice, learned to work within the general administrative framework of the colony, and met with chiefs from other parts of the Territory to exchange ideas and discuss problems.

Secondly, the structure of power, which authorized some forms of discourse and practice and prohibited others, occupied a spatial field much wider than, and very different from, ethnic Shambaai. We need only to look at the hierarchy of the Roman Catholic church to know that acceptable practice and acceptable discourse within the churches of Shambaai found their authorization at a higher level, outside East Africa. The same is true of chiefship, or of the policy on whether to admit Muslims in government-supported mission schools. These decisions were made in a complex process involving the interplay of authorities in London making policy for the whole of tropical Africa (taking competing economic interests into account), authorities in Dar es Salaam, provincial authorities in Tanga, and authorities in Lushoto District. Authorizing structures were also located within African society, amongst the peasantry. Some varieties of discourse and practice were unacceptable within Shambaai, and local people could prohibit their use. This happened in innumerable unseen ways, but it also happened in the dramatic resistance of the 1950s, through which local people destroyed the major British plan for changing the organization of daily life.

Finally, there was the corpus of discourse and practice itself, which spread not only across spatial fields, but also across domains of social activity.[15] Discussions of healing the land, we have seen, are special cases within a broader body of discourse in which ambivalent power can be put to benevolent uses only when the powerful healer is the owner of all wealth. This body of discourse and practice found expression in sacrifice to the ancestors, in domestic healing rites, and in chiefly politics. A completely different sort of example can be found in the thought of one group of peasant intellectuals of the 1950s who argued that employment for a specialized task implied formal education at that task, in school. These intellectuals cast their argument in the terms of a wider discourse which was, of course, given its classic description by Max Weber (1978), who wrote about "rational"-legal authority. After peasant intellectuals invoked this language in relation to chiefship, it was also used by Lutheran congregants in demanding an end to racially based control over the church. Rational-legal discourse has, of course, a world-wide distribution, and its full significance can only be understood through a study ranging far beyond the local social organization of Shambaai. In the same way, the discourse of ownership and ritual power can only be fully understood in all its forms, which stretch across much of East Africa.

It should be clear by now that it is impossible to write a full history of the intellectuals of Shambaai and of their discourse. I do not propose to attempt a substantial account of rational-legal discourse, nor of the structure of authority within the Lutheran church of Tanganyika, nor of the organization of the Islamic community in the northeast of the colony. The history being proposed is much more modest: an account of discourse on healing the land and harming the land in relation to wider political debates and to the history of intellectuals, within the context of larger struggles to shape society and politics in East Africa. Nevertheless, it is important that the broken threads of all the connections in space be left hanging, that we not succumb to the illusion that this is the history of "a society" and its discourse.

The study of intellectuals and their discourse is a strategy for writing about the people of Shambaai without making them into ethnographic specimens, examples of the "other." The writing of ethnography threatens to place the ethnographer as the subject, the active thinker, the giver-of-names, and the people about whom the ethnographer writes as the objects, the others, the people who are given names (Parkin 1982:xxxiii–xxxiv). Fabian's (1983) critique of anthropology is devastating: during the period of field research the ethnographer lives together with the people studied; he and they (she and they) live in the same time and place, in the same epoch, share the same world. But then the written ethnography transforms the people studied into the "others," who live far from the ethnographer's world, distant in space, and are therefore treated as though distant in time, not subject to the same historical forces as the ethnographer or the readers of ethnography.

The problem of otherness is not easily solved, for the subject matter of anthropology is cultural difference. If we define the people of a given society as different from us, then we have defined them as other, distant from us, not subject to the same historical forces or living in the same moral universe. This is unacceptable. But if we say that we are indeed coeval, living in the same era, subject to the same historical forces, struggling with the same issues, then we lose the picture of cultural variation which is the heart of anthropology.

The study of intellectuals and their discourse takes some steps towards mediating this contradiction. Firstly, it dissolves the picture, drawn from natural history, of varieties of human culture scattered around the world—what Fabian calls "culture gardens." The "society" being described, the aggregation of people at a particular time and place, is no longer seen as having a homogeneous and exotic culture; the picture is now more complex, one in which there are in fact locally shared elements of discourse and practice, in which people do speak a common language, but in which historical agents within local society use and transmit their divergent streams of discourse and practice. Secondly, the intellectuals draw their practice, and define their community, in ways that situate them within the history of the rest of the world. The Lutherans of Shambaai (or the Catholics, or the Muslims) situate themselves within a religious community which extends beyond the borders of the supposed culture gardens. Thirdly, the world within which discourse is authorized — the larger world in which peasant intellectuals define their interests — is the same world where the scholars live: a world in which crops must be sold on the world market, and one shaped by concentrations of political and economic power, the concrete form of which can be discerned in intellectual practice itself. Finally, the approach to intellectuals requires that the anthropologist (or historian) must also be situated, in relation to the stream of inherited ethnographic or historical discourse and practice and in relation to the ethnographer's own social position and interests. We cannot picture an approach in which the peasants are defined as intellectuals and the ethnographer is not.

Discourse and Peasant Resistance

Healing the land and harming the land, as an idiom in which to discuss relations between chiefs and subjects, was the language of political struggle at many of the important moments of historical conflict in Shambaai. The present work could therefore be read as a history of resistance. Nevertheless, resistance is not the central theme. The narrative is organized around the history of discourse on healing the land in its social context. We continue to focus on that discourse even at times when the relationship between chiefs and peasants is not at the center of the political stage, when healing the land is not the dominant idiom of political debate (for example, after Tanganyikan independence). It is paradoxical that a focus on discourse and its context gives us a revealing vantage point from which to view resistance.

In Shambaai, the language of healing the land and harming the land has been embedded in actual peasant struggle for much of the past century and a half. A political debate framed in these terms conceded from the start that issues of chiefship, rather than issues of trade, or of colonial control, or of the system of labor on plantations, were central. Casting the debate in terms of healing the land and harming the land had the effect of legitimizing the role played by chiefs, and of making nondynastic issues, potentially very important ones, seem marginal. In this sense the terms of debate could be seen as working in support of the colonial order through most of the British period. A study of healing the land and harming the land reveals a great deal about the basis on which Africans accepted colonial rule. If language is seen as supporting either resistance or collaboration, then healing the land lies in the balance as the idiom of collaboration. This was not invariable, however. In some parts of Shambaai in the 1950s, local people used the popularity of particular rain chiefs as an instrument to defeat British plans for the thoroughgoing commoditization of agriculture. As we shall see in other cases, the ostensible language of hegemony could be turned against the hegemonic power.

The focus on the central terms of chiefly discourse — on *healing the land* and *harming the land* — is not a narrow one; it cannot stand on its own. People struggle to escape from the bonds of their language, to define issues in alternative terms. The core discourse had the effect of defining conflicts in terms of local and dynastic issues, and of excluding from debate the larger questions about colonialism. The peasant intellectuals had no choice but to use the inherited language, but they created or adapted other forms of discourse, searched for alternative political language, redefined the issues for themselves. For this reason, the significance of debates on healing the land must be examined alongside dissenting discourse, the attempts by peasant intellectuals to escape from the prison of their own language. A study of the core terms of accepted discourse gives us a privileged place from which to explore dissent, for we understand the limits against which it presses. A study of dissent then leads us, inexorably, to a study of intellectuals within society, for the alternatives forms of discourse are socially situated in the history of intellectuals — the language of Christian evangelists, of clerks, or of Muslim teachers are alternatives, resources to be used in creating a dissenting discourse. The struggle over discourse is rooted in the social history of competing intellectuals.

Recent resistance studies, which explore the diversity of peasant ideology and experience, are the culmination of trends in history-writing which began with the rejection of the nationalist literature of the 1960s. The rejected interpretation saw heroic early resistance against colonial conquest as laying the groundwork for the postwar independence movements.[16]

Important parts of the postnationalist interpretation emerged in the work of Allen Isaacman, who emphasized two themes. He showed that the earlier literature's emphasis on military confrontation directed attention away from thousands of acts of silent, day-to-day resistance: tax evasion, work slowdowns, the destruction of European property, and desertion. He also showed the importance of divisions within African society, which made it impossible in many cases to see resistances against the Europeans as the risings of united and homogeneous African nations against the alien intruders (Isaacman 1976; Isaacman and Isaacman 1977; Isaacman et al. 1980). On occasion African rulers surrendered to the Europeans, but their subjects resisted. It was not always clear whether the primary enemy of the rebels was the European invader or the African ruler. Several recent works describe precolonial situations of incipient revolt into which Europeans blundered unwittingly, setting alight fuel which had been waiting only for a spark (Glassman 1988; Des Forges 1986; Caulk 1986). The differentiation of the peasantry proved to be crucial also in the high and late colonial periods.

Studies of internal African differentiation have become increasingly subtle. Terence Ranger's important study of peasant consciousness and guerrilla war in Zimbabwe (1985) discusses the varied forms of peasant discourse, including peasant religious discourse, which he calls "a privileged language in which reality is categorised and transformed" (1985: 185). John Lonsdale (1986) explores similar questions in trying to understand Kikuyu definitions of a moral community in the origins of Mau Mau. Beinart and Bundy describe the varying experiences of the peasantry as shaping resistance: "An individual might be appealed to as a peasant threatened with new taxes or loss of land; as the member of a former chiefdom or kinsman in a local lineage; as an elder in a separatist church; or as a recently returned migrant from docks or mines" (1987:3). The closer we get to a careful empirical concern with peasant discourse, the less uniform the peasantry appears.

Beinart and Bundy (together with the writers on everyday resistance) describe peasant ideas and peasant actions that are hidden from the public view. "The affairs of rural Africans 'away in the locations,'" they write, "were submerged, and were dropping below the gaze of government, of white sympathisers, and even of African political leaders" (1987:1). The central conflicts were "hidden struggles." Some writers on everyday resistance claim that the struggle needed to be hidden if it was to be effective. A recent book quotes Marc Bloch:

> Almost invariably doomed to defeat and eventual massacre, the great insurrections were altogether too disorganized to achieve any lasting result. The patient, silent struggles stubbornly carried on by rural communities over the years would accomplish more than these flashes in the pan (Scott 1985:28).

The patient, silent struggles are the thousand acts of everyday resistance: peasants boil their cotton seeds to prevent them from germinating, for example, or intentionally infect their coffee bushes so that crops grown under compulsion will die; they hide in caves on the day the tax collector appears and remove field markers for required soil improvement schemes.

The silence of the sources on consciousness in everyday resistance is not mere chance: it is a necessary characteristic of this form of struggle. There is good reason for everyday resisters to *avoid* stating their intentions openly if they are to be effective. The forces of government and of employers are too powerful for members of a vulnerable class to resist directly. Open resisters are fired from work, arrested, or beaten. Where rich and poor are sharply divided, the poor often come to depend on the rich for help in time of illness, or for employment. The poor person who openly dissents from the discourse of the rich loses the possibility of relying on their help. The poor person's response is not to yield, but to resist in ways which are invisible, which are organized offstage. For resistance to be effective, it *must* frustrate the historian. A thorough study of peasant discourse, however, helps in placing the precious pieces of evidence appropriately.

Everyday resistance is silent as a strategy, but not necessarily silent in fact. The public stage is controlled by the powerful. The peasant who resists can only do so offstage. According to Scott (1985) the peasant resister often achieves discursive penetration — clearly describes the forces which are affecting peasant life — but always offstage, never onstage, where peasants must be silent or they will be crushed.

The separation between action offstage and action onstage, discourse offstage and discourse onstage, is a valuable one. It acknowledges that peasants are resisting but accepts the fact that peasant discourse is, for the moment, inaudible. Not absent, but inaudible. There is a big difference between those two: the distinction between discourse offstage and discourse onstage is very different from the distinction we have already made between discursive consciousness and practical consciousness. To describe consciousness as practical is to say that knowledge is tacit and that the actor is incapable of formulating it discursively. To say that discourse cannot be seen onstage leaves open the question of whether the action emerges as practice without discursive penetration, or whether the action emerges from discourse which is merely unseen, publicly invisible.

The distinction between discourse offstage and discourse onstage is central to the rather strange process of research by which this work was created. The heart of this book is a discussion of the politics of the 1940s and 1950s. It is a period on which I never did research in Shambaai, even though I have done field research there on and off since 1966. I was, by chance, in a position to overhear offstage conversations, many of which focused on healing the land and on the politics of the 1950s. The language of onstage communication in Shambaai is Swahili. One does not usually speak to governmental authorities on any official topic in Shambaa. Much of my own nonworking time has been spent visiting in houses, stopping at village tea-houses or bars, gossiping in the Shambaa language, and listening to other peoples' conversations in Shambaa. Many crucial bits of discourse cited in this book first came up in conversations between peasants, not as statements addressed to me. I was a bystander. The central issues first appeared as a disjuncture between what was being said in Swahili at government meetings about development and nationalism (and later *ujamaa*), and what was being said (often by the same people) in Shambaa at home about rain and chiefship.

This does not mean that everything said in Shambaa is offstage and everything in Swahili onstage. The formal interviews on precolonial history which I conducted in Shambaa had an onstage character. Statements addressed to the chief or to his officials in the 1940s or 1950s would clearly have been public, onstage, even if sometimes spoken in Shambaa. One of the problems with the terms *offstage* and *onstage*, private and public, is that they assume a single context. There were clearly differences between statements in the 1950s which were meant to be heard by British district officials and others which were meant to be heard by Kilindi chiefs and not by the British. Before discussing whether a statement is made offstage or on, we need to know whose stage we are talking about.

If we see the public stage of the 1940s and 1950s as belonging to the British, then the distinction between discourse offstage and discourse onstage leads to the most puzzling and contradictory outcome: the opposite of the one proposed by Scott (1985), who would expect peasants to challenge established rule in private while paying it deference in public. In the actual event, offstage discourse accepted the basic structure of control; onstage discourse challenged it. The central discourse on rain, which focused on political issues at the local level rather than on issues of imperialism, labor, or the territorial economy, was held offstage. The discourse on healing the land depended on an assumption that the fertility of the land could be shaped by techniques outside the realm of science. These assumptions were unacceptable to the British. For the most part, healing the land was not mentioned in correspondence with the British, or in public discourse where the British were present. Indirect rule allowed Tanganyika's government to reinforce a discourse of which it claimed no knowledge. The governor, or provincial commissioner, or district commissioner would not have been able to discuss healing the land on its own terms. They coopted preexisting intellectuals as agents, and those agents carried along their own discourse. The outcome was that the colonial authorities revived a discourse they neither understood nor approved. The main debate emerged among peasants, in the Shambaa language. Only a shadow of the real debate, a pallid discussion of dynastic questions, appeared in public discussion.

The rich discourse which took place onstage, in full view of the British, was concerned with the definition of democracy, with the need for economic development, and with the real meaning of the abolition of slavery. These appear at first glance to be thoroughly hegemonic as issues, but they were not. Genovese has argued that in a slave society democratic slogans can be revolutionary, and in this case of a colonial society they were (cited in Marks 1986:365). Shambaai under colonial rule was profoundly nondemocratic; a demand for democracy was a demand for radical change. It led to debate about the means by which local people could take popular control over the direction of their own society. The discussion of development was also radical. The British in their publications for African readers claimed to be bringing education, health services, and rapid economic progress to Tanganyika.[17] Local people examined the poverty of their own local society, its lack of schools and of maternity clinics, the absence of truly wealthy progressive farmers, and asked the reasons for local poverty and underdevelopment. Local intellectuals also turned discussions of the abolition of slavery against the British. They criticized the arbitrary exercise of chiefly power over the peasantry, saying that it was a form of slavery. Resisters were able to make radical claims in public because they adopted the central terms of what might have been seen as hegemonic colonial discourse. Colonial officers found it difficult to suppress discussions of democracy, development, or the abolition of slavery. The public acceptance of discussion on these subjects made a space for radical criticism. The peasant intellectuals who used this space did not, however, limit themselves to discourse onstage. They were able to argue offstage that the particular chief who exercised arbitrary power of the sort abolished with the end of slavery had no rain.

The history of peasant intellectuals and their discourse refutes the claim that a resisting peasantry inevitably looks backwards, trying to recapture the past rather than move towards the future. To see the peasantry as backward-looking is to assess, realistically, the destructive effects of the commoditization of rural relations. When this happens, poorer countryfolk lose the customary protections of earlier periods: the old social contract is broken; a defense of that contract is appropriate, but the defense necessarily looks backwards to the social forms of an earlier era. The resistance of the 1950s in Shambaai was backward-looking in exactly this way. Colonial erosion-control rules threatened to destroy the system by which the poor borrowed land for subsistence, rent-free. The resistance movement defeated this threat — it looked backwards in defending the rights of an earlier period.

This is not, however, the whole story. Peasant intellectuals drew on their wider discursive resources to make a new critique of local conditions — a critique that accepted change as inevitable but asked that control of local politics and the local economy be left in local hands, and asked furthermore that principles of justice prevail.

One reason the myth of the intellectually underdeveloped peasant has survived is the practical record of peasant failure. Peasants have not succeeded in taking power in the independent states of modern Africa. The assumption is that this must be the result of a weak peasant world view — one which is not "systematic, 'derived,' and structured" sufficiently to carry protesters all the way to the creation of a new order.[18] In the present case, however, what was lacking was not a derived world view but the resources necessary to impose that world view on the whole of colonial Tanganyika. Peasants were forced to make alliances in order to end colonial rule, and their allies won control of the new state.

2

Tribute and Dependency
in Late Nineteenth-Century
Shambaai

The death of a king remained secret until a new king
had been installed in the night near Vugha, the capital. At dawn the war
drum *Nenkondo* sounded to announce the death of a king and the accession of a king. The people of Vugha streamed out to the Council Clearing to find their new ruler seated, wearing the ostrich-feather headdress.
This was the only time the king's subjects were permitted to state openly
their conditions for the social contract with their ruler. They greeted him
with the royal title, "*Simba Mwene*," and then shouted,

> Give us rain. Give us bananas. Give us sugar cane. Give us plantains. Give
> us meat. Give us food. You are our king, but if you do not feed us properly
> we will get rid of you. The country is yours; the people must have their
> stomachs filled. Give us rain. Give us food. . . .[1]

Once the people accepted the ruler as *Simba Mwene*, "the lion," they
knew that he would be free to take all the wealth of the land. It was
said of the Simba Mwene that "he eats the whole land" (*aja shi yoshe*).
Just as a lion might descend on a cow where one least expected it, so a
Kilindi could descend to demand tribute anywhere within his territory.
The king was *Ng'wenye Shi*, "Owner of the Land." *Ownership* in this
sense implied control over the land in its political aspect, in the same
way the "owner" of a village (*ng'wenye mzi*), its patriarch, held rights
over his progeny.[2] To be "Owner of the Land" implied the right to take
tribute from any of his subjects. Only if all the wealth of the land was
put into the hands of the king, as though his own, would he bring rain
and food. A nineteenth-century proverb has it that the king cannot be
bribed; you have nothing with which to bribe him, for all the wealth
is his.[3]

The principle that the king owned the land was discussed with me
by Mdoe Loti, a brilliant man, blind in old age, who had been present
at the royal accession of 1895. We had talked about that accession at length,

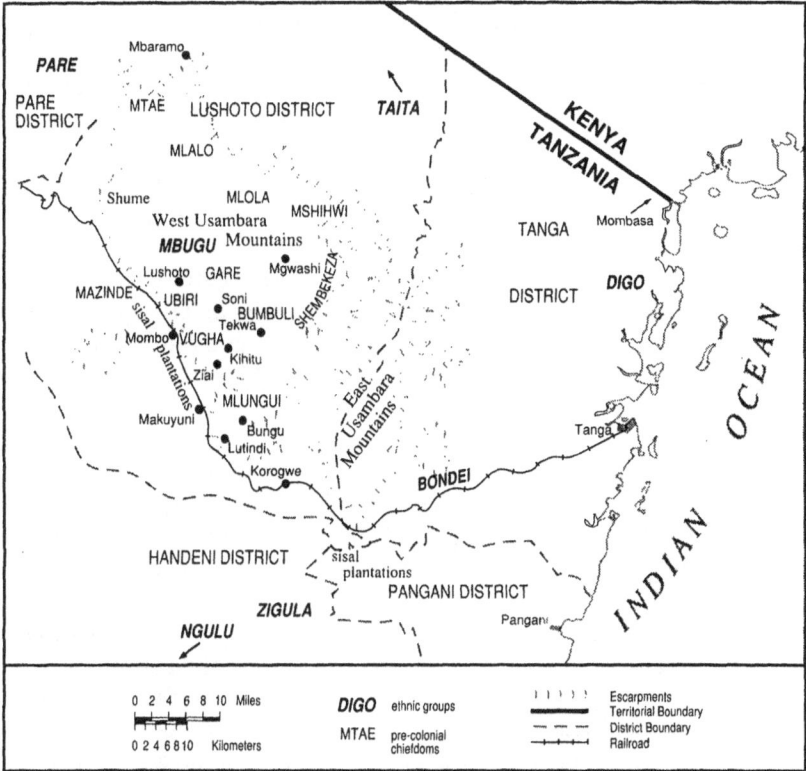

Map 1. Shambaai and Neighboring Areas

but now we were exploring the rite of sacrifice as practiced by both peasants and royals. The rite had existed in the nineteenth century and was still practiced by some people in much the same form in the 1960s.[4] The person who wished to sacrifice to his departed father invited his patrilineal relatives and then also brought a healer from outside the lineage. At the start of the rite, which took place at night, all present went out of the house in single file, circled around outside and then re-entered, singing that the house now belonged to the healer. Mdoe Loti explained, "The healer must 'build' your house as though it were his own. In the morning you 'redeem' your house, you buy it back" by paying the healer. The healer must be an outsider, just as the king is seen as an out-sider to whom the kingdom is given by the ancient inhabitants. The healer, Mdoe Loti insisted, is deceived. Of course the house is not his. He takes it over in a figurative action so that he can make the rite. Similarly, he explained, "The chief does not possess the land. He is deceived. It is not his land at all. It belongs to the people themselves. In this the king is like the healer" (Mdoe Loti 27 May 1967). It is difficult to know whether Mdoe Loti's skepticism about the king as true owner of the land had its origins in discussions of *demokrasi* which had been alive ten years earlier, in the 1950s. I suspect not. In any event it is clear that in the nineteenth century, peasants in the Shambaa kingdom said that the king had rights in all the wealth of the land, but then expected him to exercise those rights in a moderate way.

One of the central organizing principles of the myth of the founding king, Mbegha, as told in the nineteenth century, was that dangerous forms of power bring life and fertility rather than death and famine only when the powerful person is given the land as his own. Mbegha had come from the land of Nguu, where he was a ritually dangerous person. According to many versions, he had been a *kigego*, a beastlike infant whose survival guarantees that his relatives will die. Mbegha changed into a life-giving and beneficent king after the Shambaa voluntarily gave him the wealth of their land. The crucial moment of transition, in the myth, came when local people gave Mbegha their daughters as his wives, without bridewealth.[5]

Nineteenth-century chiefs took wives without paying bridewealth because the wealth of the land was theirs. The precolonial rule of exogamy held that a marriage was acceptable only if the husband's relatives were able to make the bridewealth payments to the wife's relatives. This became impossible when the two sets of relatives overlapped in such a way that they held common rights in wealth. Marrying a prohibited woman was described as "turning in upon your own wealth." Chiefs could not pay bridewealth because all the wealth of the land was theirs. They inevitably "turned in upon" their own wealth.[6]

The relationship between tribute and fertility is illustrated by an incident at Vugha after colonial conquest. The German district officer had hanged the king after forcing him to accept Lutheran missionaries near the capital. The people of Vugha saw that power had been transferred, and tried to take measures to insure the fertility of the land under the new regime. In 1897, two years after the king's death, cattle disease broke out in the village of Kighuunde, near Vugha. A leader of the local people made a request of Vugha's German missionary. "Our livestock are dying," he said. "If we are under your protection, we will keep our livestock. I would like to give you a ewe, for you to care for, and so that you will one day have a herd of your own. Then if my animals die, so will yours; if I drink milk, so will you."[7] Only if the missionaries shared ownership, only if the people of Kighuunde paid tribute, could the missionaries be expected to use their power to keep the herds alive.

The people of Vugha did not give the missionaries *all* their livestock;

they offered a single ewe. Clearly there were limits to the wealth or the labor a ruler was expected to take in return for increasing the fertility of the land. As Mdoe Loti implied, it was merely a figure of speech to say that all the wealth of the land was the king's. The actual limits were set in practice.

The king's work as a rainmaker, and popular judgments of his efficacy at making rain, will be discussed in the next chapter and in the narrative throughout this book. The present chapter began with the conditions set by Vugha's peasants: the king must give them bananas, must give them food, must give them plantains. It asks whether there were other ways, beyond rainmaking, in which king and chiefs became involved in the basic peasant economy and in questions of food security.

Tribute

The most obvious way that chiefs became involved in the peasant economy was through extraction, through tribute payment. The kingdom's boundaries, the distribution of its tribute-paying population, and its degree of effective centralization changed through time. The kingdom had its origins in the eighteenth century, along the southern rim of the West Usambara Mountains. It is probable that most of the core population at that time spoke the Shambaa language. They lived at the top of the mountain escarpment, which rose steeply out of the plains; their villages were located so that they could practice hoe agriculture in both highlands and adjacent lowlands. They also kept cows, goats, and sheep. As the kingdom grew, each neighborhood of Shambaa speakers was given a chief, who in some generations was tightly controlled by the king at Vugha and in some generations was semiautonomous. Around the kingdom's borders were areas which did not take chiefs from the ruling Kilindi lineage, but which paid tribute. Quite early, the Mbugu-speaking cattle keepers of the central highland meadows began paying tribute, although they were never ruled by Kilindi chiefs.

Around the turn of the nineteenth century, the mountain farmers at the northern rim of the West Usambaras came under the domination of Kilindi chiefs. This was the part of the kingdom which most closely resembled the original core area in economy and culture. The kingdom then spread eastwards. The Bondei farmers of the foothills east of the Usambaras came under the control of Kilindi chiefs sent from Vugha. To the east of Bondei, the lowlands stretching towards the Indian Ocean coast sent tribute to Vugha in the 1830s and 1840s, and probably earlier (Feierman 1974: chaps. 1 and 4).

Tribute payment was a matter of negotiation and of the balance between the king's (or chief's) capacity to enforce his will and the capacity as well as the desire of the peasantry to resist. Resistance came earlier in the eastern half of the kingdom, in the hills of Bondei and in the coastal zone, near the Indian Ocean, than in the West Usambara Mountains which were the kingdom's core. During the reign of Kimweri ye Nyumbai, who ruled from about 1815 to 1862, the western half of the kingdom was treated much more benevolently than the chiefdoms to the east. Chiefs in the east were freer than those in the west to take slaves from among their subjects, and to seize property capriciously. By the 1840s there were incidents of armed rebellion in the eastern chiefdoms. Even the places which remained under Kilindi control resisted paying tribute in the usual way. In 1853 a missionary, accompanied by Kimweri's *Beleko* (his major representative to the eastern provinces) and by Kimweri's soldiers, passed through a Bondei village. Kimweri, as *Ng'wenye Shi*, holder of political rights in the land, held rights in the village's wealth. The *Beleko* and the soldiers requested lodging; they had the right also to take tribute in livestock. The villagers welcomed Kimweri's men with a false report that there was smallpox in the village and that it was dangerous to enter. When the Beleko objected, the Bondei insulted him. Only the threat that all the villagers would be taken to Vugha won the soldiers lodging for the night, and even then their demand of a goat for their evening meal was refused. They ate boiled beans and bananas.[8]

Later, in 1870, these same Bondei of the eastern provinces rebelled and drove out the Kilindi altogether. They returned to a form of government in which their own local elders provided leadership. Nevertheless, the Bondei continued to accept the principle that the major Kilindi chief had a right to livestock, and would only provide rain if they respected that right. In 1884, at a time of famine, the leaders of the Bondei villages decided on their own to send one goat each to the major Kilindi rain chief whose territory was nearby.[9]

At other times peasants were forced to accept the practice of Kilindi appropriation, even while they challenged the principle. It was clear in a number of instances that men resented giving their daughters to Kilindi without bridewealth, even when they had no practical way of resisting. In numerous oral traditions marriage without bridewealth is described as "theft"— a word virtually never used for tribute collection.[10] Yet the chief's demand was difficult to resist because it was backed by superior force. The maternal grandmother of a friend of mine in Mshihwi had been married in the 1890s to chief Shatu. After German conquest the woman's brothers took her away from Shatu's village and arranged her marriage to another man, who paid them bridewealth. According to her grandson, the Kilindi complained, but her kinsmen replied, "You did not pay. You took her by force (*kwa nguvu*), and now your ability to use force has ended" (Joseph Hassani November 1966).

Even though tribute collection was variable because it depended on the outcome of negotiation between the chief's men and the peasantry, it is possible to sketch the usual extent of a chief's right to tribute at quiet times, when his authority was not being challenged in any special way, and when he was not making extraordinary demands on the peasants in his chiefdom.

Chiefs received tribute in labor, in livestock, and in food. Tribute in labor presented a special problem because the local agricultural system made very great demands on the labor of women, and also on the labor of married men. The time of the heaviest need for labor to clear or weed the chief's farms was also the most intense working time amongst the peasantry. In most instances additional labor beyond the productive needs of the households was found by looking to other age groups, aside from married men or women in their vigorous years. Health care depended on the old people, tribute labor on the young men. Mature people were less likely to work hard outside their own farms. The preference for young men was shown clearly in the chiefdom of Mtae in the 1890s: the chief was served by the young men, but the minor court officials had to be satisfied with what they described as the apathetic assistance of mature men.[11]

Each village had a special house, called a *bweni*, near its gate for boys and young men. They entered before puberty and remained until the time of marriage. At night they guarded the village's entrance gate. They were available also for collective work parties within the village, called *ngemo*. Any of the village's senior householders could call an *ngemo* of the young men. At the end of the day the host was expected to provide a cooked dish of banana- or maize-flour, together with meat. Chiefs, like the village elders, provided food for their work parties, and so in a sense they were served by *ngemo* labor.

At the royal capital of Vugha, which drew labor from the population of the whole chiefdom of Vugha, without the competing demands of minor chiefs, the young men of a particular village served as *walughojo*, "attendants," for the five days of a market cycle. They slept at Vugha, did whatever errands and jobs needed doing, including agricultural labor, and were fed at the capital. In the following market cycle the young men of another village took over. The assigned time of the king's young attendants came up once every several months.[12] In addition, at times the king's crier called out all the young men of the area around Vugha for a particular piece of farm work.

Mlalo and the other capitals were smaller than Vugha. In those places the chief's crier called out in the evening to announce that young men (or young women, or older men) were required to report to work on the following day. In the morning a horn sounded to announce the start of work. Anyone who did not report was fined a chicken, to be captured on the spot.[13]

Mature women, who were heavily burdened with farm and house work, almost never worked on the chief's farms. Instead they were required to bring firewood for the chief's wives and also for their own village young men's house. They also brought food when there was a special need at the capital, or in thanks for a good harvest.

Tribute labor was not described in the oral accounts as a heavy burden, and it does not appear to have been a focus of conflict. Tribute in livestock was the subject of greater conflict, although tribute was not the chief's sole source of wealth in livestock — perhaps not even his major source. Chiefs acquired livestock through warfare and through their role in litigation.

It is difficult to know how many cows, goats, and sheep the chiefs owned. Wealthy men in Shambaai took care to distribute their cattle widely, to reduce the risk that disease or armed attack would take the whole herd, and to avoid provoking envy. Herdsmen from outside the borders of the kingdom cared for some of the chiefs' livestock. The herdsmen included the Mbugu of the central highland meadows of Shambaai — semipastoralists who paid tribute to the king but otherwise were not governed by him (Döring 1901:90–91). Some Zigula of the plains below the escarpment served as herders to the great men of the royal court at mid-century. In 1853 a raid by the king's soldiers against the Zigula was held off because the senior officials of Vugha wanted a guarantee of indemnification if their cattle, kept in the Zigula villages, were lost. A German-period observer estimated that Kibanga, a senior chief, owned several hundred head of cattle, and then commented that a poor man owned two or three goats. It is impossible to know the basis on which he estimated Kibanga's wealth.[14]

The word for a poor person was *mkiwa* (pl. *wakiwa*), probably from the verb -*kilwa*, "to be beset with difficulties." LangHeinrich, who collected sentences for a Shambaa dictionary between 1895 and 1906, was given a sentence for *wakiwa* which implied that the division between Kilindi and others was seen as one between rich and poor, rather than between governors and governed. "We all are *wakiwa*," LangHeinrich's informant said, "and they are Wakilindi."[15] Non-Kilindi did, on occasion, accumulate greater wealth than other peasants, through service as court officials, through ivory hunting or healing, or (especially in the 1870s and 1880s) through service as war leaders or through trade. In each case, however, the right to accumulate required the chief's active consent, most commonly won through additional voluntary tribute payments. The chief's greed could easily be aroused by a rich peasant's herd, in which case the chief might descend, like a lion, to seize all the cows.

Whenever a chief faced unusual expenditures, he sent men to collect goats or cows from the subjects around. Hangers-on at the court of a Kilindi often went on their own initiative to collect tribute. They arrived at a homestead and demanded a cow or a goat. The peasant who paid was wise to follow his goat to court, to make clear the goat's source so that he would not be called upon again in the near future. Someone trying to win the chief's favor, or a group of subjects hoping for rain, sometimes voluntarily brought livestock to the chief as their "greeting" to him.[16]

The main beneficiaries of tribute, aside from the chiefs themselves, were the senior men of the court, whether at Vugha or at a lesser capital. These were not members of the Kilindi lineage. Heirs to the court officials of Vugha made it clear that their ancestors ate very well during the reigns of strong kings. In 1852 Krapf saw tribute being collected from the semi-independent coastal areas (a difficult and dangerous kind of collection) and then observed the division of the proceeds at Vugha. The tribute collectors brought back 200 pieces of cloth, which was categorized as "wealth," equivalent to livestock. Kimweri ye Nyumbai took 100 cloths. The men who collected the tribute at the coast received 42. The *Beleko*, a non-Kilindi who was Kimweri's official representative to eastern districts, received 25. The other prominent non-Kilindi officials of Vugha received 33. The senior men of Vugha had a strong interest in seeing that the king was powerful enough to collect tribute. They plotted against weak kings.[17]

Forms of Personal Dependency

The chief, as the owner of the land's collective wealth, provided an ultimate guarantee, a refuge, to individuals and local social groups at the extreme margin of survival. The local groups could not have existed in their late nineteenth-century form without chiefship to define their boundaries. Seeking refuge meant accepting a form of personal dependency on the chief, one which in some cases carried the threat that the dependent would be sold to slave traders.

A father who had no food for his children in a famine year could take them to the chief, to be fed at the court and to live as the chief's dependents. The chief could not sell them to slave dealers. After the famine's end the father would redeem his children with payments of livestock.

Women were dependent on either their husbands or their fathers for protection and a place to live. At a time when a woman decided that she would no longer continue living with her husband, if she had no refuge with father or brothers, she could flee to the court of the chief. In most cases the chief gave the husband another woman in his wife's place.[18] A young man who did not have the cattle for paying bridewealth might request that the chief pay. The young husband then worked for the chief until his debt was paid. A man responsible for adultery who, even with the help of his brothers, could not pay the indemnity of a cow and a bull calf to the offended husband, plus a cow to the chief, was forced to give a person as the chief's pawn. The adulterer would try to avoid pawning himself, so that he could work to collect the remaining livestock to redeem his dependent. A creditor, unable to collect the wealth owed to him, seized some of his debtor's property. The chief then paid the debt and returned the property but took pawns from the debtor until he himself had been repaid.[19]

In each case the chief's wealth enabled him to meet the needs of people at the margins and to make them his dependents. People sometimes said that a particular chief held back the rain, creating famine, so that peasants would be forced to sell their cattle for food, would have none left for paying indemnities, and would join the chief's personal dependents.

The existence of dependency as a refuge for people at the margins opened the way to extreme forms of exploitation when the coastal trade in slaves became important in southern Shambaai in the 1870s and 1880s. At that time some chiefs sold slaves who might in an earlier generation have been given refuge. The most brutal of the chiefs simply seized villagers and sent them off to the coast. The peasant understanding of this intensified slave trade is discussed in chapter 4. Slavery and pawnship as ways of dealing with the needs of peasants at the margins continued alongside the new slave trade, wherever it existed, and remained the predominant forms of dependency in the northern chiefdoms, even in the 1870s and 1880s.

In times of order, hearing cases and deciding on indemnities was itself a major source of chiefly wealth. At Vugha, especially in times of the kingdom's centralization, when all appeals and all murder cases were heard at the royal court, the king's share of indemnity payments was substantial. The indemnities varied with the nature of the offense, the concrete circumstances, and also the offender's demeanor before the court. If he refused to accept responsibility for offenses which were patently his own, the indemnity rose. It reached up to fifteen head of cattle in some cases of murder, with the chief taking about a third.[20]

A chief's dependents lived at his capital or at the villages of his wives. A young man of twenty years might enter the chief's own *bweni*, the bachelor house of the capital, to become a soldier in the chief's wars, fighting and living alongside free peasants. A slave soldier received a weapon from the chief, and a portion of the booty he captured. But if he was redeemed, bought free, he was required to return everything he had acquired in the chief's service.[21]

A young slave woman provided sexual services for the chief and in some cases for honored guests at his court. If the chief made her pregnant, she became another one of the chief's wives. Slave women were also given as wives to the chief's male slaves, in which case the children were the chief's (P. Wohlrab 1918:169).[22]

The chief assigned most pawns and slaves to live at the households of his wives. Each wife had her farms and her dependents to work them. She fed the slaves of her household and oversaw their work. Kimweri ye Nyumbai, who was reputed to have 300 wives, filled villages for miles around the capital with wives and dependents. The last holders of Vugha, in the 1890s, had between 30 and 50 wives each. Whenever a commoner near Vugha died, the king took one of his farms to add to the royal establishment. Lesser chiefs had fewer dependents, but almost all had some. The food grown by the chief's dependents fed visitors to the court, fed working parties, and also served as provisions for the next set of pawns.[23]

Whenever a local group pawned a member, they remained concerned with that person's well-being. The pawn held the hope of being redeemed by kinsmen. A pawn who had owned farms when free continued to own them and to profit from them. But there were other slaves who retained no rights in their own descent groups or in property; once enslaved, they were outside the politics of descent altogether. These were individuals who committed offenses against the community as a whole, as opposed to offenses (such as adultery or assault) against indemnifiable local groups.[24]

The repeated and habitual practice of witchcraft was an offense against the community as a whole. If someone was suspected of the habitual practice of *ushai*, "witchcraft," a large group of the witch's neighbors, drawn from a number of lineages, attacked the witch's village and tore down his house. They either killed the offender or took him to the chief. The chief might give them a sheep (called *the club*), sending them off to kill the witch by having him clubbed and thrown off a precipice. The sheep was then used in a healing ceremony to "cool" the danger experienced by the executioners. In other cases the chief brought the witch to live at his capital. In the late nineteenth century, Vugha had a reputation for having the largest collection of witches in Shambaai. They helped to make the war medicines of the king's armies. In any case the witch's children would become slaves of the king or of a powerful chief. All the witch's land and his wealth were confiscated. Rebels against royal power were treated in the same way.[25]

A chief had greater power to dispose of the dependents of witches than he did in the case of young people pawned for debt, or in famine, or in place of an indemnity. Witches and rebels retained no residual rights in their own descent groups. They could be sold to coastal traders for guns and powder. During Erhardt's first month at Vugha, in September 1853, the wealth and dependents of two witches were brought in to Vugha, and the witches executed. Rebels against the king's authority were treated like witches — as offenders against the whole community. Prisoners of war, also, were without residual rights in Shambaai. They too could easily be sold. Before Kimweri ye Nyumbai's death, major thieves were added to the category of slaves sold. Later, in the wars of the 1870s and 1880s, a time of the increased importation of firearms and of intense demand for plantation slaves on the island of Pemba, slaves were captured and sold with increasing ease and in ways which subjects saw as a violation of the rules of dependency. Minor thefts were made into excuses for enslavement and sale (Feierman 1974:175–76).

Pawns and slaves were useful in one of three ways at the royal court. First, they could be sold for guns and powder or for rain charms. ("Rain doesn't belong to the Kilindi," one narrative argues. "Wealth buys rain, which then belongs to the subjects. . . . The seller of a charm says, 'This rain costs a young woman,' or 'This rain costs a young man.'")[26] Second, they provided labor for the farms of the chief's household. Third, in the case of fighting men or of slave women who were made chief's wives, they increased the number of people involved in the kingdom's politics who were completely dependent on the chief, with no cross-cutting ties of loyalty to local descent groups.

Peasants, Slaves, and Social Reproduction: the Kifu Group.

On the surface, the king's subjects appear to have been divided into two quite different categories: peasants and slaves. In many respects the former resembled the peasants of today's Africa. Separate households disposed of their own product; men and women within a household held separate rights in the food produced. Land near villages was bought and sold, and peasants sometimes sold the fruits of their fields. They paid a share of their product to the political authorities, to whom they also provided a portion of the household's labor. Slaves, on the other hand (prisoners of war or the children of witches), labored under conditions controlled by the chief, subject only to the moderating effects of their own resistance. The chief sold, or beat, or killed a slave without violating accepted norms. Men and women temporarily dependent, awaiting redemption by their relatives, occupied a range of intermediate positions. The radical opposition between peasants and slaves was, however, in some senses an illusion. The definition of the most basic unit of peasant social reproduction, the *kifu* group, depended ultimately on the existence of slavery.

The distinction between *peasants* and *slaves* reflects late nineteenth-century usage in the Shambaa language. A chief's subjects were *washi*, "people of the land." The territory of each separate chief was called a "land" (*shi*), its boundaries defined by the agricultural practice of those who lived within it (see below). The chief's dependents were *watung'wa*, a loan word from Swahili. In Shambaa this was a broad general word which took in all kinds of the chief's dependents. *Nkole* or *mateka* were dependents who had been taken in war. *Washumba* were dependents who worked at the house. *Wapuna* were young dependent men who served as soldiers; the word was also sometimes used as a more general term for all kinds of male slaves. *Wandee* (s. *mndee*) was the equivalent word for young women. Every young woman living her life in a village was an *mndee*, but if people spoke about the chief's *mndee*, they were referring to a person of dependent status. The distinction was made clear by the context.[27]

Seen from the point of view of a peasant village, slaves were people who had moved beyond the margins of peasant life. They were now outsiders. Oral traditions speak of enslavement after rebellion by saying that "it causes the lineage to be lost" (*yaaza mbai*) — the lineage disappears, not to be seen again in peasant society. Members of a lost lineage might be taken away from Shambaai altogether, sold to coastal traders who provided slave workers for the coast and for the clove plantations of the island of Pemba.

Peasants pictured local society as composed of a great many small groups, each based on patrilineal descent, all of them struggling to reproduce successfully, to acquire wives for their sons, and to protect the health and well-being of the next generation of children. When a person was taken as a prisoner of war, this was a loss of human capacity, of the group's capacity to reproduce and maintain itself. It was a loss very different from the loss of capacity which came later, in the German period, when men went off to work on settler farms for a period and then returned; in that case a part of the labor of many individuals was removed, often by force. In the precolonial period all the labor of a few individuals was removed, and those people sent beyond the boundaries of local society. People who had lost a relative continued as autonomous peasants, working for their subsistence as they had before, but with the knowledge that one of their number had departed, as though in death.

Slaves who had been witches were seen as the pollution of local society, now cleaned out and removed to the court. A proverb which refers to this uses the verb -asha, "to dispose of or throw away." People speak of throwing away garbage, but they also speak of "throwing away" in the wilderness the corpse of a person who has died dangerously (kufa viwiwi), in a polluted way which threatens harm to the living. The proverb is Viwiwi vyoshe vyaashighwa na kitaa, "All dangerous, inauspicious, evil things are thrown away to the royal court." The heart of the royal court was, in this case, like the wilderness in which one disposed of dangerous corpses and dangerous medicines.[28] The most dangerous young witches, if left alive, were put in the court bweni, the young men's house which guarded the gate of the central court zone at the heart of Vugha.

Pawns, slaves, and witches all moved outside the bounds of local peasant society, leaving behind them a landscape populated by small kinship groups, whose capacity to sustain themselves remained intact. Yet the very definition of the local groups as they existed from the 1850s onwards depended on the existence of pawnship or slavery and on royal power. Local groups organized their own reproduction in a form which implied, and depended upon, the existence of pawning as a practice. The picture of two very separate strata — of a free peasantry and a stratum of slaves — was a way of defining social reality which made peasant resistance less likely. It directed attention away from the fact that slaves were drawn from the peasantry and that slavery was another form (alongside tribute) in which chiefs took peasant labor for their own use.

Pawnship was implied in the way local groups organized the payment of bridewealth, the inheritance of widows, the purchase of food in famine, and payment for healing rites. It was implied, in other words, in the ordering of social reproduction. This bears out Claude Meillassoux's contention that the crucial element in defining the mode of production in Africa is the organization of reproduction (Meillassoux 1975). It was reproduction, organized through fraternal kifu groups, which defined the characteristic social organization of nineteenth-century Shambaai.

Traditions collected at the turn of the twentieth century described how slavery, which they recognized as a recent phenomenon, began to emerge at the moment the land's ancient inhabitants gave women to Mbegha without asking for bridewealth (Karasek 1918–22:81). The predynastic precedent for establishing equivalences between rights in wealth and rights in persons was through bridewealth. Pawning was a modification and extension of the principle, established through bridewealth, that descent groups could establish relationships in which they balanced rights in persons and rights in wealth, and in which they made mutual adjustments to their capacity to reproduce. The emergence of slavery as an extension of this system brings to mind Gerda Lerner's argument that there was a necessary linkage between gender inequality in patriarchal society and the emergence of inequalities in societies divided by class (Lerner 1986).

To understand the link between reproduction and pawning, it is necessary to trace the developmental cycle by which a household grew into a *kifu* group and then disintegrated, transforming itself into a larger but looser association.

Production of food crops for subsistence was the work of the individual households, with the labor and the product divided between husbands and wives. When a woman went to live with her husband's relatives at the time of marriage she was given at least one farm of her own. The husband had his own farms, including the banana garden near the homestead, in which he hoped ultimately to be buried. The men worked on the initial preparation of the soil; the women were responsible for the harvesting. Other jobs were shared, although men appear to have done more of the sowing, and women more of the weeding (Karasek 1911:174; *NaoM* January 1892:10; Krapf 1964: part 2, 125). The woman used the product of her farm to feed her own children, and she could sell any surplus. The husband used the proceeds of his farm to supplement his wife's food if it was insufficient, although he had to take care to share equally among the women if he had more than one wife. If he cleared land near a village with his own labor, then he could sell it.[29]

As a man's sons grew to adulthood, he gave them farms of their own to cultivate. They could sell the proceeds for goats, but the father retained the main inherited wealth in livestock in his own hands. With time, tension arose concerning its disposition. It was the father's own personal wealth to be used in any way he chose, but it also represented the security and the reproductive capacity of his sons. Bridewealth was an obvious source of conflict. So long as a son remained unmarried, he spent much of his time farming for his father, who could, if he chose, marry a second or a third wife, keeping his son a bachelor. Theoretically it was possible for a son to earn bridewealth by farming and selling food, but this was very difficult.[30] Even then, a son who received bridewealth from his own earnings or from collective sources still needed his father's help in providing a farm for the new wife, and in negotiating with his bride's father. "Bring me a live hyrax" (*mpee ye moyo*), the bride's father said in some parts of Shambaai. The "live hyrax" was the groom's father.[31]

When the father died, each "house" (the word for each wife and her children) was given some of the livestock, but then the greatest number were left in the hands of the eldest son of the senior wife. These cattle were to be held as *kifu*, a patrimonial fund for the well-being of all the dead man's sons and their progeny. The uses of livestock in a *kifu* fund were narrowly restricted. *Kifu* could be used only for purposes of social reproduction — for the survival and increase of the dead man's progeny. The most obvious use of *kifu* cattle was for bridewealth, so that each son of every brother could marry a first wife. From *kifu* also would come the goat to be sacrificed to the dead father if a child was ill and the diviner's oracle called for a sacrifice. In addition, the rites of passage at various life stages (*mivigha*, s. *mvigha*), which were seen as essential for continued survival and fertility, also were paid for with *kifu*, as was collectively consumed famine food. All these uses of *kifu* wealth were life-giving ones, and they were collective. They ensured a descent group's continuity through time. A reduction in *kifu* wealth was a reduction in the capacity to survive and to reproduce. Transactions in *kifu* wealth were, in a sense, a calculus of social reproduction.[32]

The chief intervened in this calculus by imposing indemnities. Aside from the special cases of threats to the entire community — witchcraft, rebellion, and the habitual practice of kidnapping — a chief intervened only in cases where competing groups were unable to resolve their conflicting claims to wealth and reproductive capacity. If a young man was seriously injured, for example, his assailant was expected to pay compensation for "damaging his young-manliness" (*kumbania ubwanga*). However, if the assailant was the brother of the victim, the case never came before the chief because conflicting claims to reproductive capacity were not in question: both brothers drew on a single fund of common wealth. For the same reasons, incest was not a matter for the chief's court because only a single descent group's reproductive capacity was involved. In one famous case of father-daughter incest in the colonial period, the guilty man was brought before the chief's court, but succeeded in having the case dismissed by challenging the proceedings. "Which person [of another lineage] is arguing the case against me?" he asked. He was not punished by the court but was ostracized by his neighbors.[33]

The chief's demand for an indemnity, or in the case of witches and rebels, the chief's punishment, could fall only upon the offender and (assuming the offender was an adult man) on his children. It is possible that if the offender was an unmarried man, responsibility fell on his father. In the recorded cases of witchcraft, the man was killed and his children sold, but his other relatives remained unaffected. A man who shot Kimweri ye Nyumbai's tribute collectors was killed and his children sold. His other relatives were seized only as hostages; they were held until the rebel was in the hands of the king's men, and then released (Krapf 1964: part 2, 304).

In the case of an indemnity, the offender himself paid, and his children were taken as pawns. If, however, he had rights in a *kifu* fund, then the fund bore responsibility for his indemnity. As with other uses, in this case *kifu* guaranteed the continuity and survival of the group. It prevented the loss of members to pawnship or to slavery.[34]

A *kifu* group forced to pawn dependents tended to pawn young people. Adult men and women were too important a part of the group's labor force to pawn except in extremity. A man could not, in any event, pawn his wife because she remained a member of her father's group. In the famine of the late 1890s missionaries reported that husbands without food sent their wives home to be fed by their fathers.[35] The woman's position between two lineages could be played to her advantage if she received a sympathetic hearing or support in one or both places. If conditions with her husband were difficult, she could leave him, return home, and expect that her father, or her brothers, would reason with the husband about his behavior. The woman who was in an impossible position was one who was treated badly by her husband and rejected by her brothers. When this happened she could make herself a dependent at the court of a chief or, more commonly, it was said that she might commit suicide by breaking a cooking pot, in which case it was expected that she would die, and so also would the relatives she named in her oath.[36] If it was necessary to send a pawn, a woman who had left her husband to return home to her patrilineal relatives, especially distant ones, was likely to be chosen. This is a speculative point. A century later, women in that position received the least kinship support because they were raising children for another lineage, contributing to someone else's reproductive capacity.

Young men and young women, before marriage, were certainly sent as pawns. Young women were valued more highly than young men in the equivalencies between indemnity payments and pawns. My informants disagreed with one another and with the published report on the precise equivalencies, but all agreed that a young man was worth less. Three or four head of cattle for a young woman as opposed to two or three for a young man, and more of the cattle for a young woman cows, which were worth twice as much as bulls.[37] If the chief took full responsibility for a homicide payment of twelve head of cattle, he probably took four of the murderer's dependents as slaves.

The father of a son who incurred repeated indemnities was able to limit his liability by taking his son to the chief with a bull called *kighombo*, "the club." He gave both his son and the bull to the chief, saying, "Here is the club with which to kill my son."[38] The chief then took the son as a dependent, took liability for the young man's indemnities, and was free to kill him or sell him. I knew a man at Vugha in the 1960s who had been given to the king by his father about twenty years earlier, undoubtedly without the bull of *kighombo*. The son remained at the old capital, doing menial chores for whoever happened to be in power even after the transition to independence, although he was clearly free to move off on his own at any time he wished.

In the disorders of the 1870s and 1880s *kifu* groups took on the function of armed defense. They provided their women with armed escorts to protect them from kidnappers who roamed the paths seizing women to sell at the coast. At times *kifu* groups carried out counter-raids to reclaim members who had been enslaved.

If one of the brothers chose to divide *kifu*, the others had no choice but to agree. The eldest brother's benevolent administration was the key to holding it together. The autobiography of Lukas Sefu, a Christian of the 1890s, describes how, in the years before the author's conversion, his brother refused him the cows with which to redeem a slave woman he wanted to marry. Lukas received his share of *kifu* only after an armed confrontation with his brother and the intervention of a senior relative (Lukas Sefu 1911:10–13). Calculations of likely gains and losses in bridewealth payments shaped the decision on whether to support or oppose the continued existence of the *kifu* fund. A *kifu* group in Mshihwi in the 1880s, part of a larger lineage of Tetei, included one member (Mbea Vintu) who had a large number of sons. All his brothers had daughters. Mbea Vintu's brothers divided the wealth, and they all moved off to a village about five miles away, so that the one man's sons should not use up the wealth acquired for the daughters of the others.[39]

A *kifu* group inevitably split with time, after the emergence of a new generation of *kifu* groups. Even though sons of a single father tried to keep a fund of their father's wealth undivided, sons of separate fathers never held a common fund of their grandfather's wealth.

The system of indemnities, the threat of pawnship, and, in violent times, the need for defense prevented premature dissolution of *kifu* groups in the years before conquest. The possibility of owing an indemnity and losing a person was not an easy one to face alone. The *kifu* group would either pay the indemnity or work together to redeem the pawn. With German conquest in the 1890s pawning came to an end. Chiefs knew that it was dangerous to be seen holding slaves. They gave their women slaves to peasants as wives, in return for cattle.[40]

After the end of slavery, *kifu* could still be used for bridewealth, for famine food, for sacrificial and healing rites, and for rites of passage, but the threat of pawnship was past. Innumerable *kifu* groups decided to split the wealth, each decision precipitated by a particular internal crisis, like the fight over bridewealth between Lukas Sefu and his brother.

In each case the division was made possible by the removal of the threat of pawnship. Increasing economic differentiation might also have played a role in the end of *kifu*, with the appearance of wage labor. Nevertheless, the end of pawnship appears to have been crucial. Except for pawnship, all the uses of *kifu* could be met by informal cooperation among brothers of a kind which began to emerge in the German period.[41]

This understanding of the decline of the *kifu* group is a radical departure from current interpretations of the history of local social organization in Africa in the transition to colonial rule. The almost universally accepted interpretation is that colonial conquest cut off the political head of African society — destroyed the independent power of chiefs and kings — but that somehow the headless body lived. In the accepted view, precapitalist organization at the domestic level survived, and articulated with capitalist production. Only slowly did precapitalist forms erode, through generations of economic change. The evidence presented here demonstrates a fundamental transformation in local social structure at the time of colonial conquest. The forms of local mutual assistance in the colonial period, which are commonly referred to in the literature as precapitalist, were not at all the same as the precolonial ones.

The antecedents of the *kifu* group in the period before slavery are unclear. Some evidence indicates that descent groups in that early period were larger, able to bear some of the weight later carried by chiefship (see chapter 4). In any event the *kifu* group as it existed in the late nineteenth century was organized in a form which harmonized completely with pawnship and slavery.

At a larger level of scale than the *kifu* group, in the late nineteenth century, was the loose network of a number of fraternal groups, all descended from a common ancestor, which met together on special occasions having to do with death and the ancestors, and with marriage. This larger lineage survived into the colonial period without weakening significantly. After a man died, leaving *kifu* behind, he remained a dangerous force in the lives of those who had inherited his patrimony. When a diviner decided that an illness among his descendants was caused by their dead progenitor, his eldest son would arrange for a sacrificial rite (*fika ya chekecheke*) to be performed with the *kifu* group merged with the larger lineage of which it was a part. The core of the rite was a sacrificial meal shared by the dead man together with the dead of the wider lineage, making him a part of the larger group of ancestors. The wider lineage shared a common mystical fate. If a *kigego*, a dangerous infant, was born within the lineage, individuals anywhere within the lineage (not only members of the household or of the *kifu* group) were in danger of dying. The dead man's widow was inherited within this group. The lineage members shared a feast of a bridewealth goat when any daughters of the group married.[42]

Even though men of this larger group did not hold a fund of collective wealth, they were unable to claim indemnities from one another in the court of a chief. An offense by any member of this group against any other was a matter for the lineage elders. The many *kifu* groups within a lineage often contributed to the cost of one another's indemnities, or to redeeming pawns, but the contributions were voluntary, part of a larger web of reciprocity.

Food Security

Peasants called for the king to give them rain, to give them bananas, but took elaborate measures of their own to achieve food security. Their ancestors had created a complex farming system, which they continued to adapt, using three rainy seasons, variations in temperature and rainfall over three altitude zones, and irrigation. Chiefs located their capitals at places which were bound to be nodes in the farming system, and did their best to hold substantial food reserves for times of hunger. They did little, however, to organize peasant efforts at producing their own food. Even irrigation works, which required coordinated labor and so could possibly have been subject to chiefly control, remained in the hands of the peasants and their own ritual leaders.

Most villages of the Shambaa-speaking population were located between 1,200 and 1,500 meters above sea level, around the outer rim of the West Usambara Mountains. The mountains rise like an island out of the plains to this altitude. The landscape within the mountains is deeply dissected, with little level area except in occasional basins. Villagers living around the mountain rim were able to use three different altitude zones. The first, which they called *nyika*, was below about 650 m above the sea level, where grain ripened quickly in the heat. The second was *shambaai*, the highland zone above about 1,000 m, where the villages were located and the climate was suited for bananas. Rainfall here was more regular than down below. *Nyika* and *shambaai* were identified by their characteristic vegetation. The third was a high mountain zone above the villages, where crops could be planted during the cold mists of July and August.[43] The Shambaa-speaking population occupied the rim of the mountain block and the more central areas which were so deeply dissected that they had internal areas of *nyika*. The highland meadows, above about 1,500 m, were occupied by people speaking the Mbugu language, for whom cattle keeping was more important than for Shambaa speakers.

Moisture-laden air coming in off the Indian Ocean rises along the escarpment, cools, and deposits its moisture as rainfall. The rains that fall in March, April, and May fall more heavily on the southeastern slopes because they are brought by winds from that direction. The rains of October, November, and December are brought from the northeast. In each case there is great local variation because rain falls on windward slopes, which have dry rain shadows on their leeward sides.

The farmers of Shambaai work for food security by using a wide range of agricultural possibilities within their local landscape. If their main rainy season is in March, they try to find farms within several miles of their village that are better placed for the November rains, and they also keep farms high in the mountains for the July rainfall.[44] In each case the rains are unpredictable, but if the main rainy season fails, then perhaps a subsidiary rainy season might tide people over to the next year.

During the main rainy season, many farmers plant in both Shambaai and *nyika* to reduce the risk that crops in that season will fail completely. Some crops are planted only in *nyika*. In the nineteenth century these included manioc and sorghum. Bananas and sugar cane were planted almost solely in Shambaai. Maize, which was a major nineteenth-century crop, was grown in both Shambaai and *nyika*. Lowland maize ripens quickly, providing food in years when short rainy seasons lead to the failure of the slower growing highland maize. If the rains continue while the lowland maize is drying in the field, the harvest is spoiled, but perhaps the highland maize, which ripens later, will be saved. Nineteenth-century farmers planted highland maize for the first several planting seasons after clearing forest. Then, if the land was near a village, they used the land for their banana groves. If highland maize, lowland maize, March maize, November maize, and July maize all failed, then there were still marshy areas in highland basins or at the foot of the mountains which could be planted, and there were irrigated fields.[45]

The network of irrigation furrows which ran veinlike down the hills and through the gardens of Shambaai was controlled by the peasantry and had been created by their ancestors. The irrigation system increased the level of food security but was not in the chief's domain. Traditions of migration into Shambaai before the founding of the kingdom in the eighteenth century make it clear that the furrows had been dug in predynastic times. The pattern of control and of ritual leadership support this view. The men served by a furrow maintained it and decided together on the distribution of water for irrigation, in a system of rotating irrigation days. Each farmer could count on receiving water on his assigned day. Each major furrow was under the ritual control of an elder, drawn from an ancient peasant lineage of that particular spot. Water did not flow before he performed his rite of sacrifice.[46]

Control of wealth in livestock was an essential part of planning for famine, whether controlled by the husband of a household, the father of a group of adult sons, or the senior brother of a *kifu* group. Male informants insisted that it was the man's job to worry about contingent events — illness and famine — and to take the appropriate measures. Women's work was in fact central, for instance, in gathering wild foods, but was not recognized as a public or political famine control measure comparable to the expenditure of *kifu* wealth. The livestock themselves were almost never used as famine food. They were driven to wherever starchy staples were available, to be sold. A man who was a small child during the famine of the late 1890s remembers his father telling him, "You alone, by yourself, ate the value of nine goats in that famine, when we bought food."[47]

The resources of each household and each *kifu* group were distributed over a wide area. Today, the farm plots of a typical household are scattered at a number of points within a radius of about five miles from the village. The farming pattern was the same in the nineteenth century. Each household needed to reach farm plots up in the high peaks, down in marshes at the foot of the escarpment, in Shambaai, and in *nyika*, plots that were irrigated, and plots in good locations for the subsidiary rainy season.

People lived in large, permanent villages, many of which continued for centuries, which residents used as central stopping places from which to walk each day. The dwellers in each house tied a rope to the front door, to show that no one was home, and then went off to work, hoe or bush knife in hand, some to a distant farm, others to herd cattle, goats, or sheep, others to collect medicinal herbs in the forest, others to collect grass from a valley bottom for thatch, others to hunt wild game in *nyika*, still others to witness a case being argued at the court of the chief.[48]

The villages were strung along the tops of ridges or the upper parts of hillsides, with the banana groves stretching down from each homestead (*Musa acuminata, Musa balbisiana, Musa paradisiaca*, and bananas of the *Ensete* family). In the banana groves of Shambaai, the shoots reproduce continuously, and so the groves are virtually permanent, like the villages which rely on them. Banana gardens were the quintessentially male plots. A respected elder who no longer farmed and distributed his farms among his sons always retained his banana garden, in which he hoped to be buried. The major supply of grain came from women's farms, but the man's banana garden was the protection against famine. Maize might fail if the rains came too early, or too late, or if too little rain fell, but the starchy bananas of the man's garden ripened in all but the most disastrous years (Attems 1967:79).

When people moved out in the morning from their villages to their farms in *nyika* or in the highlands, they usually stayed within the boundaries of a single "land" governed by a Kilindi chief. In times of hierarchy the entire "land" (*shi*, s. and pl.) of Shambaai, governed by the king, was divided into units, each of which was called a *land* in turn and governed by a subordinate chief. The typical chiefdom, the land of one chief, had boundaries which ran up and down the escarpment, taking in villages along the rim of the escarpment as well as the unoccupied *nyika* below them. The boundaries were carefully remembered. Natural features were supplemented by markings, such as axe-heads driven into trees. In one defensive war rite, the officials of a chiefdom led a cow around the boundaries.[49] If chiefdom boundaries had run along the rim, leaving out the lowlands, they would have taken in areas of heavy population while excluding the farms to which villagers walked every day. Instead, the boundaries marked the natural limits of daily peasant movement.

Each chief's land was tied together also by a very dense network of marriage bonds. Young women freely decided whether to accept offers of marriage, except in the rare cases of child betrothal (Dupre n.d.:31a; Dahlgrün 1903:219; P. Wohlrab 1918:167; Karasek 1918–22:82). They insisted on marrying close to home so they could return to their mothers for childbirth, seek help from their brothers in marital disputes and from female relatives when they were ill. They were prohibited from marrying within the lineage, and strongly discouraged from marrying cousins outside the lineage (fathers' sisters' daughters for example). This set of rules and preferences led to the widest possible distribution of ties of relationship within a chiefdom. The territory was ostensibly populated by many separate *kifu* groups, all of them competing and each one discrete, with clear boundaries separating it from all the others. It was knitted together, however, by the practical decisions of women on where to marry. The network of alliance created a tight social fabric. Neighborhoods very much like the lands governed in the nineteenth century as chiefdoms existed before the creation of the kingdom.[50]

Within the land of a single chief, the capital provided a focus. Chiefs tried to make sure that every local *kifu* group within easy distance of the capital maintained a house there. At Vugha, the royal capital, which had a mid-nineteenth-century population of about three thousand, court officers insisted that every one of these houses be occupied by a woman every night. Vugha, like the other royal villages, and like peasant villages, was built at the top of a hill, with banana groves descending from the edge of the habitations. A missionary who visited Vugha in 1867 reported, like many other nineteenth-century visitors, that he "never saw so many bananas as are growing all about Vuga."[51] Chiefs maintained the banana groves to attract followers to their town. A new arrival would be given a bit of the royal banana grove. "After all," one aged Vugha resident explained, "the chief wanted the land to fill with people."[52] Chiefs awarded banana groves to their most important officials but then required that the groves be well maintained. Officials paid fines if the groves suffered neglect.[53]

The king held the largest concentration of the markers of senior masculine status: banana gardens and livestock. Peasants who came to serve at his court ate well. But his role in the everyday agriculture of the villages was limited. In peaceful times the chiefs maintained public order, making it possible for peasants to visit distant farms without fear of kidnappers.[54] Otherwise the king and chiefs served the people by offering refuge to those pushed beyond the margins of peasant society. The basic work of clearing forests, planting fields, and maintaining irrigation furrows depended on the efforts of the peasantry. The chief's contribution was rain.

3

Healing the Land and
Harming the Land

Kilindi chiefs were not the only rainmakers in pre-colonial Shambaai. In the kingdom's early years local descent-group leaders held important rain medicines. Throughout the kingdom's history alternative nonroyal practitioners appeared, claiming the power to bring crops in their proper season. The dominance of Kilindi rainmaking was the outcome of a contest, often a violent one.

Nor did people accept without question that rainmaking was the key to prosperity and satiety. During the last half-century of the kingdom's existence, from the early 1840s, a small but growing number of chiefs began to violate their obligations to provide refuge to dependents and began to treat slaves as commodities. It would have been possible to argue, as some peasants did at the time, that limiting the chiefly power to take slaves was the best way to guarantee survival — that rainmaking was secondary. The peasant priority on controlling slavery rather than rain ought to have become increasingly clear in the 1870s and 1880s, when the most powerful chief in Shambaai, a trader named Semboja, had no claims to rain medicine.

Through all these struggles, the language of rain medicine continued, nevertheless, to occupy an important place in Shambaai, and the Kilindi continued to be the most important rainmakers. Peasants interpreted the political struggle as bringing an alternation of drought and rich rains. Royal ritual also imposed a rhythm on the passage of time. It did not suppress the discussion of violent events and disastrous changes, but placed them within the context of a seemingly eternal rhythmed alternation. Even though the peasantry elaborated an alternative discourse based on local descent, discussion of rhythmed alternation was effective in defining many of the issues of nineteenth-century politics.

This chapter explores the terms in which rhythmed alternation was expressed — terms which form a seamless web. The following chapter explores the competition among precolonial intellectuals, which was also conflict over the definition of the most basic political issues. Neither in the kingdom's early years nor in its final decades did the centrality of the royal rhythms go unchallenged.

The Rhythmed Time of Royal Rule

If Adam had not eaten the fruit in Eden, we would die like
the moon.
Mdoe Loti, 1967.

The moon has died. The morning star shines. But it is not the
morning star; it is the moon.
From the royal accession rite, second half of the nineteenth
century.

Royal ritual was rich in verbal and visual images: of the king as a lion
that kills people and takes cattle, the king as a deadly buffalo, alone facing his hunters who were the courtiers, or the king as a patriarch governing his subjects as he would wives and children. The central organizing principle in the culturally ordered experience of the king as bringer
of fertility was neither a metaphor, nor a metonym, nor was it any other
figure of speech, nor was it a visual image. It was the experience of time's
passage as rhythmed, regular, and life-bringing, or as random, irregular,
and deadly.

The double rite of passage in which a king was buried and a new king
installed was organized so as to impose a rhythm on the passage of time,
a rhythm of the inexorable alternation of peaceful royal rule, followed
by disorder and death, and then again peace and hierachy. The rites on
which this statement is based are the ones which took place between
1862 and 1895.[1]

After the drum was beaten announcing the death of one king and the
accession of another, death and disorder came to Shambaai. For the entire duration of the moon under which the old king had died, anyone
who walked along the four main paths from Vugha — to the north, south,
east, or west — was liable to be executed (LangHeinrich 1903:251; P. Wohlrab 1918:172; Dupre n.d.). The *mshangi*, of the lineage which performed
ritual murders for the king, went to a spot at Kwe Mishihwi where the
path separates to pass above and below a large boulder. At this spot he
strangled a passerby.[2] Acts of violence were permitted; men walked the
paths only in groups. The king's men struck especially against strangers.
In 1853 outsiders within the kingdom, hearing unfounded rumors of the
king's impending death, fled while there was still time. During the mourning period, until the new king sacrificed at the royal graves, it was forbidden to till the soil or to weed the crops, to shave or to cut one's hair,
to sacrifice to the ancestors or to hold a rite of passage. It was as though
for this brief period all experience of the passage of time was subordinated to the experience of disorder attending the king's death.[3]

This was a structured disorder, for it was permitted only once the new king had been installed, so that the peasantry would not experience king-lessness.[4] The dead king was buried and the new king installed in a dou-ble rite of passage lasting four days. The care of the dead king's body and the order of events in his burial proceeded simultaneously with the multiple ritual installations of his heir along a path from Bumbuli in the east. The entire series of events was hidden: court officials installed a royal impersonator to moan beneath the covers of the king's bed; the heir trav-eled at night, and the old king was buried at night. The heir received the headdress near the capital on the same night that the king's body, not far away, was placed in the grave. So far as we know, the men in-stalling the heir, placing him on the stone seat in the ritually-prescribed village of Kihitu, made no mention of the fact that a king was being buried on the same night, nor did the men burying the king take ritual actions referring to the installation.[5]

At dawn after these events, the war drum sounded to announce the completed installation of a king and the death of a king. The drum's skin was then slit with a knife, concluding in a single action the two rites which had until then been simultaneous but separate.

The drum announced that the king died like the moon, which is cov-ered over for a period, only to reappear. The ritual was dominated by images of night, of blackness, and of the moon's floating, rhythmed re-currence. In the grave, the dead king's body was placed on the skin of a newly slain black sheep, with a black, carbon-covered piece of metal. The body was wrapped in a black cloth and covered with the skin of a freshly slaughtered black bull. The new king, meanwhile, traveled at night from the east, like the moon. As one informant explained, "The moon comes from Bumbuli [in the east]. When the moon has died, and is gone, it reappears. [It has not really died,] it is simply covered over."

Abdallah bin Hemedi 'lAjjemy, who lived in the kingdom from about 1867 to 1873, described the public events after the beating of the drum. One of the court officials displayed the new king to the people of Vugha, saying, "We know him well. The moon has died. The morning star shines. But it is not the morning star; it is the moon." The morning star, like the moon, moves from east to west, but it is a lesser body, unlike the king. One of the salient characteristics of the moon is its regularity and pre-dictability. A proverb says, *Mnyanyi ni ng'wezi, hakawa kucheewa*; "The moon is a crafty one, it never lingers."

The moon is periodically covered over and then is cleaned off by the rains, to shine again. *Fua yachunta ng'wezi*, "the rains wash off the moon," as another bit of folk wisdom has it.[6] A moon not accompanied by the rain was qualitatively different from other moons, with a name of its own: *mkungula* (LangHeinrich 1921).

The new king was covered over, like the moon, in the last ritual action before he entered the royal capital. At Fune, near Vugha, the men who had brought him westwards from Bumbuli killed and began to cook a bull they had brought with them. They laid the king on the ground, covering him with a cloth. The king's representatives, the major officials of Vugha, having seen the fire, came to eat. They grabbed and tore at the meat of the bull. Then, in the words of one informant, "they stole the king." They wandered about aimlessly, carrying him, after which one of them carried the king across the stream which ran near Fune. The men who had come all the way from Bumbuli with the successor were left behind, the king having been stolen from them.[7]

This action seems, at first glance, to be an imitation of death and succession, but it was not. Two separate elements were involved. The first, an imitation of the founding king, Mbegha, will be discussed later. The second was the covering and uncovering of the king, like the covering over of the moon. The informants were uniformly explicit that the new king was "covered over" (-ghubikwa) with a cloth; the word is the same as that used for the covering of the moon. A different word was used to describe "wrapping" a dead body in a cloth or in dead banana leaves (-gewa shanda or -gewa mashwagho). The king's progress was not a death and rebirth; it was a covering over and then uncovering, like the cycle of the moon.

After the new king appeared at Vugha, the period of disorder began, of murder on the paths, and of the suppression of productive farming. The ritual did not aim at escaping disorder, but at restricting it to its appropriate rhythmed time, so that after the next moon appeared, and after the dead king received his sacrificial meal, the land would no longer suffer the deadly effects of the king's death. In this, "the ritual attempted to make the activities of men conform to the habits of their thought" (Hubert and Mauss 1929:202), for they made the disorder fit into a moon-measured period. During the years of German conquest, the kingdom experienced two royal deaths, but it was forced to forego murder on the paths because of the presence of the Germans. The peasants experienced disorder in other ways. In November 1893, king Kimweri Maguvu died. In January 1895, swarms of locusts ate most of the crops standing in the fields. The people of Mlalo told the local missionaries that Maguvu's father had sent the locusts as mourning for his son's death. Several months later, at the end of April, Maguvu's successor Mputa died, and his death was followed on May 15 by an earthquake with three blows, which the people of Mtae understood to be the consequence of Mputa's death.[8]

The rite of accession imposed a rhythm of yet another kind on the passage of time, for the new king who walked westwards along the path from Bumbuli walked in the footsteps of the founding hero king, Mbegha, whose progress he imitated. On the way from Bumbuli, at the village of Tekwa, the new king took part in a sacrifice to the ancestors of an ancient lineage, said to have been Mbegha's allies.[9] Then the heir came to the village of Kihitu where, according to the myth, Mbegha killed a lion and thereby became a lion. The heir himself was supposed to have been born on that lion's skin. In the accession the new king was given the royal headdress and proclaimed *Simba Mwene*, "the lion," at the same place. Then the royal heir passed *Kawe Nkajatwa*, literally "the stone which is not stepped upon." This stone, which had ostensibly been stepped on by Mbegha, remained covered by undergrowth and inaccessible at all times except during the accession, for which it was cleared.

We have already seen that the officials of Vugha appeared at Fune at the moment when the heir was covered over by a cloth. In this action, the courtiers, as non-Kilindi, represented the peasantry. They were drawn to the scene by the meat brought along with the new king from Bumbuli. In the myth it was Mbegha's gifts of meat which drew the Shambaa to him, leading them to take him as king. At Fune the courtiers greedily tore at the meat and then carried off a passive heir to make him their king.[10]

The new king did not recapitulate the entire progress of the founding hero who (in the myth) entered Shambaai at Ziai, southeast of Vugha, then moved northeastward from Ziai to Bumbuli, and only then westward to the capital. Mbegha's journey was itself a mythical abstraction. The recapitulation of Mbegha's path in the rite abstracted further, casting aside parts of the journey which did not pass from east to west like the moon. Each new king reenacted the history of Mbegha, stripped of all features that detracted from moon-like rhythmed recurrence.

The effect of the double rite of burial and accession was to make structure out of contingency, to strip history of unique and unpredictable events, to make every royal reign equivalent, in some sense, to every other, and to convey a sense of inevitable recurrence—the king dies like the moon, only to rise again.

It would be a mistake, however, to conclude that rhythmed recurrence was the sole form of historicity within the Shambaa kingdom. We have already seen the centrality of ideas of descent, in the sense that a man's wealth, the patrimony he bequeathed to his children, remained under his influence even after his death. Cultural practices were also seen as a patrimony which came down in a line of descent, to be reproduced by the living in unvarying form. In this case they were called the *fika* of the ancestor: the ancestor's unvarying cultural patrimony. The lineages of hereditary smiths described iron-working as their *fika*, to be executed in unvarying ritualized form.[11] The noun *fika* is related to the verb *-vika*, "to perform a rite," or "to make an offering to the dead." *Fika* is also the word for the actual rite of sacrifice.

The cultural practice of royal rule was called the *fika* of Mbegha; its elements were to be reproduced in unvarying form. The houses of the royal capital had to be built in the ancient bee-hive style, and the beds in the *banti* style: a frame covered with the ribs of the raphia palm. In each case these were the *fika* of Mbegha, sometimes called the *fika* of Sheuta and Bangwe, the primeval ancestors of all the people of Shambaai. These two bodies of *fika* (coming from Mbegha or from Sheuta and Bangwe) sometimes merged, when the origins of all local culture were attributed to Mbegha as the founding king.

Conflict, deal-making, anger, betrayal, adultery, deception, and intimidation were excluded from the rhythmed recurrence of the rites, but not from the discursive consciousness of the people of Shambaai. I collected many dozens of narratives which recount in minute detail the political machinations of nineteenth-century political actors. The narrators explored the personalities of the individual actors: Kimweri ye Nyumbai as old and house-bound, the late nineteenth-century chief Semboja as cruel and as contemptuous of the old code of behavior for chiefs in relation to their subjects. The narrative recalled acts of cunning and betrayal: Kilindi chiefs making hidden deals with one another to assassinate their brothers.

The politics of descent were the organizing principle of narratives that recounted the history of political struggles in Shambaai. The narratives follow a continuous linear chronology from Mbegha to the present. Not every narrative covers the whole terrain, but the total genealogy is implicit when the narrator tells the history of a part. The armature of the narratives, the framework on which they hang, is the descent politics of the Kilindi lineage.[12] A university historian might be fascinated by the Bondei rebellion as a popular attempt to overthrow an increasingly exploitative system of slavery. The oral narratives, however, tie the rebellion to Kilindi succession politics and to a plot by one of the royal claimants to kill competing chiefs — a plot in which the Bondei were caught up. The separate peasant descent groups in Shambaai preserved narratives of their own internal struggles and divisions. They link up when appropriate with the concurrent royal genealogy.

The point of this is clear: the suppression of conflict and of idiosyncratic historical detail which is characteristic of the accession rite is merely one mode of organizing the public experience of politics. Other complementary modes existed. We can see two modes unfolding side by side in royal names, which fall into two generational sets: the generation of Shebughe, and the generation of Shekulwavu. Every king is either Shebughe or Shekulwavu. The names of wives, daughters, and sons-in-law are all organized accordingly within the two generations.[13] Shebughe fathers Shekulwavu, who fathers Shebughe, and so on to infinity. Yet this alternation did not prevent the narrators from using an idiosyncratic name for each king, a name which identified only that king. Kinyashi Muanga Ike, "Kinyashi Who Walks Alone" was Shebughe; he was succeeded by Shekulwavu, also known as Kimweri ye Nyumbai, "Kimweri Stay-at-Home."

The kingdom's history appears in the rites of burial and accession only as the imitation of Mbegha and as names of the dead kings mentioned in a rite of sacrifice. The rhythmed rite of burial and accession does not appear in the oral narratives, the histories of conflict; or rather the rite appears only in the distance. The narratives use a literary device to describe the experience of someone who hopes to be king but is not chosen. The disappointed heir hurries to the capital to claim the throne, but as he draws near, he hears the drum which signals his rival's installation and his own failure. The closest the historical narratives come to the rite itself is the sound of a distant drum.[14]

Nancy Farriss, in a discussion of Mayan time conceptions and a review of literature on the cultural construction of history, demonstrates that cyclical and linear conceptions of the past coexisted in Mayan knowledge, and also that such coexistence is not unusual. It might well be the norm for societies of which we have a historical record (Farriss 1987). The question is not whether cyclical and linear time coexist, but *how* they coexist. This is really two quite different questions. The first, on the way historical actors in the midst of their struggles place their own actions in an unfolding cycle, is explored throughout this book.

The second asks about the mechanism linking recurrent rites with the linear unfolding of time — coordinating dissimilar conceptualizations of a single set of events (linear and recurrent) among a single set of actors. On this, the great but long-ignored classic was first published by Hubert and Mauss in 1905.[15] They ask how rites succeed one another and reproduce themselves in time, while the myths they represent are immutable (Hubert and Mauss 1929: xxxi). Their answer is that the succession of rites exists alongside other ways of measuring duration, and is capable of imposing a rhythm on unequal durations. Nineteenth-century Shambaa knew that the reign of Kimweri ye Nyumbai was much longer than other royal reigns. They did not measure this length in years. Instead, they observed that Kimweri fathered many sons by many wives, and installed them as chiefs throughout the kingdom. He then grew so old that his son's son was ready to take the kingdom from him long before he died. The rites of burial and accession, in which violence lasts for the duration of one moon, and in which the new king rises like the moon, imposed a rhythm on the long and short durations of royal reigns. They did not negate or contradict other observations of duration, but they established a ritual context in which each reign was continuous and indivisible.

The great contribution of Hubert and Mauss lies in their recognition that rhythmed time coexists with the linear succession of particular events. The time of ritual, and of the periodic reenactment of myth, is not at all reversible time, as Lévi-Strauss would have it. The ritual does not lead people to accept that today's event is identical to yesterday's. Hubert and Mauss accept the existence of linear durations and of particular events, but then show how myth and ritual impose a rhythm on those events. In the process, consciousness of the particular historical circumstances at the current moment rejuvenates the rite and gives it renewed life.

Kuzifya Shi and Kubana Shi

The sense that rites imposed rhythmed time on the disorder of politics is too superficial an understanding in this case, for the political actions themselves — the moments of intense struggle — were permeated by a rhythm of alternation. People fought over the question of whether a course of political action would achieve the passage of the seasons like the rhythmed recurrence of the moon, bringing rain and food, or whether it would bring the time of the sun, leading to hunger. The two political conditions were also characterized as "healing the land" (kuzifya shi) and "harming the land" (kubana shi), but these were merely convenient labels. The core of the cultural configuration was in alternative patterns of the passage of time.

The identification of the larger cultural configuration, referred to here as healing the land and harming the land, and the argument for its continuity over more than a century, are based on two quite separate sets of evidence and reasoning. I identified the configuration of symbols and conceptions during the field research of the 1960s, and then followed its evolution through the 1970s. Having identified the configuration, it became clear that its separate elements, its contrasting images, existed by the second half of the nineteenth century (and very probably well before that), often using the identical words.

I will begin by describing the configuration of the 1960s, interspersing my description with detail from earlier periods to illustrate parallels. In the next chapter I will explore how these conceptions were used in nineteenth-century politics.

Kubana shi and kuzifya shi describe alternative, opposing, complementary actions taken with respect to the land. The verb -bana is used in a wide variety of contexts, with the meanings of "to damage," "to vio-late rules of proper behavior or ritual prohibitions," "to destroy," or "to make something dirty." The reciprocal form, *kubanana*, means "to quar-rel with one another." *Kubana shi* means "to harm the land," but with the damage coming from improper social behavior. The term *-zifya* means "to repair," or "to heal," or "to make better." It is used to describe the restoration of proper social relations after a conflict, and to describe so-cially correct behavior, as well as healing after illness. Thus the two terms (*-bana* and *-zifya*) have the sense of harming and repairing, but usually in a social rather than a narrowly technological sense.

In the context of royal politics, *healing the land* and *harming the land* most frequently refer to climatic conditions as they affect farming. *Shi izabanika*, "the land has been harmed," is a way of saying that the rains have not come, and that people will be hungry. On the other hand, rich crops of grain drying in the fields are a sure sign of a land healed. Dis-course about politics in moments of crisis is frequently a discussion of what needs to be done to avoid famine, and to create conditions in which the land will be filled with fields of grain.

Kubana shi and *kuzifya shi* are terms used in ordinary informal dis-course. Speech on these issues is not formulaic or highly patterned. Sentences are freely variable in style and content. In addition, the statements operate at two levels, appearing as though they were mere formalized references, simple descriptions of action, while evoking a wide range of associations through metaphor and metonymy. Edelman has demonstrated this with reference to the most ordinary and prosaic terms of American bureaucratic discourse. Discussion of "training programs" for the unemployed leads to metonymic evocation of a series of assump-tions: "That job training is efficacious in solving the unemployment prob-lem, that workers are unemployed because they lack the necessary skills, that jobs are available for those trained to take them" (1977:16). "Mental illness" implies that those who are ill cannot diagnose or care for them-selves, that authority over those so labeled must be held by people with professional qualifications, and that professionals are responsible for therapeutic intervention (on the model of medical intervention), which can lead to cure.

Because of the submerged character of evocation, informal descrip-tions of action can have, at times, an even greater capacity to shape per-ceptions than do ritual symbols. When, in a ritual, the king "becomes" a rock or is addressed as a buffalo, everyone knows that he is neither a rock nor a buffalo. But when someone says that the king has "healed the land," this may be taken as a simple statement of fact, even though it evokes at the same time a rich network of associations.

A single statement, in this evocative language, can be taken by different categories of people to have very different implications. El Zein (1974) showed this in his study of Islam in Lamu on the Kenya coast, where the identical Quranic parable of black dust, red dust, and white dust was taken by the leading families to mean that Arab descent is necessary for achieving religious purity, while the descendants of ex-slaves understood it to mean that religious purity is a gift to those who deserve it irrespective of birth.

The terms which call up different associations among different individuals or categories of political actors can also be counted on to have different implications from one historical period to another. In order to understand changes in political discourse over a long period, it is necessary therefore to understand not only what the terms of discourse were, but also what were some of the implications—the associations and the ways in which the terms shaped political issues. The purpose at this point, however, is to outline some basic regularities in the use of the terms. The changing historical context and changing implications of the language of healing the land will be discussed throughout the remainder of this book.

In the days before conquest (according to the historical traditions as told in the 1960s), so long as the king's power was not challenged, his control of the instruments of force and his access to rain charms all worked to bring the rains in their proper season. For the king in relation to his land, control over the patrimony of rain charms combined with uncontested ownership leads to benevolent results. In precolonial days, as in more recent times, it was the struggle for dominance between powerful competitors that harmed the land. Just as competition between powerful war leaders often brought the kingdom's subjects to lose their lives in war, so competition between those who made the rain could lead to famine.[16]

Action which damages the land is usually described as *nguvu kwa nguvu*, "force against force," or "power against power." This conflict is seen as occurring between Kilindi or at least between important rain-makers. Conflict between peasants is not normally described in this way because neither one has *nguvu*, "power." People usually say that envy (*uwizu*) is the driving force of the counter-rainmaker. Since the chief had to be given the entire wealth of the land to be effective as a rainmaker, any competitor who wished to take away the land would try to show peasants that his own power was greater than the chief's. He could do this by holding back the rain. Peasants could be counted on to switch allegiances at the point when they found their chief's power inadequate to bring plenty.

Once in 1966 when the time for the rains had passed and the rain had not yet fallen, I stood with a friend watching the dark clouds move quickly across the sky. "You see," he said, "there is an envious counter-rainmaker holding back the rain. When you see the heavy clouds moving like this and no rain falls you know that an *mghanga* (a medicine man or healer) is at work." The implication here is that natural forces bring the clouds at their appropriate time, but that men can control whether or not the rain actually falls.

A similar understanding was current in the nineteenth century, when holding back the rain was a cause of war. An Anglican missionary observed a Zigula war party in 1868 on its way to attack a Shambaa village. "The reason for all this was as follows: —The people on the plains had no rain; those on the hills had plenty; therefore the highlanders had used medicine against the lowlanders and must be punished."[17] The heir to a non-Kilindi lineage of fertility specialists reported that his grandmother was sold into slavery by her brother in the years before conquest because both of them had inherited the lineage medicines. His medicine would be effective only if he was its sole possessor.[18]

Discussions of the locus of power, and of "power against power" (*nguvu kwa nguvu*) as harming the land, were at the heart of political practice in the half century before conquest, as reported in the historical traditions.[19] Evidence exists for the same conception in the German period. When locusts arrived in 1894, local people told missionaries that this was a measure chiefs had taken to end German power. A German officer reported in 1908 that chiefs at Bumbuli were making medicines "to break my *nguvu*." The report used the Shambaa word.[20] According to a later oral tradition, a German officer brought all the Kilindi together to tell them he was going to hang the king. "If you have any *nguvu*, show it now," the tradition reports him as saying. "No one brought forth any *nguvu*," the tradition reports, "none at all."[21]

Kuzifya shi, "to restore the land," is used to describe actions for increasing fertility. The opposition between harming and restoring seems to imply that the land in its natural state, undisturbed by rainmakers, would always be fertile. I have never heard people speculate in this way, perhaps because the terms themselves imply the existence of chiefs with rain charms, and so it is difficult to retain the terms while challenging their premises. The land is bound to be healed when rain charms and rainmaking powers are all concentrated in the hands of the king or chief. The assemblage of powerful charms at the center of Vugha, and the perception of danger at the heart of the capital, therefore signified that the possessor of Vugha was capable of healing the land.

The term for a king's domination of his chiefs and of his competitors, so that he can heal the land, which is then fertile, is *kuzuiya shi*, "to prevent harm or suppress conflict in the land." In the historical traditions, elders say of a king who dominated the land and brought good rains, *azafunika shi, isheandue*, "he covered over the land, so that no one was willing to initiate [competitive] action." This usage was current by the 1870s. Traditions about the wars of that decade mention that chief Kibanga had the nickname *Zamgombezi*, "the medicines of the fighter," to which he answered, *zaema mafuniko*, "they cannot be covered over."[22] If this had been a fact rather than a boastful nickname, the wars would have ended, for Kibanga would have dominated all his rivals.

Peace is seen as the result of strength. When the king had real authority, he was not challenged, and he was never put into a position where he would need to use force. Violence was a sign that famine was likely, for it revealed the competition of force against force (*nguvu kwa nguvu*). This is close to the Parsonian understanding of power (Parsons 1963), in which the use of force is a sign of failure at securing generalized compliance with a wide range of obligations. The king was most effective at securing compliance when the land "was covered over" and "did not initiate action." We saw in chapter 2 the importance of the nineteenth-century principle that only if the king possessed the whole land as his own would he make effective rites for its fertility and prosperity. We saw, also, that the same principle was at the heart of the ancient rite of sacrifice among peasant lineages.

Among ordinary people, in cases of illness caused by sorcery, or in other words by one person's aggression against another, the course of treatment developed into a contest of power between the medicine men working for and against the sick person. The patient could not recover unless his supporting healer proved fully dominant, and therefore capable of ending the contest of strength.

The central principle is identical in healing within the sphere of peasant society and healing the land at the level of the chiefs. Medicine men in conflict bring death; the healing medicine man's complete dominance brings life. The implication here is that there was not a separate language of royal politics. Royals appropriated peasant language and put it to their own uses. We will examine the basis of this when we look at precolonial intellectuals.

The notion that effective power is never tested and is never expressed through the active use of force is one of those general conceptions that find particular forms of expression in different social contexts. The contrast between great power left to sleep, as opposed to imperfect power which is used, can be found in formulaic statements about old and young medicine men. I knew one very old man, in the 1960s, who took the epigrammatic name, Mzitu Mkuu, which depends on the ambiguity of the word *-kuu* to signify both "the great forest" and "the ancient forest." When

greeted, he would answer, "*Ugona mali*," ("Terrible things sleep there").
He explained that when young men learn their first powerful medicines,
they immediately test them out and kill one another. An old man knows
terrible things, far beyond the knowledge of the young, yet his charms
remain unused and untested, like the awful but unseen creatures in the
middle of a great forest. *Ubwanga*, "young man-ness," and *kibwanga*,
"in the manner of a young man," connote violence, strife, and competition.

Since dangerous forces are always at work in the land, the land is
harmed when the king's power is inadequate, but when it is equal to all
challenges, every dangerous person and charm is held in check. This idea
underlay the practice of sending all witches and criminals to Vugha. Once
they were brought into direct relation with the king's power, they were
made harmless. One man explained Vugha's character to me in the following way, when I said to him that the capital must have been a horrible place:

> It was not a horrible place. It was a place where poor unfortunates (*wa-
> kiwa*) were saved. The reason I say Vugha was not an evil place is that
> once a person who had done evil went to Vugha he stopped. . . . If you
> come to Vugha and do evil, you will be killed because of your own evil.
> The Simba Mwene resembled a rock. He was invulnerable to sorcery.[23]

If the king was ever forced to send a refugee (whether witch, criminal,
or victim) back to the court of the chief from whom he or she had fled,
it was a clear sign that the king of Vugha had not covered over the land.
The king was not invulnerable and therefore could not neutralize all dangers. The king, at such a time, was incapable of healing the land.

The alternation of periods in which the king harms the land with
periods in which he heals it—the alternation, in other words, of famine
and plenty—is related metaphorically to the opposition between male
and female in a way that brings the imagery of fertility back once again
to the temporal pattern of rhythmed recurrence. When the king "covered over" the land, his subjects experienced a "feminine farming season"
(*kiimo cha fyee*), one in which the crops were bountiful. A challenge to
the king's authority would lead to famine, also known as a "masculine
farming season" (*kiimo cha ngoshi*), because it was seen as a consequence
of force against force. Plants can also be counted as either masculine or
feminine, depending on whether they bear fruit or not. A maize plant
which grows without bearing ears is called *masculine*, as is an oyster-nut
plant which never develops a nut-filled sac. Maize which produces food
is called *feminine*.

Every piece of the interpretation to this point is based on great quantities of redundant ethnographic evidence. The contrast between thor-

oughgoing domination and force against force appears in innumerable contexts of everyday healing and of royal politics. The contrast between a feminine farming season and a masculine one is a uniformly accepted figure of speech, and one in which the associations are alive. It is not a dead metaphor. At this point I would like to mention a very interesting interpretation given by only one informant, my creative and intelligent companion Leo Hassani, who had several years of primary education. In 1967 he said:

> The sun shines every day, forever and ever. It may be covered over for a day by clouds, but it is still there, up high. We use the word "suns" (*mazuwa*) to mean "days" (*mishi*), because the sun shines every day. But rain has its proper times, like the moon. If you hear someone talk about a masculine farming season, it is when the sun shines altogether too much, for the rain has its months. A masculine farming season is *nguvu kwa nguvu*, "force against force," when those people battle one another, and hold back the rain. But the feminine farming season is a fertile one.

Drought is described simply as *zuwa*, "the sun," which rises unceasingly, even though on some days it may be hidden by clouds. The sun is fertile only if it combines with the rain's periodicity. "The sun resembles a man," the same man said. "A man is capable of being fertile every day, if he meets with a woman." A woman's fertility is periodic, and she therefore resembles the moon. In the Shambaa language (in this case with similarities to English usage) a woman's menstrual cycle is her "moon." The same word, *ng'wezi*, is used also for an irrigation channel. Many people say that a woman is fertile immediately after menstruation, by analogy with farming. "After the rain," explained one man, "you sow your seed." *Mbeyu* means both "semen" and "seed." In this way symbols which refer to the fertility of the land are rooted also in the processes of the body and of farming as it is experienced through touch, smell, the movement of one's own body. The relationship between moon and rain is treated as both metaphor and matter-of-fact. We have already seen that *fua yachunta ng'wezi*, "the rain washes off the moon."

The ties between the symbolic language of royal politics and of everyday life emerge, I am convinced, because those who created royal rites and who debated the political choices drew on the forms of reasoning and the stock of images which they knew best. The consequences of this are profound, in two closely related ways. First, the fact that the language so clearly evokes bodily experience, whether of menstruation, or of the physical activity of farming, gives discussions cast in these terms an immediate emotional energy. Second, the arguments over correct action are made in such a way that support of hierarchy among royals, and the association of competition with famine and death, carry over to support hierarchy of husband over wife, or old man over young man. Similar values with congruent justifications in the royal and the domestic contexts are mutually reinforcing.

Leo's interpretation raises interesting questions about temporal rhythms, because the masculine temporal mode in other contexts is one of irregular and unpredictable events — the luck of the hunt, or of warfare, or the uncertain outcome of conflict at the court of a chief. Leo raises the possibility that unceasing repetition, which he characterizes as *not* periodic, is also associated with masculinity.

The more usual, patriarchally accepted temporal pattern defines women's work as daily, regular, repeated, and therefore devoid of planning, as opposed to the irregular random movement of men who hold responsibility, with the king as the archetypal man. In farm work the man is expected to do heavy clearing and other work that comes at irregular intervals. It is the woman who goes to the garden each day for its continued maintenance. She is expected to walk to her garden in the morning as the sun moves higher in the sky, and to return to her cooking in the late afternoon when the sun declines. In this sense the sun gives a rhythm to social interaction. When people meet in the morning they say, *kuzacha*, "the sun is rising," meaning "I am going to do my daily tasks." On their way home in the afternoon they say *kuzashwa*, "the sun is declining." If you are hurrying home in the afternoon and do not want to talk, you need not explain at length. You have only to say, *kuzashwa*.

In old-fashioned burials, the long axis of a grave runs along a hillside. A man's body was placed lying on its right side, facing eastwards and towards *nyika*, the plains; a woman's body was placed on its left side, facing uphill and in the direction of the setting sun. The standard explanation of this in the 1960s was that women should face the hills and the setting sun so they can return home when *kuzashwa*, when the sun is setting, to cook the evening meal. Men face the rising sun so as not to delay their early morning hunting trips to the plains. Hunting, the quintessentially male activity, had all the unpredictability of the wilderness. Cooking, the female activity, took place in the safety of home and was predictable. The gender-based contrast between cooking and hunting, home and wilderness, predictability and unpredictability, was found also in rites of passage.

We have already seen in chapter 2 that among peasants, publicly recognized forms of contingency — crises which threatened the group's reproduction (except for childbirth) — were dealt with by men. Men controlled *kifu* wealth, the fraternal group's livestock, because it was they who paid indemnities to keep dependents from pawnship, they who bought famine food, ransomed dependents captured in war, and paid healers. In this respect, the king played the man's role on a much larger stage. He controlled the wealth of the whole kingdom so that he could deal with all the contingencies affecting it. He faced unexpected and threatening events by using medicines which were the patrimony of his ancestors, and by using the kingdom's wealth to sacrifice to those ancestors, to pay powerful healers to use their medicines for the land's fertility, or to purchase guns and powder.

Mbegha, as the founding hero king, was archetypally masculine, the hunter, the provider of meat (men's food), the man who "made all Shambaa into women." In the words of one informant, "His job is to make things feminine, so that they will bear fruit."[24] Kilindi masculinity was a central principle in the culture of kingship. The king was normally the most polygynous man in the kingdom. Adultery with a king's wife was treated as an act of rebellion, punishable by death. The principle of Kilindi masculinity was so strong that Kilindi daughters were treated, in many respects, as men. The phrase often used in the traditions is, *wazaghauka waghoshi*, "they became men." Kilindi women went through the young men's initiation rite. They chose husbands, while normally it was men who chose wives. In normal usage a man takes a wife (-*ghua*), and a woman is taken as wife (-*ghuighwa*). Kilindi women "took" husbands. If a Kilindi woman died in childbirth, her husband was subject to the death penalty, because "she was killed by his poisoned arrow."[25] The principle was that the Kilindi made the people of the land into women so that the rains would come in their proper season, like the moon.

The terms in this analysis cannot be ranged in neat and regular columns, with male invariably associated with sun and famine, or female with moon and fertility. The night, the time of the moon, was also a time when witches wandered naked. One way of saying that the king was irregular and dangerous, like a witch, was to say that he wandered alone at night. Social acts are more likely to bring benevolent results when visible, in the light of the sun. Each symbol — night, day, moon, sun, male, female — changed its significance depending on its immediate context in ritual or in speech.

The unvarying organizing principle in discourse about these symbols is an opposition between rhythmed regularity on the one side, and irregular, unpredictable, random events (and possibly unceasing continuity) on the other. The moon returns according to its rhythm, but whatever is irregular and unpredictable is hidden in darkness.

It is possible to see this temporal contrast as a generative principle. Individuals create new and idiosyncratic images, which are accepted and understood in public discourse so long as they remain in harmony with the core temporal oppositions.

The imagery of rhythmed time is found in the central rain charm at the heart of Vugha, the *kiza*. It is a round-bottomed earthen pot inside the royal burial enclosure, the only object there aside from the graves of kings. According to the hereditary official who cared for it, inside the pot "there are medicines, and also there is soil and the edible plant known as *eze* [pl. *maeze: Xanthosoma violaceum*]. When it rains, the *maeze* sprout. When there is drought, and the sun glares down, the *maeze* die, but beneath the soil they are still alive. Only the visible part dies." In a time of excessive drought, he explained, two court officials "pour the water into the *kiza* and remove the dead leaves. Finally, they take the dried crumbled leaves of a certain tree, and rub them into the pot. The next day it rains. I myself went, together with the Shefaya, to do this, but I don't know what the leaves were, because I was given them by the king."[26] The *eze* does not die. It is covered over like the moon in the rite of burial and accession, only to reappear.

The oral narratives describing political struggles in the nineteenth century assume that a rhythmed alternation is at the heart of actual political practice. They assume an alternation between two configurations of political action within the Kilindi lineage, and along with it a rhythmed alternation between two characteristic forms of the organization of litigation, of warfare, and of tribute. It is to these that we now turn.

Configurations of Descent and Power

The struggle by chiefs to "cover over the land," to establish themselves as dominant rainmakers, took place at many different levels within the kingdom. Each local chief worked to dominate competitors within his own territory—to prevent the emergence of competing local rainmakers who might challenge him. If the chief succeeded in suppressing competition, then he was the only local recipient of tribute from the peasants. At a wider level, it was the king's task to "cover over" the territories of all of the chiefs, to prove that he alone of all Kilindi was dominant. When the king "covered over" the whole land, then tribute flowed to the royal capital, commoners could appeal the judgments of their chiefs at the court of the king, and only the king imposed the death penalty. When king and chiefs fought, at a time of power against power, tribute did not come to the capital, commoners could not appeal the judgments of their chiefs, and many chiefs could impose the death penalty. The kingdom as a whole, therefore, oscillated between two states, parallel to healing the land and harming the land.[27]

The driving force behind this oscillation, according to the historical traditions, was the struggle for dominance within the Kilindi lineage.

Royal descent politics fell into two alternating configurations: one in which the king placed his children as chiefs in all the chiefdoms and therefore expected obedience from them; the other in which he failed to do this and struggled with half-brothers or father's brothers who refused to subordinate themselves. The history of the kingdom was therefore a long-term oscillation between the two conditions of the Kilindi lineage. Oscillation did not suppress the succession of events in a linear order, but was the framework within which those events unfolded. Traditions told by men of the royal court are quite clear, for example, that the slave trade grew rapidly after Kimweri ye Nyumbai's death (in 1862), and that it had not existed earlier in the same form. They maintain that the emergence of slave traders was to be expected at that stage in the cycle — a time when the king was incapable of dominating competitors in the Kilindi lineage.

Peasants spoke about the politics of descent, and along with it they spoke also of the politics of rain. In discussions among Kilindi, however, descent politics — the alternation between the two configurations — held center stage. Kilindi discussions did not focus on rain or on healing the land. The historical record of Kilindi discourse shows that this was the case in the nineteenth century, and it remained the case long after colonial conquest.[28]

The history of political competition within the Kilindi lineage shows that it did in fact go through a long-term developmental cycle, one which can be viewed as the unfolding of stages within a closed system. During one part of the cycle, the king as father dominated the chiefs who were his sons; during the other part, the chiefs were not junior to the king, and relations between chiefs and king were characterized by competition. The picture of alternation between two states is a remarkably apt representation of royal political patterns. Nevertheless, it is impossible to claim that we can observe rhythmed repetition over the long term, because only two cycles of oscillation were completed during the entire history of the kingdom. In addition, however, the observation is supported by the unfolding of a parallel cycle in the splinter kingdom of Mshihwi.[29]

In the best of circumstances, when the kingdom functioned as most Kilindi thought it should, which is the way it worked in the days of Kimweri ye Nyumbai, the king chose a prominent descent group from each territory, married a woman of that group and sent her children to rule there. Just as an ordinary peasant's wife received from her husband a farm to be passed on to her children, so the house of a king's wife received a chiefdom as the source of its livelihood. The eldest son (or in some cases a daughter) became a chief, and that son's children ruled small pieces of the same territory.

Political office was quite different from land or cattle as a resource to be transferred from one generation to the next. It could not be divided without diminishing its value, for political power must be concentrated to be effective. If the king wanted to provide territories for his children, he needed to remove the preexisting chiefs. The Kilindi were the only descent group which cast off members in each generation. Individual Kilindi, after losing office, became *Wakiindi wa kaya,* "Kilindi of the common hearth," and then later lost Kilindi status altogether. Chiefs resisted the loss of office, and their probability of success in resisting the king's efforts to remove them changed at different parts of the kingdom's developmental cycle.

At times when the king could not enforce his will, many of the chiefdoms became sovereign states independent of royal control. They were capable of withdrawing from the kingdom because the separate chiefs in the major territories carried out essentially the same activities as the king. Chiefs mediated disputes among peasant *kifu* groups or sacrificial groups. They assembled fighting men to defend their own territory or attack others. They collected tribute. They performed rites to bring rain. When the king was powerful they deferred, in all of this, to his overarching authority.

The degree of royal control was defined, in the first instance, by the kinship relationship between chief and king. When, as in the time of Kimweri ye Nyumbai, each chief was the king's son, the authority of father over son reinforced the king's authority over his chiefs. At such times the kingdom was effectively centralized.

By the end of Kimweri ye Nyumbai's reign, which lasted from about 1815 until 1862, Kimweri had installed his own offspring in the overwhelming majority of chiefdoms and their subunits. Abdallah bin Hemedi 'lAjjemy listed fifty-seven of Kimweri's children as chiefs of Shambaai, and thirty-six in the eastern provinces (1962: Sura 42). The actual number was much higher, since Abdallah tended to list only the senior child of each matricentral house, and not all the younger subchiefs.[30]

A father who ruled over the chiefdoms of his sons knew that any one son would find it difficult to challenge his authority. All the sons knew that once the king died they would struggle with one another for dominance. A son who rebelled successfully against the king was bound to preempt a leading position after the king's death. The sons could be counted on to fight against a brother who challenged his father's authority, because the same brother would likely challenge them in turn.

Because Kimweri's authority as a father over his sons reinforced his authority as king over chiefs, he could employ sanctions against what he regarded as improper, or more especially impolitic, behavior. The word

in traditions to describe Kimweri's application of sanctions is *-shunda*,
to punish or chastise. It is the same word used to say that an ordinary
father punishes his children. The most extreme sanction was to move the
chief from his territory to a less important one or to one in which the
position of chief was less rewarding or more difficult.[31]

In at least one case, the complaints of peasants led Kimweri to remove
a chief. Kimweri's son Semboja had gone to the chiefdom of Gare as a
young boy of about eight, with his mother's brother (a Gare man) as
guardian, educator, temporary judge, collector of tribute, and coordinator of rites for the welfare of the land. Semboja, who was later to become a terrifying slave raider, was difficult even as a child. Traditions
say that he shot poisoned arrows at the treasured hunting dogs of his subjects. When Semboja's guardian stepped down, the peasants waited for
a suitable incident to complain to Kimweri. This came when some cows
wandered into Semboja's maize garden, and he chopped with a bush knife
at their legs. After this and one further complaint, Kimweri removed Semboja as chief of Gare. The young chief was sent to a small and insignificant territory at the southwestern corner of Shambaai, overlooking
the plains at a point where Maasai speakers, moving through, were forced
to follow a path near Shambaai. Kimweri felt that Semboja's violent tem-
perament would be usefully employed against the Maasai. The situation
developed quite differently when the Maasai path became a major trade
route; Semboja moved down to the plains at Mazinde, and allied himself with the Maasai.[32]

One can see, in Semboja's career, one piece of evidence among many
others for the unshakable authority of the king in this descent configuration. Semboja's behavior was not governed by popular notions of pro-
priety. He did not hesitate at violence, nor was he anxious to avoid being
called a witch. He publicly violated the conditions of mourning after his
father's death (Abdallah bin Hemedi 'lAjjemy 1962: Sura 73). Yet he never,
so far as is known, attacked or ridiculed his father, nor did he resist when
chastised, or when sent to a minor chiefdom. If Semboja had rebelled
against his father, he would have been opposed by all his brothers.

So long as Kimweri ye Nyumbai's reign continued, he retained sovereign power over the separate chiefdoms, although his control was weaker
near the eastern edge of the kingdom. Each of the chiefs sent a portion
of his tribute to Vugha. Except for cases of witchcraft, no chief imposed
a death penalty on one of his subjects. Litigants at the court of a chief
had the right to appeal to Vugha. None of the chiefs could make war
except by Kimweri's order. The greatest rain charms were all in Kimweri's
hands. None of the chiefs could threaten to hold back the rain if Kimweri
wanted it to fall.

The oral traditions about Kimweri's years, whether told by chiefs or peasants, all agree that his reign was the best of times in the old kingdom. In the days of Kimweri ye Nyumbai, the traditions say, there were no violent raids, no unfair judgments.

> Kimweri ye Nyumbai placed sons in the chiefdoms, and he was respected. . . . Ah, in those days there was nothing but peace and good will in the land. . . . Such peace is not seen in the days of every king. It was seen in the days of Kimweri, because if a person had no wealth, if his wife's lineage was about to take her from him, he could say, "Oh king, my wife is being taken." Kimweri would say, "Go to the following place. There is a cow of mine which you may take." He didn't like to be told, "This is the son of so and so." He liked to say, "They are all my children." And when he sent a son to rule, he would say, "You are to build a village, and live nicely with your companions, so that there is no conflict. In judging cases, show an evil man his own evil. But if there is a man with no evil, don't introduce evil into his life."[33]

This was of course an idealized view of Kimweri ye Nyumbai, whose conflicts with the Zigula brought war to the land, and who at times took slaves capriciously. The tradition is saying that because he placed sons in all the chiefdoms, thus "covering over" the land, his was a time of benevolent rule. In important ways the tradition is correct: Shambaa chiefdoms did not make war against one another in Kimweri's time, and subjects could appeal their chief's judgments to the court at Vugha.

The disordered period in the royal cycle came after Kimweri ye Nyumbai's death. The transfer of kingship began before Kimweri died. He became old and feeble, no longer able to hear cases, and so he decided to pass control of Vugha to a successor. The heir to Vugha, son of the great house, had already died. Kimweri's decision was to pass on the kingdom to the heir's son Shekulwavu.[34]

It was Kimweri's success that made his grandson Shekulwavu's position untenable. The chiefs, Kimweri's sons, Shekulwavu's uncles, were all members of the same generation, sons of the same man. They would have to be removed from office in order for Shekulwavu to impose control. They could be counted on to present a unified front against the new king. If he removed any of them, it was a threat to them all. Shekulwavu's position was even more difficult than it would normally have been at that point in the developmental cycle. He took the kingdom only because of his father's untimely death. His father would have competed with half-brothers; Shekulwavu competed with his father's half-brothers, men he was expected to treat with great deference. Even if Shekulwavu's father had survived to become king, the position would have been impossible, since all Kimweri's many sons, except for the new king's full brothers, would have united in resistance. Tradition has it that Shekulwavu's father had been killed by a half-brother.

During Shekulwavu's six years as king, after Kimweri ye Nyumbai's death, he placed a close relative in only one major chiefdom, Bumbuli, which he had vacated in his own move to Vugha. Shekulwavu was not successful in removing any of the established chiefs.

Both sides — the new king and his enemies — found themselves in conflict with principles of expected behavior. Expectations of Shekulwavu were contradictory. As king, he was expected to "cover over the land," winning dominance for Vugha over the chiefdoms. As brother's son, he was expected to treat the chiefs, his father's brothers, with deference. Shekulwavu was unable to find an adequate approach. When a slave fled to Vugha from the court of the powerful chief Semboja, the king returned the slave. This violated the principle that Vugha is inviolate as a refuge; it provoked resistance by the people of Vugha. When more slaves fled, Shekulwavu found it impossible to turn them back, and Semboja was enraged (Feierman 1974:156–57). Shekulwavu's mother came to Vugha after leaving Mshuza, the powerful chief who had been her heir. He too wanted Shekulwavu removed.

The king's enemies also found themselves in conflict with expected principles of political behavior. Shambaai was a single sovereign state — a single *nguvu*, or "power." Chiefs from within the single power were not permitted to make war against their king. The chiefs therefore recruited non-Shambaa fighters — foreigners from Taita — and provided them with instructions on how to overcome Vugha's defenses. If the attack failed, the chiefs would deny involvement. The attack ended with Vugha in flames and the king in flight. A short time later Shekulwavu died, and the kingdom split in two.

Shekulwavu's close relatives created "a separate power," *nguvu ntuhu* (an autonomous Kilindi splinter state), in the East Usambara Mountains. A Kilindi of Vugha described the implications of a separate power in the following terms: "Those days it was just the same as with the Germans. If you committed a crime here, if you fled to [the British side of the border at] Mombasa, you were a free man, because Mombasa was a separate power."[35] The existence of a separate power weakened the new king of Vugha, Semboja's son. A chief threatened by the king with removal could resist by making common cause with the separate power of Shekulwavu's relations.

This outcome — an impasse between a king incapable of dominating Shambaai and a separate power incapable of defeating him — was not a new one during this period of the 1870s and 1880s. A little less than a century earlier, Kimweri ye Nyumbai's father had been just such a king, restrained by a separate power, and Kimweri's grandfather had been a centralizing king like Kimweri himself.

The pattern was a recurrent one in the history of the kingdom. A king is incapable of defeating his enemies who threaten to make common cause with a separate power; he is therefore unable to replace the chiefs of the heartland with his own men. This king's failure represents his successor's opportunity, for the next king does not have to face a unified group of chiefs. Instead, he faces chiefs who are the remnants of many different struggles in different periods, chiefs who find it difficult to join together in resistance. He places his children in all the chiefdoms and presents his successor with an impossible political problem.

The succession of Kimweri ye Nyumbai's father, Kinyashi Muanga Ike, had been the outcome of a bitter dispute which led to the formation of a separate power at Mshihwi. The threat from Mshihwi prevented Kinyashi from dominating the core of the kingdom in southern Shambaai. Like Shekulwavu, he was able to place a close relative only in Bumbuli: this he gave to Kimweri. Kinyashi expanded his base by placing his sons in northern Shambaai, where there had previously been no Kilindi (Feierman 1974: chap. 4).

Kimweri ye Nyumbai was the beneficiary of his father's difficulties. The chiefs of southern Shambaai, his father's enemies, could not easily cooperate with the chiefs of the north, his half-brothers. The war with the separate power at Mshihwi had continued so long that the two original enemies, Kinyashi and his half-brother, had died. Kimweri and the heir to Mshihwi met, and each took an oath never to attempt ruling the territory of the other. The end of the war with Mshihwi left Kimweri ye Nyumbai free to consolidate his control of the core chiefdoms. Kimweri placed his sons in the chiefdoms of Shambaai, thereby making his successor's position impossible, leading once again to the emergence of a separate power. The pattern of rule for the kingdom as a whole, therefore, was an oscillating one. The land was covered over for a period, and then followed a period of *nguvu kwa nguvu*, "power against power." The king was incapable of dominating his chiefs, and warfare continued between the king and his enemies in the separate power. Lives were lost in war, and in the 1880s, if not in earlier cycles, the upheaval of warfare contributed to the famine of a land harmed.

In the 1870s and 1880s the polity established by Shekulwavu's relatives in the east counted as a separate power because the two sides had split the lineage. No longer would the two sets of Kilindi attend mourning ceremonies together, inherit wives from one another, or sacrifice together to the ancestors.[36] Within the core of the old kingdom, however, in the West Usambaras, chiefs continued to mourn, to sacrifice, and to inherit together, but recognized that there was more than one locus of power among them.

A "locus of power," *he nguvu*, was the territory of a chief who was not subordinate to any other. Three practical tests indicated whether a particular chief's village was *he nguvu*. A chief at a locus of power did not pay tribute to a superior chief; he could impose the death penalty, and none of his subjects could appeal a judgment to a superior chief; he could decide to make war against a foreign power without consulting another chief.

This very brief summary of the definition of a *locus of power* is based on a great many oral traditions: some about tribute, some about litigation, and some about warfare. A small number of the traditions elucidate the meaning of a locus of power directly. The majority, however, simply assume the relevance of the distinction. Some traditions say that final judgment, beyond appeal, could only be reached at Vugha. When the narrator is questioned further it becomes clear that he is talking about the time of Kimweri ye Nyumbai when the entire kingdom had only one locus of power. Traditions from Mlalo, in northern Shambaai, described the chief's right to enforce judgment, with no appeal to Vugha. Further details make it clear that the period referred to is the late 1880s after Mlalo had successfully resisted an attack by non-Shambaa fighters who had secretly been sent on orders from Vugha. The practical implications of the definition never vary: if a chief does not send appeals of litigation to a higher power, if he can apply the death penalty, then he does not pay tribute, and he decides on matters of war and peace on his own.[37]

The practitioners of politics communicated an understanding of their political system to one another with the utmost simplicity, and in terms which accounted for the variability of the relationship between king and chiefs. Two distinctions account for all the relationships within the borders of the kingdom. First, some chiefs were sons of the king, and others were not. Sons of the king always regarded their father's authority as binding, since they derived their legitimacy from him. A king could remove his sons from their chiefdoms, appoint them to other chiefdoms, and replace them with other men. A king did not have the same power of appointment in chiefdoms held by brothers or by agnates other than sons. Any chief except a son could have been expected to resist removal. In chiefdoms not governed by sons, a second distinction separated chiefdoms which were under the power of a king from others which were *he nguvu* — at an independent locus of power.

The history of political struggle was an oscillation between two conditions: one in which a king governed his sons, and the other in which a struggle of power against power emerged between king and chiefs. The two conditions were closely tied to the conditions as defined by peasants concerned about rain — a land healed, and a land harmed. The simple terms for oscillating states were the core of a powerful framework of explanation. Practitioners of politics were able, at all times, to specify with precision the distribution of power from one chiefdom to another across the whole extent of the kingdom.

4

Alternative Paths to Social Health in the Precolonial Kingdom

When the people of Vugha stood before their new king to shout of their need for food some of them called out a single word over and over: *Nkaviongwa! Nkaviongwa!* "It is not mentioned! It is not mentioned!" According to an old court official, the meaning of this was that "the things done at Vugha are not mentioned because . . . they are cunning acts of domination," deadly plots against individuals, planned in the night. In a broader sense Kilindi attempted to exclude from public debate, to render unmentionable, alternative visions of political organization.

Among peasants interested in food and rain, peace and justice, the Kilindi-dominated vision of the world assigned a central place to dynastic relations. As we have seen, popular interpretation held that conflict between king and chiefs, between royal half-brothers, led to famine and war; a king's unchallenged dominance over dynastic rivals led to peace and satiety. Within these terms of discourse a peasant worked to achieve social health by giving allegiance to a powerful Kilindi chief.

Supporting a chief was not, however, the only possible path to social health within the larger society. In the early reigns, local descent group leaders held their own fertility medicines. Throughout the kingdom's history, withdrawal from under chiefly rule, a return to descent-group rule, was an imaginable possibility. It was, in fact, the strategy of people among the Bondei in the eastern part of the kingdom in about 1870 when enslavement by chiefs reached intolerable levels. The eastern peasantry threw out their chiefs and went over to government by local elders. Their rebellion shows that while the discourse on healing the land directed attention away from non-Kilindi alternatives, it did not fully eliminate either the possibility or the consciousness of those alternatives. The question of whether there was to be one theory of government or two (or perhaps more) was itself an issue open to struggle.

Serious obstacles stand in the way of understanding nineteenth-century debates. The obvious obstacle is the fragmentary character of the sources for reconstructing the thought and speech of nonliterate peasants who lived a hundred years ago, or more. In the case of Shambaai, however, some elements of a partial reconstruction are possible. We have a body of recorded oral traditions as told from the points of view of a great many local descent groups. These are complemented by scattered but important written sources from the 1840s onwards.

An additional obstacle to the attempt to move beyond a Kilindi-dominated vision is the tendency in anthropological thought to privilege a society's most central and most coherently organized conceptions, categories, and symbols. On this issue the classic French sociology of the *Année Sociologique* has had a profound influence on students of African cosmology. Attention to "social facts" and to "collective representations," as in Emile Durkheim's sociology, makes the relationship between society and received representation the subject of study. Durkheim and Marcel Mauss (1963) argued that cosmology originates in the organization of society.

The most important problem in the current context is not with the general study of society and of representations, but with the picture conveyed by most works in the Durkheimian tradition of each African society as discrete and clearly bounded, and each society's central terms of discourse as unified and coherent. The scholar's search for coherence overlaps with the drive by those who hold power within society to silence all heterodox ideas.

In the case of nineteenth-century Shambaa discourse, the scholar who simplifies, who finds unity and coherence, portrays the world as the Kilindi themselves would have liked to see it — a world in which Kilindi action in healing the land and harming the land was the sole relevant action for achieving social well-being. The way out of this unintended alliance between ethnographers and elites is to complement the study of core culture with a search for heterodox forms of discourse and practice, or at the very least a search for the patterns of social organization within which those forms grew.

Alternative Medicines

In searching the record for alternatives to Kilindi dominance it is important to make a sharp distinction between the general cultural principle underlying healing the land and the narrow application of that principle to the Kilindi dynasty. As we have seen, the underlying principle was deeply rooted in the precolonial culture of Shambaai: it was applied in healing practices among peasants, was at the heart of their sacrificial rites, and served as one of the pillars of every patriarch's authority over his dependents. The basic principle most probably existed before the kingdom's creation and would continue after its demise. The principle was that competition among holders of ritual power leads to harm and death; the unchallenged power of a ritual leader, combined with "ownership," brings life.

The Kilindi did not create the basic principle, but they merged it successfully with the politics of their own lineage. The crucial question for the peasantry was not whether ownership in general brought life, but whether one or another Kilindi chief could build a concentration of rain charms and armed might sufficient to bring peace and fertility. The great Kilindi achievement was in getting people to phrase their questions about ritual power so as to refer to royals, and not to local healers or descent-group heads. The mark of Kilindi success was that peasants said king Kimweri ye Nyumbai's unchallenged dominance over his sons gave him control over the rain, and that they also said conflicts among Kilindi in the 1880s brought famine. It was by no means automatic that the framework of the Kilindi lineage would come to bear the weight of healing the land. Kilindi success, in this regard, was the outcome of a long struggle, one which never ended.

The struggle began in the early days of the kingdom. Local descent groups fought to keep their own fertility medicines; royals fought to take them away and to establish a monopoly. Royals built their chiefdoms, in a number of cases, on the territories which already had coherent structures in the pre-Kilindi period. The territories had been organized around dominant local descent groups, with the leader of each ancient descent group responsible for fertility medicine in his own territory. The early kings worked to absorb or to destroy these predecessors.

Even after the elimination of most descent-based fertility medicine, the Kilindi failed to achieve a monopoly over rain medicines. It was impossible for them to eliminate every sort of healer who claimed the ability to bring rich crops. Chiefs were forced to fight, or to ignore, or to co-opt the autonomous holders of fertility medicine for agriculture.

Before Kilindi rule the ancient inhabitants of Shambaai were organized in villages, each of which followed the leadership of an elder drawn from its dominant descent group. If strangers chose to settle in an established village, they accepted its leader as their own. At some places the dominant lineages in all the separate villages of a cluster saw themselves as descended from a single patrilineal ancestor. In this case they accepted a single ritual leader who performed rites for the defense and fertility of the entire cluster. The villages of a neighborhood joined together in trade, in marriage, and in rites of passage, whether or not they shared common descent (see Feierman 1974: chap. 3).

The early kings allied themselves with some prominent neighborhood leaders and attacked others. In either case the Kilindi appropriated pre-existing fertility medicines. By doing so they changed the political framework of fertility medicine from one which focused on the leadership of local descent groups to one in which the central battles were fought within the overarching Kilindi descent group.

At Mlalo in northern Shambaai the Kijelwa, who sacrificed to their ancestors for the fertility of the land, continued to do so during the early years of royal rule. The chiefs of Mlalo took the Kijelwa grave site as their own. The first name they mentioned when invoking the ancestors in rites for rain was the Kijelwa forebear, Saguruma, whom they called a *Kilindi-Kijelwa*.[1]

At Ubiri, the home of the Hea, who occupied a cluster of villages, the encounter was violent. The Hea leader, Mhina, had medicines for protection in war, and he had a *kiza* — a pot with earth and plants and medicines — for the rain. Hea traditions say that on the day of a rite of passage, a young woman sent by Mbegha offered to shave Mhina, to prepare him for the celebration. Mhina raised his chin to expose his beard, and the woman slit his throat. After Mhina's successor took charge of Ubiri, Mbegha returned to the attack. According to one Hea tradition Mbegha said, "That *nguvu*, that power, is still there." He arranged to have the new Hea leader strangled and then sent his soldiers to ask, "Do you still have any *nguvu*?" The Hea descent group split into many small parts and gave up the rule of exogamy. The *kiza*, the Hea leader's rain pot, was taken to Mbegha's capital at Vugha.[2]

The Hea rain pot was not the only *kiza* in Shambaai. *Kiza* was the word for a fertility shrine that took several forms. Lesser shrines were spread widely around the mountains. In some cases the *kiza* was a pot of water and medicines placed in a garden with *king'weng'we* trees (*Dracaena deremensis*) around it. At other places it was a single *king'weng'we* at which one placed a banana shoot before planting, to make it fruitful (K. Wohlrab 1929:30; LangHeinrich 1921:169). The tree has a tall thin trunk with dark green, rubbery leaves at the top. It grows with spectacular rapidity and flourishes in the worst of droughts.

The whole of the royal grave site at Vugha was thus a rain shrine, the main elements of which were borrowed from the ancient inhabitants of the mountains. The graves, together with the rain pot, were encircled by a fence whose main posts were the trunks of live *king'weng'we* trees.

Just as the Kilindi appropriated ancient Shambaa rain medicines, in a later century the British appropriated Kilindi rain medicines, which became a support of colonial rule in Shambaai. The history of appropriation and domination is a long one.

The struggles of the early Kilindi years were not simply contests for the control of particular rain charms. At issue was the role of nonroyal descent groups in Shambaai. The Hea were a large powerful group spread over a number of villages. By the time their wars with the Kilindi were over they had been divided and scattered. They faced the Kilindi rulers as separate fragments.

The same thing happened to the Nango, recent arrivals in Shambaai during the early kingdom, whose political organization was very different from that of ancient inhabitants like the Hea. The Nango were a set of six large, related descent groups, each of which had a distincitive ritual emblem. Nango groups were not narrowly localized; they were spread through several parts of Shambaai. Nango from all over the mountains periodically joined together in a mass ritual assembly under the direction of a single leader to initiate young men.[3]

Bughe, the second king, allied himself with a faction of dissatisfied Nango for the murder of their ritual leader. Many localized Nango groups split up; their members fled to live with non-Nango affines, or in inaccessible villages. The full story of these events, together with the existence of relationships among all the people who call themselves Nango, is publicly remembered only in parts of the mountains which are far from Vugha. The survivors near the old royal capital describe themselves as members of small widow-inheritance groups which just happen to be called Nango.[4]

The Kilindi not only appropriated preexisting rain charms; they destroyed the organizational base on which those charms rested. As centralized power grew in the kingdom, large and powerful descent groups disintegrated. The late nineteenth-century pattern of social organization as described in chapter 2 was a consequence of these earlier struggles. With the decline of large, descent-based social groups, the Kilindi confronted a multitude of small, genealogically shallow sacrificial groups, each fragmented into multiple fraternal groups.

The destruction of local medicines was uneven, for in cases where autonomous war medicines were in the hands of insignificant local groups, the chiefs agreed to let them stand. Scattered around Shambaai are numerous villages which the Kilindi agreed never to enter. Each of these has a *ghaso*, a ritually dangerous assemblage of war medicines. Usually the *ghaso* is a small patch of forest left to stand in the middle of cultivated fields. It is maintained for the keeping of medicines so dangerous that they must be kept in *tunduwi*, in the wilderness. A person who enters a *ghaso* must, on leaving, undergo "cooling" decontaminating rites. The people who maintained a *ghaso* continued to argue their cases before the chief's court, but they knew that the chief's men would not enter their village to seize women or cows in an arbitrary way.[5]

Despite all Kilindi efforts, new medicines continued to appear. Even when local descent-group medicines were fully under control, individual healers rose up, often basing their claims either on medicines learned abroad or on personal charisma. Around the turn of the twentieth century, people were telling a folk tale which must have represented Kilindi nightmares. It was about a man so poor that all he had to eat was the waste from other people's sugar cane. One day, in the forest, a *kulunge* tree gave him the present of a magical ram, which granted all of his wishes. He asked for a wife and received a wife. He asked for clothing and received more than one could buy at the coast for the price of two slaves. His chief confiscated the ram, but after further events it appeared that only the poor man could win the ram's gifts. When the chief asked for anything he received manure. In the end, the people of the land made the poor man chief and sent the chief off to be a poor man (Karasek 1911:214).

We have records of an incident in 1911 (some years after German conquest), in which a nonchiefly healer made successful claims on a minor chief's followers. The healer was sleeping in the chief's house. The healer awoke in the night, loudly calling out a woman's name. In the morning he told the chief that in the night an *mzuka* spirit had given the woman to him as his wife. The chief gave him the woman, who almost immediately ran away. The healer then threatened the chief that "If in the immediate future the *mzuka* kills the cattle, don't come to me. Any misfortune whatever will have been caused by that woman" (Hosbach 1911). The surprising element here is the ease with which the healer imposed his claim. A chief's capacity to rule effectively depended on his ability to control the claims of nonroyal healers.

Before colonial conquest, a Kilindi at a locus of power was able to use his monopoly on violence to control public healers, unless they had unusual powers. A common motif in oral traditions is the encounter between the chief and a peasant master of rain medicines. After purchasing the medicines, the chief has the peasant murdered so that his knowledge will travel no further (Karasek 1923–24:25).

One method of controlling rainmakers was described during the German period by a man named Mbogo in the chiefdom of Bumbuli. He gave the following account of his own experiences, which he said happened in the days of Kimweri (probably Kimweri Maguvu, in the 1880s):

> The maize was drying up. Several men came to me and said, "You have been called to Vugha." Once there, I was held for several days. Then they opened the discussion with the question, "Why are you so dirty? Why is your hair so long? Are you, perhaps, holding back the rain?" [Long hair was in those days associated with ritual power.] I answered, "No!" The chief called out, "Grab hold of him. Shave his hair. If you shave him and it doesn't

rain, he is innocent. If the hair falls and it rains, he is . . . holding back the rain." They cut my long hair with a dull knife, without wetting it. As they did this a few drops of rain actually fell. I was required to pay a goat as a fine, and then allowed to go free (Karasek 1923–24:25).

According to the German settler to whom this story was told, in other cases the offending rainmaker was killed.

Non-Kilindi practitioners administered public fertility medicine without royal opposition in a limited number of cases: if it was defined as outside the chiefly sphere, or if the practitioners were sponsored and approved by the chief.

Irrigation, we have seen, was outside the chiefly sphere. Each major furrow had its ritual specialist drawn from an ancient peasant lineage. This man needed to sacrifice before any water was allowed to flow. In addition, peasants made their own rites of divination when choosing village sites. Once again, as with irrigation, the ritual was outside the chief's sphere.[6]

Locust rituals were seen as political and were sponsored by the chiefs. The specialists in driving locusts away came from the Pare Mountains to the west of Shambaai. They received payments in livestock from the chief, and in chickens, goats, and food from the peasantry. They acted on the fiction that they owned all the wealth of the land, taking whatever pleased them in addition to the tribute they were given. The rule was, however, that what they took to show their ownership of the land they had to consume before they left Shambaai. These healers, called *Wambagha*, had their own ritual centers in Shambaai. They maintained a *ghaso*, a patch of forest for dangerous medicines (in this case with houses at its center) near Vugha.[7]

Even though the Wambagha had medicines unknown to the Kilindi, chiefs assimilated the alien knowledge within the framework of chiefly politics. Wambagha came only at the chief's invitation. Peasants saw locust plagues as serving the interests of chiefs by increasing the number of their dependents or by helping them to bring the suffering needed as mourning for the dead.

The chiefs fought for power in an environment where many different individuals established claims to hold healing power: locust specialists, irrigation specialists, healers who treated epidemics, those who claimed special relationships with spirits at caves and trees, or with the ancestral spirits of a locally dominant lineage, and so forth.

Competition among all the holders of fertility medicines can be taken as evidence for the openness of the system of authority in Shambaai. It demonstrates also that there was competition among alternative visions of the healthy society. One competing position held that Kilindi chief-ship must be merged with control over rain medicines: chiefs must be the sole rainmakers. Another assumed that fertility medicines were to be respected wherever they were found, since they were diffused through-out society, among descent-group leaders and men of personal charisma as well as chiefs. These two positions can both be treated as variations on a single theme. They were both explorations of an underlying tension between the diffuse, uncontrollable character of ritual power and the perceived fact that public medicines would only be effective if concen-trated in a single pair of hands.

By the early 1870s a third position emerged, a much more radical depar-ture from the core definition of issues underlying healing the land. The new position was based on the assumption that rain medicines are of sec-ondary importance for achieving the well-being of the peasantry. The central question, in this view, was whether chiefly practices of enslave-ment and tribute collection were just, or whether they exploited peasants. For society to achieve health, the exploitation of subjects by chiefs must end. This alternative theory is discussed in the last section of this chap-ter. The people of the kingdom thus held an alternative conception of what was needed to achieve social health in addition to holding alter-native medicines in the system defined by the central conception.

The coexistence of multiple forms of healing, indeed of plural theories of healing, was characteristic also of the treatment of ordinary illnesses in the villages of Shambaai.

The facts of therapeutic pluralism, as observed around the African con-tinent, have come to challenge earlier pictures of neatly organized Afri-can cosmologies and well-ordered hierarchies of explanation. Robin Hor-ton, in his classic article on "African Traditional Thought and Western Science" (1967), argued that people in each "traditional" society held a coherent set of theories concerning the spiritual and material forces at work in their world. These conceptions of causality could not easily be tested or proven false, because they existed within a closed world, with-out alternative theories of causation. Horton has been criticized for com-paring science, a specialized body of knowledge within Western society, with the thought of ordinary people in African society — not comparing the knowledge of specialists in the one place with the knowledge of spe-cialists in the other. In addition, a number of recent local studies of heal-ing show the coexistence within each single society of many competing therapies and indeed of competing theories of illness causation. Many African societies appear more varied and complex than Horton had thought.

With rare exceptions (for example John Janzen's work on the history of Lemba [1982]) the accounts of plural healing traditions describe conceptions and practices as they exist in the twentieth century, for the most part after 1960. It is not yet completely clear whether therapeutic pluralism was common in precolonial days, or whether it was a consequence of either colonial intervention or increases in literacy.

In the present study of Shambaai, we are fortunate in having at our disposal numerous descriptions of cases of the treatment of illness and of therapeutic practices in the period before 1914 (with the earliest descriptions from the 1840s).[8] These show clearly that plural approaches to illness coexisted in the precolonial period. People in nineteenth-century Shambaai did not simply follow the automatic prescriptions of tradition; they used varied approaches and assessed the consequences of therapy on a practical basis. The situation can only be described briefly here. For the most part it falls outside the scope of the present book.

What is relevant here is the fact that in the sphere of personal healing, even more thoroughly than in the sphere of public medicines for rain, multiple approaches coexisted. Rain medicines needed to be concentrated in the fewest hands to be effective. New or exotic rain medicines were threats to chiefly rule, and their owners were liable to be persecuted. New medicines for the illnesses of ordinary people were much more common.

Patterns in the training of healers tended to open up healing to borrowing and innovation, for they combined extended training in Shambaai with long periods of travel and learning throughout the surrounding region. Healers in training were either the sons of practitioners, or younger men (in some few cases women) who apprenticed themselves to recognized healers for extended periods, often by taking a blood oath which established basic terms and conditions for the relationship between master and apprentice.[9]

Healers and their apprentices tended to specialize. Specialties were of several different kinds. Some had to do with particular types of presentation of illness, for example, broken bones which might be set, illnesses in a syndrome much like that caused by hookworm, or maternal difficulties in lactation. Others focused on types of causation: particular forms of sorcery, or individual *mizuka* (named illness-causing spirits sometimes found in nature and sometimes in the social world). Still other specialties dealt with the consequences of particular oaths. There were specialists, for example, who dealt with cases in which women took suicidal oaths over broken cooking pots. Other specialists performed rituals to honor dead ancestors. Most healers mastered their own specialties as well as a wide range of the most commonly used therapies.[10]

Apprenticeships continued for years. For ambitious young men, years of learning under the direct supervision of the healer alternated with years of travel beyond the borders of Shambaai. During the periods of travel, the apprentice practiced newly learned techniques and collected livestock with which to pay the teacher.

The periods of travel sometimes took the form of journeys of discovery on which healers learned new medicines, thus opening the therapies of Shambaai to many new influences from the outside. During the late nineteenth century, people spoke of the danger of illnesses which came from abroad, outside the mountains. Since these illnesses were foreign, they could not be treated with medicines known in Shambaai. Traveling healers brought home methods for treating them. It was partly in this way that whole new sets of *mpepo*, spirits with which local people became possessed, entered Shambaai in the last quarter of the nineteenth century. Traveling healers undoubtedly also brought new therapies for illnesses that were not new.[11]

Mzulei was a healer who began one day (at around the turn of the century) to shake and to sing. He traveled from one place to another in search of knowledge of cures: to Bondei, east of Shambaai, where he learned about Christianity from the Anglicans there, to Mombasa, and as far west as Uganda. He returned from his journey of discovery, took up residence in a cave, and over a period of time began to treat people for *mpepo* illnesses (Hosbach 1911).

Healing journeys were also occasions when healers tested themselves against one another, when they came to know the competition abroad. A woman named Mahimbo studied oracular speech for two years with a teacher named Kidonga, probably just after the turn of the century, and then began to practice on her own. One day, during the visit of a healer from the Zigula plains to the south of Shambaai — a healer specializing in the same spirit — she found it impossible to speak. She took this as a sign of his ritual power. The two took a blood oath with one another to resolve their potential conflict. They would then have been free also to exchange healing knowledge (P. Wohlrab 1913).

The history of healing journeys presents a picture of precolonial society very different from the closed and intellectually restricted world described by Horton. In addition, records of illnesses show that it was relatively common for people in Shambaai to explain illnesses as having what we would call natural causes, and to treat them empirically with herbs.[12]

In research done eighty years later it became clear that the central debates on diagnosis and treatment today emerge among a patient's relatives. Diagnostic authority is not handed over to a community of healers or (except in the most limited way) to diviners. Today, patients' relatives tend to try herbal remedies first before resorting to treatments dealing with spirits, or sorcery, or the ancestors, and before seeking out a diviner. Central to the naming of illnesses today is a process by which therapy managers try out types of treatments as practical tests of efficacy, and as methods of diagnosis. If a sorcery treatment works, then this is evidence that sorcery is involved. If not, the next alternative treatment is tried. Both of today's patterns — that of starting with herbs before resorting to other treatments, and that of trying out the efficacy of alternative treatments — can be perceived in the missionary records of therapies during the early colonial period. The first pattern is confirmed also in the writings of an extremely knowledgeable observer of local therapies at that time, who wrote that "In spite of the high regard in which healers are held, the Shambaa does not fully trust the healer's art. The patient begins by trying out all the medicines known to him before he allows a healer to see him" (Karasek 1911:197). The second pattern can be observed in the case records cited above and in the practice of making a pledge to the ancestors. Therapy managers of the early colonial period would make a conditional promise to the ancestor, explaining that they intended to observe the patient's condition overnight. If the patient improved, then the ancestor could count on being given a sacrifice.[13]

Missionaries described local folks casting about in difficult cases, trying one therapy and then another, sometimes asking the missionaries to try their hands at healing.[14] Local people tried out Islamic healing in the same practical spirit.

Proverbs of the early colonial period convey something of the tone in which people discussed healing. At times it was skeptical, as in the proverb, *Hufyo hufyo ne ughanga*, "Deception, deception, that's medicine."[15] Much of the emphasis in proverbs was on medicine as a support to the body's own processes. *Ughanga ni mahambo ya ng'wii*, went a second proverb: "Medicine is decoration of the body." Another proverb held that medicine is a *lwega*, the wooden prop used to support a banana plant weighed down under a heavy bunch of ripening bananas. It would be comparable to saying today that medicine is a crutch. Another stated, *Mghanga taile ni mtamu kuhona*, "The healer is recognized with his honored greeting, *taile*, when the patient has healed." In other words we know whether someone is a successful healer by observing the patient's condition. *Taile*, which is difficult to render in English, is the subjunctive of the word *to know*. It means, roughly, "May you have knowledge" (but in fact recognizes that the healer does have knowledge). He then replies, *"Na Mulungu,"* With God," recognizing that his knowledge is connected to some overarching existence. When a missionary at Mtii in the 1890s told a very old man he met along a path that God makes the rain, the old man agreed fully. "The chief," he said, "has gotten from God the power to make rain."[16]

It is clear, then, that therapeutic practices formed an open set, one to which knowledge was added with great regularity. People in Shambaai exercised considerable skepticism about therapies and were willing to try out new cures and judge by the results. Under these circumstances, it is not at all surprising that in the public sphere many forms of rain medicine coexisted, and that the Kilindi did not control them all.

Precolonial Intellectuals: Alternative Understandings

The most skeptical peasant who engaged in profound critical reflection while farming the land was not an intellectual in the sense defined in the introduction to this work. The thoughtful peasant did not for the most part engage in socially recognized organizational, directive, educative, or expressive activities, nor was that peasant's work weighted towards intellectual elaboration rather than muscular-nervous effort.

The intellectuals in this sense were limited to a rather small stratum. Specialized healers met these criteria; home healers who farmed the land and then administered medicines in their spare time did not. Specialized officials at the royal court were also intellectuals in this sense. So were the *Mlughu* (the chief minister) and the six *Wafung'wa* (the king's representatives), who represented the king's wishes to the eastern or western halves of the kingdom, heard legal cases, and negotiated political arrangements with the lesser chiefs and with local descent groups. Each *Mdoe*, the administrator working for every separate chief, also counts as an intellectual.

One of the ways a group rising towards dominance establishes the legitimacy of its position is by conquering and assimilating preexisting intellectuals (Gramsci 1971:10). This is what the Kilindi did when they brought preexisting healers, those who made rain medicine and locust medicine, into their service. Over the years, successive kings made special places among the court officials for representatives of historically important descent groups. Assimilating intellectuals was central to the process by which Kilindi made themselves the crucial actors in the drama of healing the land. The process led to the merging of explanations of healing the land with the politics of the Kilindi lineage. The Kilindi themselves would only come to be intellectuals in the present sense in the 1920s, when they became agents of the British in organizing colonial rule.

Kings and chiefs were not intellectuals before conquest, even though they engaged in organizational and directive activity, and even though their work in many cases was weighted towards intellectual elaboration. They were not intellectuals because they were struggling to maintain their own dominance, not to serve as some other group's agents or to mediate among groups struggling for dominance. Gramsci makes a similar point about twentieth-century Italy: "The entrepreneur . . . must have to some degree a certain number of qualifications of an intellectual nature although his part in society is not determined by these, but by the general social relations which specifically characterise the position of the entrepreneur within industry" (1971:8).

Were the Kilindi truly a dominant group in Gramsci's sense? The question is difficult; perhaps unanswerable. The Kilindi certainly took wealth, food, and labor from within Shambaai. In the nineteenth century, however, they worked on the periphery of (and in some senses came to support the interests of) the coastal economy based on slave plantations. Their wars produced slaves who worked on the island plantations. The Kilindi were dominant within their own autonomous world, yet in some ways they served the interests of a system in which economic action extended beyond the borders of Shambaai.

One danger with the approach to intellectuals taken in this work is that it becomes difficult to avoid merging, in one's own mind, the common meaning of the word *intellectual* in the English language and the special usage adopted here. It is possible to argue on the basis of Gramsci's definition that precolonial intellectuals existed in Shambaai, and then to carry over the general conclusion — that a precolonial African society enjoyed the contribution of intellectuals, interpreted now in the more standard sense. In order to avoid this unthinking conflation of senses of the word *intellectual*, it is worth examining precolonial Shambaai in the light of a definition of intellectuals drawn from a different sociological tradition — an analytic usage of the word closer to its standard English usage.

Edward Shils, distinguished as a sociologist and as an interpreter and translator of Max Weber's work, is responsible for the major social science encyclopedia definition of intellectuals:

> Intellectuals are the aggregate of persons in any society who employ in their communication and expression, with relatively higher frequency than most other members of their society, symbols of general scope and abstract reference, concerning man, society, nature, and the cosmos. The high frequency of their use of such symbols may be a function of their own subjective propensity or of the obligations of an occupational role, the performance of which entails such use (Shils 1968:399).[17]

Gramsci would have objected to this definition. "The most widespread error of method," he wrote, "seems to me that of having looked for this criterion of distinction in the intrinsic nature of intellectual activities, rather than in the ensemble of the system of relations in which these activities (and therefore the intellectual groups who personify them) have their place within the general complex of social relations" (1971:8). In other words, Gramsci does not discount the characteristic activities of intellectuals (which Shils defines as using symbols of general scope and abstract reference). Gramsci's approach offers us the possibility of understanding the relationship between ideas and power by studying the ensemble of social relations within which intellectual activities find their place. If one centers the definition on sets of symbols, as Shils does, it becomes more difficult to explore the intertwined character of power/knowledge. The symbols of general scope and abstract reference cannot be shown to serve one side or the other in a struggle to shape the future of a particular society. A set of symbols can be invoked by both opposing sides in a struggle, and they can be subtly reconfigured to support one position or another. The principles of order in a configuration of symbols may have more to do with the logic of the symbols than with any issues of power. Intellectuals, however, must ultimately take positions within the unfolding struggle. By studying their positions, we begin to understand the place of their discourse within a configuration of power. On the other hand, the interesting advantage of Shils's approach, as we shall see, is that it places central emphasis on the emergence of bureaucratic forms of action. These are important in our history.

Shils's emphasis on symbols "of general scope and abstract reference" shows a preoccupation, at its core, with rationalization — a key concept in Max Weber's work. For Weber, rationality had a complex network of meanings. Weber wrote about the rationalization of sets of ideas, by which he meant their coordination into a coherent and consistent system. For this reason a legal system based on a few abstract principles is more rational than one with many concrete rules. In a related meaning, a set of actions is rational if it is predictable, following regular procedures; it is irrational if unpredictable and arbitrary. The replacement of unpredictable religious ecstasy with methodically planned rituals for achieving the same ends was a "systematization and rationalization of the methods for attaining religious sanctification" (Weber 1978:538).[18] Rationality also means choice of the most appropriate means for achieving particular ends, as when a factory produces something at the lowest possible cost, given the cost of labor, capital, land, and so forth.

In Weber's view, Europe in the fifty years before World War I was moving rapidly towards rationalization. Bureaucracies were rationalized. They had officials whose recruitment was based on education and whose spheres of competence were carefully delimited (not arbitrary and personal). Bureaucracies coordinated complex activities oriented towards clearly identified ends. At the same time, intellectuals of a new type were emerging: government servants with knowledge in one or another specialized technical field. Theirs was systematized knowledge, mastered by experts in the service of government. The emergence of experts and the decline of governmental generalists was, in Weber's view, the outcome of a long process of rationalization.

Shils is preoccupied with this process. He describes the time of industrialization and bureaucratization as a crucial one in the history of intellectuals, one when a much larger stratum of intellectuals appeared than ever before, holding great influence within society.

Despite his focus on the consequences of European modernization, Shils does not exclude intellectuals from non-Western societies, nor even from nonliterate ones. "Every society has intellectuals" he writes (Shils 1968: 401). In his view, the less differentiated a society, the thinner its stratum of intellectuals, but they can always be found.

In late nineteenth-century Shambaai there were many candidates for identification as intellectuals in Shils's terms. The king's chief minister and the six king's representatives learned a substantial body of the kingdom's history. They needed to know the history of agreements between previous kings and local groups, the history of conflicts among Kilindi factions, and the history of royal oaths. If the king violated an oath because their historical knowledge was faulty, he would die. They discussed politics in terms of the general principles outlined in the previous chapter, and tended to argue both policy and court cases with reference to hundreds (perhaps thousands) of proverbs and maxims stating general cultural principles. The style of disputation in court cases called for the services of a *kiuzio:* half keeper of proverbs, half court jester. Each proverb was spoken in two parts: the person arguing a case stated the first half, and the *kiuzio* supplied the *bontokeo*, the "conclusion."

Among peasants, principles of the greatest generality could be stated at any time, but came to the fore in a systematic way during rites of passage (*mivigha*) and sacrificial rites (*fika*). Unlike specialized healing rites, *mivigha* and *fika* were a part of the life of everyone who lived in Shambaai. In the context of these rites, officiants stated general principles on the nature of death, the conditions of human reproduction, the essential character of masculinity and femininity, and the sources of fertile farming. Among the intellectuals as defined by Shils, therefore, it would be appropriate to include healers who specialized in officiating at sacrifices or rites of passage.

In addition to healers and officials, there were the leading elders of descent groups, who were expected to perform rituals and to decide on disputes in village-level hearings. And there were the poets, song-composers, and storytellers of Shambaai. Their individual names have disappeared, but we know that they existed because their songs and stories have come down to us.

One of the ironies of the Weberian categories is that healers whose techniques would seem the most scientifically acceptable, the most rational, to a school-educated reader are the least likely to be termed *intellectuals* under this definition. Their practices are not rationalized in Weber's sense. People who administered herbs tended to treat each herb as separate and concrete in its curative properties, not in terms of general abstract principles of human life and the cosmos.

Shils's extended writings on intellectuals focus on processes of modernization and the formation of nation-states. He has not written at length about nonliterate societies. In the anthropological literature the question of whether nonliterate intellectuals exist is addressed by Jack Goody (1977; 1986; 1987) in his discussions of literacy. A somewhat different set of debates has arisen, brilliantly pursued by Mudimbe (1985), Hountoundji (1977), and others, on whether it was possible for an African philosophy to exist.[19]

Goody, in a chapter entitled "Intellectuals in pre-literate societies?" argues that intellectuals exist in nonliterate societies but tend to disappear from the scholar's view. When authorship is oral it becomes anonymous. As Goody puts it, "The signature is always getting rubbed out in the process of generative transmission" (1977:27). People remember the song or the saying, but it becomes part of a collective folk tradition, anonymous, as though independent of particular intellectuals as songwriters or formulators of sayings.

Goody accepts that individual authorship existed, even if knowledge of it is lost, but he sees nonliterate authorship as being very different from the literate variety, less capable of creating rationalized knowledge. He argues that it is difficult to achieve consistency among ideas, to eliminate contradictions, without literacy (1977:19–51; 1987:69). Writing makes it possible to compare ideas with one another systematically — to account for all the usages of a word in a given text. Nonliterate people, he argues, find it difficult to arrive at a consistent, noncontradictory body of ideas.

In Goody's view the difference between the literate and nonliterate transmission of knowledge is fundamentally important. Literacy is an actual mechanism by which one can explain the differences which Horton explored under the rubrics "traditional thought" and "Western science," and which he characterized as the closed and the open predicaments. According to Horton (1967), the scientist is always aware of possible alternatives to received theory; the system is always open to the possibility of change. In traditional thought, by contrast, the system of explanation is closed to alternatives. A Horton-style argument on the basis of the present ethnographic case would claim that there was no way to disprove peasant arguments that famine was a consequence of the king's weakness. When the king was weak, people explained drought as a consequence of competition, of *nguvu kwa nguvu*, power against power. When the king was strong, drought could also be explained. People said that drought came as mourning for a royal death, or that the king wished to remind his subjects of their obligation to pay tribute. The organization of action systematically screened out alternative explanations.

We know by now, however, that alternative techniques did exist in precolonial Shambaai. Goody would not deny this. In fact he describes alternatives in precolonial Gonja (the site of his own research). Skeptics existed, he argues, but cumulative skepticism did not exist:

> What seems to be the *essential* difference, however, is not so much the sceptical attitude in itself but the accumulation (or reproduction) of scepticism. Members of oral . . . societies find it difficult to develop a line of sceptical thinking about, say, the nature of matter or man's relationship to God simply because a continuing critical tradition can hardly exist when sceptical thoughts are *not* written down, *not* communicated across time and space, *not* made available for men to contemplate in privacy as well as to hear in performance (1977:43; see also 1987:156).

There is no reason to quarrel with Goody's central points: that literacy affects the way people reason in society and that there are real differences in socially accumulated knowledge between precolonial and industrial societies. Nevertheless, Goody understates the degree to which alternative ideas found a systematic and cumulative basis in precolonial African societies. Alternatives found a basis in healing institutions. Many kinds of healers lived and worked within the same small area; this meant that ordinary people were able to compare the efficacy of the varieties of healing. Healers traveled widely in the course of their training; this led systematically to an awareness of varieties of healing as an open set of alternatives. Nonroyal fertility specialists competed with the chiefs; this made it possible for peasants to compare alternative techniques for healing the land. The form of society preserved the openness of intellectual alternatives, even while the absence of writing changed the way in which people compared those alternatives.

The academic oral historian's technique depends upon the existence of alternatives to orthodox views of history and of social health. Reconstructing the history of struggle in the early kingdom becomes possible only because some groups within society disagree with the accepted view. In Shambaai, for example, the myth of Mbegha, the most fundamental narrative exposition of the eternal character of relations between rulers and ruled, stated that the heroic first king never used violence against the people of Shambaai, who freely invited him to be their king. We have seen that descendants of the Hea group preserve systematic knowledge of the first king's violent conquest, thus providing an alternative to official history.

Because the precolonial authorities treated alternative knowledge as dangerous, we know that it was powerful, not merely of private concern, not merely an ethnological curiosity. We have already learned of narratives describing the healer who comes to the chief's court carrying new rain medicines. After he gives up the medicines, the chief orders his execution, so that his knowledge will travel no further.

A second set of narratives, the story of the Nango group's early struggles with Mbegha's son, is rarely told at Vugha. A friend there admitted to me that his father once told parts of the larger story, but then insisted on his son's silence. "Leave that alone," the father said. "That can lead to the annihilation of our descent group."[20]

In the case of royal accession and burial, knowledge of the rite was transmitted by a number of separate descent groups. Each descent group along the new king's path or involved in the old king's burial controlled only one piece of information within the larger body of ritual knowledge. To assemble a rationalized picture of the rite it was necessary to consult elders of all the groups involved, each preserving knowledge separately. This I did, but then my picture of the whole rite, based on coordinated knowledge (Feierman 1972: chap. 5), was different from anything which existed in precolonial Shambaai. For knowledge to have been authentic, it would have had to be partial.

The fact that bodies of alternative knowledge were often blocked off, isolated, or suppressed demonstrates awareness of its dangerousness. But the suppression of alternative knowledge was only partial. This is shown by the existence of many kinds of traveling healers in the nineteenth century and the survival of descent-group traditions on into the 1960s. Heterodox knowledge had its social bases; it therefore had contexts within which to accumulate.

To argue that alternative knowledge accumulated, that the world of knowledge was not closed, is not to say that there is no difference between the character of precolonial science in Shambaai and the science of university physics departments. The entire social organization of knowledge is different. Knowledge is shared among physicists on a worldwide basis, with scholars everywhere basing their work on identical documents, techniques, and definitions. The institutional framework of science is not, however, an automatic consequence of literacy. The ancient transition from nonliterate to literate forms of knowledge was a gradual process, intertwined with institutional change. Goody recognizes this in his more recent work (1986; 1987); he stresses the gradual character of the changes wrought by early literacy. But the reconsideration of early literacy has not been matched by a historically based reconsideration of nonliterate knowledge, of the possibility that alternative bodies of knowledge can be transmitted by competing groups of nonliterate intellectuals, and not only by competing written texts.

Paths to Social Health During the Prelude to Conquest

The social context of political discourse changed rapidly during the thirty years before the German war of conquest of 1888. During these years the form of dynastic history unfolded as before: the ordered hierarchy which had characterised Kimweri ye Nyumbai's reign was succeeded after his death in 1862 by a period of intense competition among Kimweri's sons and grandsons. This period of disorder was the recurrence of an earlier pattern, the unfolding of that part of the dynastic cycle in which a land healed was inevitably succeeded by a land harmed. Even though the form of dynastic competition remained the same, its content changed. The character of relations between peasants and chiefs entered an altogether new era, as did the process by which chiefs built their forces to win the dynastic competition.

As seen from within the households and descent groups of Shambaai, chiefship had a double face: it was both a refuge and a source of danger. A father who had no food for his children, a woman fleeing her abusive husband, and a criminal who could not pay the required indemnity all found sustenance and protection at the court of their chief. The price was to place oneself or one's child into the chief's hands as his personal dependent for a period, until the debt could be made good or the indemnity repaid. The chief's court was, however, a dangerous place. A dependent who angered the chief could be punished arbitrarily. At the worst of times, the chief brought down famine onto the shoulders of his subjects, thus forcing them to win their survival by bringing him dependents. Vugha, the royal capital, was known as a refuge and a place of false witness, a place where poor unfortunates found sustenance, and the abode of all Shambaai's witches. This dual character had long existed. Under the best of conditions, when the chief had healed the land, people had enough food and were able to settle their cases without losing children. When the chief had harmed the land, famine and litigation drove men to pawn their children. Women were carried off for ransom in war.

During the 1860s, 1870s, and 1880s the overall balance of the system of refuge and dependency shifted. Wars followed one another unceasingly. Chiefs who needed to sell slaves to buy guns and powder enslaved their subjects for ever more trivial offenses. They began to break the rules of dependency that made it improper for the chief to sell pawned dependents. By the late 1870s a woman in the east was sold for stealing two vegetables. In this new era chiefs turned against their subjects. In one war of this period the chiefs of Bumbuli and Shembekeza returned from fighting against the separate power in the east without having taken sufficient slaves and cattle. They turned against a small part of their own territory, rich in cattle and women, and simply took their own subjects for sale. According to a man from Mazinde, in those days "If you had a lot of goats and a village full of children, off you all went" (Feierman 1974:177–78).

The greater the extent to which the world of peasants and the world of slaves appeared to be separate, as in the earlier years of the century, the more fully acceptable peasants found the political world in which they lived. The slave might originate amongst the peasantry, a person forced to take refuge with the chief as a result of bad luck or bad judgment. Even when the group lost a member, those remaining at home continued to sustain themselves and to reproduce. The person who was gone altogether, to the coast, had moved beyond the borders of the peasantry's moral universe. Now however, during the period of increased insecurity, slaves were leaving so quickly that it was difficult in some groups to maintain the moral separation between slave and citizen, and difficult therefore to continue treating the chief's court as a place of refuge. In some parts of the kingdom this led peasants to question the central premise: that the chief's court was a place of refuge, security, and sustenance.

The struggles that determined the kingdom's fate in this period have been described at length in *The Shambaa Kingdom* (Feierman 1974) and are mentioned here only to the extent necessary to illuminate the relationship between changes in leadership and interpretations of healing the land.

The decades leading up to German conquest were a time when the coastal caravan trade in slaves and ivory became increasingly important in the region's life. Within the kingdom the contest for power, the age-old dynastic game, now hung on a struggle for preeminence in trade relations. The chiefs who assembled the most effective fighting forces in this period were the ones who could purchase the largest supplies of guns and powder and could call upon the armed assistance of trading partners from outside Shambaai — Swahili, or Maasai, or Zigula.

No longer did the leading chiefs hold as their main qualifications owner-ship of rain medicines or the practical capacity to sustain impoverished peasants. By the 1870s the holder of Vugha was a Kilindi who was not heir to any of the major rain medicines. He was Semboja's son Kimweri Maguvu. Semboja, we have seen, was Kimweri ye Nyumbai's son, of a minor house which received none of the old king's important rain charms. These went to a few senior sons. The most powerful charm included a part of the dead ye Nyumbai's body. This went to Shekulwavu, who was driven out of Vugha by Semboja, and whose heirs established a separate power — a separate splinter kingdom — in the east.[21]

The fundamental shift in the roots of political power from the capacity to feed peasants to the capacity to trade gave increasing influence to a set of intellectuals who had previously been only marginally important in the affairs of Shambaai: literate Muslims, most of them from the coast, outside the borders of the kingdom.

Islam was a basic qualification for full citizenship in coastal society in this period. In coastal documents non-Muslims of the hinterland are described as *washenzi*, "barbarians," as opposed to freeborn *waungwana*. An escaped slave or an up-country trader who lived at the coast and wished to be treated as an equal converted to Islam. According to Jonathon Glass-man (1988), who explores the role of Islam in Swahili caravan organiza-tion, the auspiciousness of a departure date was decided by a teacher of Islam. Fasts and holidays of the Islamic year were observed along the way. A religious teacher, he reports, would not be accepted at the coast until he had traveled with a caravan to the distant interior. We can see that the spiritual leaders of Islam made journeys part of their training in much the same way as the healers of Shambaai.[22]

Muslims were not new to Shambaai in the 1880s. Back in the reign of Kimweri ye Nyumbai, a Muslim healer lived at the royal court.[23] In the decades after his death the major chiefs engaged the services of lit-erate coastal Muslims, who wrote letters to the Sultan of Zanzibar and to the leaders of coastal towns and also negotiated on behalf of their Kilindi patrons with authorities on the coast. The most famous of these Muslim scribes and diplomats was Abdallah bin Hemedi 'lAjjemy, whose Swahili history of the kingdom is a major source for the period's events. By the 1880s Kilindi chiefs had skills mastered only by visiting scribes in earlier periods. Kimweri Maguvu, king at Vugha, was literate in Swahili in Ara-bic characters. Twenty years earlier, Shekulwavu, his predecessor as king at Vugha, had been unable to speak Swahili.[24]

Conversion to Islam among the Kilindi began by the 1840s in Bondei but had still not come to the heartland of Shambaai at the time of conquest. Abdallah bin Hemedi 'lAjjemy described an early Muslim Kilindi of Bondei, Mwelekwanyuma Mwenye Hatibu: "He was a devout Muslim, who fasted and prayed, and paid his dues and gave alms and built mosques in every one of his places" (1963:Sura 72). In Shambaai, by contrast, the oral traditions maintain that no one said prayers or fasted for Ramadhan until after German conquest. Semboja and Kimweri Maguvu may have called themselves Muslims at times, but they continued to eat pork and to sacrifice to the ancestors (Feierman 1974:200).

There is no evidence that the growing importance of Islam was an issue of great significance to the peasants of Shambaai. Much more important to them was the emergence of a form of politics in which the security and the sustenance of the peasantry counted much less than previously. Semboja's rule was revolutionary, a radical departure from the social contract under which Shambaa peasants offered the chief their support in return for rain and for food. Unlike Kimweri ye Nyumbai, whose armed strength was in the massed armies of Shambaa countrymen called from their homes by war drums, Semboja depended on Kimweri's ancient enemies, the Zigula, to provide the fighting men for Mazinde, his capital. Shambaa citizen-soldiers were constrained from preying on the peasantry by loyalty to their own villages and descent groups. Zigula fighters did not hesitate to take slaves in Shambaai. The slaves could then be sold for guns and powder and for trade goods with which to reward the mercenary soldiers.

In the inherited language of Shambaa statecraft, the wars of Semboja's time were the expected consequence of a land harmed. After Kimweri ye Nyumbai's death, the Kilindi descent cycle led inevitably to warfare and to the division of the kingdom — the foundation of a separate power. According to the conventional wisdom and the record of past disputes, in another generation power in Shambaai would be so fragmented that a new king would be able to overcome the divided opposition and place his sons in all the chiefdoms, thus restoring the land to hierarchical order, so that it would be healed.

The peasants did not hold a single uniform interpretation of what was happening; conflicting interpretations coexisted. The hegemonic interpretation of the period's history, one repeated in many traditions, is given in the following quotation from a former court official:

> The Arabs traded with Semboja. Their merchandise was people. That is why the Arabs found a way of entering the affairs of the Shambaa. The Arabs were not involved in our affairs in the days of Kimweri ye Nyumbai. Their merchandise was people. In the days of Kimweri ye Nyumbai there were no enemies.[25]

In other words, the slave traders came to Shambaai *because* the Kilindi were at a competitive moment of their cycle. The particular form of the trade in slaves was an accident, a contingent event, but the long-term structure, in this interpretation, was that of Kilindi descent.

Academic historians describe a fundamental change in the organization of the region's economy in the nineteenth century. Sugar, grain, and clove plantations grew up, creating a substantial local demand for slaves (Sheriff 1987). The web of exploitation in which Shambaa peasants were caught had a broad regional component alongside the local relations between chiefs and peasants. The folk model of harming and healing the land adequately portrayed only the local half of the pattern. It treated plantations and the international market as elements beyond the system. If for Europe or even for India the interior of East Africa was beyond the economic periphery, for the folk theorists of the Shambaa kingdom, the coastal and island plantations were beyond the periphery of their world, not forces to be taken into account.

The sense of trade as external found expression within the *kifu* group, which saw departed slaves as having moved beyond the periphery. It found expression also in the spatial organization of Vugha. The capital was a representation of the whole kingdom; its section represented parts of the kingdom. Outsiders slept at *Mamuungwana*, literally "the place of the freeborn coastal people," outside the capital limits. The houses of *Mamuungwana* were square, like their prototypes at the coast, whereas all the rest of Vugha's houses were round, built in the local beehive style. Here too the coastal traders were external.

Even though Semboja was the quintessential new trading chief, he did not ignore Vugha or the politics of rain. He tried to take Vugha for himself and was forestalled only by a united strategy among the Kilindi to install his son Kimweri Maguvu. Even then Semboja was concerned with the politics of rain. He arranged for Kimweri to make the blood pact with the son of Mshuza, heir to the major rain medicines at Ubiri. At the necessary times, Kimweri sent cows from Vugha to Ubiri with a request for rain, which was always honored with the appropriate rites.[26]

The interpretation of Semboja's actions as the consequence of a land harmed was not the only one at the time. The second interpretation, given less frequently in the traditions, is that Semboja was a completely deviant kind of political leader. "The one who broke the ritual prohibitions (*miiko*) of the Kilindi is Semboja, when he sold people and made war."[27] Local people, in discussions with Semboja, were reported to have said, "Once you have finished killing all the people of the country, who exactly will you rule over?"[28] This is a way of saying that Semboja's actions make no sense when judged according to the ancient social contract, which assumes a community of interest between rainmaking chiefs and tribute-paying subjects.

There was an element of nostalgia in this position, as there often is in peasant politics at times of rapid economic change. One of the central trends in peasant resistance during the transition to capitalism, a trend often noted by scholars of peasant resistance around the world, is a refusal to accept the destruction of ancient aristocratic guarantees of the peasantry's right to subsistence.[29] The Shambaa peasant argument that Semboja was not behaving like a proper Kilindi chief, not healing the land, was just such a position.

Many individuals and small fraternal groups resisted the new slavery. We know of their actions even though we have little record of their words at the time. A woman named Maukindo resisted when being taken along a lonely path in Mshihwi by the men who had captured her. She attacked them, threw some of her captors off a precipice, and fled successfully to the safety of her family. A *kifu* group at Vugha made a daring counter-raid to reclaim their women from kidnappers based at the trading town of Makuyuni in the plains. The son of their leader, in his oral account, insisted that the Vugha of his father's time, the time of kidnappers, was not a fit place for any ordinary person to live.[30]

Within Shambaai a revolutionary return to rule by local descent groups did not prove possible. Nevertheless, individual groups struggled to carve out autonomous spheres. Some powerful men became slave traders on their own, subject only to paying the chief to ignore their activities. In other cases a fraternal group fortunate in the number and skill of its fighting men took over a strategic outpost on condition that they be exempt from tribute. They were able also to escape attack by slave raiders. By doing this they created a small sphere of descent autonomy, although one very different from the descent rule destroyed by the Kilindi a century earlier.[31] The people of Bondei, who occupied a substantial part of the kingdom's territory, overthrew Kilindi rule in their rebellion some time after 1868, called *Kiva*, which means "rebellion," or "resistance," although Farler (a missionary who lived in Bondei at the time) translated *Wakiva*, the people of *Kiva*, as "republicans" (LangHeinrich 1921:168; Farler 1879:85).

The rebels ultimately came to reject the fundamental premise of the discourse on fertility, even though they did not reject the notion that Kilindi chiefs owned effective rain medicines. The premise they rejected was that competition for rain medicines was the most important factor shaping the well-being of the peasantry. They acknowledged that the Kilindi owned powerful rain charms. After the rebellion succeeded, they continued to bring gifts to Kilindi on some occasions with requests to make rain, but they never agreed to come back into the Kilindi state.

They insisted on independent rule by the elders because there was a much more important issue than control over rain charms. The central issue for the Bondei was the breakdown of the separation between peasants and slaves. By the 1860s it was difficult for Bondei to imagine the chief's court as a place of refuge where fathers took their hungry children to stay for a while and then return home. The rebels argued that the chiefs' people were ignoring the rights of peasants, treating them as though they were slaves. Here is a list of Bondei grievances at the time of the revolt:

> The capture of our children and their being given in marriage by force without our receiving dues or cattle.
> Their slaves and guards robbing people whom they meet in the road.
> If a man is accused of witchcraft no evidence is called but he is killed and his children are taken and sold.
> If they want food they send men into our towns to take goats and chickens and if the owner says a word he is beaten.
> If one of their wives has parents they do not allow her to visit her father or mother (Abdallah bin Hemedi 'lAjjemy 1962: Sura 169).

The Bondei refused to allow their revolt to serve the politics of healing the land, even though this is what one Kilindi faction tried to convince them to do. Shekulwavu's brother Chanyeghea called for the rebels to destroy Semboja's power so that the kingdom could once again be unified under the main heir to the hereditary rain medicines, but the Bondei rejected the appeal to the principles of healing the land. One of their elders sent the following message to Chanyeghea:

> The Kilindi are born liars. Do not rely on the word of any of them, it will not be true. . . . Now we agree to do as [Chanyeghea] asks; but when he is in power and has the dominion he will turn on us and say Pay me your dead. You have killed my uncles, you have taken their property, you have sold my brothers, you have given my uncles' wives in marriage, now hand over the adulterers. . . . Now we have driven out the Kilindi, we have taken their property and given their wives to others. We have become their enemies and even if we accept this matter we will never make with them any agreement whatever. That is our decision (Abdallah bin Hemedi 'lAjjemy 1962: Sura 156).

After the uprising the Bondei returned to rule by elders.

At the heart of the struggle were the intellectuals: the political and ritual advisors who worked at the courts of chiefs. Below them were the armed men who enforced the chiefly will. We know very little about the recruitment of advisors in Bondei. In Shambaai the most exploitive of the chiefs recruited advisors and soldiers from among outsiders, in many cases Zigula from the plains to the south of the mountains. Zigula could be counted on to be loyal to the chief and not the people, with whom they had no special ties. In Bondei, in many cases, it appears that Bondei people themselves served as court advisors and as soldiers, enslaving their own people. This would have put them in an impossible position with their own relatives, who were the victims. Perhaps for this reason the chiefs' Bondei supporters appear not to have stood by them when the rebellion came. Chiefs were left exposed, without supporters; some were killed, and others fled. Tumba, the Kilindi chief who most easily survived *Kiva*, was served by a corps of Zigula soldiers.[32]

The history of *Kiva* demonstrates that the kingdom's peasants were capable of rejecting the central premise of Kilindi politics: that struggles among royal rainmakers are the events which determine peasant well-being. The rebellion did not merely attempt to replace one set of rainmakers with another. It was based on the premise that issues of rain were not as important as issues of slavery and of the arbitrary exercise of chiefly power. The Bondei peasants threw out the Kilindi and returned to government by descent-group elders.

Seventy years later, when peasants rebelled against Kilindi rule (this time as part of a colonial order), they called for Shambaai once again to be governed through a federation of peasant descent groups. This was a language of rebellion with ancient roots.

5

Colonial Rule and the
Fate of the Intellectuals

When the Germans conquered Shambaai in the 1890s, they seized control over the destiny of kings and chiefs and took for themselves the governmental power to decide who should live and who should die.[1] But the Germans were not powerful enough, or not willing enough to spend massive resources, to govern the area through an entirely alien administrative staff — to place a European administrator in every ward or chiefdom. They relied on Africans to serve as the crucial linking agents between the European over-rulers and the mass of the African population. This was not a peculiarly German strategy. All of Africa's colonial rulers, including the British who took Tanganyika after World War I, employed local African administrators. What varied from place to place and from one regime to another was the choice of African agents: clerks, or traders, or chiefs.

The colonial regime's choice of African agents — of the intellectuals who served them — would profoundly influence the changing character of African life. The Europeans lacked the knowledge of African society to control day-to-day affairs on a practical basis. They did not understand African culture from within, and therefore could not reason with local Africans to convince them of the wisdom, or even the acceptability, of particular policies. They chose African agents who used their own words to support the colonial policies they administered. When the Europeans chose a set of agents, they were also choosing a form of African discourse; if they chose chiefs, then their policies would be justified in chiefly language. By choosing the agents, the colonialists shaped the language of African politics in powerful ways. Yet their own impact was one they did not fully understand (because of their ignorance of African culture), and therefore one they did not control in its particular form.

In some cases the colonial rulers coopted preexisting leaders from within African society, as when they used chiefs or coastal Muslim traders as agents of colonial rule. In other cases they trained Africans to learn the traditions of European intellectuals, of Christian teachers or evangelists, for example. In any event the African agents of European rule brought

Map 2. Tanzania, December 1960

with them historically conditioned patterns of behavior, understandings of social reality, and definitions of the good society. When their tradition was an alien one, it entered the fabric of African society by this process, and shaped the terms of local political discourse; when their tradition was African in origin, discourse was reshaped from within, for now its context and significance were altered.

In colonial-period Shambaai for all the years up to 1947, African politics and political ideas revolved around European choices among three sets of local agents: members of a Muslim commercial and religious stratum, literate men who were mission-educated, and Kilindi chiefs. German governmental authorities destroyed chiefship and came to rely instead on members of the Muslim commercial stratum. German missionaries struggled unsuccessfully to replace Muslims with Christian clerks in government service. When the British took over they turned the German pattern upside-down. They restored a chiefship which appeared by then to have breathed its death-gasps. And they made tentative beginnings towards a Tanganyikan future dominated by Christian functionaries and teachers.

The colonial choice of African agents had important consequences for economic practice, for the appropriate shape of African political discourse, and even for the choice of language (Swahili or Shambaa) to be spoken in daily administration. The German choice of Muslim agents brought about a close association between administration and commerce, for Islam had long been associated with trade and with patterns of interaction which tied people together across the lines of local language. In the German period, Shambaa who moved to trading towns in the plains below Shambaai, or who became involved in commerce, felt it appropriate in many cases to learn the practice of Islam. In this period the language of Muslim traders, government clerks, *akidas* (African agents of German administration), and Shambaa travelers was Swahili. The German choice of Muslims as agents was in harmony with colonial policies calling for rapid economic change in the northeast of the country.

The British decision to remove the *akidas* and replace them with Kilindi chiefs, with some influence in the hands of Christian clerks/teachers, harmonized with a larger decision to slow the process of economic and ideological integration across political or linguistic boundaries. The core conceptions about healing the land and harming the land carried strong localizing implications. Peasants who looked to their chief for rain understood that their prosperity or poverty took shape within the boundaries of a single chiefdom. A merchant who moved back and forth between mountains and plains, interior and coast, could not have held so localized a view of the sources of prosperity. When the British removed members of the merchant stratum from office and replaced them with chiefs, they shifted the focus of political debate towards a local one. It will be shown that they tried also to limit and localize patterns of African trade.

The Christian evangelists, clerks, and teachers also had an intensely local focus in many ways, even though they took part in a universal religion. Most Christians were members of a Lutheran church whose early missionaries worked to create Shambaa forms of Christianity. The missionaries were especially concerned to find rich sources of expression in the Shambaa language for Christianity's core conceptions. They aimed at creating vibrant prayers and sermons in the Shambaa language. Seen from within Shambaai, the British expectation that literate Christians would grow in influence complemented the choice of chiefs as agents. It helped to consolidate the language of ethnicity and to focus political concerns at the local level.

Gramsci defined intellectuals as "the dominant group's 'deputies'" (1971:12). In this sense chiefs who served Europeans in the colonial period were intellectuals; chiefs defending their own interests a century earlier were not. To say this is not to claim that chiefs of the 1920s used their intellects to a greater extent than did chiefs of the 1820s. Rather, the point is to explore the implications of a separation between those whose interests were ultimately at stake, and those who performed organizational, educative, or directive tasks. To understand the political forces at work and also the terms of popular political discussion — to understand consent and resistance — it is not enough to know who was dominant in each period: chiefs in the 1820s and British plantation owners, trading companies, and government in the 1920s. In each case the terms of the debate were shaped in profound ways by those who were not dominant but who occupied mediating or interstitial positions within the structure of power and who used knowledge for socially recognized ends.

What is more, intellectuals who were members of a group or category with a history, intellectuals whose characteristic practice and discourse were inherited from the past, followed a course shaped by past practice. They were not molded as though from raw clay by the dominant group.

Among the intellectuals who served the colonialists as agents, each set enjoyed some degree of autonomy. Chiefs derived a certain degree of autonomy from their mastery of rain medicines. This was one of the central paradoxes of the British period, for the British used chiefs in order to borrow their legitimacy: the overlords assumed that peasants' respect for the chief's rain, combined with ancient habits of deference, would lead to smooth acceptance of colonial orders. Yet in practice the chiefs with the greatest reputation for rain were the most free to resist colonial orders. They knew that they held the loyalty of their subjects, even without colonial support. Some school-educated men also enjoyed a degree of autonomy. Not all educated African Christians held government jobs. Those who retired from wage employment or who preferred to stay home and farm enjoyed a greater degree of autonomy than the clerks. They criticized the orders their employed fellow-clerks were bound to support. Muslim clerics and traders, too, enjoyed some autonomy, limited only by their need for government permission to trade.

Each set of intellectuals shaped discourse in the interests of their colonial masters. But each set also exercised its autonomy to turn that discourse against the rulers. In the 1940s and 1950s chiefs with the greatest popular support, because of their reputation for rain, were also the most successful at resisting colonial economic plans, which were then described as harming the land. The peasantry, told by the British that "traditional" rule was important, fondly recalled alternative traditions of rule by lineage elders. The mission-educated peasants/clerks argued in favor of literacy and Christianity, but also pointed towards the deep contradictions between democratic values and colonial domination, and even, in some cases, approvingly recalled the precedent of English regicide. The colonial rulers determined who in African society introduced the terms of political debate, but they could never determine where that debate would end.

The German Destruction of Chiefship

At first, German policy towards chiefs near the settler farms and plantations in the northeast of the territory was contradictory. The highest priority, of course, was to eliminate any possibility of effective rebellion. Beyond this, however, the government attempted to preserve chiefs as agents, because of the popular loyalty they inspired; yet government officials gave precedence at the same time to the interests of settlers and planters. The chiefs were made to confiscate land and to recruit forced labor, earning the contempt of their subjects and destroying the loyalty which made them useful.

The German presence was established at the coast during the 1880s; the Kilindi leaders knew by December 1889 that German power could not be resisted. That was the month Bushiri bin Salim, leader of the great coastal war against the Germans, was executed. Semboja and the other chiefs knew that they could never assemble as large a fighting force as the one which had just been defeated. In 1890 Semboja agreed to serve as a German agent, as did Kibanga further east. But German acceptance of powerful, potentially autonomous agents was only a temporary phase, for with continued chiefly autonomy came a continued capacity to resist.

The first Germans at the royal capital of Vugha were missionaries, not the army or other government agents. The Evangelical Lutherans who settled at Vugha had already been welcomed by the chief of Mlalo, one of whose goals was to resist the domination of Semboja and of the royal capital. It is probably for this reason that Semboja's son, Kimweri Maguvu, at Vugha, had earlier refused access to the missionaries. They were able to press their case only after his death in 1893. Maguvu's successor, Mputa, also tried to keep out these agents of the northern Kilindi. "Whoever wants to hear God's word," he told them, "can go to Mlalo."[2] The next missionary action was even more threatening, for Kimweri received an order from the German station chief at Mazinde that the missionaries were to be allowed to settle at Vugha, which they did in February 1895.[3] In March Semboja died, and then came disaster.

During the last week of April 1895, Lieutenant Storch, the station chief, staged a drama to demonstrate to all Shambaai that German power was supreme. He arrested the king, took him to Mazinde, and then pronounced him guilty of murder for having killed the lover of one of his wives. Storch ordered at the same time that every Kilindi chief be brought to Mazinde. The chief of Mbaramo, who was too ill to walk, was brought on a litter. Before most of the Kilindi of Shambaai and many of the important men of Vugha, the Simba Mwene was hanged. It was this act which the elderly courtiers at Vugha in the 1960s who had been alive at the capital in 1895 described to me as transferring power from the Kilindi to the Germans. Lieutenant Storch, nicknamed *Matungika* ("the piercer," or "the stabber," because of the hook under the corpse's chin), is quoted in one typical oral account as having said to the Kilindi, "If you have any *nguvu* let me see it now." *Nguvu*, as we have seen, was the term for sovereign power in precolonial political discourse. No one showed *nguvu*, and control passed from the Kilindi.[4]

The people of Vugha reacted to Mputa's death with panic. Many slept out in the open for several nights, hidden in thickets, for fear of what would happen to them. Once the initial period of panic had passed, the officials of Vugha arranged a rotation as if for casual court service. People of different quarters took turns attending the church which had been built about two miles from the capital.[5]

Even after Mputa's death, Storch needed an African agent, and chose a Kilindi. Storch had clearly not thought that his execution of Mputa would destroy all Kilindi power. His understanding, under the influence of Baumann's book and perhaps of the Mlalo missionaries, was that he was destroying the "Semboja Party," as he called it, while preserving some chiefly authority at Mlalo and among the eastern Kilindi.[6] Seen from the Kilindi point of view, the king's right to execute a man who challenged royal masculine predominance by adultery was close to the heart of sovereignty, but it is unclear whether Storch understood this. The Lieutenant did, presumably, count the monopoly over life-or-death decisions as important to imperial sovereignty. It is clear, at any rate, that chiefship in some form could have survived even the execution of Mputa.

Kilindi rule could not, however, survive the use of chiefs to transfer large areas of land to the conquerors, or to organize compulsory labor for German employers. This is what came next. When Storch chose to give Kibanga and Kinyashi, leaders of the eastern Kilindi, control of Vugha, he would have known what they had already done in the east. Kibanga, brother of Vugha's ruler of the 1860s (Shekulwavu), had already at this point leased 400,000 hectares to the Rhine-Handei Plantation Company for a hundred years at less than two cents per hectare per year. Shekulwavu's son, Kinyashi, sold areas larger yet to the German East African Company (Iliffe 1979:126).

Storch installed Kibanga at Vugha on 6 June. Almost immediately a German arrived at Vugha and leased large areas of land for coffee. On 28 June a representative of the German East African Company arrived at Vugha with the assignment of buying all land not actually under cultivation. Kibanga who either had learned from his experience or cared more about the land of Shambaai than about land in the east, refused to sell. By early September Storch became disillusioned with Kibanga and replaced him with Kinyashi. Within a few weeks Kinyashi sold land near Vugha to the mission; three previous rulers had refused. Between 1895 and 1906, 162 leases were given for land in the district, most of them presumably during Kinyashi's years at Vugha.[7] Kinyashi also used his authority as Simba Mwene to call out labor for the conquerors. According to the missionary LangHeinrich, "Kinyashi had boasted that he could send his people wherever he liked. They were his slaves. At first hundreds, even thousands, went out at his request. The villages were empty for a time. But people's own fields declined and they grew angry."[8]

Even though Kinyashi's installation at Vugha in September had been greeted with public celebration, and Kinyashi had boasted of his own power, by the following February (1896) the new ruler appeared to missionaries as a pathetic figure. The mission held services to consecrate the chapel built on their newly purchased land. Kinyashi attended, but sweated with anxiety the whole time. Then the lion-king decided to leave without eating, begged permission from the missionaries, then wavered, asked permission a second time, and then a third, and finally fled. By July a missionary heard a woman loudly singing at Vugha, *Kigono cha shimba, chagona nguluwe,* "Where once a lion slept, there is now a pig." The king should be like a lion, who eats the meat of the whole land as tribute when he covers it over, but Kinyashi was like a pig who roots up the crops. It must have been at about this time that Kinyashi stopped performing rites for the fertility of the land at the court.[9] Vugha declined in this period; in 1897 more than half the houses of Vugha were empty. In September 1898 a great fire destroyed half the capital, and no one made any attempt to rebuild.

The years 1897 to 1899 were a time of disaster. Rinderpest swept through the mountains killing cattle in 1897. Locusts came, and then a very long drought, with the famine made worse because it followed years of upheaval and loss in which reserves had been depleted. The famine was disastrous at Vugha. Throughout the mountains people died of hunger at the roadsides, as they went searching for food. A smallpox epidemic broke out among the uprooted population. This was also the time when jiggers first spread to Shambaai and brought serious illness, since people did not know how to treat the infestation. Some of these plagues are remembered as punishments meted out by the Europeans. One oral informant told the story of a German planter who, when faced with local refusal to work on his farm, sent to Germany for an earthen pot full of jigger eggs. He broke the pot in a village adjacent to the estate to punish the recalcitrant workers.

Kinyashi lived isolated and broken through the time of the famine. In better times he would have fed Vugha with royal reserves. Now he was forced to beg the missionaries for enough to feed his own family. In 1902 Paulo Mnkondo, a commoner and mission adherent, was made provisional chief official of Vugha in Kinyashi's place.[10]

The one significant attempt at the time of conquest to find the means to transform chiefly rule, and to preserve it under German power, was made at Mlalo. There both chief and missionaries decided for a brief time that a Christian-Kilindi alliance was possible. In the end the alliance failed because the missionaries were ambivalent about leaving their early converts under the authority of a non-Christian chief and unable to provide the chief with full protection from governmental demands or discipline.

Shekinyashi, chief of Mlalo, promised his cooperation to the colonial authorities in 1888, before the coastal resistance had suffered its final defeat. He hoped for assistance in resisting Vugha. The Mlalo Kilindi claimed that Kimweri Maguvu at Vugha had threatened them with war if they allowed missionaries to settle. By mid-1891 Johanssen and Wohlrab, the first Bethel missionaries in Shambaai, settled at Mlalo, where they found themselves caught with loyalties divided between the chief, who was their protector, and the first converts, who were to be the founders of the Christian community in Shambaai. The ambivalence of the missionaries and of the chief continued after Shekinyashi's death in 1894 and the succession of his son Kinyashi (the same name as the king of Vugha in 1895, but not the same person). In 1895, for example, the missionaries helped a Christian named Mussa to reclaim from the chief a goat which had been taken as tribute. But when Mussa argued publicly with Kinyashi a few weeks later, the missionaries explained to the entire court of Mlalo that obedience to authority was Christian policy. The missionaries tried to resolve their conflicts with the chief of Mlalo without involving the station chief at Mazinde. Kinyashi seemed at moments to be at the brink of conversion to Christianity.[11]

The missionaries, however, lacked the power to protect their ally from harsh or unrealistic government demands. In August of 1900 Kinyashi fled toward the English border. Wohlrab's explanation of this was that "The decline of princely dignity, which has come more and more with the evolution of chiefs into government officers with oppressive duties, has made their position seem a burden." The precipitating event was an order that all local bulls be done away with so that local cattle could be cross-bred with European cattle. Seven months later Kinyashi wrote to Wohlrab in abject distress: "My lord, my teacher, I am a fool, like a crazy person, for I have gone without taking leave of you."[12] Kinyashi ultimately returned and resumed his duties as chief, but never again in alliance with the Bethel missionaries. Now he was a devoted Muslim.

Once it was clear that the missionaries could not offer adequate protection, Islam was the choice of the most important chiefs; it was a religion of influential outsiders, but unlike Christianity it avoided the implication that converts had gone over to the Europeans, and it did not bring resident German missionaries who could report to the district officer. Important chiefly conversions to Christianity came only later, during the English period, under very different conditions. In the German years, in any case, the situation of chiefs was hopeless, whether they held the missionaries at arm's length, as did the kings of Vugha during the early 1890s, or whether they contemplated Christian conversion in the manner of Kinyashi of Mlalo.

With chiefs in rapid and obvious decline, and with famine and disease leaving behind them weakened survivors, it was a time when explanations of healing and harming the land were in crisis. It is especially difficult to know what people were thinking and saying on the subject during this period. It appears from the oral accounts, in hindsight, as though the crisis never occurred, because conceptions of healing and harming the land were restored with the reinstatement of chiefs by the British in the 1920s. Missionary records of the German period are helpful so long as we understand that the missionaries themselves were seen as potential rainmakers. People spoke to them not as confidants, but as powerful and dangerous men.

Mputa's execution in April 1895 appears to have been the event which precipitated the crisis. Before then, the Kilindi were seen by a broad range of people as controlling the condition of the land, whether the Kilindi served as chiefs (as in the kingdom's heartland), or as nongoverning rainmakers (among the Bondei and Mbugu). British missionaries in the east saw people from Bondei going to Kinyashi in 1894 (before his return to Vugha) to learn what the condition of the crops would be like during the coming farming season. In January 1895 some Mbugu explained to a missionary that the famine would free the land of Europeans, who would be driven back to the coast. A month later the people of Mtae, to the northwest of Mlalo, explained that the famine was a chiefly stratagem to consolidate control.[13]

After Mputa's execution many people, including Kilindi, began to wonder whether Germans had replaced chiefs as rainmakers: since Germans had the power, they must also control the crops. Early in 1896 Kinyashi of Vugha asked the two resident German missionaries, Lang-Heinrich and Gleiss, to pray for rain. They did so. In 1898 people in Mtae tried making a communal rite; when five people died within a few days of its completion, the local missionary was asked, "Why is God angry with us?" The missionary held a day of prayer to try to stem the advance of the plagues. An Mbugu leader at the same time told Johanssen of Mlalo that the Mbugu were not interested in the Christian religion but wanted to pay cattle to ransom themselves.[14]

In 1899, after the great famine had been going on for a year, a peasant at Mlalo told a story to Johanssen about a giant named Hunju. The missionary recorded it as an interesting folk tale, but it is likely the story was being told as a parable, in warning. It is the following tale:

Once upon a time there lived an enormous monster named Hunju who made all men his subjects. When he entered a town and made his demands, whether for cattle or people, he was given whatever he wanted. No one dared come near to him, and no town even made the attempt to drive him away, or to kill him with an arrow shot from afar. His size was indescribable, for when he went through the ocean he did not need to swim, and when he caught a sea monster with his hands he held it up high, roasted it in the sun, and then ate it. He used a giant tree as his toothbrushing-stick. One day when he was going through the land he entered a town and demanded a herd of cattle to eat. The terrified people pleaded that he have mercy on them: they could not give him the cattle, for they had none. But Hunju became furious and accused them of hiding their cattle. He left in anger and resolved to make an example of the people, so no town would ever have the courage to hide something from him. He climbed a mountain and lifted a stone slab large enough to cover the whole town. He put it on his head and went down the mountain to flatten the town. God saw him going there and was displeased by the arrogance with which Hunju held himself to be God-like. God therefore made a hole at the spot where the slab rested on Hunju's head, so that it broke through with a terrible jolt and left the remainder resting on Hunju's shoulders. He tried in vain to lift the stone and pull his head through, to get rid of the load. It would not budge. As far as his eyes could see there was only stone slab; his hands could not bring food to his mouth. He spent three months without eating, for he was enormously strong. When he then tried to rise to his feet he died. The load had killed him.[15]

Johanssen was being told that even the Germans could destroy themselves if they went too far in exploiting the weak.

With the crisis of Kilindi authority, and conditions of extreme distress, the missionaries acted as alternative chiefs, especially during the late 1890s, when the power of chiefs had eroded without new arrangements having crystallized. In times of famine before the conquest the chiefs had fed the hungry, who became their dependents. Now this was the missionary's job. When the great famine of 1899 to 1900 was at its height, missionaries at Vugha were bringing in 100 loads of food a month. Mission stations swelled with those in need.[16]

Mission adherents also expected protection from government demands. In the 1890s missionaries did not hesitate to send their people, letters in hand, to the district officer with requests that local officials be overruled. Döring at Mtae even provided sanctuary to the defeated forces of the chief in 1897 after a pitched battle with the newly appointed agent of the Germans (*akida*); the capacity to give sanctuary had been a clear diagnostic sign in the preconquest period that an independent locus of power (*he nguvu*) existed. On some occasions (especially in the 1890s) missionaries negotiated with the local chief over the work responsibilities owed by Christians. In some instances, when the expectations of adherents were not met they left the Christian community. In 1903, when a local Christian official at Vugha was unable to meet a government demand that he provide 300 porters, he asked the missionaries for help. They recruited Christians in order to save the official's job. Some of the porters, however, left the Christian community.[17]

Because the missionaries exercised power within local communities, they were able to take in people who had been cut loose from the local web of relationships. Once again, this had been a chiefly function a few years before. Lutindi, which later became a mental hospital, began as a home for over a hundred freed slaves, although these did not become the heart of the mission community. Many of the exemplary early converts were outcasts who came from the vicinity of the mission stations. Shedafa of Mlalo had been mentally disturbed in a violent way when the chief deposited him at the mission station. Marko Kaniki, one of the most famous early Christians, had been accused of his wife's death and driven out of Shambaai. When he returned after working at the coast, he found refuge at the mission. The Christian community at Mlalo solved the problem of finding wives for Christian men by welcoming women who had left their husbands. The first converts at Mtae were lepers, but many other early Christians were ordinary men and women.[18]

Even though Bethel missionaries were willing to assume quasi-chiefly authority, they were only slightly more capable of consolidating their position in African politics than were the chiefs themselves. The reason was the same for both chiefs and missionaries. The needs of the settler economy took precedence over those of chief or mission. Missionaries were unable to protect their followers from onerous labor demands. From the late 1890s until 1904 each settler was allocated a certain number of villages whose headmen had to provide labor (Iliffe 1979:152). When the Governor abolished the system in 1904, a campaign was undertaken to eliminate all small hamlets. The population was to be concentrated in large accessible villages for ease of labor recruitment. This led to such abuses that Johanssen, at that point head of the Bethel mission in Usambara, argued before Governor von Rechenberg in 1907 in support of a system of labor cards, compelling every local man to work thirty days for a European in each four-month period. With this one modest exception, the settler economy was beyond mission control. The missionaries complained that their work had ground to a halt because most Christian men were off doing compulsory labor.[19]

Christian and Muslim Intellectuals in the German Period

The Lutheran mission's strategy in responding to the difficult conditions for Africans was to try creating an elite of artisans and clerks. Their motives in providing occupational education were mixed: they were responding to a threat that Catholic orders would win government favor by filling a need for artisans; they planned to provide a Christian counterbalance to the government's secular school at Tanga; they wished to place educated Christians as local officials, to reduce the growing influence of the government's Muslim agents; and they wanted to ensure that Christian Africans would set an enviable example of prosperity at a time when most African men were destined to be poorly paid laborers. The artisans and clerks could, in fact, pay officials to find substitutes for compulsory labor (LangHeinrich n.d.:30).

In 1901 the Bethel Mission opened a middle school near Mlalo. At about the same time, the mission was creating a network of artisans' shops across Shambaai. By the time the Great War broke out, the mission had two large carpentry shops, a number of smaller ones, a book press and book-binding shop, a wheelwright's shop, three shoemakers, a number of trad-ing shops, tailors, and so forth.[20]

The mission succeeded over the longer run in creating a Christian elite of government employees who would, forty years later, help to articulate a new political ideology in opposition to both the Kilindi and the colo-nial power. In the years between 1900 and 1914, however, it appeared as though the African agents of colonial rule would be predominantly Muslim, and quite probably the language of African politics would draw on Islam.

The administrative district which had Shambaai at its heart was one of those districts where the role of colonial *akidas* first emerged. The *akidas* were appointed as tax collectors alongside Kilindi chiefs in the late 1890s; with the collapse of chiefly authority, *akidas* took on a wider range of administrative tasks. The majority of them were Muslims; some were from the coast, and others were former slaves (in some cases slaves of chiefs) who were among the first educated at the time of conquest.[21]

The missionaries struggled, generally unsuccessfully, to undermine Muslim officials and replace them with Christians. In 1900 they convinced the German district secretary to refuse letters in Arabic script from the tax collector at Bumbuli. At about the same time, the mission agreed to educate clerks for government service in return for a commitment that the district authorities try to appoint Christian officials. At Vugha in 1910 the mission attacked the government appointee, Ngelesa, by bringing at-tention to his practice of taking child brides.[22]

Differences between mission and government focused not only on re-ligion but also on language and culture. The missionaries saw themselves creating an ethnic church which would undertake education, prayer, and evangelism in the Shambaa language. They printed primers and Bible stories in Shambaa from 1892 on, helping at the same time to standard-ize the Shambaa language, and to establish the speech patterns of Mlalo as literary Shambaa. In 1908 they held an exposition at Vugha of the material culture of the Shambaa, working further to give coherence to Shambaa cultural identity.[23] The government through the German pe-riod was working in a very different direction — teaching Swahili to its officers and drawing many *akidas* and government clerks from the Swahili-speaking coast.

Decades before colonial conquest, Islam had begun to spread in at least some of the places where coast and interior had been integrated in a network of exchange. Both the economic integration and the spread of Islam accelerated rapidly, side by side, under German rule.

The well-watered plains at the southern edge of the mountains were taken for plantation agriculture, mainly for sisal and some rubber.

Nyamwezi workers were brought in, and the plains quickly assumed their character as a place where men from a wide range of backgrounds met and worked together — a character with continuities to the precolonial period. According to some mission accounts, workers from the mountains who went down to the plains found it difficult to get preferred jobs unless they converted to Islam.[24]

The integration of the local economy into the regional one was taking place in several ways at once; forced labor was only one of them. Loss of land to the settlers led to problems of subsistence, with the resulting economic need intensified by government measures which forced peasant men to work for Europeans. Fallow periods and food production were declining disastrously by 1912. At the same time, between the late 1890s and the War, imported consumer goods were becoming increasingly popular; people produced crops for sale so that they could buy imports. Oil lamps, clothes, boots, and cigarettes were in common use among people living in the plains near the Mazinde military station in the 1890s. By 1907, according to LangHeinrich, most people in the southern parts of the mountains wanted cloth, varying in style with the fashions of the coast; most houses had oil lamps and blankets. People in those parts of the mountains earned money not only through labor for Europeans, but also by selling food and sugarcane wine in large quantities for plantation workers in the plains. Railway construction, which was completed to Mombo by 1905, used labor and increased the region's exports. At the same time, the hardwoods of Shambaai were taken to be burnt in the locomotives.[25]

The areas of the most intense trade, especially between mountains and plains, were also the ones in which Islam spread most easily. Railway construction workers who suffered shortages of food in the plains climbed the mountains to purchase food at Bungu, on the southwestern edge of the mountains. The women of Bungu, adapting an ancient pattern of food trade in the new context, descended regularly to Makuyuni, on the railway, to sell food at high prices. Makuyuni and Bungu quickly became centers for the spread of Islam. Muslim African traders at Makuyuni, who were agents for Indian wholesalers, served as teachers of Islam and proselytizers. Traders also began to make converts in the mountains in the area around Bungu. By 1909 many people around Bungu were fasting during Ramadhan. It is clear from oral accounts that a teacher of Islam settled further into the mountains at a village near Bumbuli before the War broke out.[26]

Islam spread through an alliance between traders and *akidas*. At Bungu the process of proselytization which was begun by the traders was carried forward by Akida Tupa, whose brother (a trader) built a mosque there in 1910. At Kwa Mponga it was the *akida* who served as the teacher of Islam and dispenser of Muslim medicinal charms.[27]

By the end of the German period, Islam and Christianity were both spreading to ordinary peasants in the mountains. Islam seemed characteristically to be the religion of *akidas* and traders and of people from diverse parts of the territory living side by side in the plains. The religion was associated with the Swahili language, with the union of plains and mountains, with interaction among people drawn from many local cultures, and most generally with processes of economic and social integration. Christianity in Shambaai, drawn in similarly general terms, was a religion of ethnic exclusivity, of the Shambaa and German languages, and of the work of teachers, clerks, and artisans. The missionaries themselves perceived these divisions. They tried, with little success, to create a group of Christian *akidas* and traders. Their defense of the exclusivist position, among people converting to Islam, was that Christianity preserved Shambaa customs, while Islam represented everything foreign.[28]

The British Choice of Agents

By 1914, when German rule in East Africa was coming to an end, *akidas* and traders had won influence as brokers in the Usambaras. The boundaries of Shambaai and of the kingdom had declined in their significance to the local population as a result of the regional integration of trade and labor. The British in the 1920s tried to restore a sense of narrow boundaries and selected a different set of brokers. The British rulers made a paradoxical decision in favor of the *Volks*-ideology which had been favored by Lutheran missionaries of the German period; this was also a decision in favor of the Kilindi and of Christian clerks, and one which limited the influence of African traders.

None of this happened instantaneously upon conquest. Local government in British Tanganyika was decisively shaped only during the governorship of Donald Cameron, who came to the territory in 1925. He arrived in Tanganyika determined to introduce indirect rule: the integration of indigenous political authorities as subordinates in the colonial administration. Cameron's enthusiastic support gave indirect rule the status of a "cult" in Tanganyikan administrative circles.[29]

One historian of indirect rule in Tanganyika explains that "Cameron remained highly sensitive to the broader political pressures that could be withstood by a colonial government only if it had an ideology of its own."[30] In this case the immediate threat in 1925 was that Tanganyika

would become part of a united East Africa dominated by Kenya's settlers, with Sir Edward Grigg, then governor of Kenya, as the governor-
general. In any event, Cameron had been convinced of the effectiveness
of indirect rule during his time in northern Nigeria.

Years later, in his memoirs, Cameron described the central problem
of administration as finding the means (in his words) "for communicat-
ing with primitive and ignorant people; we must in fact 'administer the
people' whereas in the United Kingdom . . . it is . . . sufficient to administer the law" (1939:77). Indirect rule would undertake administration through chiefs whose positions had "foundations in the hearts and
minds and thoughts of the people" (1939:94) but who would never hold
sovereign power. The chiefs were not to play the role of native princes,
as in Buganda, where a treaty relationship existed between African rulers and the British; chiefs were to serve instead as subordinate administrators or influential mediators (Iliffe 1979:319ff.).

The key to indirect rule, according to Cameron, was king-worship
without royal power. The Tudors, as interpreted by Trevelyan, were his
model (1939:109):

> The keynote of Tudor Government had been King-Worship, not despotism.
> Monarchs without an army at the centre or a paid bureaucracy in the coun-
> tryside were not despots, for they could not compel their subjects by
> force. . . . The power of the Tudors, in short, was not material but meta-
> physical. They appealed sometimes to the love and always to the loyalty
> and "free awe" of their subjects (1939:109).

Ranger shows that this appeal to king-worship was part of a broader process in which the colonial rulers imposed newly invented European royal
traditions on Africans and at the same time invented African royal traditions for their African subjects (1983).

The main work of the chiefs under the new system was to hear cases
and to collect taxes. Chiefs and their councils, designated as *native authorities*, collected tax from the territory's subjects, forwarded it to the
government, and received a rebate of 25–30% to be used for financing
local needs. Local expenditure was limited (in the years before World
War II) almost exclusively to the salaries of the chiefs and their staffs and
to very small expenditures for services (McCarthy 1982:18). In Shambaai,
for example, the Usambara District Native Treasury estimates for 1936
allocated 12% of recurrent expenditure to medicine, a game trapper, forest guards, agricultural instructors, and hide driers. The other 88% went
went to clerks, chiefs, headmen, and their messengers.[31]

The immediate job of Tanganyika's government in 1925 was to create
a set of clearly bounded administrative units, each focused on local po-

litical and religious ideas inherited from the precolonial period. To the extent that the government succeeded, it created the subject matter of British anthropology in the years after 1925. Tanganyika's government needed to find "tribal" groups with clear boundaries for administrative purposes; the functionalist anthropologists tended to study bounded tribes. The government encouraged king-worship, not the preservation of ideologies which encouraged political competition. The functionalists have been criticized for undue emphasis on political consent. The government wished to sustain a stable and coherent traditional culture; the functionalist error was in finding exactly that sort of coherence and inertia.

The shaping of the anthropologists' vision was neither planned nor sought by Tanganyika's government in the 1920s. The creators of indirect rule preferred to rely on research done by administrative officers (Lackner 1973; Malinowski 1929, 1930; Asad 1973; Mitchell 1930; Myres 1929; see also Cell 1976). The parallel understandings grew out of a convergence of assumptions between anthropologists, who tended to treat each local society as a distinct scientific specimen, and colonial administration, which preferred discrete administrative units, each with a separate political ideology. The parallels also emerged from the field method, which was in some ways the great strength of functionalism. Anthropological researchers based their conclusions on evidence collected during periods of field observation which lasted for years. They distrusted historical evidence, which seemed both pale and unsystematic next to knowledge gathered through direct observation. Since the societies which they observed under indirect rule were stable, conservative, and relied on coherent traditional ideologies, the anthropologists reported their observations accurately within the narrow spatial and temporal limitations they had established.

At the heart of British policy was a contradiction capable of undermining chiefly rule. All political debate among Africans was to be organized at the local level, not at the level of the territory as a whole. Yet the territory was in fact an economic unit. Provinces provided one another with labor and with produce. Events in one part of the territory (or one part of the Empire, for that matter) affected the well-being of the rest. If subjects debated the affairs of the territory as a whole, then chiefly questions would recede in importance.

Cameron wrote that replacing communal relations among Africans with narrowly economic ones "destroys tribal instinct and produces, if left to itself, something more akin to the slave system found in the West Indies half a century ago."[32] The makers of indirect rule tried to achieve an impression of stasis in the rural economy, even though radical changes were in fact taking place. The rapidly growing core of Tanganyika's economy in the 1920s was sisal production, organized on plantations of which the smallest were about 1,000 hectares. The labor force grew quickly. The rough rule of thumb was that it took one worker one year to produce one ton of sisal fiber, and production grew between 1912 and 1938 from 17,000 tons to 103,000 tons. The great majority of the men working on the plantations migrated for periods from the poorest parts of Tanganyika. The sisal growers exerted pressure on the Agriculture Department to avoid introducing commercial crops in these areas. The source regions for sisal migration presented a superficial picture of economic conservatism of the kind recommended by Cameron, beneath which they were undergoing drastic change. A survey of Ngoni men in 1953 revealed that 90% had engaged in seasonal migration. These men were expected to return periodically to their homes and to retain "tribal" loyalties, attachments to the seemingly static communities from which they migrated (Tambila 1974:3, 13, 18, 20; Rodney, Tambila, and Sago 1983; Iliffe 1979: 301–5).

Africans in other parts of the territory met their growing cash needs by producing commercial crops for export. Here too there was a contradiction between the need for increased production and for rural stasis which would support the impression that peasant well-being derived from the decisions of chiefs and councillors. The government tried to ensure that every African peasant met food needs from the resources of the isolated household, or at most from within the district. Officials made a distinction between subsistence crops and economic crops, and required peasants to grow adequate quantities of food crops, no matter how extensive their other economic activities.[33] A food supply drawing on all the districts of Tanganyika would lead to rural differentiation, driving some Africans off the land, and separating them from their "tribes." It would also erode the sense of awe and metaphysical attachment to a local chief. In cases like that of the Shambaa kingdom, in which the king's reputation depended on rain, an external food supply was at odds with chiefly authority.[34]

A related policy prevented Africans from trading across district or provincial boundaries (McCarthy 1982). Wider trade was to be in Asian or European hands. The immediate justification was one of bureaucratic convenience: local authorities could collect taxes more easily at a limited number of district markets serving local taxpayers. Farmers could sell their crops and pay local taxes with the proceeds. The effect was also to reinforce the peasants' perception that prosperity depended on local forces and to prevent the emergence of African networks reaching across district boundaries. Once again the government suppressed consciousness of wider integration.

Competition under Indirect Rule:
Chiefs against Literate Peasants

The introduction of rule through chiefs took different forms in the diverse parts of the territory. In some places chiefship had survived German rule; in others it had never existed. In Shambaai the goal was to restore a system which had been broken. Kinyashi, heir to Kimweri ye Nyumbai's grandson Shekulwavu and chief at Vugha during the disastrous late 1890s, became the first Paramount Chief of the postwar period. Local British officers thought his reputation as a rainmaker would inspire the awe on which this new colonial system depended. They reported in December 1925, during the period in which the Shambaa were being consulted on their choice of leaders under indirect rule, that the short rains broke on the day of Kinyashi's appearance at Mlola (a subchiefdom capital), provoking "extraordinary demonstrations." In January 1926 a lion appeared at Vugha, the first seen there in some time. It killed a cow fifty yards from Kinyashi's house, left the carcass uneaten, returned the next night, and was easily shot — another excellent omen.[35] In some places, the British blew life into the cold embers of Kilindi dominance. According to a man who had been present at the meeting restoring the chief of Mshihwi, a great many local people argued against restoration. The British official then asked, "How many of you are relations of the Kilindi?" Of course, almost everyone was. He said, "If the Kilindi are made to leave this country you will all have to leave; you are mixed together as one people."

The three years during which Kinyashi held office, from 1926 to 1929, were years without famine, and Kinyashi's reputation today is as a great rainmaker. Kinyashi himself, during his years of office, apparently took his work as a rainmaker seriously and made a strict separation between rainmaking and political power; he saw himself as holding one but not the other. This was a separation which, as we have seen, was earlier made by Bondei rebels of the 1870s, who overthrew their Kilindi chiefs but continued paying tribute for rain. Now, in the British period, Kinyashi's subjects knew that he could not make war, could not sentence people to death, and could not freely collect tribute. Kinyashi himself refused to accept gifts from subjects whose cases he judged, and saved his entire salary, counting it carefully from time to time so that when the district officer fired him, he would be able to return it all.[36] Uneducated chiefs like Kinyashi were, in Cameron's vision, needed only for a period. The next generation of chiefs and their councillors were to be both educated and Christian. He was an enthusiastic supporter of the plan to rely on missions for colonial education. "The future place in the world of the people of Tanganyika," he wrote, "depended very largely on their becoming Christianised" (1939:167). The expectation of Tanganyika's rulers was that as time went by, the ideology of chiefship would weaken, and Christianity would then serve as an alternative support for the social order. According to the authoritative statement of British educational policy of 1925, which Cameron called the "charter of education" in Tanganyika, "Education should strengthen the feeling of responsibility to the tribal community. . . . Since contact with civilization — and even education itself — must necessarily . . . weaken tribal authority and the sanctions of existing beliefs, and in view of the all-prevailing belief in the supernatural which affects the whole life of the African it is essential that what is good in the old beliefs and sanctions should be strengthened and what is defective should be replaced. The greatest importance therefore must be attached to religious teaching and moral instruction."[37] Muslim religious teaching was not to play this role: the government gave subsidies for educating Africans in Christian schools but not in Muslim ones; in Shambaai Muslims (with the exception of sons of chiefs) were virtually excluded from education beyond the lower grades.

Conflict over the religion of local political brokers had begun during the German period as a dispute between mission and government on the religion of *akidas*. In the 1920s Christian converts took up the fight for a Lutheran chief. According to the *Annual Report* of 1928, Kinyashi, "owing to his inanities and prehistoric mentality is losing the respect of his chiefs and the younger generation." Quite probably this reflected the views of local Christians. At the same time supporters of a Christian Kilindi, Billa Kimweri, descendant of Semboja, sent letters to Kinyashi threatening him with death. Kinyashi resigned in May 1929, and was succeeded by Billa who died in August. Shebughe Magogo, a member of the Semboja branch, then took over.[38]

The conflict between Christians and Muslims did not go away. There were moments of intense tension in the 1930s, when supporters of Billa's children, who would have served as Christian chiefs, attacked Shebughe Magogo, who was Muslim and uneducated. One of Billa's relatives was locked up in 1934 for having a drum beaten to call Shambaa together to remove Shebughe Magogo.[39]

The conflict deepened after World War II, now as a movement by literate men who in many cases had been either soldiers or employed as minor functionaries in the civilian government. They were acutely aware that Shambaa were lagging far behind other Tanganyikans, especially the people of Kilimanjaro or Buhaya, in education and in economic progress. They argued that local backwardness would be corrected only if the most competent literate men were in charge of local government.

The British, by choosing chiefs and literate clerks as their two main sets of agents, had defined the lines of conflict for the postwar period. A bitter political battle unfolded between the two groups from 1945 to 1947, leading to Shebughe Magogo's abdication. Later on, the battle between the chiefs and the functionaries would ultimately be resolved by the victory of educated functionaries over chiefs in the political movement which won national independence.

Improvement associations of the ambitious literate men sprang up as the war ended, at first simply calling for *maendeleo* (Swahili for "progress") without attacking chiefs. Between 1944 and 1946, the ambitious young men founded at least five improvement associations. Bondei, Shambaa, and Zigula servicemen formed a society to plan a public library and to improve medical services, housing, and agriculture. Lushoto men founded a reading club and private library. Samuel Chamshama, a government clerk, took the lead in founding the Usambara Association. And government employees founded the TAGSA — the Tanganyika African Government Servants' Association. The names and constitutions of improvement societies changed over the next few years, but many of the original leaders remained active.[40]

For these men, education was a central demand, the key to progress. The poverty of education had created a generation of *watu wa nyuma*, "backward people." The area was particularly poor in education because it relied on German missionaries, who were forced to withdraw twice in a thirty-year period. Lutheran schools, which had taught more than 3,000 pupils in 1912, served only 1,500 in 1946.[41]

Increasingly, in 1946 and 1947, the men of the improvement associations saw the Simba Mwene Shebughe Magogo as a major obstacle in the way of progress. What they wanted was not simply to change the chief. They wanted to introduce new political principles, some of them drawn from the European stream of their education, and some a reinterpretation of democratic elements in precolonial politics. Even education was, as they saw it, a democratic weapon. The District Commissioner understood this when he wrote in 1947 that "The Sambaa Union are pressing for more schools and if they succeed in their object their demands in twenty years time will be much greater than asking for the removal of the ruling personnel of the Native Authority."[42]

Education was the only legitimate qualification of Tanganyika's British rulers (the illegitimate one being race). The African functionaries, if well educated, would ultimately challenge European rule. Julius Nyerere and the nationalist movement did this ten years later. The use of African education as a weapon against European domination came into play also in Shambaai's Lutheran church in the late 1950s and early 1960s, when African church leaders fought to remove their inadequately educated German head of church.

In 1947 leaders of the Lushoto Local African Association told the district commissioner they wanted an African leader who had "proper education" in the work of government. Only such a person would understand that subjects were not at all like slaves. In another letter, the same authors said "our rulers should be chosen strictly for their intelligence." This was a plea for opening careers to men of talent and not restricting careers to men of chiefly birth.[43]

Alongside the democratic demands for a government open to all educated people, irrespective of race or chiefly lineage, could be found antidemocratic strains in the same discourse — calls for control of government only by those who had the proper qualifications. The long-term implication of this position, if followed to its natural conclusion, was that educated Africans would ultimately rule over the uneducated. This implication is clear in a 1947 letter by the president and secretary of the Lushoto Local African Association, the former a worker in the Forest Department and the latter a "tribal dresser" who administered medical first aid. Both were peasant farmers. They wrote as follows: "In our opinion only someone who is expert at a particular kind of work is able to judge a person's competence at doing that work. In matters of modern government, the only one able to judge a person's work is someone with the appropriate education in that work." This statement reserves authority for those with technical competence. We will see that the conflict between technical competence and democracy was a central issue in Tanzania after independence. Here it is foreshadowed in the words of peasant intellectuals: men who earned their living as farmers and supplemented it with the wages of minor government jobs.[44]

The peasant-clerks, -teachers, and -functionaries who opposed the king found democratic precedents in their own picture of precolonial African society. They recalled the years before Mbegha came to Shambaai — before the Kilindi dynasty — as a time when ordinary people were governed within their own villages by their own elders. An alternative to chiefship, or to government by the educated, could be found in government by the elders.

The actual direct conflict between the African clerks and the king in the postwar period came to a crisis after an initiative by the British provincial commissioner, who shared with the functionaries the conviction that chiefs in the postwar world would need some education in order to work effectively at their jobs. In March 1947 the provincial commissioner, on safari, decided that "The Shebuge is evidently not a fit man and is no longer able to perform his duties." Shebughe Magogo was permitted to remain in office, but was to be given a "prime minister" from among the literate peasants.[45] The provincial commissioner's brief note gives no indication of his thinking—whether Shebughe would have been incapable of carrying on under any circumstances, or whether (as is more likely) Lushoto now needed an educated leader to carry out postwar economic plans.

The district commissioner announced this new plan at a meeting two months later. He named the one man he knew to be competent, with whom he had shared work during all his time as commissioner: the Native Treasury clerk, Samuel Chamshama. From Shebughe's point of view this was a horrible choice. The clerk had worked for Shebughe in 1937 and had written a coolly intimidating letter asking Shebughe to pay his debts to a minor Indian trader. Samuel Chamshama was one of the main organizers of the Usambara Association, the organization of literate peasants critical of development in Shambaai under Shebughe.[46]

It was Shebughe Magogo's objections to Samuel Chamshama which provoked the prophetic defense of bureaucratic values: "Only someone who is expert at a particular kind of work is able to judge a person's competence at doing that work. In matters of modern government, the only one able to judge a person's work is someone with the appropriate education in that work." It is worth quoting these words again, for in 1947 they were spoken as the language of rebellion against rule by a poorly educated chief who was holding back competent young men. The words were therefore democratic in their implication. The same words spoken again fifteen years later, after independence, would resound as a call for all power to the technocrats. Democratic language emerged in that later period with very different terms.

The meeting at which the district commissioner announced the new policy and appointed Samuel Chamshama was held in the midst of a popular battle (discussed in what follows) over who was to govern the small subchiefdom of Lushoto. One candidate was unpopular but had Shebughe Magogo's support; the other was a rainmaker with wide popularity. The district commissioner pronounced Shebughe Magogo too old and infirm to carry on, named Samuel Chamshama chief minister (*Mlughu*), and then announced that the new *Mlughu* would decide on Lushoto's chief, with the Simba Mwene to serve merely as a ceremonial installer. Shebughe refused to accept his *Mlughu*, thus opening a period of constitutional crisis, with the literate Christian peasants (and many others) of Shambaai on one side and the Paramount Chief on the other.[47]

The district commissioner's announcement that the *Mlughu* would choose Lushoto's chief seemed like a fundamental change of regime, nearly equivalent to the German execution of Mputa at Vugha fifty-two years earlier. The Paramount Chief, the other assembled Kilindi, and the new literate men all concluded that authority would probably now pass from the Simba Mwene to a literate commoner. Each previous district commissioner had served as the main support of the Simba Mwene at Vugha. The present one threatened to put power into the hands of a commoner, and by doing so to change direction in the colonial choice of African agents.

German conquest had transformed chiefs into servile agents who were then replaced by *akidas,* who were in turn replaced under the British by chiefs with an administrative and ceremonial role. Now, in 1947, literate men hoped it was their turn to lead — that it was a time of transition from the dominance of chiefs.

The literate peasants saw this transition as meeting the needs of all Shambaai, which in their view had fallen behind other parts of the country under the leadership of Shebughe Magogo. They attacked him for not having brought *maendeleo,* "progress," to Shambaai. The clearest statement of their position comes in an undated list of accusatory questions presented anonymously to Shebughe Magogo, probably on 30 June 1947.[48] The letter judges Shambaa to be "backward people," *watu wa nyuma.* "Usambara," the rebels wrote, "has no education whatsoever. . . . Usambara has no midwifery. Shambaa women give birth in miserable circumstances. Many Shambaa women die in childbirth. Why are there no maternity clinics? . . . In what year were anti-erosion rules introduced? How are they applied? Why are there no meadows for pasturing animals? . . . How many schools are there in Usambara? And how many missions? What is the population and how many children attend school? In Usambara how many children are there who do not attend school?"[49]

The authors, using veiled language, accused Shebughe Magogo of having murdered his predecessor, the father of Abrahamu Mputa Billa, who in 1947 was the Lutheran pretender to the throne. The Paramount's supporters attributed these accusations and other acts of resistance to the Lutheran church. When Shebughe Magogo's supporters gathered at Vugha in August 1947, they "requested that Bwana Shebuge write a letter to the leaders of the Lutheran Mission to ask them whether friendship is at an end, and whether enmity and back-stabbing are all that remain. The most notorious leaders of the rebellion are drawn from this church."[50] Some British administrators of the 1950s felt that resistance was the work of those "prepared to indulge in pipe dreams of extending Lutheranism through a Christian chief" (Molloy 1971:82). But the issues of "progress," of education and development, were not narrowly Christian ones. Many Muslims wanted their children educated, were disturbed by discrimination against Muslim children at school, and by the fact that Muslim school-

children were subjected to Christian religious teaching.[51] A majority of
known rebels against Shebughe Magogo were Muslims. Many Muslims
supported Kinyashi's sons at Vugha, the Kilindi line which inherited the
kingdom's most important precolonial rain charms.

Another stream of dissident political language that existed alongside
the discussion of education and progress and merged with it in interesting ways was the language of predynastic lineage rule. On 6 June, the
day after Shebughe Magogo announced that he would not accept the
district commissioner's nominee as *Mlughu*, Isaac Kilo and Saguti Sabali
wrote praising non-Kilindi rule. In 1945 they had been President and
Secretary, respectively, of the Tanganyika African Government Servants'
Association. They wrote as follows:

> The British government came, desiring to install a legitimate government
> and to put a stop to the government of akidas, which was illegitimate.
> Because it was a government of foreigners, ignorant of the true history of
> the inhabitants, it asked at each place, "Who were the original rulers?"
> Then came an event which causes us to grieve, and it is this: what was
> the intention of the Shambaa elders, when they told the government, which
> only wanted to know the truth, that the Kilindi had been the original rul-
> ers of Shambaai? . . . You elders . . . before Mbegha came to Shambaai
> were there no rulers? Undoubtedly rulers existed (although none with the
> power to rule the whole of Usambara). It is senseless to speak obscenities
> which destroy your own reputation. Let us be open about the errors of
> the Shambaa elders.[52]

The authors of this letter went halfway toward challenging indirect rule.
They questioned the legitimacy of the Kilindi but accepted the premise
that local people need a traditional government and colonial help in establishing it. As the authors stated the case, the correct choice of local
notables leads to autonomy and progress. The authors knew, perhaps even
without conscious reflection, that if their article was to be accepted by
a government newspaper it must be phrased in terms acknowledging the
government's good will in serving its subjects. Government control over
the newspaper helped to shape debate. The authors concluded by proposing a complete shift in the choice of government agents from those
chosen for royal birth to new leaders chosen for intelligence, by which
they meant education. Their letter began by supporting a new tradition-
alism but ended as a demand for control by literate leaders.

The demand for education, the demand for modern material progress
(*maendeleo*), and even, we have seen, the demand for a return to pre-
Kilindi tradition, all were to some degree hegemonic: they all accepted
the fundamental value of the British contribution in East Africa. "Prog-

ress" and "education" were brought by the British. So, paradoxically, was the pursuit of traditional African forms of government.

If the discussion of African tradition could be shaped to support British colonial rule, so could praise of British democracy be shaped to reject colonialism. Isaka Hoza did this. A man who earned his living as a peasant farmer, he was one of the most eloquent rebels. He invoked British democratic ideas in their extreme form:

> In 1629 there was a king of England named Charles. The king did not listen to the advice of those subjects chosen by the people to explain the needs of the country in the council which is known as "the Houses of Parliament" until the present day. Because his subjects did not like his character, in other words his refusal to accept criticism on any matter at all, they forced him to close down the council. . . . But because of the heroism of a man named Cromwell the king's strength came to an end. . . . The people saw that it was better to die than to obey commands of this sort, made by one man alone. . . . In the end he died by having his head cut off in the year 1649. This is the story of a king whose deeds are very much like the deeds of our king in Usambara, who is concerned only with himself and his own children. He refused the good advice given by his subjects that a *chama* [political association] should be made of all Usambara, so that his subjects would have the unity to conduct the affairs of the country. And now that his strength is nearly gone it is said that he has begun to collect his Kilindi relatives and to make a *chama* of the Kilindi by themselves. This is complete foolishness which will bring war between the Kilindi and the Shambaa who are owners of the land.[53]

This last phrase is a fascinating democratic inversion of the king's title as "owner of the land" (*ng'wenye shi*). In the precolonial period this meant, as we have seen, that the king controlled the territory in its political aspect and especially that he had the right to take tribute. Now it was the Shambaa as opposed to the Kilindi who were described as the owners of the land (*wenye nchi*), using the Swahili cognate of the Shambaa term. This is consistent with Isaka Hoza's central positions: that the king ought to take the advice of his subjects; that it is better for the land's people to die than to accept arbitrary commands; and that sovereignty resides among the people.

Rain Politics in the Resistance to Shebughe Magogo

The movement against Shebughe owed much more of its success to large-scale popular associations (*vyama*, singular *chama*) focused on rain than to the smaller *vyama* of literate men pressing for modern progress. The political issues capable of moving thousands to act revolved around competition for chiefship among men with greater or lesser reputations as rainmakers. In this sense the British appropriation of chiefship worked effectively. Even when the peasant associations openly opposed British decisions, they did so in terms of the conceptions of chiefship reimposed by the British — conceptions which had the effect of focusing political protest at a local level and on dynastic issues.

Shebughe Magogo inspired little enthusiasm among commoners who wanted rain. He had not inherited the major rain charms, which belonged to Kinyashi's line, and in addition he suffered a serious disability. Senior men of Vugha described Shebughe Magogo to me as a *kilema*, a "person with a ritually significant deformity," in his case of a *chaa*, a "finger" or a "toe." In the precolonial period a *kilema* was prohibited from entering the royal burial enclosure or from coming into contact with the most important royal charms. Shebughe's reputation was not helped by the famine early in his reign, caused by locusts in 1932 and then drought in 1933. Peasant resistance to British-imposed coffee growing rules at Vugha fed into the popular assumption that Shebughe would be unable to heal the land.[54]

Shebughe's disabilities made it impossible for him to deal with the central contradiction of his position. He held neither the rain charms nor the force of arms necessary to impose his will on the rest of Shambaai, outside Vugha, and yet he would measure his success as Simba Mwene by the extent to which he could dominate the separate subchiefdoms: Mlalo, Ubiri, Bumbuli, and the others. Only if he could dominate those, would he become a fully credible successor to Kimweri ye Nyumbai, the great nineteenth-century king. When Shebughe tried to remove chiefs, and when the local chiefs he removed were themselves renowned rainmakers, his actions fed popular discontent and led to the growth of the popular *vyama* of resistance. It was the resistance associations, working to protect local rain chiefs, which created the large-scale protests leading to Shebughe Magogo's abdication.

That Shebughe was acceptable to the British and the rain chiefs unacceptable was symptomatic of a more general contradiction inherent in indirect rule. The system of administration was meant to build on the free awe which subjects felt for their traditional rulers. Yet in Shambaai, the district officers (and Shebughe himself) were most frequently in conflict with those Kilindi whose claim to the loyalty of subjects was unchallenged. The chiefs least favored by the government were those with reputations for controlling rain. Shebughe did all in his power to remove chiefs who won greater popular support because of their rain than he did. These were also the leaders who were offered tribute by their subjects and who felt free to ignore the wishes of the district officer.

The conflict between Shebughe Magogo and a rainmaking chief was clear at Mshihwi, which had precolonial claims to a status as a separate *nguvu*, a splinter kingdom independent of Vugha. For brief periods Shebughe would give in to popular pressure and accept the chiefship of Mnkande Kimweri (grandson of Shatu), who had a great reputation as a rainmaker. Then Shebughe would find an excuse for removing Mnkande, only to be faced with popular resistance over cotton growing, or taxes, or the water demands of sisal plantations.[55]

The one exception to the general picture was Daudi Sozi of Bumbuli. He had rain charms, and yet he was praised by district officers through the first twenty years of his service. According to some of Daudi's intimates, he tried to remain a cooperative colonial servant because he feared coming to the same end as his father Kibanga, who had been killed by the Germans after serving them. Sozi was one of the few major chiefs to convert to Christianity.

At Mlalo, healing the land came to be identified with opposition to British rule. In 1933 Hassani Kinyashi succeeded his father as chief. Hassani was famous as a rainmaker. He therefore felt free to serve his subjects well and the colonial administration poorly. District records complain of Hassani Kinyashi's record as a tax collector. Hassani's obstinate independence became intolerable during World War II, when chiefs were expected to provide manpower for the military and for plantations. In 1942 the chiefs provided censuses of the men in their territories, listing the number fit for work on plantations, for military service, or for staying at home. The other chiefs of Shambaai claimed that one third of their men needed to stay home; Hassani placed 86 percent in this category. Hassani Kinyashi was forced to revise his census and was then fired, to be replaced by Ali Chankoa, tax clerk at the district capital and son of a minor chief.[56]

Hassani Kinyashi's removal from office generated resentment against the Simba Mwene, Shebughe Magogo, who was ultimately responsible in popular opinion for selecting local chiefs within his kingdom. The women of Mlalo, according to an oral account, feared Hassani would leave the country as had his predecessor in the seat. One close observer of the events at Mlalo reported in an oral account, that the women said, "'If you go to Mombasa, who will cause the rain to fall? Are we to be finished off by famine?' They refused. Then Chankoa took the seat and famine fell on the people's shoulders." One of Chankoa's relatives explained, "When Chankoa went into the great house the drum would beat by itself, for he violated the ritual prohibitions of the great house." The people of Mlalo did not want him. They said, "We want food."

For as long as Hassani Kinyashi was out of office, Mlalo's people went hungry. In the 1942–43 growing season the local rains failed totally; in

1943–44 they were very poor; in 1944–45 the rains were average; in 1945–46 the failure of the rains was made more devastating by locusts and then a late frost, which wiped out the few remaining crops in high areas. But drought and locusts were not the worst of the problems. Up until 1943 Irish potatoes had been the great crop of northern Shambaai, the area for which Hassani Kinyashi made rain. In one peak year the area had exported 330 tons of potatoes, and in 1942 it aimed much higher.[57] But then a potato blight struck in 1943, and wiped out the crop in 1944. In 1945 there were no potatoes.

The agricultural authorities appear not to have asked whether the potato blight had caused Mlalo's observable poverty, which they saw as a consequence of soil erosion and poor husbandry. In 1946 Hans Cory, the government sociologist surveying the site of the future erosion scheme, told Mlalo's elders that soil erosion was sapping Mlalo's fertility. Weren't the crops smaller, he asked, than they had once been? Their view was that the soil had lost none of its fertility. Only rain was lacking, and by "rain" it is clear that they meant general control over the fertility of the land, including potato blight. They did not explain to Cory that the problem could be fixed if Hassani would return. There is no doubt they thought so.[58]

A deputation of Mlalo men went to the district officer in April 1946 and threatened to squat outside his office until Ali was removed as chief. The district officer convinced them to go home, but then the women of Mlalo came close to ransacking Ali's house and setting fire to it.[59] The officer, together with Shebughe Magogo, held a public meeting at Mlalo attended by a crowd he estimated as 5,000. "It became apparent that the people of Mlalo were almost without exception unanimous in their wish to get rid of Zumbe Ali." At a second meeting, the officer asked for a public statement of Ali's deficiencies as chief. The officer's account records a few minor points of grievance. According to Ali's son, the officer called out, "List for me your chief's derelictions at duty." "His derelictions," the people responded unanimously, "are that he has no rain." The officer wanted Ali to continue as administrator, with Hassani Kinyashi occupying the shrines and making rain. Hassani refused, and after more meetings attended by thousands of people, the district officer restored Hassani Kinyashi to his seat in August. Hassani returned to his shrines, and the late rains of 1946 were in fact bountiful ones.[60]

The agricultural authorities, having waited for a resolution of the dispute over chiefship, now pressed for the adoption of their erosion-control scheme. The experts had produced a series of draft schemes, beginning in 1942, none of which had been adopted. The Governor, in February 1946, rejected all the draft Mlalo schemes because they would provoke resistance by displacing population.[61] The provincial commissioner, similarly, saw erosion control as undesirable because it was likely to provoke political agitation. But then in August 1946 he reconsidered, after a meeting with the agricultural experts. "At this meeting I was pressed by all of them to reconsider my opinion." The central reason was that the new agricultural officer was on the spot, ready to go to work.[62]

The compromise plan called for a modest beginning, including an agro-socioeconomic survey of the Mlalo basin and a demonstration project in a single ward, for which Shita was ultimately chosen. The experts would show, in a small demonstration area, that eroded hillsides could be made to bloom. The households in the scheme would be asked to remove all their livestock from grazing in farmland between plantings, to grow fodder crops, to plant and maintain contour hedges, to realign cattle paths, and to refrain from farming near water courses.[63] The scheme provoked immediate resistance, most of it passive. The scheme moved ahead only because it used an enormous amount of labor, most of it from outside Shambaai, to rehabilitate a small area of farmland.

Three years later, Tanganyika's governor, Edward Twining, summed up the scheme's failings:

> The area selected consists of some 600 acres and is in an excellent position to be a demonstration plot, but did not appear to me to be atypical. The work which has been done at a cost of £9,000 is certainly spectacular. There at a glance you see an example of everything in the armoury of the jargon of the Imperial College of Agriculture put into practice. It (may?) indeed be an agricultural masterpiece. It is certainly a psychological blunder. It seems that those in charge used methods which can only be described as a return to direct rule, without perhaps the ruthlessness which the Germans would have used.[64]

Twining was now the second governor to condemn the scheme, which continued with a life of its own, spreading in its unpaid form to the whole of Shambaai, because the agricultural experts seem to have been capable of acting independently of their political superiors. Within Mlalo, Hassani Kinyashi worked behind the scenes to frustrate implementation.[65]

Hassani understood, as did his subjects, that he owed his position to the people of Mlalo and had won it despite the opposition of British administrators and of the Paramount Chief, Shebughe Magogo at Vugha. It was Shebughe who had decided to fire the chief of Mlalo back in 1942, bringing four hungry years, and Shebughe who accompanied the district officer to the riotous meeting of April 1946, at which Mlalo's people paid him no attention. When, a year later, Shebughe found himself under attack, his Paramountcy threatened, the Mlalo people would oppose him again. The central issue was rain.

In southern Shambaai, similarly, it was a dispute over rain within a subchiefdom which precipitated popular opposition to Shebughe. The opposition, once mobilized, went on to win Shebughe's abdication. It became part of a larger movement which made common cause with the associations demanding education and progress. The larger movement ultimately challenged British rule and elaborated complex and ambivalent positions on the desirability of kingship.

The official TANU (nationalist party) history of Lushoto District, written by local people, asks how the African Association first became involved in local political conflict. Even though their answer does not mention it directly, rain was at the heart of the matter. This is their account:

> Here is how the plot to attack Shebughe Magogo began. In the sub-chiefdom of Lushoto there was a chief named Daffa . . . who had become old and decided to retire from work.
>
> Remarkably, he did not allow the people to choose a chief. Instead he made a private decision to choose his own son Mtoi Daffa.
>
> The people of Lushoto dissented, and argued that the just course would be to give the seat to a person named Kimweri Kibanga. The Paramount Chief was drawn into the battle.
>
> The Sultan decided that Lushoto's chiefship ought to go to Mtoi Daffa, thus agreeing with the old chief Daffa's decision.
>
> The Sultan's decision enraged the people of that sub-chiefdom, and when people elsewhere in the district heard of this case, they also decided to reject Paramount Chief Shebughe Magogo.[66]

The chiefdom of Ubiri (the precolonial chiefdom, which took in most of later colonial Lushoto) had played a central role in the 1880s in providing rain for a large area of Shambaai, including Vugha. In those days, when Semboja's rainless line occupied the royal capital, the king would send a cow to Mshuza of Ubiri, with a plea that he make rain. Shebughe Magogo, the Simba Mwene in the 1940s, emerged from that same branch of chiefs without rain. His subjects therefore needed to look elsewhere for help. Some undoubtedly paid tribute to the heirs of old king Kinyashi, the alternative royal line at Vugha. Shebughe Magogo, unlike the king of the 1880s, did not send his men leading a cow to Ubiri and pleading for help. Instead, he worked to undermine the rainmakers of Mlalo and Lushoto. People in many parts of the district therefore feared they would go hungry.

This interpretation differs from the archival accounts, which portray the 1947 struggle against Shebughe Magogo as a battle for education and "progress" (*maendeleo*), and as a contest over whether Shebughe would accept a literate chief minister. The literate peasants and peasant-clerks in postwar improvement associations did, in fact, help to lead their fellow mountain folk in the struggle to force Shebughe Magogo's abdication.

But the occasions when they found a following—when, as in Lushoto and Mlalo, hundreds and even thousands of people came out — were usually times when rain was an issue.

The progress-oriented Usambara African Association rejected the leadership of Shebughe Magogo, but the point at which it attracted mass support was the moment when the *chama* supporting Mlalo's rain chief joined up. The *chama* had its origin as an association fighting to bring back Hassani Kinyashi as chief. It then continued to work for healing the land by opposing the spread of Mlalo's erosion-control scheme. This *chama* joined *en masse* in the fight against the rainless Simba Mwene. In April 1947 it linked up with the Usambara Association to fight for the Paramount Chief's overthrow, bringing along about 3,000 dues-paying members.[67]

It was the district commissioner himself who then unwittingly drew Lushoto's rain *chama* into the struggle against the Simba Mwene. The district commissioner met with hundreds of angry Lushoto people on May 2, all of them concerned over subchief Daffa's retirement and the apparent succession of a nonrainmaker. Only three days later (May 5-6), the district commissioner held a district-wide assembly of chiefs to consider the crisis of the paramountcy. He then linked Lushoto's rain politics with the district-wide conflict between the literate men and their Paramount, thereby ensuring that the local *chama* would become active in the wider political arena. The district commissioner pronounced Shebughe Magogo too old and infirm to carry on as active Paramount, named the literate clerk Samuel Chamshama Chief Minister (*Mlughu*), interviewed the two candidates for Lushoto's chiefship, and then announced that the new *Mlughu* would decide on Lushoto's chief; the Simba Mwene was to serve merely as a ceremonial installer. The Paramount refused to accept his *Mlughu*; Lushoto's aged chief returned to office but proved unable to collect taxes; police were brought in for tax collection; and Lushoto became a main center of resistance to the Paramount.[68]

As we have already seen, many local people interpreted the district commissioner's action as showing that the British were switching their support to a new set of agents—the literate men, many of whom served as clerks and minor functionaries. This happened just at the time when Shebughe Magogo was under severe attack by the rain *vyama* of Mlalo and Lushoto. The literate men and the rain *vyama* easily made common cause.

In the dispute over Shebughe Magogo's Chief Minister, the most important rainmaking chiefs took the side of their followers and of the Usambara African Association. At a meeting on 4-5 June 1947, Shebughe Magogo rejected the district commissioner's choice of Mlughu, and tried to win support for his own choice. Most of the subchiefs, including the major rainmakers Hassani Kinyashi of Mlalo and Daudi Sozi of Bumbuli, opposed the Paramount's choice and supported the position of the literate men. Later in the month (23 June), when hundreds of people gathered at Lushoto in open rebellion to demand Shebughe Magogo's abdication, most subchiefs did nothing to restrain the rebels.[69]

The Paramount's closest advisors were puzzled and angry. They wrote to the subchiefs: "We were astonished to see that you sat silently while your people organized to remove Shebughe Magogo from the honored seat in which you placed him. . . . [We are] beginning to wonder whether perhaps you can be counted among the rebels yourselves."[70] If the chiefs disciplined the rebels, they might themselves become targets of resistance. So long as chiefs did not break with their followers, they held some hope of healing the land. Among the rainmakers in particular, the tie between chiefs and their followers held.

The *vyama* continued to press for Shebughe's abdication through the cold mists of July 1947 and on into August. They demonstrated loudly at a meeting held by Shebughe Magogo in Korogwe on July 25, then threatened to bring thousands of demonstrators to Vugha in early August.[71]

The Paramount's courtiers found it impossible to understand British inaction. In their view the challenge to Shebughe threatened the kingship and with it the entire character of authority in Shambaai. They took the nineteenth-century principles seriously; the king's body is inseparable from the kingship, and therefore abdication is possible only if the king dies: *kubushwa ni kufa,* "abdication comes only through death." The king's authority is inalienable, like the authority of a father over his children:

> The elders [of the royal court] were astonished at seeing actions more extreme than any seen since government in Usambara began. They found the absence of any normal punishment remarkable. The elders discussed this in the light of customary law, for anyone who uses abusive language in addressing his father, or another person, is brought to justice and fined. For what reason, then, is this matter left alone and not brought to justice, and why is its punishment unknown?[72]

If subjects are allowed to rise up against their king, then children might be able to rise up against fathers. Shebughe's supporters wrote anxious letters to the district commissioner through early August, demanding that he send police to arrest and punish the rebels and thereby rescue authority in Shambaai.

The battle between the *vyama* and Shebughe Magogo went on through August, September, and October. The district-wide *chama* became a branch of the Tanganyika African Association — the forerunner of TANU, representing Africans in the whole of Tanganyika — only to have their actions in the chiefship dispute repudiated by the central TAA. After further mass meetings and local organizing, Shebughe Magogo abdicated his seat at Vugha on 22 November 1947.[73]

Shebughe's allies and courtiers saw his abdication as a betrayal by the British. If the government had not wanted him to abdicate, then why had they refused to prosecute the rebels? The court officials had provided evidence of crimes and could not understand why the evidence was ignored. Shebughe had the support of the district's white settlers. The settlers' association wrote to the chief secretary in Dar es Salaam pointing out "the unwisdom of an action which undermines the prestige of an age-old native regime."[74]

Shebughe's abdication grew out of the internal contradictions of indirect rule in Shambaai. The British wanted to appropriate to themselves the awe in which subjects held their chiefs, yet found the most awe-inspiring chiefs inconvenient allies. These chiefs were secure enough in the support of their followers and dependent enough on their followers to resist unpopular administrative orders. Indirect rule foresaw gradual transition to rule by literate Christians. The literate peasant farmers moved beyond the discourse intended for them by colonial policy — a conservative discourse revolving around Christian values and "tribal" values. They held alternative visions — of transferring sovereignty to the peasant majority, or of putting administration into the hands of the best-educated, or of ending advancement on the basis of birth to a chiefly line. In 1947 the rain chiefs, the popular peasant associations which supported them, and the aspiring literate commoners all joined together. The ultimate consequence was the Simba Mwene's abdication.

6

Royal Domination and Peasant Resistance, 1947–1957

The decade following Shebughe Magogo's enforced abdication was a period of major conflict over the government's Usambara Scheme for erosion control. Had the scheme succeeded, it would have created a stratum of wealthier peasants, and it would have increased the commercialization of land transfers. The scheme intensified political conflict in Shambaai and further sharpened the political divisions that emerged after World War II.

The two coalitions that emerged during the years of the scheme defined the district's movement into independent nationalist rule. On the one side was the Paramount Chief Kimweri Mputa Magogo, son of the abdicated Paramount, and a descendant of the trading chief, Semboja. Kimweri, like his father, faced the problem of governing Shambaai without control over major inherited rain medicines. Kimweri tried to create a coalition which included merchants, prosperous farmers, and devout Muslims. On the other side were educated peasants, many of whom had held minor posts with the government. They became part of a large and powerful coalition driven by the energy of peasants, especially women, whose subsistence was threatened by the Usambara Scheme. The two most prominent rain chiefs, Hassani Kinyashi of Mlalo and Daudi Sozi of Bumbuli, descendants of men who had been Semboja's enemies, won the support of peasants defending subsistence against commercialization. Mlalo's chief was himself an important Muslim leader. Even though the great rainmakers were themselves government chiefs, unable to oppose the scheme openly, they were a natural political focus for the scheme's enemies.

The peasant-clerks and the defenders of subsistence supported TANU (the Tanganyika African National Union), the nationalist party which brought the nation to independence in 1961. The rain chiefs gave the party their tacit support. The new government abolished chiefship and placed power in the hands of bureaucrats. Few of the peasant-clerks had adequate education to enter the bureaucracy. After independence they were to be cast aside in favor of men with greater education whose local roots were weak. Because the peasant-clerks led a popular movement, however, their discourse was a major influence in the later period.

The peasants who fought to protect subsistence, and who provided the political movement's energy, won a great victory: they defeated the Usambara Scheme and prevented the implementation of its most threatening elements. But they were unable to win autonomous control of peasant affairs under the independence government. The characteristic government of the bureaucrats that came to rule Tanzania thus grew out of the struggles of the 1950s in Shambaai and in places like it all around the territory.

These were events of the greatest importance, and they form the subject of the next three chapters: the present chapter is a narrative of the events with some attention to context, the second an exploration of how peasants understood the economic issues of the 1950s, and the third a discussion of innovations in political language.

The Installation of Kimweri Mputa Magogo

The years of struggle opened with the appointment of Kimweri Mputa Magogo, son of Shebughe Magogo, to take his father's place. This was a victory for a small group of court officials at Vugha who argued that the Paramount's abdication threatened all authority in Shambaai. The way to restore authority was to name Shebughe's son to serve in his father's place, and to punish his father's enemies. The son was well-educated, not vulnerable to the charges that had plagued his father: that an uneducated man was unsuited to administer the kingdom in modern times.

The district's new commissioner, D. M. Piggott, completely agreed with the courtiers. He quickly showed that he would not tolerate popular intervention in chiefly affairs, except through the government's chosen channel of chiefs' advisory councils. "Then a new D. C. came in, a harsh one named Bwana Piggott," one literate rebel remembered, ". . . one who frightened local people . . . and listened only to the words of the chiefs." Piggott, together with the provincial commissioner and the secretary for African affairs chose Kimweri with no Africans present. Kimweri was initially to be subchief of Vugha, with the understanding that he would ultimately become Paramount. On 23 February 1948 Piggott held a meeting at Lushoto to announce the choice, which was accepted in silence. According to Piggott, "I explained that the Sub-Chief was chosen on traditional lines and was of the right family and educated. Also that there were probably many there who had other ideas but would just have to accept it. . . . I explained also that the remedy for the disturbed state of the country lay in their own hands to disown the *chama*. If it continued to interfere in politics it could be declared illegal and members could thereafter be arrested."[1]

Piggott made good on his threat to arrest *chama* members during the disturbances after Shebughe's death on 21 May and the decision to install Kimweri as the next Paramount. Protesters slept out at the district capital, demanding that the decision be reversed. Piggott then ordered the subchiefs to arrest and try Kimweri's critics.[2]

Kimweri himself tried to find a positive basis on which to begin building support. His devout attachment to Islam held some promise, for many of the prominent rebels against his father were Lutherans, yet Muslims far outnumbered Christians in Shambaai. The emphasis on Islam also reinforced Kimweri's emerging friendship with African traders, for a number of merchants were prominent in the community of Islam. The main public ceremony marking Kimweri's accession was a Maulidi: a celebration of the birth of the Prophet Muhammad. On this occasion Kimweri began his inaugural address as Simba Mwene with the following words:

> *Alhamdu LiLlahi Rrabi L-Alamiina, Waswalaatu Wasallamu Alaa Sayyidinaa Wanabiyyanaa Wamawlaana Muhammadi Waalihi Waswahbihi Wasallam . . .*
>
> Praise be to God, Lord of the Worlds. Benediction and peace be upon our Lord, Prophet, and Master Muhammad and upon his family and companions. . . . We are here to praise God and Muhammad his Prophet, the benediction and peace of God be upon him. May he protect us when we are in doubt and distress, difficulty and discord, and facing ordeals . . .[3]

On later occasions the district commissioner provided transportation and introductions for Kimweri's trips along the East African coast to attend religious celebrations.[4]

In this postwar period when, as we shall see, the government encouraged territory-wide economic integration, the alliance between chiefship and Islam had the potential to bring Kimweri added support. His devotion to Islam was deeply rooted in his own convictions, not a mere political pose. In addition the set of associations was a convenient one, especially for this Paramount Chief who did not control major rain medicines, and who would therefore be rejected by subjects who took seriously the localizing implications of indirect rule. If subjects accepted that all of the kingdom's prosperity took its shape only within the borders of the old kingdom, and if that prosperity depended completely on the personal qualities and inherited medicines of the Simba Mwene, then it was clear that the kingdom could not prosper under Kimweri. Kimweri could claim instead to be fostering the prosperity of region-wide trade and the growth of capitalist agriculture among his subjects. For these claims, the Muslim associations were useful ones.

Nevertheless, the division between Kimweri's friends and his enemies did not fall along simple religious lines. Many of the peasants who were normally inactive in politics but wanted a chief with rain, and who came to resent the government's scheme for transforming peasant agriculture, were Muslims. There were Lutherans on the Chief's Council who supported Kimweri and Muslims in the Citizens Union who fought him. Hassani Kinyashi, the chief of Mlalo and Kimweri's enemy, was a Muslim who encouraged the founding of a Muslim Association in his chiefdom. In 1949 Kimweri deported a Shehe who held a protest meeting.[5] In addition, many of East Usambara's Anglicans were on Kimweri's side. Anglican schoolteachers were among the leaders of the association of Kimweri's supporters.

After accession, Kimweri's immediate job was to build a coalition of supporters. His friends learned from the rebels that the *chama* as an organizational form — the association with voluntary membership — was an effective political vehicle. They called their conservative *chama*, which first met in July 1948, *Tumaini la Ushambaa*, "The Hope of Usambara." It included African peasant-traders among its early leaders. The Hope decided at its first meeting to go into the business of buying peasant crops, with a large trader of Korogwe guaranteeing a loan for that purpose of 3,000 shillings (at a time when a laborer's salary was 16 shillings a month). A few years later the largest peasant-trader in Shambaai, who ultimately came to own a chain of shops, wholesale businesses, and bus lines, served as the vice-president of The Hope of Usambara. The same man was president of an association to further Islamic education. The Chief's Council turned to The Hope when it needed semiofficial nominations for a representative of the district's African traders. Members of The Hope of Usambara gained influence with the district officer and had his help in protecting their interests when school buildings were to be constructed on commercial land, or when pieces of estate land were handed over for African cultivation with the help of government tractors.[6]

Several months after Kimweri's accession, an important peasant-trader wrote a letter asking him to revoke the trade licenses of Africans who served as fronts for Asian traders. The writer, and other Africans, intended to supplant the Asians altogether. Piggott agreed that in the future every African trader would need to have a letter from his subchief attesting that the business was his own and that he was not merely the agent of an Asian.[7]

This decision gave chiefs the power to deny trade licenses to their enemies. Traders were politically vulnerable in any event because they almost inevitably crossed the ubiquitous legal barriers restricting trade. The profits to be gained by evading government monopolies were substantial. In 1949, for example, the government required African coffee farmers to sell their crops to a designated exporter at one-third the price paid by merchants in Tanga.[8] The men able to circumvent the legal marketing system quickly became rich. The illegal coffee trade is, of course, difficult to document, except through anecdotal knowledge acquired over the years. Such trade was undoubtedly important in the politics of the period, but I must emphasize that there is no evidence that Kimweri knew details of the illegal trade or cooperated in it.

The illegal trade in grain must also have been substantial, although I have no direct knowledge of individual traders. The sisal estates, which needed maize to feed their workers, illegally purchased hundreds of tons in Shambaai each year, with the government's full knowledge, because it was clear that peasant farmers would not sell at the official grain storage price. The official government monopoly ended in 1955.[9] Lumber was another source of illegal income. Africans sold many more cubic feet of tropical hardwoods than they were permitted to remove under government pit-sawyer licenses.[10]

British and American critics of Tanzania's economic policy pretend that marketing monopolies, administered prices, and distortions of peasant production all originated with African socialism. In fact they were at the heart of colonial economic administration and important for colonial-period politics.

The system of licensing and the predominance of illegal trade pushed peasant-traders in Lushoto District into an alliance with their chiefs. In a society where dense social networks transmitted personal information almost instantly, a merchant whose every act was illegal could not afford to be a political opponent of the chief. The records of the 1950s are filled with cases in which members of the Usambara Citizens Union (UCU), or TANU, or the local *vyama* were arrested on manufactured charges. An illegal trader would have been especially vulnerable if he had been an open member of the UCU.[11]

The more far-seeing merchants tried to maintain good relations with both sides in the political conflict. According to nationalist reminiscences, some peasant-traders gave open support to Kimweri and at the same time made secret contributions to rebel organizations. Some traders who were unable to get government permits committed themselves fully to the side of the rebels. Mohammed Singano of Gare, for example, had been convicted in 1942 for trading in vegetables at a time when European farmers held a legal monopoly. Nine years later he appeared as an organizer of a mass march on Vugha to remove Kimweri. One of the early rebels in Bumbuli was an illegal cloth trader on a small scale. But the success-ful African traders appeared in Kimweri's camp.[12]

The vulnerability of African traders in this period made it very diffi-cult for them to play an independent role in the political struggles lead-ing up to independence. In some parts of the territory traders overcame the obstacles and were active in the nationalist movement. In all cases, however, the tight regulation of trade left traders in a weak position in relation to local authorities. They would undoubtedly have had much more influence in the early period of independence as counterweights to the bureaucrats if they had not been so constrained under colonial rule.

The district commissioner did not intervene in the politics of coalition-building. Kimweri took the initiative at drawing in merchants, Muslims, and Anglicans. The commissioner was concerned instead with the gen-eral prestige of the Paramountcy, with its formal institutional structure, and with the instruments of coercion. Money was to be the source of prestige. In 1950 Kimweri received a large salary increase and a 13,000 shilling box-body car. "Both of these improvements," the *Annual Report* explained, "aim to increase the Chief's standing and authority among his subjects and to discourage the efforts of the chama."[13] In 1953 Ki-mweri attended the coronation in London, the smooth progress of the trip marred only by the difficulty provoked by an invitation to a cocktail party at the Dorchester Hotel during Ramadhan.[14]

The British strategy depended also on creating an institutional frame-work for the Paramount's coalition-building. At about the time of Ki-mweri's accession they created a *Bawanjama*, a "Chief's Council," along with a pyramid of Subchiefs' Councils. The *Bawanjama* included sub-chiefs, subchiefs' courtiers, and men nominated to represent special in-terests (one person each of Pare and Mbugu ethnic backgrounds, repre-sentatives of medical people, teachers, a historian, and a merchant).

Kimweri worked to bring prominent women onto the *Bawanjama*, which decided in December 1948 to add four women immediately. Pig-gott, the district commissioner, thought the move ought to be delayed, but then permitted it to happen, although it is clear that he found their presence disturbing. He complained in 1949 that their "zeal for mater-nity and child-welfare sometimes verges on the excessive."[15]

The district commissioners of the late 1940s and early 1950s used the police, the courts, and the jails to control the chief's opponents. Mr. La Touche, a superintendent of police, began investigating local popular associations in 1947. From the middle of 1948, about the time Kimweri became Paramount, the government banned public meetings of the Tan-ganyika African Association and instructed chiefs to try members of any association which did not have their own approval. Leaders of the *chama* were occasionally beaten and locked up for brief periods without due process. In January 1952 when Salehe Shauri (a key leader of the *chama*) wrote to the district commissioner complaining that a chief had arrested him falsely for a nonexistent debt, the commissioner noted in his minute at the bottom that this was "the infamous Salehe Shauri" of the chama, and that "No action seems to be called for by us on this."[16]

As events unfolded in the years following 1948, the administration's support and Kimweri's coalition were not strong enough to control the opposition, or even to slow its growth. The government's compulsory Usambara Scheme for the transformation of peasant agriculture in Shambaai made the Simba Mwene's position untenable. It was impossible for Kimweri to save his Paramountcy or to win popular support so long as he administered the hated scheme. In order to understand the political issues at stake, we must first sketch the dilemmas of peasant agriculture in the period and the general policy of which the scheme was a part.

The Agricultural Background
to the Usambara Scheme

The new element in the late 1940s was intense pressure on land and labor, not at all like the situation in the 1920s when cultivators in many parts of Shambaai did not fall short of land, when they enjoyed greater latitude in planning their work, and when food was plentiful. By the 1940s population growth put a strain on resources. District borders which in 1920 took in no more than 80,000 people held two and one-half times that number in 1946.[17]

Population growth accompanied a transformation of the rural economy. The mountain people of the 1920s grew crops to feed themselves and their children, but could choose to sell the surplus to sisal plantations with thousands of workers to feed in the nearby plains. In 1927 the local cultivators of Tanga and Lushoto Districts produced enough to feed 50,000 workers and to export an additional 758 tons of food. The hungry people of Handeni, an area of recurrent famine, made up their food needs in 1929 with Lushoto's surplus.[18]

The herds of those years found grazing land, especially in areas where the farms abandoned by German settlers had not been taken over by other Europeans. Old men, now free of the war dangers of the twenty years before 1895, and having survived the sweep of famine and epidemic since then, could watch the number of their progeny and of their cattle increase. Young men could choose between caring for cattle, raising food, or working on estates — coffee in the mountains, or sisal in the plains. Most kept to their own farms and worked for whites only when short of cash. The days of Shambaa sisal workers were to come thirty years later.[19]

The central economic transformations of the 1940s began earlier, as small changes from the time of German conquest onwards, at the insignificant margins of livelihood. The Lutheran missions at Mlalo, Mtae, Vugha, and Bumbuli gave Arabica coffee seedlings to their adherents at various times. The missionaries felt a paternalistic desire to see their adherents prosper. In 1980 a serene old Christian, Mzee Ismail, living at a village near Bumbuli, described his beginnings as a coffee farmer. He worked as Pastor Gleiss's personal servant from the late 1920s. The pastor held back most of Ismail's wages, which he would only pay out to buy farms for the young Christian, and then only to make direct payment to the seller. By 1928 local people owned 45,000 coffee trees in Shambaai, not a large number, but a beginning.

The cash crops of the 1950s, coffee and vegetables (supplemented by wattle and tobacco), spread mainly through peasant initiative. Despite the mission role in introducing coffee, Muslims emerged among the largest producers in the years after World War II. Polygynous men recruited family labor more easily than monogamous Christians. The Africans of Lushoto District, who exported about 5.5 tons of coffee in 1936, were marketing 140 tons two decades later.[20]

Vegetable farming also spread from small interwar beginnings. Shambaa men sold vegetables at the Tanga market by the early 1930s (Baker 1934:52) and probably earlier. Then the war stimulated enormous expansion, even though the authorities expected European farmers to be the main producers. In the actual event, African farmers were soon responsible for 90% of production, but were expected to sell their crop through European planters. By 1944 Shambaai exported 1,000 tons of vegetables. Later, tonnage fell when the government stopped buying, but then rose again to hold steady at 500–700 tons through most of the 1950s. Two other commercial crops supplemented vegetables and coffee in the postwar economy: tobacco for consumption within East Africa — a centuries'-old trade crop — and wattle bark.[21]

The expansion of sisal, peasant cash crops, and erosion control, along with population growth, all consumed land in the postwar years, moving the economy rapidly towards land scarcity. Sisal plantations expanded onto the best plains land, which might have served the overflowing mountain population. The plantations attracted immigrants — enterprising workers from other parts of the territory who settled permanently with their families at *mwisho wa shamba*, just beyond the borders of the estates. By 1948 the recent arrivals formed 20% of the Luengera Valley's population, between East and West Usambara (Mhando 1977:120). In

the mountains, cash-hungry farmers changed their food plots and grazing land over to coffee or vegetable farming. Food plots shrank in any
event because the government pressed, from the 1930s, for peasants to
take more and more land for contour hedges to control erosion. Cattle,
now deprived of grazing, trampled the hedges, frustrating government
agents and farmers.[22]

It is difficult to state precisely how scarce land was in postwar Shambaai. Agricultural officers certainly thought it was, but their judgments
were often wrong during those years. Nevertheless, numerous indirect
indicators suggest that land shortage was significant, and, what is more
important, they illuminate how that scarcity affected the shape of the
local economy.

Land cases rose rapidly in frequency, especially at Bumbuli and Gare.
African squatters, who were tolerated in forest reserves and on European
estates so long as land was plentiful and the squatters not too numerous,
now found they were unwelcome. The government tried to remove squatters from Shume in 1947, with forest evictions in other places continuing
in the early 1950s. In 1952 Ambangulu Estate placed new restrictive conditions on squatter occupation.[23]

District administrators estimated in 1952 that one-third of all taxpayers worked at some time during the year for sisal estates or for contrac-
tors on estates. Young men from Mlalo went off to work at Nairobi, Tanga,
and Mombasa.[24] Some men stayed in town for years. These virtually
always retained their share in farms at home — in food *shambas* for women
left behind and in coffee land worked by the stay-at-home brothers. The
number of men who held land in the mountains almost always exceeded
the actual number living in the mountains. The system resembled a bank
with obligations to account-holders that were larger than liquid assets.
The bank functions because only a few customers at a time demand their
money. Pity the day in Shambaai when everyone moves home.

One great threat to continuity in the peasant economy came from the
loss of grazing land. Herds increased at just the time grazing shrank. By
January 1942 Chief Daffa of Lushoto decided to convert a large area of
pasture at Ubiri into farm land.[25] The pasture research officer at Mlalo
in 1945 reported that cattle had no room for grazing, "in some cases hardly
any room for walking or even standing."[26] Popular perceptions confirmed
the expert judgment. The radicals of 1947, listing grievances against the
Paramount Chief, demanded: "Why is it that there is no pasture land
for our animals?" Good political management, they thought, would ensure a proper balance between pasture and farming.[27]

The scarcity of land led to a scarcity of women's work time. The more
scattered farm plots became because of scarcity, the further women had

to walk to reach them, and the further away also were the wild areas in which women found fuelwood. The enormous increase in male labor migration also placed more pressure on women's work time.

The government's agricultural officers saw the problem as one of soil erosion rather than one of scarce land and labor. They thought that declining yields in Shambaai were causing the crisis of scarcity and that with proper techniques the land could once again be made to bloom.

Planners assumed that the land would not be able to support the area's future population. They therefore introduced plans for labor-intensive erosion control, for removing land from cultivation, and for moving people out of the mountains. Saving the land from degradation was the urgent priority, so that a limited number of cultivators could continue to prosper.

New plans would require cultivators to build ridges on their land to prevent erosion, to remove all steep land (sloped more than twenty-five degrees) from annual cultivation, and to plant elephant grass for stall-feeding cattle to solve the problem of lost grazing. But for a woman pushing at the limit of her labor time, the requirements of ridging were disastrous, and for people short of land, it was unthinkable to remove steep farms from use.

Where would the displaced mountain people go? The early government plans called for building small factories in the mountains, staffed by dispossessed farmers. Then the hope was for plains settlements using tractors to clear land, but most plains land was poorer than the officials imagined, and sisal took the best. In the end, the men of Shambaai were to become a sisal-growing proletariat. As the district commissioner explained in 1951, "It has often been suggested that some form of industrial outlet will have to be supplied to absorb some part of the rapidly increasing population. This outlet is not however so urgent as it would appear at first sight. Already the many sisal estates that ring round the mountain area offer an immense field of varied and well paid employment for many years to come."[28]

The Policy Background to the Usambara Scheme

The plan to increase agricultural productivity and industrial productivity by moving peasants off their land was a departure from interwar economic policy, which put its greatest emphasis on preserving the stability of peasant life. This was part of a more general shift in Tanganyika's direction in the postwar years, with roots in the 1930s. The labor advisor to the secretary of state for the colonies wrote, after a visit to East Africa, that the region needed a new economic framework: "The fact has to be faced . . . that the former balance has largely disappeared; subsistence from the tribal land, and cash from exportable goods or wages, is no longer the generally applicable solution of the African's needs" (Orde-Browne 1946:20). The rural policy that made each district, and even each house-hold, self-reliant in meeting its food needs had been coordinated with a labor policy which relied on migrant men temporarily away from their subsistence homes.

Now, in the postwar period, the government wanted to raise the efficiency of industrial or plantation laborers and to raise farm productivity at the same time. Erosion control was tied to a set of policies regulating agriculture in general, as well as wage employment, urbanization, and the politics of chiefship.

Along with the shift in policy came a "second colonial occupation"— a vast increase in the number of colonial officers, and therefore in the capacity of government to impose change. Two-thirds of Tanganyika's administrative officers in 1950 had been appointed since 1944 (Iliffe 1979: 443; Cliffe 1972). The change was not only one of numbers. The expansion reduced the influence of omnicompetent district officers and increased the reliance on technical staff within each district. Erosion control was now the special project of agricultural officers who used chiefs as subordinate functionaries — a means to the central goal of improved farming.

Britain in the postwar years incurred enormous debts to the United States and pushed to expand production of raw materials in the colonies to take the place of imports from the United States and other parts of the world paid for in dollars. They spent more than £35 million in Tanganyika during the late 1940s on an ill-fated scheme to grow groundnuts using machinery. Out of the same desire to increase production, the government doubled the number of settlers in Tanganyika between 1948 and 1958 (from 10,648 to 20,498) and increased the amount of land alienated for settlement. The government also encouraged progressive African farmers — the ones investing in land, labor, and machinery — to grow larger quantities for the market. White settlement and the expansion of capitalist African farming would necessarily undercut the self-sufficiency of some peasant farmers by reducing the amount of land available in particular localities and by encouraging some peasants to work as laborers rather than on their own land.[29]

Another way to increase overall levels of production was through soil conservation methods. These would enable peasants to produce more (whether for market or subsistence) without using more land. Conservation measures would also preserve the soil for future generations. At this time planners around British-controlled Africa were imposing conservation schemes as a response to the many sources of pressure on the land: expanded African production, the rapid growth of the African population, and the growth of competition by European settlers for the land. Soil conservation was a way of fitting more Africans onto a small amount of land (Anderson 1984; Beinart 1984). Planners did not want to drive peasants off their land wholesale, for this would create a large and explosive pool of unemployed in the towns. The planners were later to discover that erosion control was itself capable of causing political explosions (Throup 1988).

Those peasants who did leave the land were expected to become members of a newly stabilized work force. Colonial planners had two different reasons for moving towards stabilized labor in the cities. The first, as Frederick Cooper has shown, is that casual migrant labor proved to be a dangerous form of labor organization (1987: chap. 6). Men who were sometimes workers, sometimes farmers, and sometimes members of the urban unemployed had rich networks of social ties beyond the workplace. In strikes in the West Indies between 1935 and 1938, and then in Africa after that, migrant laborers showed themselves capable of using their roots in the wider community to draw nonworkers into labor disputes. If there was no clear separation between workers and nonworkers, then labor disputes easily expanded into politically dangerous riots or general strikes.

Second, a migrant labor force was an unskilled one, no longer adequate for the period when factories were expected to produce goods within the empire to take the place of goods imported from outside, paid for in dollars. Manufacturers needed to keep workers on the job long enough for them to develop skills and then beyond that to give a good return on the investment in skills. This could only be done if women and children came to the place of work, having broken their ties with self-sufficient farms. Manufacturing did not grow rapidly in Tanganyika, but workers from the north of the territory worked in Kenyan factories, and others settled permanently with their wives and children near the sisal estates, which also wanted a more stable labor force. Once again, policy needs were mixed, for permanent workers needed expensive housing, education, and health services for their families, and expected higher pay. If employment shrank, or if job-seekers settled in town without finding jobs, a large body of dangerous urban unemployed could grow up. Employers and administrators wanted a carefully modulated proletarianization. As late as 1956 the chairman of the Rhodesian Selection Trust suggested that Northern Rhodesia's copper-belt workers (some from Tanganyika) ought to be stabilized without becoming urbanized, meaning that he hoped workers would remain on the job for their whole working lives but then return home to the countryside after leaving work (Prain 1956).

The postwar economic changes, taken all together, transformed the earlier dual system, in which women provided subsistence on farms at home while men earned cash, either at a distant workplace or by growing a set of commercial crops separate from and complementary to the subsistence ones. Men would now settle at the workplace with their wives and children, breaking the link between low wages and the subsistence agriculture which subsidized them. The specialized production of food crops would be needed to feed workers and the new city dwellers. Credit would be available for progressive farmers to expand rapidly, and not merely to produce a small margin over subsistence.

The dual system now under attack had from its start been the economic base of indirect rule. The changes subjected chiefs to intense pressure, first of all in a very practical way — by requiring them to administer conservation rules to control soil erosion, for example. More generally, the new economy put chiefship in a contradictory position, in several important ways. The administrators of the 1920s had intended that chiefship would reinforce old political ideas about the moral causes of prosperity and well-being. The restoration of chiefs in Shambaai in the 1920s confirmed peasants in their assumption that harming the land and healing the land controlled hunger and satiety. Now British administrators were looking for new educated chiefs who would convince people that their well-being depended on controlling soil erosion. Indirect rule had also tried to reinforce the perception among local farmers that local forces, defined within the boundaries of small political units, determined well-being. In the new context, however, some people from within any particular locality would need to migrate to a workplace outside those old boundaries and possibly give up the land which had been the basis of subsistence. If the logic of agricultural productivity required, a farmer could be asked to give up a piece of land within an old chiefdom and take distant land in return. Another of the basic elements of indirect rule was rural homogeneity. Each farmer worked for subsistence and then a bit besides. All were in the same boat, all dependent on their chief for prosperity. Agricultural improvement and specialization of production to the places where it was most advantageous, and in the hands of the most suitable farmers, split apart that homogeneity of interest and left the chief as an arbiter of forces in powerful conflict.

Planners were well aware that they were buying economic change at the cost of local political stability. The labor advisor to the secretary of state for the colonies explained that the new economic policies would undermine chiefship and the politics of tradition in East Africa, but that the upheaval was unavoidable:

The time has now come when a departure from traditional methods must be contemplated, and the desirability of a new adjustment to modern requirements must be considered in view of the increasing inadequacy of the old economy. Such a change would entail numerous implications; a large measure of departure from tribal custom and tradition would be inevitable, and the administrative problems involved would be complicated and difficult (Orde-Browne 1946:24).

When the colonial government decided in the 1920s on a political and economic course for Tanganyika, they had an approximate sense of their preferred direction for the future of local political expression. The peasant economy was to remain relatively unproductive, the politics localized and stable, and the political culture to be based on local forms expressed in local languages. Educated Christians would be the only counterweight to cultural localism. This elite would never threaten to incite political upheaval because they would necessarily be few in number and inspired by conservative religious values. After World War II the policymakers decided to aim for higher economic productivity and therefore to abandon the economic basis of localism, but they hoped the majority of people would continue to focus their political passions on local issues, direct their frustrations at local leaders, and use traditional political language to do this. Peasant political leaders refused to accept the narrow role planned for them. They thought for themselves; Tanganyika's course was not at all easily predictable.

The Introduction of the Usambara Scheme

When Kimweri Mputa Magogo took office as Paramount, the erosion-control scheme was still limited to Mlalo, where it was having severe difficulties in its pilot phase. The British hoped the new Paramount would help to move the scheme forward over what appeared to them the passive opposition of Mlalo's chief, Hassani Kinyashi. The agricultural officers, in their eagerness to move the scheme forward, placed Kimweri in an impossible position of conflict with one of the great rain chiefs of Shambaai. Hassani Kinyashi was the rainmaker whose removal from office in 1942 was followed by four years of famine, then by huge popular demonstrations demanding his return to office, and finally by his return.

In later years, through all the struggles of the movement to independence, Hassani never lost the support of his subjects. I was at Mlalo in 1966, five years after national independence, a time when Hassani had already been pensioned off as a subchief. The people of the chiefdom continued to provide him with labor tribute in the hope that the drought which followed his retirement would not be repeated. In that same year Hassani ran for election to the District Council. His opponent claimed that Kilindi in general and Hassani in particular were irrelevant to the needs of Shambaai. Hassani refused to campaign. Within electoral boundaries which included the oldest Christian community in the mountains, which was also one of the largest, the old chief won the election 1496 votes to 80 (Mnkondo 1968:16). He won even though nationalist sentiment was at its peak and the constituency substantially Christian, because he was capable of healing the land.

At the start of Kimweri's reign, the young king, with no reputation for rain and little popular support, was expected to discipline Hassani Kinyashi. The results were bound to be disastrous for Kimweri's reputation. In August 1948, two months after Kimweri took office, he visited Mlalo together with the provincial commissioner. They held a meeting attended also by the district commissioner, the provincial agricultural officer, the provincial medical officer, and others. The provincial commissioner announced that chief Hassani Kinyashi would be left in office only to make rain and that he would be given an administrative assistant to be paid out of his wages to handle all practical matters. According to the commissioner's account,

> Kimweri Mputa Magogo said a few words exhorting the people to back up the scheme under the new organisation. . . . At this point Sub-Chief Hassani asked for permission to speak. He pointed out that he was not a rain-maker, which caused considerable surprise to all present, and that if the Government thought him inefficient he wished to resign forthwith. I at once accepted his resignation. . . . It is interesting . . . to note that when dismissed in 1942 he declared openly that he would cause a drought in that same year.[30]

Kimweri Magogo thus found himself linked in popular understanding with the erosion-control scheme and with Hassani Kinyashi's resignation, both of them intensely unpopular among the vast majority of local people. The Paramount probably saw Hassani Kinyashi's resignation as a positive step towards achieving Vugha's long-term goal: the subjugation of the Mlalo Kilindi.

In 1949 the district authorities chose as Hassani Kinyashi's replacement at Mlalo a headman who had been willing to use force in imposing the erosion-control scheme. As soon as the new man became subchief, he removed any of the headmen who did not support the scheme. The result, according to Governor Twining after his visit to Mlalo, was that the Agricultural Department achieved "100 percent hostility to the scheme" on the part of local people, who detested it. Local Africans explained to Twining that they had "no intention of cultivating the land in the way . . . expected of them."[31]

When resistance grew strong enough to stop the Mlalo project altogether, the authorities decided to apply the scheme to the whole of Shambaai. They wanted to escape from the politics of Mlalo's chiefship and from the awkward beginnings of the pilot scheme. The expanded working plan drawn up in February 1950 explained, "It is desirable that the scheme should lose, absolutely and at the outset, any local connotations of the kind which grew around it during the demonstration period in the Mlalo Basin. Every sub-chief and every sub-chiefdom must be implicated if *general* interest and acceptance are fostered rather than local alarm."[32]

Implementation of the scheme began in 1950. In July Kimweri's council approved the scheme rules. In the months that followed every subchief's council was to select a single headman's area (a *jumbeate*) as the first demonstration unit. Each taxpayer was required to put a measured area of land under tie-ridge cultivation, with the area to be increased in each successive year, and with additional *jumbeates* to be added in successive years.

The scheme rules were intended from the start as a way to inform cultivators that they would lose land. The agricultural authorities took the first practical steps by placing markers to define any land steeper than twenty-five degrees. "The beacons will serve as notice to all concerned that the exclusion of the hill sides above the beacons from cultivation may take effect within a period of six months to one year. . . . The erection of the beacons will be the first overt sign to the people of a selected Jumbeate that their traditional land-usage is to be curtailed. The period of warning will give any family seriously affected an opportunity to seek a supplement of land elsewhere."[33] The agricultural authorities knew that land was in short supply, and that "the application of the land utilisation principles themselves must accentuate the existing shortages at least temporarily."[34] The planners of the late 1940s expected the Shambaa to need large amounts of additional land (some said a million acres) for a stable and prosperous agricultural system.[35] The additional land was to be found in the vast underpopulated lowlands around the edges of the mountains and in neighboring Handeni District.

As the scheme progressed, it became clear that adequate additional land would not be found. Agricultural officers experimented diligently in the plains, but found that much of the available land was saline, that rainfall was inadequate for secure agriculture, that the bits of well-watered land had already been taken by sisal estates, that water was inadequate for irrigation, and that the planned crops failed.[36] The monthly agricultural reports on experimental plots in 1952, for example, describe efforts at Sekilago, where maize was a total failure, baboons took the groundnuts grown on nonsaline plots, and nine plots out of ten made substantial monetary losses. At Mombo, only five experimental plots out of forty-seven made a profit. The buckwheat was spoiled by cattle, the Indian millet by birds, the groundnuts cut across by ants, and the maize dead except on a few plots.[37]

After the experiments, the district authorities reported in 1953 that the land situation in the district (which at that time included the large sisal estates and barren plains of Korogwe subdistrict) was as shown in Table 6.1. The awareness that plains land was insufficient for dispossessed mountain people came only after the scheme had been enforced for some time. In the early days, as we have seen, the scheme was meant to send Lushoto's people the message that they ought to find land outside the mountains.

Resistance began immediately. Women invaded a number of subchiefs' meetings in the early months of the scheme to make clear their opposition. The *District Annual Report* described them as "squads of well rehearsed female stormtroops, who chanted in unison their dislike of ridge cultivation."[38] Opposition was especially intense in Mgwashi, where many of the men would not help with ridging because they preferred to cut wild sisal, at which they could earn three times the usual unskilled wage. In October 1950 Mgwashi's women came to a required work party carrying tiny weeding hoes inadequate for the assigned tasks.[39] At the same time, the men living near Lushoto sent their cows off to the plains, closing down their business of selling milk to the Europeans and forcing Lushoto's settlers to do without milk in their tea.[40] Men all over the moun-

Table 6.1. District Commissioner's Estimate of Land Availability,
       Lushoto District, 1953

Land Utilization	Acres
Total area of Lushoto District (including what is now Korogwe District)	1,717,000
Total area at present unsuitable for crop husbandry, supporting live-stock, of which 90,000 acres reclaimable by expensive capital projects	1,003,000
Total area alienated	364,400
Total area of government and Native Authority Forest Reserve	153,100
Total African-controlled land under crops	153,000
Balance remaining for grazing, food crops, for approximately 45,000 head of cattle, and for Shambaa expansion	43,500

Source: PVH, "Mlalo Rehabilitation Scheme," p. 246: D. C. Lushoto (R. H. J. Thorne) and A. O. Lushoto to the Royal Commission.

tains raised confusing disputes about land ownership, making it difficult to enforce ridging. They resurrected old boundary fights, or claimed to own only tiny fragments of land, smaller than the required half acre. In 1951 the people of Vugha sabotaged the scheme by uprooting the banana plants used as field markers.[41]

Mlalo, where the conflict started, was one of the subchiefdoms where resistance was kept under control during the early days of the Usambara Scheme. The district authorities insisted on imposing the Scheme, but then also returned Hassani Kinyashi to office in November 1950. The influential peasants of Mlalo asked Hassani Kinyashi to present himself to the district commissioner as a supporter of the scheme. They in turn would modulate their resistance so as not to threaten Hassani's hold on office. In any event the commissioner was not eager to challenge Hassani, whose temporary replacement as subchief had been so unhinged by the opposition that he went down on his knees with gratitude when given permission to resign.[42]

The result of the agreement between Hassani and his subjects was that Mlalo, which had once supplied a large number of *chama* members, had only 191 members of the Usambara Citizens Union in January 1951, out of 3354 registered members. When the scheme's arduous demands led to resistance at Mlalo, as they did in 1952, the rebels made no move within their subchiefdom; rather, they planned to march on Vugha to remove Kimweri Magogo, the Paramount Chief, who had no rain and who had earlier removed Hassani from office.[43]

At the court of the other great rainmaker, Daudi Sozi, in Bumbuli, compliance was negligible through the early months of the scheme, and Sozi tried to evade responsibility by leaving the district officer with the impression that he was senile and incompetent. Then in March the district officer had sharp words with Sozi, and compliance began to improve, although even then some foot-dragging continued.[44] I discussed this period with many people at Bumbuli, none of whom suggested that Sozi was to be blamed for the scheme, even though he prosecuted people for land-use violations. A man who had been an intimate employee of Sozi's through the scheme period explained that everyone knew Sozi could not refuse to enforce the rules "because his father had been killed by the Europeans [in the German period]. Sozi would say, 'If I refuse, they will kill me, too.'" As in the case of Mlalo's people, the subjects resisted on their own, accepted the punishments given out by their chief, and worked to undermine the Paramount, who had no rain. As at Mlalo, few joined the Usambara Citizens Union.

At Vugha the popular opinion of the commoners, as remembered in the late 1960s, was clear: Kimweri Mputa Magogo did not control the rain. Even Kimweri's former courtiers agreed that this was the case. Back in the days of the scheme, Kimweri was the main target of popular anger. We have seen that he made the mistake at the very start of his reign of implicating himself in Hassani Kinyashi's temporary removal from office in Mlalo.

Kimweri Mputa Magogo likened himself to a nineteenth-century king, with his central aim to attack and remove sitting chiefs. He wanted to reach that point in the cycle of royal power when the king's own men would govern all the local chiefdoms. Kimweri explained a year later that "the seat which I have taken is the stool of Kimweri ye Nyumbai [the nineteenth-century king]. It was he who placed chiefs in each locality in Shambaai without asking for a vote or tracing out lines of birth. It is that custom which I received as a patrimony from Kimweri ye Nyumbai and which I continue to practice at the present time."[45] The nineteenth-century king had been able to impose his men on the chiefdoms because he held the major rain charms and because he had fighting men to enforce his will. His twentieth-century successor had neither.

Even though Kimweri Magogo had no armies to send into the field, some of his subjects assumed that because he was Simba Mwene, he must have the power to kill. In 1968 a young man at Vugha described how dangerous Kimweri Magogo had been. This was an account of an incident some years earlier involving a *kagho*, a protective medicine against sorcery, brought by a healer.

> She placed medicines along every path and road, so that sorcery charms would not get past. At that time Kimweri had a friend at Korogwe named Ngatiyani. The Simba Mwene was holding a celebration, and his friend Ngatiyani brought a huge number of *maandazi* (fried cakes) so that the people have them with tea. Ngatiyani's Mercedes climbed the mountain road, but then went over the edge and fell. When you got there you saw *maandazi* spread out all over. Kimweri wanted to try sorcery against us on that day, when his friend brought *maandazi* filled with medicines. But the protective *kagho* worked, and the car crashed.

According to this account, the *kagho* thwarted Kimweri Magogo's attempts to murder his subjects. Some men, in their recollections, interpreted the erosion-control scheme in similar terms, as Kimweri's plot to move Shambaa out to the plains, where they were likely to die of disease. In both cases the narrator presumed that Kimweri had the power to kill.

The popular presumption of Kimweri's power to kill was not effective enough, without the open use of violence, for Kimweri to impose his will on the chiefs. Kimweri Magogo removed Hassani Kinyashi from his position as chief of Mlalo, but could not eliminate Mlalo's *chama*, which once again merged the demand for rain with opposition to the erosion-control scheme. Kimweri, as we have seen, was unable to prevent Hassani from returning to office.

The weakness of Kimweri's support made him dependent on the British and left him with no choice but to enforce the scheme. This made him the object of the bitterest opposition from subjects in the areas near Vugha, who argued that he was harming the land and threatening subsistence. In July 1950, the month when Kimweri's council passed the scheme rules, the provincial commissioner at Tanga received a letter signed "From All your Subjects in Usambara." It began with expressions of respect and promises of obedience but ended by saying, "And now all of us, people of this country of Usambara, we say in a loud voice before the Lord God and before our Government that we have made ourselves completely ready — within a very short period we will strangle that person Kimweri Magogo."[46] In August and September of 1950, men from a number of chiefdoms in southern Shambaai gathered at Ubiri near Lushoto to organize a *chama* to remove Kimweri.[47] In September Isaka Hoza, one of those men, found himself arrested at Vugha on trumped-up charges, jailed, and beaten. In March 1951 the local subchief at Vugha reported finding 10,000 shillings which had been raised in contributions for paying a man who would agree to murder Kimweri Magogo.[48]

Even at this time the people who opposed Kimweri did not usually describe their actions as attacks against chiefship. Jaha Mtoi, one of the central organizers of the *chama* at Ubiri, was a proud Kilindi himself, senior to Kimweri in the dynasty, and disturbed by the Paramount's actions. The commoners among Kimweri's enemies felt free to oppose him because in their eyes he was not a chief at all, but merely a paid employee of the British. They had seen Kimweri's father, Shebughe Magogo, in the same light: "His main job is to wait for the end of the month to collect his salary."[49] Now, in 1951, they wrote that Kimweri was an *akida*, like the agents imposed by the Germans — men without local roots. "Remember the words of Bwana D. C. Piggott when he said, 'The Government, together with the Mlughu and six elders of Vugha, has chosen a ruler of Shambaai. As for all of you Shambaa, whether you want him or not is your own affair.'"[50] Kimweri's most vehement enemies thought he was willing to lose the land of Shambaai in return for pay and perks. Kimweri saw himself as a true representative of Shambaa interests, preventing disastrous losses to the Shambaa by serving the British loyally, so that he could control them.

The Usambara Citizens Union

The peasant focus on chiefship and on the relationship between the dynasty and its subjects derived in part from government action shaping the *chama*. In 1948 district authorities outlawed the local African Association and destroyed its connection with the Tanganyika African Association (TAA) in Dar es Salaam.[51] Leaders of the TAA were thinking about territorial issues rather than parochial ones. Association with them might have led local peasant intellectuals to understand their own problems in national terms. The ban in Shambaai was meant to prevent just this outcome.[52]

In 1951 the rebels against the Scheme and against Kimweri wanted to get help from outside Shambaai, but having lost the option of joining up with the TAA, they chose allies who reinforced their tendency to define issues in dynastic terms. They decided at a meeting in January to send representatives outside the district to consult with leaders of the Kilimanjaro Union (KU). The KU focused on Kilimanjaro's own local issues having to do with chiefly control over land allocation, with the inadequacy of local expenditures for schools and development, and with the need to win control over chiefship back from Tanganyika's colonial rulers. The KU in this period wanted to install an elected Paramount Chief who would be responsive to the wishes of Kilimanjaro's Chagga people and not to the orders of British administrators (Rogers 1972: chap 8).

The *chama* leaders returned home from Kilimanjaro to found the Usambara Citizens Union (UCU). It was like the Kilimanjaro Union in two important respects: it directed attention towards local issues (in this case the Usambara Scheme), and it expected that chiefs would provide leadership so long as they were popularly chosen and responsive to popular wishes. For this reason the sources of chiefly legitimacy remained central to the political debate. In the draft bylaws, the conditions of UCU membership were strictly ethnic: only indigenous people of Usambara were eligible for membership, with others restricted to nonresident status and even then accepted only after two witnesses had provided references. The shape of the Usambara Citizens Union as a resistance movement showed the profound influence of indirect rule, with its emphasis on chiefly politics and bounded ethnic groups.[53]

In spite of this, the administration saw the UCU as a serious threat. In May 1951 the district commissioner declared the organization illegal and consented to the imprisonment of five UCU leaders. These actions drove the Union underground, although it reappeared at a later stage, and its most active members continued to work against the scheme and against the Paramount.[54]

The suppression of the UCU left district authorities free to intensify scheme enforcement. They placed new *jumbeates* under scheme rules in 1952, even though they were leaving some people landless.[55] It would have been difficult to create a plan more likely to drive peasants to revolt.

When open resistance came, as it did during the cold months of 1952, it was directed against Kimweri Magogo as Paramount Chief and not against the British, and it used precolonial means of communication. During the month of August, men at a number of places around Shambaai — Mlalo, Gare, Soni, and Bumbuli — began to plan a march on Vugha to remove Kimweri Magogo. They attacked Kimweri because his council had passed the Usambara Scheme rules, and because he used the weight of his office to support them. In meetings at Mlalo for the north of Shambaai and Soni for the south the rebels agreed to go home, to wait until 2:00 p.m. on 26 August, and then to beat drums at places around Shambaai, calling people out for a march on Vugha.

Drums had been used in the precolonial period for assembling a fighting force against invaders. Back in the Bondei revolt of the nineteenth century, the rebels had counted the time until they acted by tying knots in banana fiber, with one knot to be cut off each day before the revolt. In the abortive revolt of 1952, the rebels wrote letters to one another and used calendars and watches to coordinate their actions, but the sound of the war drums was to move all countryfolk into unified action for what the rebels described as the "penetration" of Vugha.[56]

The revolt failed. At each of the four centers, a handful of men beat the drums, but the peasant army never appeared and never marched on Vugha. Perhaps the great body of cultivators needed a more radical political program. The Wakiva of the 1860s had risen en masse to remove all the Kilindi, not merely to replace a single chief. But in 1952, in order to succeed in removing all chiefs or in ending the Usambara Scheme, local forces would have needed first to remove the British, and this must have seemed impossible. The political goals of the revolt were neither radical enough nor practical enough. The rebels, caught in the rhetoric of dynastic politics, fought to remove Kimweri. But if they had succeeded, Kimweri's place would have been taken by another Paramount, and the scheme would have gone ahead. The language of indirect rule served its purpose: it directed the revolt into narrow channels.

The rebels at Gare were immediately arrested and taken into the custody of the chief, Hamisi Mwanyoka, whose house they had burned on the night of 27 August. Hamisi's main claims to authority were personal loyalty to Kimweri Magogo and a willingness to use repression against his subjects. In fact the person found guilty of burning Hamisi's house was a Kilindi with a more appropriate claim to the seat at Gare then Hamisi himself. At Vugha, the rebels had to deal with Kimweri's own agents. Even at Mlalo, however, the rebels were arrested. Hassani Kinyashi would probably have liked to see the Paramount deposed, but it was impossible for any government agent, even one who controlled the rain, openly to support popular rebellion. Eleven of the rebels, many of whom had been among the founders of the Usambara Citizens Union, were held in jail. They were tried in Tanga for conspiring against the lawful power and authority of a chief, for attempting to undermine the lawful power and authority of a chief, and for contravening the order of a Native Authority. In January 1953, all were sentenced to three months' imprisonment with hard labor.[57]

With the rebel leaders imprisoned and the opposition disarmed, district authorities were now free to push the Usambara Scheme rapidly forward. The scheme, which had expanded only slowly between 1950 and 1952, now quickly spread to cover additional territories. By the end of 1954 three-fourths of all the small administrative units (*jumbeates*) were covered by the Scheme.[58]

Local peasant resistance, which had been fierce, filling the courts in 1952 (the year of the drum-beating and the abortive march on Vugha), cooled after the imprisonment of their leaders in 1953 and then intensified again in the following year, as we can see from the chart of criminal court cases in Table 6.2. Lushoto's Annual Report attributes the 1954 increase to wider application of the scheme rules. The numbers therefore indicate something about the level of enforcement as well as the level of resistance. Noncompliance and resistance on the individual garden plots were accompanied by a resurgence of organized resistance which, in the short time of a few years, was to challenge the existence and legitimacy of colonial rule in Tanganyika.

Table 6.2. Criminal Court Cases at Courts of the First Instance,
    Lushoto Division

Year	Number of Cases
1951	1740
1952	2262
1953	1349
1954	2177
1955	1724

Source: TNA, 72/62/6/IV, 12A, Lushoto *Division Annual Report* (1954), and TNA, 72/62/6, 21A, *Usambara Scheme Annual Report* (1955).

The mid-1950s were years when the political respectability of resistance grew rapidly among the peasant intellectuals of Shambaai. In 1954 Kimweri's own chief minister (*Mlughu*), Zem Shemsanga, joined the opposition. By early 1956 the renowned rain-making chief of Mlalo, Hassani Kinyashi, was publicly welcoming Julius Nyerere to the court of his chiefdom. Nyerere had been to the United Nations in New York to argue the case for an independent Tanganyika. He was intent on drawing local resistance associations into his movement for national liberation. By 1957 thousands of Shambaa would be paying monthly dues to the Tanganyika African National Union (TANU), the political party which was to govern an independent Tanzania.[59]

The rapidity of political change was not at all expected in the Shambaai of 1954, although Zem Shemsanga's change in allegiance from Kimweri Magogo to the rebels was a significant step. He had been a mission teacher, then Chief Minister to Shebughe Magogo during that king's abdication struggle in 1947. After that he was an officer in The Hope of Usambara, the conservative political organization formed by the friends of Kimweri Magogo; then he was Kimweri's tutor in the English language, and then once again he served as *Mlughu*, this time for Kimweri Magogo. Now, in opposition, he had the advantage of understanding Kimweri's court from the inside.[60]

Zem worked closely in opposition with Theodore Isaka, a former "tribal dresser" who fought Kimweri from the start and experienced arrest, beatings, and harassment. Theodore Isaka was searching for a strategy that would achieve popular goals yet somehow reduce the threat of arrest. One of Theodore's reasons for shaping the Usambara Citizens Union as an ethnic movement, in imitation of the Kilimanjaro Union, is that the KU leader seemed well accepted by the British authorities. As Theodore saw it, Petro Njau was a "best friend" of the Governor.[61]

Theodore Isaka, Zem Shemsanga, and others worked to win government registration for the Usambara Citizens Union. Under the Registration of Societies Ordinance, passed in 1954, any group denied registration was banned from political activity. Even though the UCU was ethnically based, and the British, as we have seen, had pushed all local politics in an ethnic direction, the local authorities denied registration because they mistrusted UCU's leaders, and they also suddenly found ethnic resistance threatening.

The British were caught up, just across the Kenya border, in the war they called *Mau Mau* and which they characterized as a tribal war. They kept a wary eye on political movements and local incidents of violence in Shambaai, in fear of Mau Mau's spread. They also carefully watched all Kenya-connected Africans in Lushoto district. The Shambaa enemies of the Usambara Citizens Union accused it of "a feeling of Mau Mau."[62] The district authorities brought in the assistant superintendent of police from Northern Province to make special investigations. The paramilitary Mobile Company, based in Tanga, was in the district on and off from June.[63] Theodore Isaka's dream of building a political movement without bringing down repression on its founders might well have seemed unattainable.

At this point Theodore Isaka and Zem Shemsanga found a solution to their problem, one which had already been tried on Mt. Meru. They collected money, hired a lawyer, and submitted a series of protest petitions to the Trusteeship Council of the United Nations, beginning in August 1954. Tanganyika (unlike Kenya) was a trust territory; the United Nations therefore served as a forum that was independent of the government in Lushoto, or Tanga, or Dar es Salaam, or even London. The Trusteeship Council did not in the end call for changes in the administration of Shambaai, although the petitions might have had an effect in making the district commissioner more circumspect than he might have been without U.N. supervision.

With the paramilitary Mobile Company in place and all open challenges to Kimweri Magogo suppressed, the district agricultural authorities moved ahead as quickly as possible to implement the Usambara Scheme. In 1954 local chiefs tried great numbers of their subjects for criminal violation of the scheme's rules. Areas subject to the rules expanded more rapidly in 1954 than in any other year. The government attempted to achieve scheme coverage of all peasants in 1955. The main measures were a phased introduction of tie-ridging on slopes that were not very steep and the replacement of annuals with perennials on steep slopes.[64]

The scheme drove cultivators into the arms of the resistance. The district commissioner reported a "hardening of herts" (sic) against chiefs who did not have rain.[65] Even as their popularity grew, the leaders of the resistance tried to find publicly acceptable forms of organization. In February 1955 the Kilimanjaro Union opened a branch at Mombo in order to provide the Usambara Citizens Union with an organizational shell. To the district commissioner, any political organization which included Theodore Isaka and Zem Shemsanga was unacceptable. He repeatedly called the UCU leaders to meetings at the district office, which they found threatening. In August he had Shemsanga and Isaka arrested for a few days.[66] They continued to send petitions to the United Nations. All the while, a consensus grew among the local peasants that both Kimweri and the scheme were unacceptable. Difficult as it is to detect rapid shifts in opinion using the available sources, the growth of opposition is clear.

The Defeat of the Usambara Scheme

The struggle between peasants and the British entered a new phase in January 1956 with Julius Nyerere's arrival in Shambaai. His plans called for him to visit Korogwe, Mombo, Vugha, Soni, Lushoto, Mlalo, Bumbuli, Bungu, and Vugiri.[67] Local people were deeply impressed that he was touring the country openly, not in prison, even though he openly said the words which peasant intellectuals sometimes thought but feared to say. As Theodore Isaka explained, "The Shambaa were amazed that this person [Nyerere] could say openly to the government that they ought to leave so that we can take charge of our country ourselves." The Usambara Citizens Union leaders were convinced, at some point either during or after Nyerere's visit, that the needs of Shambaai would be met by a national movement.[68]

When local people tell stories about the visit of 1956, as they often do, they talk about Nyerere's special friends and local contacts — people like Theodore Isaka — and then also about the reactions of men in the Kilindi dynasty. Kimweri prohibited Nyerere from using the Vugha marketplace to speak; the chief of Bungu forbade his subjects to attend the local meeting. Other chiefs, rainmakers like Hassani Kinyashi or Daudi Sozi who were secure in the support of their subjects, did not oppose Nyerere's visit. Control over the rain went together with acceptance of secular nationalism.

Even though Nyerere was allowed to speak in January of 1956, district authorities effectively banned TANU for most of the next two years. They refused to allow meetings unless chiefs could attend to instruct people on the Usambara Scheme. They arrested men collecting money for TANU[69] and also imprisoned Zem Shemsanga for a period. They kept the Motorized Company in the district for most of 1956. The district commissioner denied TANU's request for legal registration with a justification that deflected hostility to Kimweri Magogo. The commissioner explained that TANU's leaders did not enjoy Kimweri's trust (*TANU na Wananchi Lushoto* 1975:10–11).

At the same time, the district commissioner loosened up restraints on the Usambara Citizens Union, which he may have seen at this point as the lesser evil, preferable to TANU. The UCU held a meeting in April and opened an office in August.[70] The distinction between the UCU and the local TANU is in some sense artificial. When former participants from Vugha remember those years, they speak of the *chama*, "the association," and it is unclear (unless they elaborate) whether they mean the Usambara Citizens Union, the earlier Tanganyika African Association, or TANU, or any of the very local aggregations of peasant political activists. It is natural for the organizations to merge in memory as "the association," for a coherent core of local leaders moved from one organization to another as conditions required. One of the citizens union leaders at Vugha described how, at a certain point, the UCU simply became the local TANU organization. Seen from Mlalo or Bumbuli, the picture looks slightly different; people from those places who had not been in the UCU joined TANU, as did some new people in southwestern Shambaai.

By mid-1957 the peasant resistance, working together with TANU, changed the political landscape of Shambaai. They forced the British to abandon the Usambara Scheme, which ended as a functioning plan on 30 July 1957 with the abolition of penal sanctions for rule violations. The Native Authority dismissed fifty-seven scheme patrolmen who had become unpopular as scheme enforcers. The entire staff of British agricultural officers left in 1957 and 1958; their association with the scheme had made it impossible for them to work in Shambaai. In an election to the *Bawanjama*, Kimweri Magogo's Council, fewer than 15 percent of the electorate voted. After TANU won its first election in 1958, the agricultural officer wrote, "It would appear that the Native Authority have lost control over a certain section of the people."[71] Indeed they had.

7

The Struggle over Erosion Control:
Women's Farming and the
Politics of Subsistence

The fight against the Usambara Scheme was a battle to preserve the social safety net for poor peasants and to retard the emergence of a fully capitalist agriculture. The defeat of the Usambara Scheme therefore shaped crucial elements in the local economy for the remainder of the twentieth century. Acceptance of the scheme would have left prosperous farmers free to expand land holdings and to charge rent for subsistence land which, always until then, the poor had been able to borrow without payment. The poorest farmers, many of whom would have been driven off the land under scheme rules, fought successfully to preserve the right of every resident of Shambaai to the free use of land for subsistence. The right to land carried with it the benefit of participating in a network of kinsfolk who helped one another through the daily crises of rural life.

The Consequences of Erosion Control

The requirements of the erosion-control scheme seem modest when measured against the present claim that they would have brought revolutionary change to Shambaai. The scheme did not claim to be changing the rules of land tenure. The most significant aspect of the scheme was the requirement that moderately steep land on mountain slopes be put under tie ridges running along the hillsides. The ridges were about a meter apart from ridge-top to ridge-top, with similarly spaced ridges running down the hill face. The ridges were called *matuta*, a word which even now can evoke memories of struggle among those who lived through the period. The overall pattern of *matuta* was a grid of raised squares. Rainwater filled the depressed center of each square and then sank slowly into the earth instead of streaming off the hillside. In a sense the *matuta* were an alternative or a supplement to the work of rain chiefs who were

181

expected to bring gentle rains which would slowly soak the hillsides.

If the regime of *matuta* had survived, it would have brought some benefits to the wealthier of the men, who would now receive rents or labor for subsistence land. We shall see that the burden of constructing *matuta* did not fall most heavily on these men, for they could afford to build tie ridges using hired labor or collective work parties. The regime of *matuta* threatened people who were poor in land, in cash, and in social support, especially women. It struck with special danger at women whose husbands were away (most of them on sisal plantations) working for wages.[1]

The central danger of erosion control was that it would deprive the poor of their rights to land in Shambaai. It was this real threat which gave force to the bitter complaint that the British had drawn a plan to drive the Shambaa out of their mountains. The regime of *matuta* was bound to convert land freely available to the poor into a category of land used only by cash-cropping men.

At the heart of the matter was the division of the gardens of Shambaai between two categories. There was land with permanent crops or permanent improvements: coffee farms on which the trees were a long-term investment, or vegetable farms on which peasants invested money or labor in terracing. These were almost always reserved for men's use, and rights in use were guarded carefully. The owner who made an investment in trees or in terracing expected to reap its profits. He did not intend to lend out this land. Coffee was often planted in the banana garden which, we have seen, was the masculine garden, and which would in some cases have been saleable even in the nineteenth century.

The second type of garden was treated very differently. This was the garden which was sometimes left fallow and sometimes planted in maize. Even in the nineteenth century many such plots were allocated to women by their husbands. Maize was planted on land without permanent improvements, land whose first purpose was to win subsistence, even if harvests beyond subsistence needs were sold for cash. Putting in *matuta* on this land converted it to land of the other type. The peasant farmers of Shambaai were not conservative in technical matters: local men voluntarily and spontaneously terraced vegetable plots. Peasants resisted building ridges on subsistence land because this would convert it into men's cash-crop land unavailable for flexible seasonal land loans and unavailable also to people poor in land.[2]

The rule of peasant land use in Shambaai in the 1950s was that no one with local roots, no matter how poor, should be forced to go without maize land for subsistence. Proletarianization, the creation of a landless class, the process of driving people out of the mountains, was unacceptable in Shambaai. Any peasant who did not have enough maize land could expect to borrow land rent-free from a neighbor. The system survived into the postindependence period. During a village study in 1979–80, the poorest women of the village confirmed that their right to free subsistence land was respected. In one case a divorcee was even given the use of a tea farm by her brother for meeting her cash needs, but this loan of land in the improved category was an unusual act of generosity. Access to unimproved subsistence land, however, was still accepted as every resident's right. This was so at a time when land was much scarcer than it had been in the 1950s. It remained the rule in most (but not all) of Shambaai right up until the end of 1988.[3]

Matuta threatened the guarantee of subsistence because they were a capital investment, a permanent improvement which took land out of the category that could be lent out freely. If the owner of the land built tie ridges, he would be reluctant to lend out the land rent-free, for he had now made a substantial investment in it. The poor person could no longer use unimproved land without building *matuta* herself because it was illegal to farm without *matuta*. If the poor person built tie ridges it meant that he or she was investing in someone else's land and guaranteeing that the land would never again be available for loan. Owners were especially reluctant to lend improved land to the person who had made the improvements. Under local land-use rules a borrower who improved the land in one year and used it in the next established a strong claim to ownership. A land-poor person faced the possibility of building *matuta* anew year after year, each time leaving the owner with permanently improved land on which to farm in the future.[4] If the poor had actually done this with any frequency they would have emerged as a new, intensely exploited, rural underclass.

This interpretation of *matuta* as a threat to the subsistence guarantee helps to make sense of the main characteristics of the protest. There was, first of all, the fact that the most intense protest came from women,[5] and it was the poorer women who were threatened most severely by the loss of guaranteed subsistence land.

Secondly, the great fear through this period, publicly expressed on many occasions, was that the Shambaa would be driven from the mountains down to the plains. The problem is to identify who were these threatened "Shambaa." A set of economic life histories collected in a village near Bumbuli, together with knowledge of the economic life histories of a number of men near Vugha, shows that some peasants were making substantial profits at coffee farming in the 1950s and using those profits to add many new pieces of land to their holdings. Successful coffee-farming men were adding mountain land; they were not threatened with its loss.

Nor were their wives, who were relatively numerous in Muslim coffee-growing households. Those threatened with loss of mountain land were households at the margins, people with little commercial land and with only minimal subsistence land, dependent on the subsistence guarantee.

A third characteristic of the protests becomes comprehensible when we see *matuta* as a threat to subsistence land. This was the enormous pressure exerted by peasants in the 1950s to open up new land for maize cultivation and for fallow — the sort of land available under the subsistence guarantee. That struggle will be described later in this chapter.

Alongside its powerful impact on the land-poor, the regime of *matuta* made agricultural planning difficult for all farmers, including prosperous ones, because it limited their ability to exploit the multiple possibilities of their complex agricultural system. Chapter 2 describes that system, in which cultivators plant maize in three different altitude zones using three different rainy seasons. Each part of Shambaai has its main rainy season, but farmers seek out bits of land appropriate for use in a subsidiary season, to tide themselves over the hungry season when the main crop has not yet come in, to provide a reserve stock of food in case of drought during the primary rains, or as a way to use household labor which is underutilized during an off-season. Farmers are careful observers of the characteristics of particular pieces of land, and choose the farm plot with the most appropriate soil and rainfall characteristics for their immediate needs. Each situation — each mixture of crops and rains and seasons — has its optimum piece of land. A farmer would have to be very wealthy in dispersed plots to have the optimum garden for each farming requirement as conditions change from year to year. A wise farmer knows which neighbor owns which plot, and borrows the appropriate bit of soil as needed.

Matuta made it difficult for farmers to continue with flexible agricultural planning based on borrowed land. It made no sense for a peasant to borrow the optimum piece of land for one season if it meant constructing tie ridges and then leaving them behind for the land's owner. *Matuta* were inappropriate in any event for land used only occasionally. The first year required the heaviest labor investment, with additional labor required for repairs in successive seasons. It was inefficient to allow *matuta* to lie fallow for several seasons, for they would then need to be rebuilt from the start.

In an extended set of discussions about the practical aspects of building *matuta*, strong contrasts emerged between accounts given by some people that *matuta* were crushingly heavy work, and descriptions by others that the burden was manageable. The informants, all of whom had lived through the struggles of the 1950s, agreed that building tie ridges was men's work, but a number of women reported that they had, in fact, taken over the heavy labor themselves because their menfolk were ill or absent.[6] The perceived inappropriateness of the requirement that women do this work reinforced the sense among these informants that the labor was heavy beyond endurance. Some people described the farmers, men and women, who suffered physical breakdown while working on the tie ridges: farmers who vomited blood, or suffered heart attacks, or collapsed with stabbing pains in the chest or side.

Those who spoke about the work as tolerable never actually described doing it themselves. They mentioned individuals who hired workers to build *matuta* or more frequently they referred to the collective labor known as *ngemo*. Ten or fifteen men would join together to prepare the garden of first one and then another of their number. When a man's turn came his wife provided food for the working party. A man who was absent (perhaps at work on a sisal plantation) or a young man who was infirm did not usually take advantage of *ngemo* labor.

The pattern of labor organization meant that people who were well-off found it much easier to build *matuta* than did people already under stress. The term *well-off* here is deliberately broad, for it refers to resources of kinship support as well as resources of cash or land. R. H. Tawney compared the situation of a poor peasant to that of a person up to the chin in water, in danger of being drowned by the slightest wave.[7] The regime of *matuta* made waves. The changes in both land use and labor which came with the imposition of the Usambara Scheme made it impossible for the worst-off of the peasants to continue working their own land.

The fact that the subsistence guarantee has survived leaves us with an intriguing riddle concerning the actual process by which people lose their rights to land in Shambaai. The process which is typical in other places around the world is for the poor peasant to sell land until there is none left — no place to grow food. In Shambaai even if a peasant sells his or her last plot, the right to guaranted subsistence land remains. How then are people driven off the land? The answer to this question emerged during a study of the health-care crises of all the households in a large village in 1979–80. People left the village because they lacked cash or kinship support, not because they lacked subsistence land.

A parent with a sick child or with a shortage of hungry-season food before harvest needed money to pay a healer or money to buy food. In some cases the money came from a cash crop farm plot — perhaps a tea or a sugarcane garden — or it came from relatives, most often brothers or other patrilineal kinsmen. The person who had no regular source of cash and no adequate group of supporting kinsmen was driven to find work. Many people chose to stay at home in their village and to eke out cash needs day by day, farming on a piecework basis for others. Day labor was, however, a slippery slope: each day spent earning money for short-term needs was a day spent away from the laborer's own farm. Resources left for facing the next crisis were likely to be even smaller.

The balance of food needs and cash needs created a hierarchy of households, from those best able to weather a crisis on downwards. The best-off households had cash-crop land which produced a regular income, and were situated in the midst of a rich network of supporting relatives. Households without agricultural sources of cash were worse off, the precariousness of their balance depending on the health of both partners: the wife at home farming on subsistence land and the husband away earning cash. The most desperate of the households were headed by women, especially women separated from a network of supportive men. Even if such a woman had guaranteed access to subsistence land, she had no regular source of income to meet the crises of daily life.

A household which shifts from farming to day labor in order to survive still retains access to a whole network of mutual assistance: the help of women who bring firewood and water when the woman of the household is ill, and even in many cases help from neighboring men in providing health care. A household which faces departure from the mountains, leaving Shambaai altogether, fears losing the last vestiges of communal social security.

Back in the days of *matuta*, the households best able to cope with the new colonial demands were of two kinds. They either had substantial cash incomes or they had resident men with supportive brothers. Ideally they had both. In the first case they could hire workers to help build the tie ridges. In the second they could form cooperative men's work groups. In other words the strongest households, the ones best able to survive, least marginal, had the easiest time meeting the new requirements. The female-headed households with no cash land (and perhaps also no subsistence land) were hit the hardest and faced the possibility that they would have to leave the mountains.

The 1950s were a time when large numbers of men were leaving wives and children at home and going off to earn cash, usually at wages too low to ensure the security of families. We have already seen the district commissioner's estimate in 1952 that one-third of all taxpaying men in the district worked at jobs tied to the sisal plantations. The wages on sisal plantations were never adequate for meeting more than the most minimal home needs.[8] Wives of the men who had left were in a difficult position in the years of *matuta*. They were not served by cooperative work parties if their husbands were absent. Even if the men returned home in the dry season to help with cultivation, additional erosion-control work extended the unprofitable home stay significantly. In cases where erosion control fell on the wives, this was a double disaster: men ought to be at home preparing fields, and they were not; and now the work of field preparation was very much more difficult. At Mgwashi, the most intense moments of women's revolt against erosion-control work came with complaints from women about their absent husbands.[9]

Erosion-control measures must also have affected the balance of remittances between absent husbands and their farming wives. The village study of 1979–80 showed that absent husbands who sent money to their wives did not, in most cases, specify how the money was to be spent. The wife could use it to hire a farm laborer to prepare fields, or to buy clothes for her children and herself, or to purchase hungry-season food. In many cases the wives chose to do the men's work of preparing fields rather than hire labor, so that they could use the money for current consumption. Since the field-preparation season was also the beginning of the hungry season, the choice was sometimes one between hired labor and food. The probable effect of erosion-control measures was to force women to work even harder at field preparation, and at the same time to spend money (if they could) for added labor. They must have worked harder and eaten less, even if their husbands sent cash.

The pressure on women's work time was in any event becoming more intense in the 1950s, with increasing land shortage. It was the spatial arrangement of mountain life that made the problem so intense. We have seen that the large permanent villages are located between warm lowland plots and the cool gardens of the high mountains. Spreading the plots through rain and temperature zones reduces risk of total crop failure. But it also places heavy demands on the women who work on farms many more days of the year than men. Women walk miles through the mountains to their plots. As farmland became scarcer in this period, women were forced to walk further. Many of the main farm plots of Vugha's women in this period were already several miles from the villages, and the enforced scarcity of the scheme was bound to increase the distances.

The rising densities also made it difficult for women to find fuelwood. The higher the density of the nucleated settlements, the more time women needed to spend going to a wild area for fuel. After World War II, the rising population densities and loss of rough land must have lengthened the time spent on gathering fuel. By the mid-1970s the surveyed women of a single village were each spending between six and twelve hours a week collecting fuelwood (P. and A. Fleuret 1978).

Planners understood that the Usambara Scheme would make additional demands on women's work time. According to the district officer, "Women on whom the bulk of agricultural work falls were particularly asked to attend" the meetings introducing the scheme in the subchief-doms.[10] None of the scheme's documents acknowledge, however, the difficulties implied by the additional work demands.

Peasant Interpretations of *Matuta*

A woman who remembered the heavy burdens of building *matuta* said that the real point of erosion control was that "Your Shambaa ways were not wanted." A local Kilindi who still saved a colonial newpaper picture showing him as an efficient scheme enforcer agreed: "People saw it as an enormous burden because they understood it to be a foreign style of farming."

The contrast between "a foreign style of farming" and "the Shambaa way" referred to a multitude of elements: to the way a person's body feels in the act of farming, to the way a field looks, and also to the shared sense that all of us, the people we know who call ourselves Shambaa, have a right to live by farming in Shambaai, a right to be helped through the difficult times which inevitably come, a right to subsist.

One man said that he could not tell me in words why farming *matuta* felt wrong; he could only show me. He picked up his hoe and went outside. He demonstrated that when a farmer follows the Shambaa way he stands on a hillside facing uphill and works consistently, always facing in the same direction. He establishes a rhythm as he moves along the hillside, and always faces in the same direction. Then the man demonstrated work on *matuta*. First he faced uphill and began to build a little ridge, then he stepped across it to face downhill so that he could continue to raise soil onto the ridge from the other side. Then he turned sideways to begin making a linking ridge at right angles to the original one. Then he stepped across the linking ridge to continue from the other side. His movements were uneven, disorganized, and lacking in any regular rhythm.

Everyone agreed that *matuta* were foreign. The disagreements, the direct contradictions among participants, came on the question of whether *matuta* were humane, or whether they were administered in a way that imposed impossible burdens. On this there were disagreements of fact. One woman whose husband was ill during the 1950s, and who was therefore excused from erosion-control requirements by the local chief, said that no women ever worked on *matuta*. Other women remembered the terrible pain of doing the work themselves. Still others spoke of women who had been driven to abandon farming altogether. They said that if a woman did this she stayed in the village and lived off food bought with her husband's wages, or from the produce of her husband's banana grove, or possibly from maize stolen in the night from other people's farms.

The retired colonial headman described the scheme as one which paid full respect to the principles of the moral economy. In his version of what had happened no old person, no sick person, and no woman worked on *matuta*; if a person had no land and needed to borrow a farm, cooperative work groups came to relieve the poor person of the burden of digging alone. This was the subject on which people disagreed: whether the foreign way of farming could be practiced humanely, within the capacities of the poor and the weak.

On questions of humane practice, exemptions issued by the chief or headman came to occupy a central place. If he issued too many, the agricultural officer objected. People who found themselves unable to meet the requirement that they build *matuta* could focus their anger on the chief, who enforced the regulations with more or less enthusiasm, and who used his judgment and his political sense in distributing the limited number of exemptions.

We have already seen that chiefship occupied a central place in the politics of *matuta*. Where local people saw their chief as a rainmaker, serving their interests and not European ones, they did not hold him responsible for enforcing scheme rules. They made a distinction between the hated *matuta*, which were foreign, and the chief who defended subsistence and "our Shambaa ways." Where local people doubted a chief's capabilities as a rainmaker, they accused him of serving foreign rather than local interests.

In Bumbuli and Mlalo, where famous rain chiefs held office and administered the Usambara Scheme, their subjects attributed the scheme's abuses to the British. The rain chiefs were held guiltless. Bumbuli's people resisted *matuta* offstage, without opposing their chief. Those who remember *matuta* do not hold Daudi Sozi responsible. "It was not Chief Daudi's doing," said a woman who had resisted *matuta*. She used the precolonial language of sovereignty in explaining why: "It was the work of the land's *nguvu*"— the work of its holders of sovereign power, in other words of the British. A Bumbuli man found his appropriate image in a different realm. He described Europeans as the owners of a business in which Daudi Sozi was a mere employee. In any event all the Bumbuli people with whom I have ever discussed the subject separated Daudi Sozi as the revered rainmaker from the work for which he was not held responsible: imposing *matuta*. In Mlalo, we have seen, peasants remembered telling Hassani Kinyashi he ought to present himself to the British as a supporter of the scheme so that he could remain in office to make rain; they would take resistance into their own hands.

Where the chief was not a rainmaker, notably in the case of the Paramount Chief Kimweri Mputa Magogo at Vugha, the peasants saddled him with responsibility for the scheme and merged their demands for rain with their opposition to the scheme. When the conflict of the 1950s came up in casual teahouse conversations at Vugha in 1967 and 1968, three identifying characteristics of the period were mentioned many times: the burdens of *matuta*, the problem of a king who had no rain, and the prominence of the *chama*, the resistance organization which would ultimately change the political landscape of Shambaai. In resistance documents of the 1950s, Kimweri is accused of being an *akida*, a representative of an alien government, not of the Shambaa.[11] The rain chiefs followed the Shambaa way; the rainless chiefs were accused of serving foreigners.

People understood that if the chief controlled rain, the scarcity of land and labor would recede as a problem. Women who this year walk further to their farms than last and further for fuelwood must make do with smaller farms. They know that they will see their children sated, nevertheless, if the rains fall at the right time, gently but with fullness. Gentle rain is the best measure for erosion control and the best guarantee of rich crops. In 1968 I walked with a literate twenty-five-year-old along a steep hillside cleared for maize. I pointed to the hillside and asked whether he approved of the farming technique; wouldn't the hillside erode? "The land never erodes," he said to me, "if the rain is made to fall gently." Of all the possible measures to improve yields and soil quality, good rains were the most immediately effective. It is for this reason that people struggled to place rainmakers in the chiefdoms.

The chief's rain was, of course, not only rain which fell from the sky. It was the effect of actions by Kilindi rulers on subsistence. Kimweri enforced *matuta* and *matuta* threatened subsistence. The danger that people would be driven from Shambaai, that they would be unable to survive, was taken to be a consequence (or perhaps a further sign) of Kimweri's rainlessness.

In the nineteenth-century rite of accession, Vugha's peasants said, "Give us food. You are our king, but if you do not feed us properly we will get rid of you." The peasant judgment of the 1950s was that Kimweri was not giving the people rain, and that he must be removed.

The identification of *matuta* with things foreign, undermining the Shambaa way of doing things, did not mean that the peasant movement was a xenophobic one, rejecting everything alien. The central question was whether any particular practice or institution enabled local people to survive on their land, enjoying the support of their mountain communities at times of need. Throughout the 1940s and 1950s many people in Shambaai, especially the peasant-clerks, demanded the rapid improvement and expansion of school education. They pointed to the prosperity of the Chagga and Haya in the most economically advanced parts of Tanzania, who were also relatively advanced in education.

For peasants looking to escape from land scarcity, education was a part of the solution, a substitute for *matuta*, for it eased the generational transition in landholding. The problem was that as a man's sons grew to maturity, they often found that his landholdings, adequate for one household, were insufficient when divided four, or five, or six ways. Under these circumstances some sons left the mountains for long periods while retaining the right to cultivate the land they left behind, on loan to their brothers.[12]

Departing young men were better off if educated because they had a chance to win jobs as clerks or government functionaries. The income for those jobs was regular, not subject to seasonal fluctuations, and was likely to continue over the long term. The cash-earning son might help with money to provide medical care for his stay-at-home brothers, their wives and children. They in turn looked after his farms, guaranteeing the prosperity of his rural retirement. Most other cash-earning possibilities for sons who left the farm were unattractive: sisal work was too heavy to go on with for years, and the pay was low; farming outside the mountains threatened to remove a brother from the network altogether. But the clerk or functionary, especially if he worked near home, might earn enough to buy additional farms, leaving the entire group of brothers richer. Literate work, along with successful trading, was the best way to escape the downward spiral of land hunger and cash hunger.

Alongside education and rain as measures for dealing with land scarcity and agricultural decline was the peasant demand that large tracts of land under European control be returned to African hands. If only the Shambaa were allowed to cultivate the land of their own mountains, the measures for erosion control would become unnecessary. Local people had a sense that if artificial colonial obstacles were removed, the expansive land use patterns of the nineteenth century could realistically continue. In the nineteenth century, when a chiefdom's population expanded, the local folks felled forest and moved into fallow. A continuation of this pattern in the 1950s would mean expansion of cultivation into forest and fallow, opening up new lands to feed a growing population and to replace worn-out land. The problem was that forests had been made into government reserves, that the largest pieces of fallow were owned by Europeans and off-limits to Africans, and that Europeans threatened to take even more land, which might possibly drive many Africans out of the mountains altogether.

A Citizens Union petition of 1955 argued that the removal of colonial restrictions on entering the forest would solve the pressing agricultural problems. "From 1930 until now," they wrote, "settlers do not want their lands to be grazed or cultivated by Africans, therefore the Wasambaa collected together to those poor areas left for them. Since it is so the Gov't. would allow the Wasambaa to penetrate the forest reserve and that when they clear the forest the equally grow forest to the poor area left. This would do good to Wasambaa than the planned relegation."[13] The English of this quotation is difficult, but the point is clear if by *relegation* we understand the movement of Shambaa out of the mountains. The Citizens Union leaders argued that if local people were allowed to clear forest and to leave worn out land fallow so it returned to forest, then there would be no need for "relegation."

The threat of being driven from the mountains, as local people saw it, was not merely a consequence of increasing African population pressure within finite land resources. Peasants feared that the Europeans were about to expand and take away the land of Shambaai. In this view the removal of Africans under the regime of *matuta* was merely the first stage in this process: erosion control was a way of removing Africans in preparation for European settlement.

Local people feared European encroachment on African land because of what they saw happening in their own district and because of what they heard about the Meru land case (following the eviction of African homesteads from two tracts of land in 1951 to make room for European settlers) and about the fate of the Kikuyu in Kenya, whose land loss had driven them to rebel in "Mau Mau." Within Lushoto, fears of land loss became more intense when local people saw that in the late 1940s and early 1950s British district authorities were welcoming a "steady stream" of settlers from Britain.[14]

Peasant protesters saw it as the responsibility of the chief to defend land within the borders of Shambaai against alien encroachment. In this sense the chief's job as a source of rain for subsistence coincided with his job as defender of territory. Many local people suspected Kimweri of collaborating in a plan to take away their land, for it was he who enforced Usambara Scheme rules.[15] Kimweri himself, reflecting in the late 1960s on the history of the scheme, said that he believed some of the rebel claims—that Europeans wanted to take the land and to drive out the Shambaa. He remembered traveling in the plains with the district commissioner and coming to a spot where the commissioner looked around and said, "This would be an appropriate place for Shambaa to live." Knowing that this was the goal, he kept watch (as he saw it) to make sure that the Shambaa did not lose land unnecessarily. Kimweri and the rebels differ in their memories of his personal role. The rebels saw him as an *akida*: a representative of foreign forces, an agent of the British who was willing to sell his own land for pay and perks. As they saw it, he violated the community of interest between a rainmaking chief and his subjects, and in this way harmed the land. Kimweri's own view was that he managed to thwart the British, who would have inflicted much greater damage had he not remained as Paramount Chief and resisted them. For example, he remembered a time when the district officer wanted to declare Soni, between Vugha and Lushoto, as a township. This would have harmed the land rights of Africans in a substantial and densely populated tract of Southern Shambaai. Kimweri insisted that the officer bring the matter before the Bawanjama, the chief's council, and then refused to deal with the issue unless the officer supplied a map of exactly what land would actually be taken. As Kimweri saw it, his alert action prevented the loss of land. The Native Authority in this period — Kimweri's machinery of government — also purchased a substantial set of ex-enemy estates, which they rented to peasant farmers, in this way alleviating land hunger.[16] Only by staying in office and suffering the criticism of his fellow Shambaa was Kimweri able to save them from a worse fate. This is how Kimweri saw it.

Local people undertook the defense of their land by direct action. In the 1950s peasants encroached on uncultivated European land in a series of incidents which drew government attention. They fought also to retain earlier squatting rights in spite of increasing pressure to evict them. Squatters had long provided labor in return for rights of continued occupancy. When land became scarcer in the 1950s, many estates tried either to remove squatters or to increase the amount of labor required for them to stay. In 1950 the large Ambangulu tea estate tried to increase the number of required labor cards for squatters. Squatters, in their turn, pushed for the exclusion of non-Shambaa from the estates, for outsiders would make the land shortage more acute. In the forest reserves, it was the government rather than private employers which fought to control squatters. In 1952 the Forest Department threatened to evict militant squatter leaders from the Shume forest, just south of Mlalo, after squatters resisted labor demands.[17]

Local people saw the movement of squatters into the forest as part of a wider struggle to bring the land of Shambaai back into the hands of Shambaa. It is clear from peasant actions in the transition to independence that local people expected a European loss of power to mean that forest land would be released, unused estate land would become available as peasant fallow, and perhaps even cultivated estate land would move to African control. If these things happened, then the threat to the subsistence guarantee would disappear. The poor would not be driven out of the mountains. Seen in this way, it is clear that nationalist political ideas of the 1950s amongst the people of Shambaai had a social and economic content.

Peasant expectations, reinforced by the success of encroachments when the European grip weakened in the late 1950s, made TANU's job more difficult when it took over, for TANU did not take over the tea estates, and could not open the forests to indiscriminate felling. After independence, TANU people had to explain why they had turned around to oppose totally free land use. In some cases they explained the 1950s assault on land use rules (in looking back) by saying they had never challenged the wisdom of erosion control, but had only objected to the arbitrary and discriminatory way it had been imposed. As they saw it, Kimweri's men imposed scheme sanctions as punishment for political dissent. It was this political use of the land rules, along with the racial privilege accorded white farmers, which was unacceptable. Erosion control was necessary, but in a different context.[18] The job of the independent government in controlling erosion and preserving forests would be made especially difficult by the expectations raised in the political struggle leading to independence. In the late 1950s *Mwafrika*, the national newspaper with TANU connections, warned its readers, over and over, that *uhuru*, "independence," would mean harder work than ever before.

Nevertheless, the farmers of Shambaai kept their eyes on forest and fallow, expecting to take hold of it once they got rid of both the British and Kimweri. The transition began before independence. In 1957 white settlers trying to sell properties at Ubiri found no buyers, and squatters simply moved in.[19] After independence, the government found it necessary to distribute the fruits of *uhuru*. In 1963 the Agriculture Department decided to give peasant farmers 30,000 acres from the Shume Forest Reserve, in 10-acre plots to be farmed following soil conservation principles. In a short time the land supported five times the planned population. Some people got no land, some got 2 acres, and some 20 acres (Molloy 1971:61–62). The Agriculture Department quickly gave up on erosion control in Shume, but the project had met some of the political expectations of local farmers.

Opening up forest and fallow remained a central peasant goal. Ten years later, that same goal gave shape to the politics of *ujamaa*. In one of the earliest Lushoto successes for the Arusha Declaration, the peasants of one locality eagerly offered to create an *ujamaa* village. Expatriate academics, who could not separate their support of the policy from the content of their observations, pronounced the village a striking success. The villagers, some of whom were quite well off by local standards, concealed most of their land ownership to convince district authorities and university researchers that they were desperately poor in land and also eager for cooperative agriculture. The government released 2,400 acres of forest land for a village farm, ostensibly cooperative. The village won a major prize from a sympathetic West European government. Most important of all, the villagers had achieved their central goal: breaking open the boundaries of forest and fallow.

The centrality of *matuta* in provoking resistance — the centrality, in other words, of popular opposition to the forced march towards land commoditization — raises the question of whether the resisters saw themselves as fighting on a broad front to hold back the advance of capitalist agriculture in Shambaai. I think not. If such a battle had been fought, peasants would have resisted the growth of cash cropping, which changed the tenure status of increasing numbers of garden plots. At no point did this sort of resistance take place. In years of conversations on farming I have never heard anyone suggest that farmers ought not to use their land to plant coffee, or tea, or vegetables if these crops are profitable. Using land for tea is accepted, indeed admired as a mark of enterprise, even if it removes land from the stock which may be lent for subsistence.

In questions about differentiation within peasant villages, as in the peasant response to erosion control, the central value being defended was not equality among peasants, nor was it a defense of production for use as opposed to exchange. The central value was peasant welfare: health care for the sick, and the promise of continued subsistence in the mountains for all peasants, even the weak. According to my observations in the 1960s, prosperous coffee farmers were never criticized for taking up commercial farming. This was accepted as admirable. They were criticized only if they did not use the profits to help meet the needs of less fortunate relatives. A neighbor at a village near Vugha in 1967 and 1968 held extensive and profitable coffee farms. From the profits he paid school fees for the children of poor relatives. His benefactions were held up as examples of proper behavior. Even when prosperous men were stingy and were resented, their commercial farming was never criticized as inappropriate. Only their unwillingness to help was resented.

Whatever the differences among richer and poorer peasants, the world of the Shambaa was on the whole a world of shared poverty. Large-scale accumulation backed by government power was in European hands. Under these conditions, farmers took pride when one of their fellows rose above the mass. In 1967 I knew a man near Bumbuli who, some years earlier, had become the first in his part of the mountains to own a bus. The men who mentioned this to me said they had been thankful that a local African rose to a level previously achieved only by whites.

Survival in Shambaai had never depended on equality, not even in the precolonial period. It had depended on the obligation of senior men to use wealth for continued social reproduction. Now, in the era of commercial crops, it was cashlessness which threatened social reproduction, driving people out of the mountains and removing them from local kinship networks. Subsistence for all Shambaa would be maintained so long as the cash-rich respected their obligations.[20] Part of the emotional force behind the rejection of things foreign flowed from the sense that the Shambaa way was to form a network of support, to keep one another alive in the mountains.

British Interests

In the confrontation over *matuta* each side, the Shambaa peasants and the British administration, had a set of inviolable interests which limited the possibilities of creative compromise. On the Shambaa side, no political position could win mass support in the 1950s if it threatened the maintenance of basic subsistence for all the people of Shambaai. Compulsory *matuta* were just such a threat, and so they had to go. The irreducible minimum that the British protected was the economic well-being of the major estates, mainly sisal but also (increasingly in the 1950s) tea.

I take this position about British policy even though I have not read any document which states that the interests of the plantations were to take precedence over peasant interests. The primacy of estate interests is demonstrated by a series of decisions taken through the 1950s: despite the increasing scarcity of land for peasant agriculture, government officials continued to allocate uncultivated land to incoming estates; agricultural officers encouraged peasants to grow coffee, known to be unprofitable in Shambaai, and prevented peasants from adopting tea, which they reserved for estates; the authorities took strong measures to control sisal workers' unions and to prevent their politicization.

The mountains of Shambaai in the 1940s had tracts of land owned by Europeans but not yet cultivated, and others which had previously been owned by Germans, now under the Custodian of Enemy Property (C.E.P.). Uncultivated European-owned land adjacent to overpopulated African land provoked intense resentment. Unfortunately for the land-hungry local peasantry, much of the C.E.P. land was transferred to Euro-

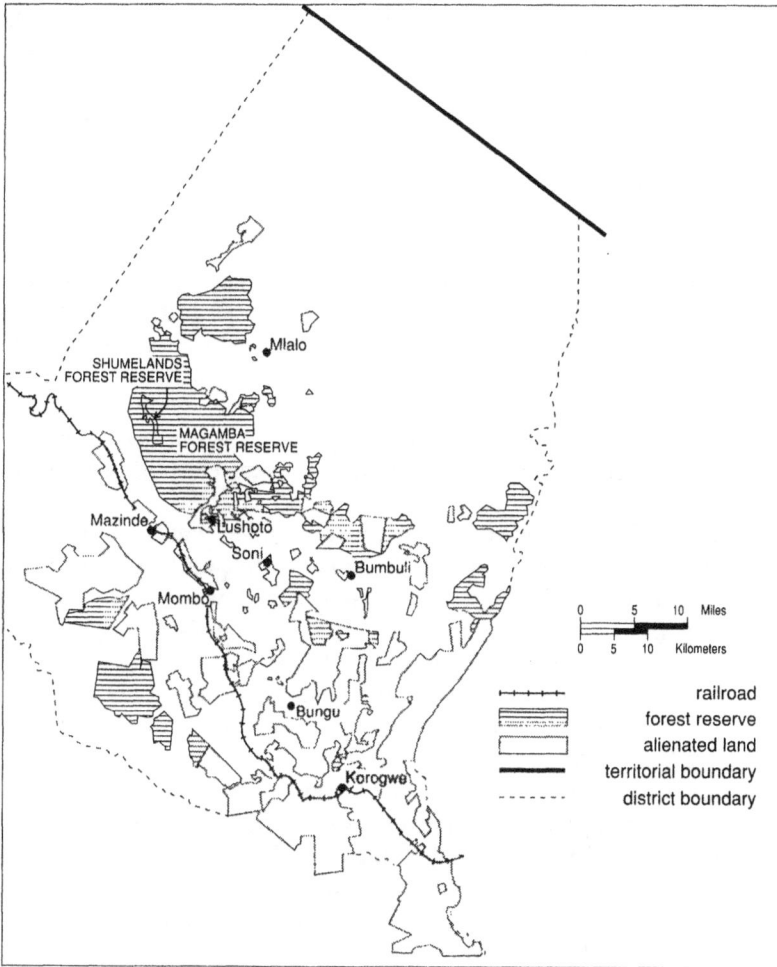

Map 3. Lushoto District, Alienated Land and Forest Reserve, 1961

pean ownership at the same time that *matuta* were imposed as the only possible solution to intense African land hunger. Of course, local people wondered why this enemy property (their fathers' land, taken by the Germans) went to foreigners.[21]

Tea companies based in India responded to that country's independence in 1947 by establishing plantations in other countries, thus reducing the new Indian nation's bargaining power by developing alternative sources of supply. In the late 1940s and continuing into the 1950s these interests cleared large tracts of land in Shambaai to expand their production. The 1950s were also boom years for sisal, with estates clearing additional pieces of well-watered land in the plains — land which peasant producers had hoped to take as their own. Estates as well as peasants encroached on land they did not own. Gomba Estate, for example, paid a fine of 20,000 shillings as penalty for its encroachment on a 600-acre tract, but then retained occupation of the tract, which it now leased from the government. These were years also when small-scale British settlers were taking land in Shambaai.[22]

The dominance of estate interests can be seen also in the decision to allocate unprofitable coffee to the peasant sphere and profitable tea to the sphere of the estates. If the ultimate result (although not the intended purpose) of *matuta* would be to bring about the capitalist tranformation of Shambaai, this decision made it less likely that the mountain people would greet the transformation with prosperity. The one certain consequence of the regime of *matuta* was that many men of Shambaai would become available to work as laborers.

As early as 1928 agricultural authorities concluded that the Usambaras were unsuited to the economic production of coffee, and that tea would be more profitable.[23] Coffee yields per acre were low, the soil was poor for the crop, pests and disease were prevalent, and rainfall in most localities was marginal with wide fluctuations.[24] From the 1930s onwards, estates switched over from coffee to other crops, especially tea.

In the 1930s tea estates urged the government to discourage tea production by African smallholders (Mhando 1977:96). Since tea producers need to get their leaves to a processing factory soon after they are picked, smallholder tea production is impossible without large-scale efforts to provide access to a factory and regular transport. This the government did not provide. It is no mere coincidence that December 1961, the month of Tanganyika's political independence, was the first month peasants in Tanga Province (and probably in the whole of Tanganyika) ever sold green tea leaf.[25]

A de facto situation emerged in which estates held a monopoly on the profitable crop, tea, while government, especially in the 1950s, encouraged Africans to plant the unprofitable one, coffee. Statements that coffee is not an economic crop appear in the *District Annual Reports* and *Agricultural Reports* over the years. In December 1953, for example, Dr. G. B. Wallace, a plant pathologist from the station at Lyamungu, visited Shambaai and reported to the Agriculture Department staff that coffee in Usambara was uneconomic except at the inflated prices then current.[26] The next month, January 1954, European staff of the Agriculture Department began to train African instructors to help expand African coffee produc-

tion in Shambaai, even though the estates of Shambaai had been uprooting coffee to plant tea, quinine, and tung oil.[27] Several years later, after
peasant resistance defeated the regime of *matuta*, the European staff ini-
tiated a publicity campaign to push the least controversial erosion-control
measures: terracing vegetable plots, planting wattle, and planting coffee.[28]
The justification was that even though coffee would be uneconomic in
the long run, it was good for erosion control. The effect was to encourage
Africans to make a long-term economic investment in a perennial crop
which the agriculture staff knew was bound to fail. This never became
a political issue because coffee was popular with peasants in the 1950s,
when prices were high; by the time failure became apparent, the British
were gone.

The Politics of Plantation Labor

The possibility existed in the 1950s that more radical forms of peasant
discourse and political action could emerge if the people of Shambaai
made common cause with workers on the adjacent sisal estates. A unified
movement might have been able to challenge the underlying conditions
which shaped both plantation life and peasant life. This never happened.
The sisal unions remained separate from peasant politics and from TANU's
nationalist politics, even though most sisal workers were themselves both
peasants and nationalists.

Three different kinds of oppositional politics were practiced within
Lushoto District in 1950s. There was the peasant resistance movement,
focused on issues of erosion control, chiefship, land scarcity, and land
alienation. There was the nationalist movement, which questioned the
British right to rule. And there were sisal plantation workers' unions,
which organized bitter strikes, especially between 1957 and 1959. The
period's politics are defined by the linkages created among these three.
The peasant resistance movement established a tight bond with the nationalist movement, but not with the sisal workers, even though many
of the peasant men themselves worked on sisal plantations. The separation between peasant politics and sisal workers' politics weakened both
groups. The peasants lost the possibility of winning help from economically strategic sisal workers. The plantation workers could not hope for
the most vigorous peasant support at the time of strikes. The sisal unions
were cut off also from nationalist politics. Their isolation in this period
is a fact of fundamental importance for the later shape of Tanzanian
socialism, yet it is rarely noted in the historical literature. The colonial

government's enforced separation of TANU and the sisal unions reduced the later influence of organized labor within the government of newly independent Tanganyika.

Farming in Shambaai and labor on the plantations were two halves of an integrated economic pattern. In the 1950's women cultivated food crops as well as they could in the mountains, while the men tried to find ways to earn cash. The men who were better off owned coffee land, or commercial vegetable plots. The poorer men, or the younger ones, went to work on the estates. The women's food economy, however, was not strictly for consumption: it too was shaped by estate needs. The estates purchased large quantities of maize grown in the mountains; in August and September of 1953, this amounted to 354 tons.[29] This sale happened at a time when Shambaa were being urged (under some circumstances required) to use plains land for planting cassava, a crop far less nutritious than maize. The total economic pattern (and in most cases each individual household) included men's cash crops, women's crops for consumption, men's and women's food crops for sale, and men's wage labor.

One of the reasons the conditions of labor never became a central political issue in Shambaai is that local men who worked on the estates never saw them as the possible source of a lifelong income, nor even of substantial savings for buying land or taking up trade. They were a place at which men could earn current income for a period.[30] The work was hard and poorly paid. For an ordinary person, the only practical and secure way to live for a lifetime, into old age, was to farm the land. When people complained bitterly about the land shortage, they did not say that the British were taking land so as to drive them to work on the sisal estates (which would have been a plausible explanation of what was happening). They complained instead that the British were driving them to cultivate farms in the plains.

The moment of bitterness did not come when men went off to work on the estates, leaving their wives or their fiancées at home in the mountains. The moment of bitterness came when wives felt they might some day need to leave the mountains and farm in the plains.

The threat that women would be forced to leave the mountains was the most feared consequence of the larger economic pattern. For resistance organizations to be fully effective, they needed to address the full context in which local impoverishment emerged. The peasant resistance groups addressed the different parts of the total pattern in very different ways. The micro-*vyama* — the small subchiefdom political unions — were capable of dealing only with the most local affairs. They most often attributed their problems to the *zumbe*, the chief, and beyond him to Kimweri. At the next level of larger scale, the Usambara Citizens Union protested mainly against Kimweri and his policies. But its members understood (as did the members of the smaller *vyama*) that overall British control was the heart of the problem. For changing this, only a nationalist movement would do. Of the movements that existed, only TANU was capable of discussing political control, agrarian issues, and labor relations all at the same time.

The sisal workers' trade unions might have served as an alternative organizational base for men who wished to challenge the larger pattern of European control. Only if the unions had become openly nationalist would they have been able to address the full range of issues which concerned their members (although even then, women's issues would have been excluded). For sisal workers from Lushoto, pay and working conditions were only a small part of what they wanted to win. They wanted to take away the plantations' land; they wanted to stop the plantations from polluting the streams which supplied ordinary folks' drinking water; and they wanted to remove European plantation managers or owners.[31]

Even though union members held a nationalist vision of their goals, the unions proved incapable of creating a program to match that vision. The government's Labour Department worked hard to ensure that nationalist unions not emerge. It discouraged political involvement by unions and tried to cut off contacts between union and TANU leaders. When workers went to consult Oscar Kambona, who was organizing for TANU, they were soon afterwards visited by police. The message was clear: keep away from political involvement (Friedland 1969:117). The same message was communicated in numerous other ways. Union leaders knew that they could not take positions on political issues and retain Labour Department recognition.

The employers, meanwhile, tried two different strategies for shaping worker politics. One was to bring in chiefs as intermediaries. In the aftermath of the bitter Mazinde Estate strike of 1958–59, the Tanganyika Sisal Growers Association considered bringing chiefs to visit from labor supply areas. In the employers' view, the more influential the chiefs were, the less influential the unions would be (Bolton 1978:183). This strategy was largely ineffective.

The second employer strategy was to fight TANU in electoral politics. The management of Mazinde Estate hired enterprising young men in Lushoto District to recruit members for the anti-TANU United Tanganyika Party (UTP). One man of my acquaintance (at one point a Village Chairman for TANU's successor party, Chama cha Mapinduzi, or the CCM) admitted to having made a substantial living out of the very generous capitation fees the Mazinde management paid for new Shambaa members of UTP. To judge from the stories I heard in widely separated parts of southern Shambaai, paid UTP recruiters spread out in significant numbers.

During the most intense period of sisal strikes, the government took measures to channel all protest into trade unions which, while profoundly nationalist in motivation, were completely apolitical in tactics and in their public discourse. In January 1957 the district officer of Korogwe Division (the part of Lushoto District in which plantations were located) sent the Tanga Motorized Company to close the Korogwe TANU branch and twenty-nine sub-branches. He also confiscated all TANU funds, and in October the district authorities banned all TANU activity. Korogwe's *Annual Report* notes that with all TANU offices closed, the emphasis of politically active people shifted to sisal unionism.[32] The years when TANU was banned in Korogwe (1957–59) were also the years of the most intense strike activity ever, and years of intense political activity throughout Tanganyika. The ban therefore seems to be a crucial event in party-worker relations, for it cut off the possibility of nationalist unionism, which was a natural vehicle for migrant workers whose sphere of oppression was not defined narrowly by the boundaries of the workplace.

I have not seen documents stating government motivations for banning TANU in this period. The ostensible reason was the party chairman's statement that TANU was now the government, and agricultural rules were therefore no longer in force (Bennett 1962:22). At other times these actions would have passed without so drastic a reaction. The effect of the ban is clear on a set of issues much broader and more important to the British than erosion control. The ban tended to cut off TANU from plantation workers and their concerns, and it fostered a narrow, bread-and-butter (or rather *ugali*-and-*mchuzi*) trade unionism, of a kind which did not survive in the independence period. The short-term effect was to push the sisal labor force away from migrancy: to make it better paid, more skilled, and less casual, and therefore presumably less concerned with agrarian issues (Iliffe 1979:541). The estates decided that under these political conditions they would pay the workers more but demand more work and reduce the numbers of workers. Reduction in the total number of sisal laborers intensified the difficulties experienced by the agrarian poor. The unemployed men returned home, placing even more intense pressure on the land of Shambaai.

The long-term effect was to weaken the influence of workers and their unions within the new government of independent Tanganyika by preventing the emergence of nationalist unionism and a thorough-going alliance between TANU and the unions in the period leading up to independence. This strengthened the likelihood that bureaucrats would emerge as fully dominant.

Matuta in the Politics of Independence

The politics of the 1950s gave agriculture its characteristic shape in Shambaai over the decades that followed. The defeat of *matuta* preserved the guarantee of subsistence land for the poor and slowed down the process by which land became a commodity. In this sense the peasant resistance leading to independence was fully in harmony with the policy of the government that the peasants installed in power, for Tanzania during its socialist period placed restrictions on buying and selling land. The peasant guarantee of subsistence land and the restrictions on renting land for annual food crops continued on through the late 1980s. No one has measured the precise effects. It is likely that proletarianization was slowed, as was investment in improving food-crop land. Wherever they could, peasants penetrated the forest, bringing new land into the old system. Fallow cycles became shorter. Over the long term, the pressure of land scarcity and of market forces appeared inexorable. By the end of 1988, land for planting annuals was being rented for high prices at Mlalo, in the north of Shambaai, although not yet in other parts of the mountains. If the practice spreads to the rest of Shambaai, the revolt against *matuta* will prove to have been a holding action.

8

Gender, Slavery, and Chiefship: Peasant Attempts to Create an Alternative Discourse

The Usambara Citizens Union, as we have seen, was tied to the politics of rain and the politics of the hated Usambara Scheme in a very peculiar way. This political association won a large number of members in Gare and Vugha, places where government chiefs had no claims to control the rain.[1] Citizens Union leaders in those places were not limited by the same constraints as peasant rebels in Mlalo or Bumbuli, where rainmakers held office. The UCU leaders could build a popular movement to oppose chiefship as an institution without seeming to attack rain chiefs. They left implicit the message that only the rainless chiefs, enforcers of the Usambara Scheme, were under attack.

The ambiguity of the attack on chiefship under these circumstances left UCU leaders free to speculate on the ideal Shambaa form of government and, in the process, to create new forms of political language. They discussed the character of chiefs who were responsive to colonial masters, and of chiefs who represented the popular will; they explored local history to find precedent for nonroyal leadership and discussed the process by which a wise elder came to be known for his wisdom without the formality of elections. They also talked about the difference between the arbitrary authority which characterized a regime of slavery and the acceptable authority necessary for social continuity.

It is difficult to know, for the years of Citizens Union influence in the early and middle 1950s, just how widely the language of the rebels spread among the men and women of Shambaai. This *chama* was an illegal organization for most of the years of its existence, and for those years continuous records have not been found. Nevertheless, we know that it had thousands of members during its brief periods of legality (3354 in 1951), and that the leaders were fully integrated within peasant society.[2] Virtually all derived an important part of their livelihood from peasant farming. Neighborhood kinship patterns made it likely that each active UCU member shared some ties of descent or affinity with nearly every

204

other individual living within a radius of several miles (Feierman 1972: chap. 3).

A review of archival notes, combined in many cases with knowledge drawn from personal acquaintance, made it possible to review some details of the activities of sixty-eight Citizens Union leaders. Of these, forty-seven are known to have had some education, although in almost every case this was limited to primary education, supplemented by brief periods of job training. Many or all of the remaining twenty-one leaders may also have been literate, but the data on their education are lacking. Most of the leaders were occupied primarily with farming at the time they were members, but many had been minor functionaries in the past: clerks, tribal dressers, or forestry guards. These were not members of an isolated elite; they were an integral and influential part of the village communities in which they lived and farmed.

It is a paradox of the period that the political language created by Citizens Union leaders had its broadest effect on large numbers of people in Shambaai only after the organization declined. This happened when the UCU became submerged in TANU, the Tanganyika African National Union, which won national independence and had its first major impact in Shambaai in 1956. TANU spread through the entire district; unlike the UCU, it grew rapidly even in the domains of the major rain chiefs. TANU grew in influence just as peasants were seeing the benefits of their own resistance to government authority, for this was the time the Usambara Scheme went rapidly into decline, to be abandoned finally in 1957. Kimweri's Native Authority was clearly on the defensive. The consequence of these victories as they unfolded was to open up, among many peasants, speculative discussions on the political future of Shambaai and more broadly on the nature of the good society. We know that the new ideas played a real role in peasant life because they became a basis for peasant action.

In 1954, at a time when the Citizens Union was still not a legally recognized organization, its leaders sent the first of a series of petitions to the Trusteeship Council of the United Nations. The language of the petitions defines important new issues in the period's political discourse, yet preserves alongside these the earlier ways of defining political issues. In the manifestoes of the mid-1950s a single message, ostensibly clear and coherent, often breaks apart on closer examination to reveal several divergent or contradictory messages.

The authors of the Trusteeship Council petitions, for example, appeared at some points to reveal themselves as strong supporters of chiefship but at others showed that they rejected chiefly rule or found it irrelevant. The cover letter to the opening petition states boldly that

> The Washambala are no longer in favour, nor do not require any more to be under the rule of the present ruling clan "wakilindi" cost what may, and as we are prepared to offer nothing but, sweat and tears.
>
> We have and are still suffering from various cruelties and can easily been seen from the attached information, and we are badly longing for "Better no rule than cruel rule."
>
> We are prepared to elect our own Shambala peasant to take the throne, then being under the said rulers.

This is a passionate declaration of independence, a rejection of chiefship. But then the actual petition, after listing concrete grievances, concludes as follows:

> It is to the knowledge and belief of every Shambala peasant that all these drawbacks are mainly caused by the chief — as he is not not [sic] right one to the throne according to customary laws as per attached history.[3]

The authors continue, in this and succeeding petitions, to chronicle the history of the dynasty on page after page.

If the readers weigh issues simply according to the quantity of prose, then the selection of the Paramount Chief is clearly the most important issue discussed in the petitions. The peasant petitioners inform the Trusteeship Council in great detail about the circumstances of Kinyashi's abdication as king in 1929, about negotiations between contenders for the throne in 1944, about the role of Shebughe Magogo's father-in-law in the royal election of 1948, about the proper clans for the Paramount's electors, about the privileged place of Kinyashi's dynastic line, and about many other events surrounding the selection of a Paramount Chief.[4]

The contradiction between the declaration of ethnic Shambaa republicanism and the absorbing preoccupation with dynastic politics conceals a second, more profound, contradiction. Beneath every word of the petitions lies the central assumption of indirect rule: that the local politics of Shambaai determine the well-being of the Shambaa people. Perhaps, as all the petitions argue, the solution to Shambaa problems will lie with the selection of a new Kilindi king, from a different dynastic line. Perhaps, as the 1954 cover letter argues, the Shambaa need to select a non-Kilindi "to take the throne." But the political focus is always local; the politics of Dar es Salaam or London are largely irrelevant.

But the petition makes a mockery of this assumption, for it is addressed to readers in New York, not Lushoto. The petitioners know that their fate is decided on a very large political stage. Members of the *chama* had written, in an earlier letter to a British member of parliament, "We Shambala people have found that nothing will be done locally unless directions are issued from the United Kingdom."[5] The U.N. petitions widen the stage even further to include the world community.

The language of healing the land and harming the land, of chiefship and rainmaking, does not appear at all in the petitions. It is unclear, if we take only the petitions as evidence, whether the writers found the issues of chiefs as rainmakers irrelevant, or whether they judged these issues significant but inappropriate for a United Nations audience. Fortunately, the opportunity arose to clarify this issue.

In April of 1980 a young man came to me with a note from his uncle, a man who had been a member of the *chama* in the 1940s, one of the original organizers of the Usambara Citizens Union, and a coauthor of many key Citizens Union documents, including U.N. petitions. The nationalist, whom I shall call Mulonda Haki, decided that he needed a scholar with a tape recorder to preserve his memoirs. We had many hours of discussion about the history of his career and about his political ideas.

Mulonda Haki had worked as a "tribal dresser," the forerunner of today's Rural Medical Aide, from 1929 until 1948. In those days tribal dressers needed only a few years of education. Nevertheless, he took both education and evangelical Christianity seriously. He found time, even during his political years, to teach his nephew and other neighboring children reading and writing. When I saw the old man's house, it looked part dwelling-place, part chapel, with a crucifix on the front. We spoke in Shambaa rather than Swahili.

Mulonda Haki's political language returns repeatedly to two main themes: the need for democracy and for a return to the ancient form of rule by lineage elders. At some points the democratic language is drawn directly from English, as with the word *demokrasi*. Mulonda Haki says, "It became clear [in the days of TANU] that we needed to gather together a government of the people, *demokrasi*, of the people themselves, not a government chosen by one person." Mulonda Haki recalls the speeches Nyerere gave in the mountains in the 1950s: "The most important thing he said was that we must end the shame brought to us by being ruled. It is a terrible thing to be ruled — embarrassing, shameful. . . . You cannot decide for yourself, or build for yourself. You must have things built for you. You are told when to stand up and when to sit down. That is shameful."

Mulonda Haki also uses the precolonial language of power, but he carefully chooses a historical reference point when commoners were in charge. "Kimweri Mputa Magogo was placed at a locus of power (*Hantu ha nguvu*), not at a place the Shambaa would want if they themselves chose." In the nineteenth century Vugha's men hoped the king would occupy the sole locus of power, to avoid the competition of power against power which led inevitably to famine, warfare, and rapacious tribute collection. They rebelled if the king proved incapable of consolidating power. The closest precedent for Mulonda Haki's language is in the mythical moment when the Shambaa welcomed Mbegha, the founding hunter king — a moment reenacted in the accession when the courtiers of Vugha chose the new king. Under colonial rule the District Commissioner chose the king. The commoners of Vugha had no real say. The king therefore represented the District Commissioner. Some nationalists say that he was an *akida*, like the appointed agents under German rule, not a king.

Mulonda Haki draws also on the heritage of Shambaa self-rule, from the years before Kilindi domination. "The Usambara Citizens Union gathered together lineages of the Shambaa, to give authority to the mature men of the lineages (*waghoshi wa chengo*). That was its central goal — to install *watawa* and *wafung'wa* and a *mwambashi*." These were titles taken by senior village men in the years before or during chiefship. Commoner notables had an alternative place in the history of rebellion. We have seen that the Bondei of the eastern kingdom rose up in a precolonial rebellion. In some villages they threw off Kilindi domination and replaced it with the authority of patriarchs. There is no evidence that the nationalists of the 1950s thought of *Kiva* when they spoke of *waghoshi wa chengo*, "mature men of the lineages." Unlike the nineteenth-century Bondei, who had experienced only a few decades of Kilindi rule, the nationalists of Shambaai recalled distant traditions of rule by patriarchs.

Up to this point Mulonda Haki's assessment might easily have been drawn from Usambara Citizens Union documents which he himself wrote. During the hours of discussion after his narrative, however, Mulonda Haki revealed curious contradictions in his assessment of chiefship. His position was very different, at some points, from the position of the Citizens Union documents. His words are worth quoting:

> SF: During the years of your movement did people want to drive out the Europeans, or did they want a chief who had rain?
>
> MH: During the days of the Usambara Citizens we wanted to remove the chiefs.
>
> SF: To remove the chiefs?
>
> MH: Completely. . . . The kingship inherited from Mbegha would not do. It was no good because it belonged to a private individual. It belonged to one man relying on his own power [*nguvu*]. When it was a matter of removing one local chief and putting in another, he consulted his own thoughts. Because of that he was unable to get along with people.
>
> SF: But then why did people want Mashui [to become subchief of Lushoto]?
>
> MH: They wanted Mashui because they trusted that he had rain. . . . Even now people tend to say that rain belongs to the chiefs. Not all chiefs have rain. It goes by houses [of Kilindi]. . . . The house of Kinyashi of Mlalo, of Mashui, of Sozi, of Kinyashi at Vugha.

SF: Do you think that those things make sense?

MH: People hold them. People hold to them in their hearts. They choose to.

SF: What about you?

MH: I have the preference to say that if even you and I pray to God he will give us rain. If the sun shines down on us threatening hunger, and then you and I say, "Lord God give us rain," he will give us rain. I have that preference. But those people [the Kilindi] have incredible cunning. They have their special things. If you saw their special ways you would be amazed.

In this quotation Mulonda Haki begins by saying that in the early 1950s, the Usambara Citizens Union rejected chiefship altogether. Then I change the subject to ask about a popular battle over chiefship. I succed in drawing Mulonda Haki right into language about rain and chiefship, for he then specifies which branches of the Kilindi actually do have rain: "Not all chiefs have rain," he says. "It goes by houses. . . . The house of Kinyashi of Mlalo, of Mashui, of Sozi, of Kinyashi at Vugha."

At a later point in the conversation (not quoted), Mulonda Haki tells me that the two most important rainmakers escaped the trap of arbitrary rule. Daudi Sozi at Bumbuli and Hassani Kinyashi at Mlalo never lost their followings. Both welcomed Nyerere during his struggle to create a popular movement. According to Mulonda Haki, if things went wrong these chiefs knew they could resign their government jobs without losing authority. This, of course, is what happened in the end.

Back in the quoted section, when Mulonda Haki moves on to discuss the houses that have rain, there are undertones of support for chiefship. I therefore press him on whether chiefs control rain. His answer is again contradictory. He trusts that anyone can pray for rain, but knows that chiefs have special and powerful techniques for controlling the seasons: "They have their special things," he says. "If you saw their special ways you would be amazed." The contradiction found expression in political action. After the *uhuru* government abolished chiefship, Mulonda Haki and other TANU men of Vugha sued Kimweri Mputa Magogo for the royal headdress, which they wanted to transfer to Kinyashi's sons, heirs to Vugha's rain charms. They lost the case.

Back in the 1950s, none of the Trusteeship Council petitions or the minutes of Usambara Citizens Union meetings mention healing the land and harming the land, or chiefs' control over rain, even though these were issues of some importance for Mulonda Haki and other UCU leaders, and even though the issues had a profound impact on the shape of the UCU as a political movement. Whatever the personal views of the

UCU leaders, who probably diverged in the degree of their individual scepticism on rainmaking, they would all have known that it was inappropriate and counterproductive to write to London or New York about healing the land. Including this issue in petitions was probably never discussed: it was a subject discussed in Shambaa, not Swahili or English, a subject discussed among neighbors in informal conversation, not at voluntary association meetings that followed parliamentary rules of order, and a subject discussed in spoken language, not in writing.

Mulonda Haki, in his initial answer to my question, rejects chiefship in a much more thoroughgoing way than did the first United Nations petition. "During the days of the Usambara Citizens we wanted to remove the chiefs," Mulonda Haki said. "The kingship inherited from Mbegha would not do." This was the political position taken by the Citizens Union in 1956, two years after the first petition. The UCU called for the complete abolition of the royal dynasty. They wanted a return to the "traditions and customs of the local inhabitants" in which (as they remembered predynastic history) the Kilindi played no role. Instead a group of *watawa* (commoner leaders) were to serve under a "chairman" named the *Muambashi*. The *Wafung'wa*, defined by the UCU as lineage heads, were to play an important role. And the *walau*, in this account, would serve as a kind of public opinion survey team, drawing together reports on the opinions and needs of the common people. The central feature of this imagined past and future was its responsiveness to popular opinion.[6]

This populist version of Shambaa customary government accepts many of the fundamental premises of indirect rule, including the sense that the institutions of local government ought to be derived from local ethnic tradition. "The Chairman wanted to know," in a UCU meeting of 1956, "whether this Citizens Union ought to operate following the customs and traditions of the inhabitants of Usambara or whether it needed to operate following foreign traditions. The meeting shouted out with one voice that foreign traditions were not wanted in running the affairs of the Usambara Citizens Union."[7] At a momentous debate four years later between Kimweri's followers and TANU district leaders over the constitution of a new District Council, each side claimed to remain faithful to *mila*, the true inheritance of ancestral custom (*TANU na Wananchi Lushoto* 1975). The emphasis on "tribe" and on custom had been even stronger in the days of the UCU.

This was, however, ethnic tradition within an unseen but assumed national framework. If, in the early nineteenth century, officials of the Shambaa kingdom imagined themselves at the center of the political universe, some 1950s peasant rebels saw the Shambaa as one ethnicity among many, part of a nation of "tribes." They gave the Presidency of the UCU in 1956 to Petro Njau, a Chagga, not a Shambaa. Njau had tried to extend his Kilimanjaro Citizens' Union to the Meru, Arusha, Iraqw, and Maasai, as well as the Shambaa. It was Petro Njau who asked "whether this Citizens Union ought to operate following the customs and traditions of the inhabitants of Usambara." When he heard the strong affirmative answer, he needed to ask what were the customs of Usambara, for he did not know. He was an outsider. Petro Njau pictured his Tanganyika Citizens' Union as a national movement which would introduce a general Council of Chiefs as a supreme advisory body to the government. His nation was an agglomeration of tribes.[8]

Paramount Chief Kimweri Magogo had asked, a year earlier, why the UCU leaders needed to leave Usambara and go to Kilimanjaro to find a leader for their ethnic movement. They responded that Usambara did not have any leaders who were as well educated as Petro Njau. By *education* they meant formal schooling. Usambara needed a "beneficent teacher," they said, a *mwalimu mwema*. At this time Petro Njau was the *mwalimu* they chose. He was, of course, superseded by Julius Nyerere, who became much more widely known as Mwalimu.[9]

The choice of *mwalimu* as leader was important to the Citizens Union when it rethought the bases of indirect rule. This had, of course, been a form of rule by chiefs over "tribes" according to custom, with educated clerks and teachers playing a secondary role. The UCU proposed to continue a government of tribal units according to custom, but in their new variant of indirect rule they would shift authority away from chiefs, with a consequent gain for teachers and clerks. The new Tanganyika was to be governed by educated functionaries working within a framework of tribes. In the actual event, the functionaries won power but rejected the ethnic framework inherited from the colonial period.

The Usambara Citizens Union never openly challenged the British right to govern Tanganyika, nor did they reject the notion that Africans could only advance under European tutelage. The UCU's acceptance of British rule was, in part, a strategy for winning government registration and avoiding arrest. It also reassured potential members that they could join without risking government retribution. A poster published in 1956 was headed, "Resolutions of the Usambara Citizens Union, *Which Have Been Accepted by the Government.*"[10] The minutes of UCU meetings, written to be read by British administrators, sound genuinely accepting of British overrule. A senior officer of the union emphasized at a 1956 meeting that Africans need European education, monetary aid from Europe, and European work discipline in order to achieve real progress.[11] Petro Njau, in his speech at that meeting, described the Governor as a teacher of democratic values. On the UCU's public poster, Resolution Number 3 was "To become truly civilized."[12]

It is difficult to know how to interpret the union's ostensible support of British rule. The Shambaa participants with whom I have spoken remember the union as fiercely anticolonial, and the vigor of British repression supports their claim. If that is the case, then the written words and the public spoken words of the time (for there would have been observers reporting to the authorities on speeches) were merely a smoke screen, a diversion. Nevertheless, words spoken or words written, even if only for official consumption, have a powerful effect on all who hear them.

The great appeal of Nyerere (and of TANU), like the appeal of the other great African nationalists of the period, was that he said openly what many common people knew, but what other leaders feared to say: that British rule needed to end so that Tanzanians could govern themselves.[13]

The power of Nyerere's message lay in its audacity, for he was the one leader who questioned the legitimacy of the entire colonial enterprise. Local leaders risked jail if they protested against the local agents of British rule. The peasant intellectuals did not dare to attack the British, yet Nyerere openly told them to leave. He broke the final taboo, said the words that were unacceptable in colonial society, yet still walked as a free man. Nyerere also resolved the final doubts among local leaders about the appropriate spatial focus of their political movement. "He convinced us completely," Theodore Isaka said, "that our own *chama*, the Citizens Union, was incapable of fighting to win the whole of Tanganyika." Only TANU would do that.

Nyerere opened a debate on the shape of the nation. Alongside this debate, a rich discussion continued to deepen and broaden on the nature of the good society as defined in local Shambaa terms. The late 1950s were a time when Shambaa cultivators talked with remarkably little constraint about their political alternatives. They reviewed institutions, customs, and values, both local and exotic, in trying to find a just alternative to the rule of chiefs.

When older people heard Nyerere talk about *uhuru*, "freedom" or "independence," they also knew *uhuru* in their observed experience as the release from *utung'wa*, "slavery" or "pawnship," which in their thinking presupposed an entire system of descent-group rights in persons. The reader will remember that in the nineteenth century most violations of the law were treated as damages inflicted by members of one descent group on another, to be redressed by paying compensation. If the offenders were unable to pay, the chief paid in their place and then took as *watung'wa* an appropriate number of the group's people to balance his expenditure. These *watung'wa*, "slaves" or "pawns," lived at the chief's court, or in some cases they were sold to coastal caravans. *Watung'wa* taken in this way could also be redeemed by their relatives; the same was true for war captives and people given as pawns for food in famine.

As seen from within Shambaai, *uhuru*, emancipation from pawnship, implied also the end of a social order in which chiefs and elders held rights in persons and in which men and women stood before courts of law as members of descent groups, not simply as atomized individuals. *Uhuru* resonated with overtones of individual responsibility, of young men and women standing on their own, independent of their fathers.

In 1955 Daniel Nehemia Ndago, a member of the Usambara Citizens Union from the subchiefdom of Bungu, was taken off in handcuffs by the chief's messenger because his father owed a debt of seventy shillings. He was being punished, also, for his politics. He wrote to the district commissioner,

> You are a free person. Because of this, I believe that you will be disturbed to learn that I am still a slave of the Kilindi. . . . According to my knowledge, in European government, and especially in English practice, a sentence is passed on each individual lawbreaker, not on an entire lineage, as was the custom under Kilindi rule before European government came to this land. The Kilindi used to sentence an entire lineage because of the one lawbreaker in their lineage.[14]

Nehemia paid the seventy shillings, only to see the chief harass him further by returning with a witchfinder to search his house and loft for sorcery medicines. In the passage quoted, this literate peasant drew the precise parallel between precolonial slavery as an affair of descent groups and his own arrest for his father's crime. Other people in the same period saw any arbitrary personal exercise of chiefly authority as characteristic of a slave regime. Petro Njau wrote that the Shambaa expected him to remove *utumwa*, "slavery" (in Swahili), from the land.

Because the move from *utung'wa* to *uhuru*, from slavery to freedom was linked to the decline of descent as the basis of a jural group, the contrasting terms also carried connotations of tradition and modernity. Back in 1947 the leaders of the local African Association wrote that "Up to the current time there are local rulers serving under the honoured Union Jack who have no modern education at all and who still think that citizens are merely slaves."[15] For people who understood society in these terms, it was natural to follow the leadership of a *mwalimu*, a school-educated teacher, in trying to win *uhuru*, "independence." Slavery was seen as traditional and parochial, not modern and cosmopolitan. The authors of the first Trusteeship Council petition wrote of their case that "international laws and logic allow even a slave to fight for his freedom."[16]

In one important sense the discussions of slavery were hegemonic discourse, in subtle support of colonial values, for they were a rejection of what was seen as African (the descent group) in favor of what was seen as European (the jural individual). One of the central legitimacy claims of the continent's colonial rulers was that they originally came upon Africans practicing slavery, which they abolished.[17] When TANU demanded *uhuru*, it found a way of using the colonialists' own language against them. Nyerere's demand for *uhuru* carried an implicit message to the British: "You claim to have given us *uhuru* from slavery," he might have said, "but the bondage from which we need to emancipate ourselves is colonialism. Now is the time for us win true *uhuru* for ourselves."

In the experience of the peasant political leaders, turning the ideology of *uhuru* against its creators was not enough. Even while local leaders rejected the way precolonial lineages defined rights in persons, they defended the lineage elders as the true holders of customary authority in Shambaai. According to Mulonda Haki, "The central aim of the Usambara Citizens Union was to gather together the lineages of the Washambaa so that they would place the descent-group elders (*waghoshi wa chengo*) in positions of authority." This is confirmed by the minutes of UCU meetings.

Yet descent-group elders held precisely the sort of authority that UCU leaders rejected in other contexts: authority was ascribed, not achieved; patriarchs made arbitrary decisions about the lives of their progeny and their women; the patriarch as a person fused with the authority-bearing role.

The peasant rebels of Shambaai debated about the contradictions in their understanding of lineage rule, and they appear to have changed their public positions over time. Throughout the debate, they emphasized status achieved by elders and not status inherited by them. In Usambara Citizens Union discussions in 1956, the men who were knowledgeable about precolonial government explained that the "*Muambashi* ['the Chairman'] is never chosen. He is a person who has become known over a long period . . . for his wisdom and trustworthiness before the eyes of all people, and it is important for him to know the customs, practices, and laws of his land." The *watawa* similarly become known for their intelligence and good deeds, not for their birth. The knowledgeable men appear to assume, without stating openly, that masculinity and old age are necessary qualifications for the role of *Muambashi* or *Mtawa*, and that the consensus in local society is so strong that leaders can simply emerge without an open process of choice.[18]

This view changed by 1960, four years later, when peasant rebels, now constituted as the district's TANU branch, drew up a formal draft constitution for district government, a widely circulated document printed on green paper, and therefore called the *Green Paper*. They placed much greater emphasis than formerly on democratic election, on measures which clearly separated the person from the office, on representation for specialists in health and education, and on separating administration from the judicial process. In other words, they moved much further in the direction of what Max Weber would have described as rational-legal authority, of a kind which would harmonize with bureaucratic patterns of administration. In spite of the fact that the district constitution of 1960 retained the precolonial titles of *Muambashi, Mtawa,* and *Mfung'wa,* the document reveals a complete victory of school education over oral education. When faced with the practical job of creating an administrative structure which might actually be implemented (as opposed to the hypothetical structure of 1956), the influential men of the district adhered to a rational-legal order.

The authors of the *Green Paper,* the constitution of 1960, saw the emerging nation as entering a stage of political progress for which the old standards would be inappropriate. By this time the local nationalists were undoubtedly influenced strongly by TANU's positions. They wrote in reference to the Paramount Chief: "With respect to the political progress of contemporary Tanganyika, it will be completely impossible to have a hereditary life-long ruler who has no fixed period of office."[19] They therefore proposed to replace the Kilindi Simba Mwene with a *President* (their word) known as the *Muambashi* (also their word), to be elected for three years by secret ballot according to universal adult suffrage. The village elders were also to be elected by secret ballot. This was a departure from the position expressed in the Citizens Union debates several years earlier, that leaders would emerge through a subtle process of informal consensus-building in which men became known for their wisdom and good judgment.

Elections meant the end of the principle *kubushwa ni kufa,* "the only abdication is death." The principle fused person and office, and its end meant a rejection of this fusion. The principle was applied to the kingship, which would have been much more difficult to challenge had the king been an accepted rainmaker. The same challenge to the fusion of person and office could as easily have applied to the position of lineage elder, to which it was never applied.

The fusion of the king's person and office was challenged in another way, by an attack on the public status of the king's personal household. In the nineteenth century the household officers were seen from a royal point of view as serving the well-being of the whole land; for example, they tried to prevent adultery with a royal wife, which was an act of rebellion. Now, in 1961, the rebels played on the ambiguity of a situation in which the king was sometimes perceived as a mere office-holder; they attacked his right to maintain a personal household at public expense. This seemed legitimate according to bureaucratic norms, and yet clearly stung the Paramount. In the movement towards independence, the king's council changed its composition. In 1961 it decided to institute the *Green Paper* constitution. The British provincial commissioner announced that no funds were available to run the council along the new lines. The council's TANU members responded by firing all the officials who cared for the king's magical charms or concerned themselves with the affairs of his household. The reason for their action, as they later explained, was that "work such as this ought to be paid for by the king as a private person and not out of public funds." Kimweri Magogo countered by convincing all the council's employees (and not merely his household officers) to go on strike. The new TANU elite called in members of the TANU Youth League as strikebreakers and held public meetings around the district to explain their position. The strike collapsed, and shortly afterwards, in August 1961, the new council form was introduced, along lines laid down by the *Green Paper.*[20]

The Shambaa TANU leaders wanted to rationalize local government in yet another fundamental way, by separating judicial authority from the authority of the executive. They wrote in the *Green Paper:*

> In past times, and continuing up to the present, the Simba Mwene and the chiefs have been judges in the courts while acting as rulers of the country and also at the same time sitting as councillors in the Usambara Council. . . . Because the rulers of Usambara arrogated all these kinds of work to a single individual, major misunderstandings emerged in the land. This way of doing things cannot suitably continue, given the political changes occurring in Tanganyika.

The authors of the *Green Paper* rejected as obsolete the notion that the Simba Mwene and the chiefs held undifferentiated personal authority rather than restricted and carefully specified authority as officeholders. In other contexts these *chama* leaders described arbitrary, undifferentiated, personal authority as characteristic of *utawala wa kitumwa,* the "slave regime" of royal and lineage rule in precolonial days. Now that the days of *uhuru* were near, authority would reside in offices, not in persons. When the Citizens Union and the Lushoto peasants' TANU branch rejected the notion that lifelong undifferentiated authority inhered in the persons of chiefs and elders, they helped to open up the possibility that local people could challenge the intimate connection between public authority and masculinity.

As we have seen, the gender basis of public authority had a long history. The myth of Mbegha pictured the founding king as supremely male, a man who had the capacity to make all Shambaa (whatever their sex) into women. "Making [men] into women" was the Shambaa idiom for successful domination. The origin myth of the Mshihwi splinter kingdom describes that kingdom as autonomous, "a separate power," and also as inferior to Vugha. The myth itself expresses this by saying that the founders of Vugha and Mshihwi each killed a lion; Vugha's lion was masculine, Mshihwi's feminine. By saying that the king of Mshihwi was a lion, the myth-tellers specified his independent power — the lion could take the meat of tribute for itself; by saying it was in fact a lioness, the myth-tellers made it clear that Mshihwi's power was inferior to Vugha's (Feierman 1974).

The king's authority over his subjects was described at times like the authority of a polygynous husband over his wives. In this patriarchal view, so long as the one male held effective authority, peace prevailed. But (as the public language of precolonial Shambaai had it), if commoners or subordinate chiefs challenged the king, or if polygynous wives squabbled and challenged their husband, then public order declined.

Political language in this form still existed in the period of nationalist debate, and of course it survived into the years of national independence. I collected twenty-six variant tellings of the Mbegha myth between 1966 and 1968, all of which held the language constant in which one man (the first king) made all local people into women, dominated them, and thereby brought fertility to the land (Feierman 1974: chap. 2). The image of the chief as husband and the local people as wives had the effect of emphasizing the direct tie between the women of Shambaai and their rainmaking chiefs, unmediated by nonroyal men. The women, as the principle food producers, had reason for intense concern about the rains. Oral reminiscences about Hassani Kinyashi, rainmaking chief of Mlalo, usually describe women as the ones most concerned about losing him. It is they who make massive collections of food or firewood or shillings to convince him of their loyalty. In one of the accounts, the women plead with Hassani not to leave, saying, *Mwetigwisha fua ni ndai?*" ("[If you leave] who then will make rain for us?") *For us* in this case means *for the women of Mlalo*. Hassani is seen as making rain for the women. Similarly, at Bumbuli, oral accounts describe work parties in which the women labor en masse at Daudi Sozi's farms and then are drenched by rain on their way home. This is a recurrent patterned image to describe Daudi serving his people as rainmaker. But the image has the women as beneficiaries. As with Hassani, this is an unmediated relationship between Daudi and the women. An unmediated relationship between Daudi and the men would not require comment; it would be normal. But relationships between public authorities and the women would, in other contexts, be channeled through husbands or brothers as intermediaries.

Women in all parts of Shambaai combined their powerful interest in rain with deep hostility towards the Usambara Scheme for erosion control. The scheme's labor demands fell most heavily on the women, and they resisted directly. The invaded the *zumbes'* courts chanting slogans against the scheme, they appeared for work parties carrying minuscule hoes useless for scheme work, and they spread information about the scheme's flaws. The Usambara Scheme officer wrote as follows in 1950, the year of the scheme's introduction:

> At Mbaramo [at the northwestern tip of Shambaai] a harridan who had recently immigrated from Mlalo told us that everyone knew that Shita had been given to the Europeans. From Mbaru in Mtae there is a similar rumour circulating that Mbaru has been handed over to the Europeans. . . . At Mlola we had the Pare Women 'ploy.' We will have some more of this, until someone is slapped down firmly.[21]

The writer doubted that women's resistance had staying power in the face of punishment.

It is difficult to know precisely what stratagem the officer referred to as "the Pare Women 'ploy.'" In Pare, to the northwest of Shambaai, with close links to Mbaramo, Mlalo, and Mbaru, local people had organized resistance against *mbiru*, a system of graduated taxation. In early January 1945 thousands of Pare (somewhere between three thousand and ten thousand) descended on district headquarters demanding that *mbiru* be repealed. The crowd stayed for weeks. The women's uprising began in Usangi, one of the chiefdoms, when the district commissioner arrived for discussions with the local chief. A crowd of about five hundred women appeared, demanding an explanation of the events at the capital. The commissioner tried to leave without addressing the women. Enraged, they mobbed (and according to police reports, stoned) the assembled officials. Two days later, women surrounded the chief's house singing songs and ultimately battling police. A series of demonstrations continued into 1946 (Kimambo 1971, forthcoming; O'Barr 1975–76). Movement between Pare and Shambaai's northern tier was common, so some Shambaa women had been in touch with their Pare counterparts. The northern tier of Shambaai, and especially Mlalo, also resembled the part of Pare where the rebellious women lived in its relatively heavy dependence on labor migration. O'Barr (1975–76) thinks politically active women emerge where men are absent as labor migrants. This is not clear in Shambaai, but certainly Shambaa women who farmed in the absence of their husbands must have found scheme labor especially annoying.

The women who resisted appear in the archival materials of the period as an undifferentiated mass. Even when they achieve individual
distinction, they are *unnamed*, as for example in the case of the "har-
ridan," or vicious hag, of the scheme officer's report. This is partly a question of the way significant public acts were defined, and partly a question of literacy. Men are named in the archival materials if they were
literate and wrote letters to the provincial commissioner or petitions to
the Trusteeship Council. They are named if they held positions in recognized organizations, and they are named if they were arrested for crimes.
Women's political resistance did not usually lead to arrest, because women
were usually seen as having no public standing. Neither in the precolonial
nor in the colonial period did women pay tribute or tax. Women's political organizations were informal; in practice they were not required to
register with the government and did not invite prosecution. And wom-
en's literacy was limited by the preferences of parents and of educational
authorities for boys' education. In 1946 about 30 percent of the children
in Lutheran mission schools were girls, but these were concentrated in
the lower standards. Only 11 percent of the children in Standard 6 were
girls.[22]

For this reason among others, women did not appear among the literate leaders of the Usambara Citizens Union. Nevertheless, in the poster
of 1956 announcing the ten "Resolutions of the Usambara Citizens Union,"
Number 10 was "To protect the rights of women so that they are equal
to those of men."[23] A Tanzanian woman to whom I showed this resolution (the late May Balisidya) doubted that it meant Usambara Citizens
Union men were proposing to wash pots.

The resolutions and other actions of the period were nevertheless significant. For the first time in the modern history of Shambaai, women
were being defined as full public citizens, at least in theory. Several years
later, when the *Green Paper* proposed open elections for the positions
of Muambashi and elders, it accepted as a candidate anyone who is "a
taxpayer or a woman over the age of 21." The Shambaa debates of the
1950s about individual rights, slavery, and *uhuru* carried profound implications for the definition of women's place as autonomous public actors. Citizens Union and district TANU positions were, as we have seen,
internally contradictory yet open in important ways to radical change.

Citizens Union discussions in 1956 pointed towards a regime of local
notables (*watawa* and *wafung'wa*). These had been male positions in the
precolonial period, and the unstated implication now was that leaders
would be drawn from among men of mature years. In the TANU *Green
Paper* of 1960, one of the district's councils was to be called the *Gosi*,
related to the word *mghoshi*, "mature man." Nevertheless, the UCU pro-

gram called for gender equality, as we have seen. TANU leaders did the same, and the TANU *Green Paper* specified that women could run for office. Lushoto's correspondent to *Mwafrika*, a newspaper with close TANU connections, reported a 1959 council election in the following terms: "The women of Usambara used their ballots wisely, showing that they can be given equal rights with men."[24]

The debate about slavery, *uhuru*, and lineage values touched women in important ways. Arbitrary control by one person over another and authority based on birth were characteristics of the lineage regime related to slavery, and therefore to be rejected. The rights of precolonial chiefs to take wives without paying bridewealth and to take their choice of unmarried young women seemed to many in the 1950s archaic and improper.

In 1957 two men protested against an unpopular chief, reporting that he forced a divorce on a man so that he could take the wife for himself. The government in which this could happen was described in Swahili as *utawala wa kitumwa*, a "slave regime," in which rulers held arbitrary rights over the intimate persons of their subjects. The case is especially interesting because of its ambiguities. The protesters were men, and it is unclear whether they saw the chief as violating the woman's right to control her own body or (more likely) as violating the husband's rights in his wife.[25] Even in the latter case the objection to slavery or pawnship (*utumwa*) opened up important possibilities for change in the conception of women's place in society.

Peasant women organized themselves on gender lines, as women, to work towards national independence. Nyerere, in his January 1956 visit to Shambaai, was accompanied by the leader of TANU's women's section, Bibi Titi Mohamed, who had been a singer in one of Dar es Salaam's popular women's dance organizations. TANU had hurriedly decided to form a women's section six months earlier, after a visiting British Labour politician told leaders that the absence of women was a source of party weakness.[26] When Nyerere, Bibi Titi, and the other leaders reached the chiefdom of Bungu they heard about the warning, issued by the chief of Bungu, that anyone attending the TANU meeting would suffer terrible punishment. The warning frightened off even the Citizens Union members; Nyerere found no audience. According to the locally produced TANU district history, the women of Bungu, angry at their husbands' spinelessness, refused to cook. According to Bibi Titi's own account, they refused to fetch water or to farm. The men of Bungu, faced with a revolt by their wives, sent representatives to meet with Nyerere at the main town of Korogwe, to beg him to return. He agreed to speak at a mission station part of the way towards Bungu. The TANU leaders addressed a huge crowd in pouring rain. Women stood in the rain, babies wrapped in cloths on their backs, using banana leaves as umbrellas. Bibi Titi's car slipped in the mud some distance from the meeting. Then she fell when trying to walk on the treacherous, muddy path. She stayed with the car and climbed onto it to deliver her speech to an audience of women and men who had come from the meeting.

Accounts of these events differ from one another in their gender imagery. An oral account by a leader of the Citizens Union who was present does not mention the women at all, only that the people of Bungu sent messengers asking Nyerere to return after the first failed meeting. Nevertheless it is clear that gender issues are on his mind, for he describes how Nyerere went on, at the next stop, to say that the men of Tanganyika should not be governed by the British "as though they were women." It is clear that Nyerere did not actually say this, for "making men into women" is a Shambaa figure of speech with precolonial roots, used to describe the exercise of sovereignty. The official TANU district history, written by local men, places the same image in a different context. It says that the women of Bungu "decided to resist their men, and said they would not cook food for their husbands, because these men were timid and cowardly like women" (*TANU na Wananchi Lushoto* 1975:1). This is a variation on the theme of men made into women, saying that if men are made into women in the public realm, then the gender hierarchy within the household is destroyed. The third version is Bibi Titi's, as generously provided by Susan Geiger. According to Bibi Titi, in a transcript of her interview with Geiger:

> The women urged their leaders to bring Mr. Nyerere, and told them they also wanted to meet the strong woman. They said they wanted to see Bibi Titi in Vugiri. "We have heard and read about her but we have never seen her. If you don't want to listen to the strong words of Mr. Nyerere, that is up to you. We want to see Bibi Titi, our colleague."

In this account the women are seen as occupying their own sphere, and they want to see Bibi Titi, who is a leader in that separate sphere. This is in sharp contrast to the two male versions, which describe the women's action as a consequence of the men's failed masculinity.

It is impossible to point to a crystallized and coherent peasant discourse in the 1960s and 1970s growing out of the debates on slavery and descent-group rights in persons during the independence period. Women were admitted to jobs in the public sphere, and women's cooperatives played an important role in the local economy, especially during the 1960s. But debates which linked the intimate level of the household with the character of public social control remained marginal. They did not become part of core peasant ideology under the new regime. The relationship between the descent group and the person remained a central cultural concern, but the domain of its expression was not in public politics. Instead, local people altered the forms of healing rituals to express new perceptions and new concerns regarding this relationship.

Some elements of pre-independence peasant discourse survived into the period of independence, but these elements came to serve purposes very distant from those intended by the peasant intellectuals. Arguments supporting the rights of women were combined with others, current in peasant society from the 1940s, that leadership positions ought to go to people who achieved competence through education rather than through racial or chiefly birth. Women's rights and other goals that had been discussed among the peasantry would ultimately resurface in rural society as elements in programs imposed by the ruling party from above and shaped by the gender assumptions of party and government personnel (Geiger 1982).

The dominant group in independent Tanzania did not invent a wholly new ideology; it borrowed elements from a number of places, including the discourse of the peasantry, but then imposed upon them its own principles of organization. Peasant ideas now served new purposes.

The peasant intellectuals of the 1950s, who were effective actors on the national stage, found themselves removed from positions of influence in the 1960s in ways described in the next chapter. They were at their most effective during the period of TANU's rise because the nationalist party at that time needed their help. The immediate interests of most peasant intellectuals in Shambaai coincided, in the 1950s, with the immediate interests of the stratum that was rising to national political dominance (see Gramsci 1971:213). In the mid-1960s the interests of TANU, now the heart of the bureaucracy, diverged from the interests of ordinary people in the countryside.

The failure of peasants to win political control for themselves is often attributed to intellectual weakness, to an inadequate understanding of objective conditions. The peasants of Shambaai were influential in the 1950s and then lost influence in the 1960s not because they lost intelligence during that decade, but because their allies parted company with them.

9

Chiefs and Bureaucrats: Independence and the Fate of the Intellectuals

TANU's electoral victories of 1958–59 and 1960, and national independence which followed so quickly on their trail, led to the steep decline of chiefship throughout Tanganyika and to the dominance of educated functionaries. The years just before and after independence (which came in December 1961) marked a formal transition for the nation's intellectuals, more dramatic than the evolution which came before it. As we have seen, indirect rule as established in the 1920s based its dynamic on the shifting fortunes of a context between chiefs and educated Christian clerks. Cameron and others at the top of Tanganyika's government expected the clerks and teachers to become more powerful as the years passed; they expected the chiefs to weaken.

The postwar years pushed that double process along ever more rapidly. The pressures for moving the economy on to a more productive basis threatened the influence of chiefs. When plantation and urban workers moved towards permanent residence near the workplace, leaving their country homes behind, their home chiefs lost authority over the daily lives of these subjects. Erosion-control schemes in Usambara, Uluguru, and other places around the territory forced chiefs to serve as enforcers of unpopular regulations. When TANU introduced the demand for self-government and democratic rule, the government used chiefs as a shield, to be held between the aggressions of the nationalists and the defensive position of the British. Through the postwar years chiefs lost support.

The educated functionaries in the meanwhile lived in a very strange sort of shadow world. They suffered a double disadvantage if they wished to assert leadership: they were cut loose from local roots and prohibited from taking part in political activity. Men with secondary educations, who held the highest administrative positions open to Africans, usually moved from one place to another across Tanganyika in the line of work. Many of these men had lived through peasant childhoods but now found no opportunity to lead the rural folk from amongst whom they were drawn. If we scan a list of the educated Africans from Tanga Province who achieved high positions after independence in the early 1960s, we see that only two out of seventy-six remained in their rural home districts for most of the 1950s.[1] A typical career saw a young man from Lushoto or Handeni go off for schooling in Dar es Salaam, or Tabora, or Kilimanjaro, then to work elsewhere in Tanganyika. These men might, in the process, achieve a national vision of Tanganyika's problems, but they had only the weakest political base with their home folks.

The second disability of the functionaries was the rule of 1953 prohibiting civil servants from participating in political activity (a rule later waived in the case of chiefs). A few important leaders stayed outside the civil service in the 1950s to work full time for TANU; Julius Nyerere and Oscar Kambona were the most notable of these. But those who remained in the civil service were apolitical, cut off from their roots if they had rural origins, and they moved from one place to another around Tanganyika, forbidden to play a political role.[2] This pattern left the rural branches of TANU — the key to its political success — in the hands of leaders who, for the most part, had not attended secondary school, and whose social origins in other respects varied from one district to another.

The chiefs, meanwhile, suffered disabilities which were at the opposite pole from those of the new functionaries. The new functionaries were never able to sink local roots; the chiefs always did. The new functionaries were not to participate in politics; the chiefs were expected to do so: the role of chiefs was inherently political, for they were the enforcers of order. In the 1950s it was the chiefs who prohibited meetings, locked up peasant rebels, and enforced erosion-control rules. Even though the peasant rebels did not take charge of government after independence, Tanganyika's new African rulers understood that peasant rebels had been a central source of the nationalist movements's energy.

During the transition to independence, the chiefs' control over local administration violated TANU leaders' sense of the fitness of things. In October 1961 Nyerere described his discomfort at finding the chief in control each time he visited a district headquarters. He regretted seeing that the peasant rebels still remained impoverished outsiders:

> It is always a government affair. I am met by the provincial commissioner and by the district commissioner both of whom are likely to be colonial officers, the very men who TANU fought but a few years ago. I am introduced to them by other government officers who are also usually expatriates. I am then introduced to the chiefs and to the officials of the native authority and again I am meeting men who either opposed TANU or who carefully stayed out of the political struggle. Then off to one side I notice a few chaps in torn green shirts wielding banners but looking somewhat forlorn (Pratt 1978:108).

The chaps off to one side were, of course, the TANU activists of the 1950s.

In public debates on the future of chiefship, as in this quotation from Nyerere, TANU leaders focused on the degree to which chiefs had openly supported or opposed the independence movement. The country's new rulers were doing a kind of public political accounting. It did not help the chiefs' cause that a Convention of Chiefs had joined with the government in 1957 and 1958 to explore proposals meant to moderate the most dramatic effects of majority rule. The Governor, Sir Edward Twining, called together a convention of fifty-seven representative chiefs in May 1957 (among them Kimweri Magogo). In his opening remarks, Twining regretted that the territory had recently been experiencing a new phenomenon of "a political party composed largely of people whose tribal links hade been loosened, and who had not got the proper respect for the Native Authorities and Chiefs. Most of their ideas came from outside Tanganyika, put into their heads by people who did not have the true interests of the territory at heart."[3] In this situation, the pace of change was very fast and, according to Twining, "it would be dangerous to make it too fast." The only hope for stability was from the tribal system, which was the "very sheet anchor of the life of the African people in the territory."

The chiefs wanted to create a constitutional role for themselves in the Tanganyika of the future. They explored the possibility of creating a house of chiefs as the upper chamber of a bicameral legislature. The United Tanganyika Party (UTP), which was doing its best to block TANU's path to power, also adopted the idea of a bicameral legislature, with the upper chamber to include outstanding people of all races. The UTP expected the chiefs to play a central role in the new Tanganyika (Taylor 1963:158; Glickman 1972:135). The chiefs' collaboration with the UTP, like their collaboration with Twining, cost them dearly in the years after independence.

Later, after independence, when TANU people reviewed the chiefs' records, they also recalled actions in support of *uhuru*: Chief Fundikira of the Nyamwezi ran for Legislative Council with TANU support in 1958. The Convention of Chiefs adopted TANU's political program in March 1959, although by that time it was clear that TANU was unstoppable. Individual acts of chiefly support were remembered and honored, but the entire score was kept.[4]

The national scorekeeping, however, was not the central consideration in decisions on the future of chiefship. Much more important was the new government's desire to build national institutions and to transcend local loyalties. Back in 1954, before the Convention of Chiefs, TANU's founding document pledged to fight "tribalism and all its isolationist tendencies amongst Africans and to build up a united national-ism" (Glickman 1972:134). Or, as one member of the National Assembly put it in 1963, "Our aim is to remove all that tribal business to be citi-zens of a single nation."[5] As Nyerere saw it, local loyalties were capable of feeding resentments over economic inequalities. The missionaries built schools in some parts of the country and not others, so that the Haya people, the Chagga, and the Nyakyusa were better educated than people in many other local groups. This could lead to ethnic conflict and reli-gious conflict.[6] In addition, hereditary chiefship violated the central demo-cratic ideals of the equality of all citizens and their equal opportunity to act autonomously. The democratic central government of Tanganyika would be based on political forms new to Tanganyika: "There is nothing traditional in the Central Government of Tanganyika today," Nyerere said (Nyerere 1960:44). The very nature of traditional status, inherited at birth, was wrong for the new Tanganyika.

Nyerere pictured a Tanganyika of villages drawn together for direct democracy; the authentic model for democracy was direct participation by citizens in the Greek city-state. Here is how Nyerere described Greek political practice in the central TANU publication which defined democracy in 1959:

> The ancient Greeks lived in small towns. Each town was a complete "na-tion" with its own government. They did not have kings or *watemi* [chiefs]. Their governmental affairs were considered and decided in a meeting of all commoners together. Authority and responsibility did not rest with a single individual or a small group of citizens, but rested with the entire citizenry together. The Greeks called this governmental arrangement "Demokratia," that is, government by the citizens, in order to distinguish it from royal government and others.[7]

Democracy in this view was participatory and direct.

Why then did the industrial countries give the name *democracy* to a system not at all like the ancient one? One common answer to this ques-tion is that representation, through election, has taken the place of direct participation. This was not Nyerere's view. He explained that democracy can only truly be identified by its foundations. These are *usawa*, "equal-ity," and *uhuru*, "freedom," which Nyerere defined as "the condition of living, acting and thinking without obstruction. A slave has no *uhuru* because he is unable to live as he wishes, to act as he wishes, or even to think as he wishes."[8] Colonial subjects are not *huru*, nor are they treated as equal by their colonial masters, for whom skin color is a mark of in-equality. In ancient Greece, according to Nyerere's formula of 1959, the citizens who met together to dispose of affairs were free, and they were equal. A couple of years later, in 1961, Nyerere discussed the fact that Greece was a slave-owning society "which excluded masses of human beings from its idea of 'equality,'" but at this earlier point his emphasis was on the freedom and equality of Greek citizens, and especially on freedom and equality as the elements of continuity in democracy from the time of the Greeks to that of the European parliamentary democracies (Nyerere 1967:104).

Chiefship was incompatible with the equality of citizens, in the nationalist view. As we have seen, Shambaa peasant intellectuals of the 1950s said this, and so also did the foundation documents of TANU's ideology. In the series of TANU position papers, an essay on forms of government followed immediately after the one on democracy, and it explained the demerits of chiefship and monarchy. "The ancient Greeks," it said, "did not like this form of rule, for it is not democracy."[9]

Of royal rule, it said,

> This is a type of government which follows a line of descent. There is one descent group within the country which is not the same as any of the others. It is a superior lineage. This lineage permanently provides one person to rule the country. This person might be called the King, the Queen, the Mtemi, the Sultan, the Kabaka, or any other title.
>
> Secondly, that ruler has true governmental authority. Thirdly, he holds authority until he dies, or until he hands over to his heir from among his children or from his lineage according to their rules of inheritance.
>
> This type of goverment is government by one person, not democracy. It is evident that a person who holds authority because of his birth from a particular father and mother and who cannot be removed except by death can, in the ordinary human way, be trusted only with difficulty to protect the freedom and equality of the citizens.[10]

The king, in a monarchy "is not a person. He is equivalent to a small God."

What is remarkable in all of this is how close the positions of TANU and Nyerere were, in this period, to the thought of peasant intellectuals, including the disparaging description of the king as a small God. Nyerere must have drawn intellectual nourishment from the debate on democracy which, as we have seen, had been intense in Shambaai (and presumably other parts of the countryside) since 1947, and probably earlier, well before his appearance on the public stage. We are accustomed to the notion that ideas flowed from educated leaders to the peasantry, as indeed they did in the late 1950s when, according to oral accounts, peasant farmers eagerly bought and read TANU newspapers, and carefully studied Nyerere's definitions of political terms. But it is equally clear that ideas flowed from the periphery to the center. Discussions of seventeenth-century British regicide, which had been current in Shambaai in the 1940s, appeared in the parliamentary debates of independent Tanganyika in the 1960s.[11]

The democratic Greek city-state appears to have been part of Nyerere's vision of villagization, which ultimately became one of the core elements in the national program of *ujamaa*. The link between village democracy and village socialism inhered naturally in Nyerere's view that equality was one of the two defining foundations of democracy. Ancient Greek equality became linked in Nyerere's thought with the equality of the pre-colonial African village. Four years before the socialist initiative of the Arusha Declaration, Nyerere described villagization as essential for the technological improvement of peasant agriculture and for the creation of direct democracy. In his inaugural speech to Parliament when Tanganyika became a Republic, he said,

> Living together in villages will also help to perfect our plans for democracy. It is true that our current government, the central government together with local government, is chosen democratically. But because we live in scattered locations, our democracy still has its flaws. First, it is difficult for us to meet together and to make decisions on our affairs, especially those concerning village life. Because of this, we leave matters to be decided by our chosen representatives. Often, however, because of distance we are unable to see our representatives and to ask them what matters they are discussing and deciding in our place. Living in villages will lead to true democracy in the matters which concern each village.[12]

Direct democracy at the village level was important for popular control over local affairs and also for communication with elected representatives.

Political independence — victory over the colonialists who had tried to make skin color the basis of domination — left the new government free to move against its internal discrimination on the basis of birth to a chiefly lineage. The elimination of chiefship unfolded inexorably from the moment Nyerere became chief minister under the British in 1960. It unfolded in a multitude of local changes, and only later as the consequence of sweeping decrees. Soon after Nyerere took office, his British civil servants urged him to leave chiefs and headmen in place for the sake of stability in rural administration. They also wanted to leave civil servants in their positions as provincial and district commissioners (Pratt 1978:108). This was galling to the mass of TANU's members, who had taken control of Dar es Salaam but now found their most bitter enemies still in charge of practical administration.

The solution was to move towards piecemeal change: to create local plans for making every one of Tanganyika's rural councils democratic, directly elected. As with so many of Tanganyika's dramatic changes in the transition to independence, this one had its roots in postwar colonial policy. The British wanted to provide a channel of expression for educated young men in the districts, and also for the expanding group of white settlers. They therefore gradually began replacing native authorities with autonomous district councils, but without abolishing the positions of the chiefs, who retained control over law and order, and retained the power to issue oral or written orders and rules. In 1960 and 1961 local councils began to remove the most bitterly anti-TANU chiefs from office. Then, in 1962, the power to administer law and order was taken from all chiefs. A series of amendments to ordinances destroyed the basis of chiefly authority. By February 1963 all the powers of the Native Authorities had been transferred to District Councils. The framework of indirect rule had been dismantled (Cole and Denison 1964:83–85; Bienen 1970:67).

When Nyerere was sworn in as president of the Republic on 9 December 1962, he appeared to take on some of the marks of chiefship. When he arrived at the National Stadium in Dar es Salaam, the drums of the royal house of Mwami Theresa Ntare of Buha sounded a rhythmic welcome. Chief Petro Itosi Marealle greeted the president and prayed that God would bless him. Then Chief Mazengo presented Nyerere with a robe, so that "the favour of your leadership be spread all over the country in the same way as this long robe has spread all over your body," with a spear for the protection of the citizens of Tanganyika, and with a shield for the defense of the country from enemies. The president left to the sound of the Haya great drum, after being anointed by Chief Mazengo with a mixture of flour and water. The chiefly emblems did not become a permanent part of Nyerere's public persona. The swearing-in ceremony might be seen as an aberration in the president's presentation of himself, or as a moment of transition from the era of chiefship and indirect rule to that of secular "modern" presidency.[13]

One question that remained after the end of chiefship was whether former chiefs were to receive pensions or in some other way to be compensated for loss of jobs. Local chiefs, as they departed, raised the question with administrative officers. The issue was resolved on a national level by the test case of Thomas Marealle, former Paramount Chief of the Chagga, who sued Kilimanjaro District Council for breach of contract, claiming that local government was obligated to pay him the salary and benefits of a lifetime in office. In October 1963 the High Court awarded Marealle 919,900.00 shillings. Six weeks later the government introduced a bill in the National Assembly to overrule the court's decision. "Government," Rashidi Kawawa said, "must have the power to stop a few people who want to suck the blood of many others."[14]

The end of chiefship was part of a larger policy aimed at keeping ethnic loyalties strictly out of the political arena. No ethnic political organization, irrespective of its nationalist credentials, was to be allowed to exist. Nyerere was watching the agony of the Congo in this period, and he was determined that "we can't have another Katanga here" (Iliffe 1979:569). In 1960 and after, TANU rejected its allies of the 1950s if they were organized on an ethnic basis. The Meru Citizens Union, for example, had brought the idea of nationalist struggle to much of northern Tanganyika by fighting the Meru Land Case all the way to the United Nations. Kirilo Japhet, who presented the Meru case, became TANU chairman for the Northern Province. Nevertheless, in 1961 TANU's Deputy Secretary General announced that the Meru Citizens Union had been closed down. For similar reasons TANU denied affiliation to the Chagga Democratic Party, forcing it to disband in 1960, even though it was composed of TANU loyalists, and its president, Solomon Eliufoo, became minister of education. Nyerere ordered the destruction of the Sukumaland Federal Council, the organization of TANU's loyal allies in that part of the country (Iliffe 1979:568–69; Bienen 1970:26; Glickman 1972:131).

The political files of Tanga Province for 1962 show that local administrative officers took great care in the transition to independence to put ethnic associations under surveillance, and to destroy them where possible. In the words of the regional administrative secretary, "It is Government Policy that all tribal societies of a political nature should not be allowed to be registered as their existences are against the declared intention of the Government to unite all small tribes of the Territory into one big nation."[15] The administrator's policy declaration bears the indelible mark of indirect rule, for it assumes that Tanganyika is a nation of tribes, even though it announces that tribal politics are now illegal.

Within Shambaai local people abolished the formal institution of chiefship during the transition to independence, yet preserved and guarded the ethnic basis of local politics, at least over the short term. The battle between peasant rebels and Kimweri had been so bitter that the local TANU did away with chiefship before the law required. The initiative was a local one, moved along (but not defined) by national policy; local rebels were therefore free to define their own preferred institutions of government. These institutions self-consciously imitated two very different models, both at the same time: European democracy and predynastic lineage rule. The *Green Paper* constitution (discussed above), which outlined their program, called for the election of officers who would hold the titles of pre-dynastic notables: *Muambashi*, *Mfung'wa*, and *Mtawa*. The notables were to hold their offices in a very untraditional way: for fixed terms and through elections based on universal suffrage.

In August 1960 the District's TANU, having had four of its members elected to the *Bawanjama* (the king's council) in 1959 and then thrown off by the district commissioner, presented the *Green Paper* as its constitutional proposal for the future government of Shambaai. The council at this point had a majority of official members, appointed to their positions by Kimweri or by the British. The *Green Paper* proposed that the officers be elected by secret ballot for terms of two or three years, with a few officers (for example the medical officer and the agricultural officer) to serve ex officio. Quite probably the most shocking declaration of the *Green Paper* was that the king's title, Simba Mwene, had no meaning at all, and that the idea of an office like the king's, which was either inherited or held for life, was inappropriate for modern times.[16]

Kimweri and the British administrators would have liked to hold back the movement towards a new council form, but this was impossible at a time when the nation was moving rapidly towards independence under a TANU government. In October 1960 Kimweri appointed a committee, equally divided between his personal supporters and TANU men, to recommend changes for the future. The meetings of this committee could not have been easy, for its members included two subchiefs who were notorious for their persecution of peasant rebels and alongside them some of the rebels themselves, including one man who had been a member of the resistance *vyama* from early days. The committee was torn from the start. Kimweri and the British provincial commissioner wanted the least possible change, and excluded the *Green Paper* from consideration. But TANU pressure from above (from Rashidi Kawawa as minister for local government and housing) gave the TANU members courage to refuse compromise. There were stormy meetings of the whole *Bawanjama;* TANU alleges that Kimweri packed the place with his supporters. The resolution unfolded after the meeting of May 1961 at which the TANU members fired Kimweri's household officials. Kimweri called a strike of council employees, which was then broken by TANU's Youth League. Shortly afterwards, in August 1961, the new council with a TANU chair met for the first time.

A photograph of the occasion shows Kimweri Magogo, eyes and mouth held rigid, visibly upset at the passing of his power, standing alongside Julius Nyerere. Kimweri later moved outside Shambaai altogether, down to a cattle camp in the arid wilderness beyond Mombo, at a place called Mlembule. It was too painful, his friends said, for him to continue living as a private citizen at Vugha, where so recently he had ruled. I visited Kimweri in the wilderness several times in 1967 and 1968. He was very much thinner than he had been in photographs taken during the 1950s. The weight loss, too, was attributed to the loss of power. Later Kimweri left the cattle camp to resume a fuller life as a Tanzanian.

The *Bawanjama's* rapid transformation, and Kimweri's striking defeat, should not be seen as a total defeat for chiefship or for the Kilindi in Shambaai. Some of the chiefs who inherited rain charms continued to earn the devoted support of their followers in Shambaai. Several chiefs continued, through the 1960s, to receive tribute labor from women in their chiefdoms, and to eat the meat of bulls brought as "greetings."

The core ideas of chiefship survived in relation to the rainmakers, and also in a surprising way in the imagined picture of the real locus of power. Real power, the equivalent of the precolonial Simba Mwene's, the power of life and death, did not reside in the district; it resided in Dar es Salaam. In the 1960s, but also in 1980, I heard old men refer to Nyerere as the real holder of power, equivalent to the king. In the imagination of some people, Nyerere roamed the countryside in the middle of the night, bringing death to his enemies. The precolonial image of the power-holder as a buffalo, bringing death, does not itself die easily. The imagery of power is not easily transformed when the power itself changes hands.

The defeat of the chiefs left Tanganyika as a nation of peasants and bureaucrats. The underdevelopment of the economy had a leveling effect, leaving the nation with few peaks and valleys, and with few categories of Africans having won the privilege or prominence on which to build future leadership. We have already seen that colonial policy in the 1920s aimed to prevent the emergence of substantial inequalities among peasants; in all periods it was directed at limiting the autonomous political role of peasant intellectuals. Labor unions of the colonial period were weak, isolated, and apolitical, and religious leaders were kept under careful control. There were, it is true, great numbers of African traders with many active in TANU, but most traders operated at a very small-scale retail level (Iliffe 1979:542). An important path toward both accumulation and political influence for African traders was through cooperatives. But the colonial government kept these under the strictest control. In all this, there were strong continuities from the British period to the TANU period. The British had been careful to restrict the emergence of alternative forms of leadership, aside from chiefs and salaried government employees. The TANU government closed down the public role of chiefs, narrowing the charmed circle of public participation until it included only the salariat. The new government was as careful as the old one to eliminate the emergence of alternatives. The TANU government restricted the emergence of a trading class, closed down independent labor unions, constrained the public role of religious leaders, and most important of all, kept peasant organizations under the strictest party control.

The argument here is that the bureaucracy held very great power in the Tanzania of the 1960s and 1970s, and that this state of affairs grew out of a colonial situation in which the only Africans with substantial collective influence were chiefs and clerks/bureaucrats. The chiefs lost power, leaving the clerks/bureaucrats in charge. The history of colonial-period intellectuals shaped the fate of the nation in fundamental ways. The triumph of an undemocratic bureaucracy was not the only possible outcome; the process was not inevitable. To understand why popular control failed, however, it is not enough to study the history of constitutional liberties as words on pieces of paper, although such words when they exist must be valued. The failure of popular control is a social history — the history of sectors of socially-rooted leadership within Tanzania which might have built up sufficient power to challenge the bureaucracy. Had these challenges been successful, they might have created spheres of popular freedom. The political form and social content of those freedoms would have varied considerably, depending on which group won autonomy. A Tanzania in which peasant organizations won influence, independent of the bureaucrats, would have been radically different from a Tanzania in which merchants were powerful, or one in which trade unions or marketing cooperatives were a dominant force. In each case one could imagine a concrete set of social policies and ideological tensions. But in the actual event, the British worked very hard during the colonial period to prevent the emergence of autonomous labor unions, cooperatives, or peasant organizations. And the Tanzanian bureaucrats did their best to finish the job.

Given the economic structure of colonial Tanganyika — a country of smallholders who grew crops for consumption or for sale — the likely third force (alongside chiefs and clerks) would have been the traders who bought crops from peasant farmers and sold them consumer goods. We have already seen that colonial regulations were meant to limit Africans to very small-scale, localized retail trade. The wholesale trade and large-scale crop purchasing remained in the hands of non-Africans, in many cases Asian traders.

When Africans did participate in large-scale trade, most substantially in the 1950s, they were involved mainly through cooperatives. These originated in the struggle by Africans (in many cases traders) to create their own autonomous trading organizations in order to win back control over marketing, which the government had given to non-Africans. But the colonial government found cooperatives easy to control and for this reason favored them, for they were the economic equivalent of indirect rule's Native Authorities and the forerunners of parastatal corporations. Cooperative officers were only partially independent of governmental control. They were, in some ways, like government functionaries.

Colonial-era cooperatives were in ambivalent positions. They were vehicles through which local Africans fought for their interests, but at the same time they were agents of government-established marketing boards: the Bukoba Native Coffee Board, the Moshi Native Coffee Board, the Lint and Seed Marketing Board (for cotton), and others. The boards designated cooperatives or private traders as official purchasers of peasant crops, at prices arranged with the government. Cooperative officers served as the African intermediaries who introduced the government's desired farming techniques, and who controlled quality in the purchased export crop. The government kept primary cooperative societies to a size that could present no challenge to chiefly authorities. It also prohibited the cooperatives from participating in politics. Each cooperative's trading operations were kept under strict government supervision, on threat of being deregistered by the Registrar of Co-operative Societies.[17]

As the economic structure of independent Tanzania evolved, the contradictions of cooperatives emerged: they were organizations controlled by government while ostensibly serving peasant members. Over time, the officers of the cooperative unions became privileged members of the bureaucracy — creatures of the government, not at all members of an autonomous commercial class, and certainly not peasant intellectuals, organically bound to small farmers. Cooperative officers became members of the salariat (Coulson 1982:149–52, 278, 280, 320, 321, 341, n.14).

In the years immediately after independence, the government rapidly increased the number of cooperative societies. In most cases these were single-channel marketing organizations — the sole legal purchasers of peasant crops. Their monopoly testifies to the weakness of African traders in the independence government, for a strong trading class would not have tolerated the complete loss of legal trade in the country's major products. The cooperatives themselves lasted only for fifteen years as autonomous organizations. At first, the officers of cooperative unions held positions of great economic power which had been created by government order yet were not subject to careful government control. The officers were free also of control by the peasant members of primary societies, because the unions were not democratic in their organization. Cooperative union leaders thus enjoyed power without responsibility. The result was inefficiency, in some cases corruption, in most cases unprofitable operation, and in almost all cases poor prices paid to peasants. The government responded in 1976 by nationalizing all the cooperative unions, turning them into parastatal corporations. A parastatal is an enterprise owned, in part or in whole, by the government, which appoints directors to its board. This was a constitutional form inherited from the colonial period, when the marketing boards were parastatals. Parastatals enjoy considerably greater independence, in accounting and in terms of employment for officers, than government ministries. The result is that co-operative officers have been transformed, over time, into privileged members of the governmental bureaucracy.

For these managers it is a golden (rather than an iron) cage, but the result, up to the early 1980s, was the total dominance of bureaucrats. This was the final consequence of a process which began when indirect rule set up clerks (but no other group and certainly not traders) as a counterweight to chiefs. The process was not a simple one, but for a time the outcome was: the emergence of a nation of peasants and bureaucrats.

The continuity between colonial and postcolonial constraints on the emergence of autonomous African intellectuals can also be seen in the history of trade unions. These had been relatively weak until the 1950s. It had been difficult to organize Tanganyika's workers, who until that time had been few in number and rurally based, as much concerned with the fate of their rural homes as with the issues of the workplace.[18] Nevertheless, the 1950s saw dramatic increases in union activity, at times expressing profound nationalist sympathies.

After independence, the new government and party took drastic measures to avert the emergence of an independent union movement with its own autonomous set of leaders. The central conflict, in the years immediately after independence, concerned the pace with which the government's work force was Africanized. Nyerere argued for a slow transition, whereas the unions (along with elements in the army) were pressing for Africans to move quickly in taking over expatriate jobs. The government's response in 1962 was to ban strikes and to establish machinery for compulsory dispute settlement. Then in 1964 the government centralized all trade unions in the National Union of Tanganyika Workers, whose general secretary and deputy secretary were to be appointed by the president of the Republic. The less docile of the unionists were imprisoned — Christopher Tumbo of the railway workers in 1963, and a number of others after the army mutiny in 1964 (Coulson 1982:137–40; Bienen 1970: 208–9, 271–72, 371; Martin 1976:91).

Another possible base for emerging intellectuals was in the religious communities, which quickly promised to become involved directly in the affairs of the state. Once again, the bureaucrats took vigorous action to exclude alternative intellectuals from active political participation.

Because the colonial government had put much of the territory's educational structure into missionary hands, most members of the educated governing elite were Christian. Muslims were, for a period, largely excluded from high government positions. The long-term solution was to secularize education, which also had the effect of narrowing the sphere of public policy in which religious leaders were involved by removing education from that sphere. In the short term, TANU's response was a double one: to coopt Muslim leaders in an Elders Section, and to close down discussion of religious questions in the realm of politics. Sheikh Takadir, the first head of the Elders, was expelled from TANU and ostracized by its leaders for questioning whether an election slate had enough Muslims on it. TANU threatened periodically to close down AMNUT, the All-Muslim National Union. Most important of all, in the crucial parliamentary election of 1965, the first after independence, election rules strictly prohibited any mention of religious or ethnic issues (Bienen 1970: 59–60, 69; Glickman 1972:135–37).

In the context of this book, the most important set of intellectuals who might have established a sphere of autonomy beyond the limits of bureaucratic control were the local leaders emerging from amongst the peasantry. The entire policy of *ujamaa vijijini, ujamaa* "in the villages," appears at first glance to have been directed towards giving greater power and influence to rural intellectuals. In fact, peasants did gain power for a period. It seemed possible that autonomous peasant intellectuals, not directly controlled by the bureaucrats, would create their own rural institutions. Government functionaries perceived this possibility as an intolerable threat; they responded by bringing all *ujamaa* villages under party control. The crucial event was the tragic decision to close down the Ruvuma Development Association (RDA).

The RDA emerged in the south of the country as a union of spontaneous village settlements, organized on cooperative principles, which sprang up at about the time of independence. The villagers worked some farm plots individually and some communally. Over time, the communal plots grew. The largest of this handful of villages, Litowa (which grew to about sixty families), became self-sufficient in communally grown food, built its own water supply, drastically lowered its infant mortality rate, and created a new school syllabus to teach its young people the skills they would actually need to be successful as villagers. The RDA received money from Julius Nyerere to purchase a mill for grinding maize flour and from a Swiss charity to purchase a local sawmill. They operated both mills successfully. In 1969 the national party Central Committee met to consider the fate of the RDA. They were disturbed that the maize mill paid higher prices for peasant maize than the government-approved cooperative, that an autonomous group of peasants outside party control, living near the Mozambique border in the midst of a war, was receiving aid from Europe, and that the peasants of the association had been effective at resisting government plans for the compulsory planting of tobacco as a cash crop. The Central Committee therefore voted to disband the Ruvuma Development Association and to confiscate the grain mill, the sawmill, the mechanical workshop, and the vehicles and equipment (Coulson 1982:262–71).

The decision to declare the Ruvuma Development Association an illegal society was much more than a local decision. At the same meeting, the Central Committee ruled that all *ujamaa* villages would now be controlled directly by the party. In spite of this policy, peasant intellectuals continued, of course, their struggle to follow their own path. A governmental policy of control over peasant life is never equivalent to the reality of control. The struggle between peasants and the government over control of rural life had been at the core of colonial politics, and that struggle continued in much the same form after independence. The Societies Ordinance, which the British had used in the 1950s to close down popular associations of peasant rebels, including TANU branches, now became TANU's instrument in outlawing the Ruvuma Development Association (Martin 1976:35). The peasants resisted in the earlier period, and they would continue to resist now, after the transition to TANU rule. The Shambaa have a proverb about the inevitable costs of government: *Waghanga woshe waavya mpome*, "All healers draw blood." Peasants know what to expect; they must look out for themselves.

Six years before the defeat of the RDA, rural district councils had been brought directly under party control. Here the crucial contest occurred in Buhaya. An ordinance of 1962 gave the minister for local government the power to dissolve town or district councils; local elections were essentially advisory. In April 1963 a number of young men, most of them TANU members, defeated the official TANU candidates in an election to the Buhaya District Council, in the northwest of the country. A majority of the new council (including some of the official candidates) refused to accept the party line. After considerable debate within the national party, the minister for local government nominated an entirely new council. Once again, the national party and national bureaucracy denied leaders outside the government the right to political independence (Cole and Denison 1964:85–89; Dryden 1968:72–75).

The government did not succeed in eliminating the existence of competing groups of intellectuals — individuals who by virtue of their social positions played organizational, directive, or educative roles. Christian pastors and priests, Muslim *walimu*, traders and local healers continued to be influential outside the orbit of state control. But their capacity to influence policy was limited. They were vulnerable to government interventions such as the regulation of healing or trade, or the termination of religious control of schools. In light of these patterns of development, it is no surprise that positions of leadership in independent Tanzania were concentrated among formally educated government functionaries.

In June of 1960 a reader wrote to the Kibogoyo column of the TANU-affiliated newspaper, *Mwafrika* (4 June 1960), asking why the educated men, who were afraid to fight for independence, were about to reap its benefits. The awareness was remarkably clear in 1959 and 1960 that independence under TANU would mean the rise of educated government employees. *Mwafrika,* a newspaper read carefully and passed from hand to hand in Shambaai (and presumably in many other parts of the countryside), reported each week on scholarship opportunities abroad, on Africans advancing to unprecedented heights within the civil service, on the names of Africans heading overseas to study, and on developments in the salary structure of expatriate administrators. There was some labor news, but almost none for the whole of 1959 and 1960 about developments in the countryside. *Mwafrika* had a regular poetry column, with some of the poems devoted to office routine, files, typewriters, and desks.

One of the main prizes at stake, in the movement towards independence, was a bureaucratic jobs. A clerk in Tabora who wrote a letter to *Mwafrika's* editor was worried about the fact that government clerks, who have the best understanding of work in offices, were not getting enough of the new jobs.

> These days we see that many Africans who do not come from among the clerks . . . are taken to study in Europe, and others are given high positions here in Tanganyika without going to Europe to study. The thing which distresses us, for our part as clerks, is that it is our brothers who are not clerks who will get the benefit of important positions like Field Officers, Labour Inspectors, Co-operative Officers, Public Relations Officer and so on. . . . Clerks are people who have special knowledge of work in offices, and therefore ought to be thought of for higher positions and to leave the clerks' jobs for women.[19]

The clerk's proposal became, to some degree, a reality. More of the poorly paid clerks' jobs became women's work, and many male clerks advanced rapidly in government service. In a survey of Tanzania's highest elites of the years 1963–68, 35.7 percent of elite members, virtually all of them male, had worked at first in clerical occupations (McGowan and Bolland 1971:81 [Table 17]).

The triumph of the functionaries came despite the fact that most of the original generation of TANU activists had too little education to move into the new jobs. Some members of that original generation were farmers, others held petty government jobs as messengers or tribal dressers, and some, in parts of the country, were traders. These people were ultimately left out of the new jobs. The changeover began in 1958 with TANU's decision to introduce secretaries appointed from national headquarters into the local party branches around the country. Some of the first secretaries appointed were peasant activists, but as time passed it became clear that educated secretaries would be more likely to follow orders from headquarters and to sustain the flow of paperwork than were the early party workers. In the provinces and districts, a division slowly evolved between TANU chairmen with roots in local politics and TANU secretaries, who were educated. Then in 1962 the government appointed area commissioners and regional commissioners to replace British district and provincial commissioners, respectively. Every regional commissioner, appointed by the president, was ex officio the TANU regional secretary, a member of Parliament, and a member of the party's National Executive Committee. The commissioners were drawn from among the better-educated party functionaries — from among party secretaries rather than party chairmen. Virtually all commissioners came up through earlier white-collar jobs. In 1964 the final major stage came in the merging of the political rulers of Tanzania and the educated bureaucracy. Civil servants, who had been prohibited since 1953 from joining political parties, were now given permission to join TANU.[20] Meanwhile, African employment in the civil service grew explosively. In 1960 there were 453 Africans in senior- and middle-grade posts in the Tanganyika civil service; by 1967 this number had grown to 6,379. The total number of such posts grew from 3,000 to nearly 8,000 (McGowan and Bolland 1971:46).

The rulers of Tanzania were overwhelmingly salaried administrators. This is demonstrated clearly by survey research done in the 1960s. Three times during that decade, researchers from Marco Surveys, a private survey research firm, interviewed the members of what it judged to be the new Tanzanian elite. The research team studied government staff lists, directories of commerce and industry, and the membership lists of professional, cultural, and welfare organizations and societies. Then it drew up a list of members of the elite, defined as men and women who earned over one thousand pounds a year or held a position of great responsibility, including important jobs in government, trade unions, cooperative unions, or religious or voluntary associations. It then interviewed the members of this elite. The research undoubtedly underestimated the importance of private African traders and leaders of Muslim brotherhoods, because these would not have appeared on lists. It would also have ignored the core issues of social dynamics — whether wealthy African farmers, for example, were accumulating farm land, or the fact that all trade unions were being brought under government control. Nevertheless, the picture of the elite is revealing.[21]

More than half the members of the elite in 1967 had "higher civil servant" as their primary occupation (53.3 percent), with "politician" next

(16.4 percent). If to these we add "party activists," "teachers," and "voluntary association [i.e. cooperative] leaders," the total comes to 84.7 percent. Agriculturists made up 0.5 percent of the elite, and laborer-traders another 0.5 percent. If we look at the primary occupations, in 1956–60, of those who were to become members of the elite, a similar pattern appears. Taken together, clerks, college students, teachers, cooperative leaders, and higher civil servants were 68.4 percent of the total. Party activists, politicians, and professionals were the next largest groups. In 1967 significantly more than 80 percent of members of the elite had attended secondary school, in a country where secondary-school attendance was the privilege of a minute part of the population (McGowan and Bolland 1971:33,34).

The salaried class, with its roots among the clerks of indirect rule, was so powerful in the early years of independence that it was able to prevent the emergence of alternative nodes of power, whether among the traders (who were preempted by the cooperatives, which were then destroyed), or among the trade unions (which were made part of government), or among the *ujamaa* villages (which were allowed to exist only under party control, and some of which were ultimately to have salaried managers imposed by the government). Later, after the Arusha Declaration, the salariat expanded within vast and numerous parastatals.

The central ideas were those of classic bureaucracies. We have already seen them foreshadowed in the public ideas of Shambaa clerks of the 1950s. They thought that position-holders needed certifiable educational qualifications, that positions within the bureaucracy would have clearly marked spheres of competence, and that the person was always separate from the office. As always with ideal types, these understandings about office did not always match lived experience. Alongside bureaucratic ideas went those of *ujamaa*, a rich and important body of thought which is outside the scope of this work.

Ujamaa is important, however, for understanding why intelligent people of good will who wished to serve Tanzania worked very hard to build a bureaucratic state. Many educated Tanzanians believed passionately in the goals of *ujamaa*: to eliminate poverty and disease from the lives of ordinary Tanzanians in the countryside and the city; to bring an adequate standard of living to all Tanzanians, not merely a privileged few; to avoid the emergence of forms of exploitation which accompany the growth of concentrated private wealth; to escape from dependency on the powerful nations of the West — nations which had proven by their actions in southern Africa that they were insensitive to exploitation based on racial domination and insensitive also to the inhuman use of cheap labor by capitalist enterprises. The self-evident value of Tanzania's national aims made it seem worthwhile to impose them from above, to build a strong state at all costs, even if the costs included frustrating the drive for autonomy by leaders from amongst the peasantry or the working class.

Back in 1960 the fully articulated ideology of *ujamaa* had not yet emerged, but it was already clear that bureaucrats would ascend and take control of the nation. Competition became intense for the education that would give entrance to the bureaucracy. Even at that time it was not a simple matter of self-serving men chasing after material gain. Many Tanzanians thought that education was the key to building a new and more prosperous nation (G. M. Wilson 1966: 449).

Within Shambaai, the time of the transition to independence and of the struggle to end chiefship was also a time when Shambaa Lutherans fought a mortal battle for control over their church. In so crucial a transitional period for the history of intellectuals, one would expect the church, as the most important educational institution, to be the object of struggle. The Lutheran Church held a dominant position in the educational system of Shambaai during the colonial period although the Native Authority, increasingly in the 1950s, began to build its own schools. From that time, some of the wealthier coffee-growing Muslims encouraged their sons to go as far as they possibly could in school. Nevertheless, the great majority of clerks and schoolteachers were Lutherans, and the church was able to control the mobility of the schoolteachers into higher levels of administration, for the church had its own channel to scholarships abroad. The struggle to control scholarships raised the stakes in what would, in any event, have been a powerful movement to reduce European missionary influence.[22]

The key figure in the struggle was a German missionary named Heinrich Waltenberg, who had arrived in 1930 as a humble deacon to serve in the church mental hospital at Lutindi, in the extreme south of Shambaai.[23] He had local ties at the time of his arrival, for his father-in-law had been a missionary in Shambaai. Waltenberg is remembered even now for the fluency of his Shambaa. When other Germans were deported or interned during the war, Waltenberg remained free, and his influence grew within the local church. He became church president in 1956.[24] Waltenberg retained a core of loyal Shambaa followers to the end, whether because of the force of his personality or because of his skill at disposing of patronage. His enemies accused him of dispensing, as personal largesse, contributions that came to the church as an institution. There is no question that so long as he was head of the church, his allies prospered and his enemies won few rewards.

The events that precipitated struggle were the church's decision early in 1961 to adopt episcopacy and then to name Waltenberg bishop, to be installed in 1962. Waltenberg promised to step down as soon as a suitable African was available to take his place, but many of the Shambaa who knew him doubted that he would ever agree that an African was suitable for this highest position of leadership. A movement emerged within Shambaai to challenge Waltenberg's rise to episcopacy. The Shambala African Lutheran Teacher's Union (SALTU), founded in 1956, was critical of Waltenberg through the late 1950s. Pay and conditions for African teachers were poor, the church fired teachers without much cause, and missionaries did not share information about church management with Africans.

A crucial break came in 1961, when Waltenberg fired Silas Shemdoe (a teacher) and removed Olimpa Shauri (an influential pastor at Mlalo) as church vice-president. He was punishing them for ignoring the channels that ran through him; they wrote directly to the National Lutheran Church in Minnesota, in the United States. A dissident congregation began meeting in a self-help chapel at Mlalo in 1961. Later, in 1962, they now insisted on sharing the regular church building, and they had Olimpa Shauri's help. At Vugha, the dissidents had taken over the church from the start. When Waltenberg sent a carpenter to nail shut the front door of Vugha's church, he was met by a group of congregants who told him that he would not survive to see another day if he nailed the door. The carpenter reconsidered and left.

In the end, the government resolved the conflict, and since the government was at that point in populist African hands, the solution was a populist one. In January 1963 the opposing sides met with the area commissioner (a Shambaa TANU activist), the regional commissioner, and Oscar Kambona, who was then minister for home affairs. This group arranged a short-term compromise. But then in the first half of 1963 the government forced Waltenberg to leave the country. To maintain an appearance of even-handedness, and presumably to clean out European interference in African affairs, the government also deported three European missionaries who had been friendly to the rebel cause.

The aim of the church rebels was to reclaim for Africans control over their own religious community. The general issue at stake, therefore, was one of human dignity and spiritual autonomy. But there were immediate practical issues under dispute also, and of these the most important was control over scholarships. These gave entry into the higher levels of the salariat, or into church leadership. By 1957 the Lutheran teachers' union (SALTU) expressed dissatisfaction with the scarcity of scholarships abroad, and with the fact that Waltenberg controlled access. The minutes of most SALTU meetings after that return to the question of scholarships abroad. When a representative of America's National Lutheran Council visited Shambaai, SALTU asked to meet with him so they could get facts about the scholarship situation, unmediated by Waltenberg. One reason for pressure from within the church for joining the Lutheran World Federation, which it did in 1959–60, was to improve the prospects for scholarships abroad. And there is no question that Waltenberg used his control over scholarships to maintain discipline. When asked at a SALTU meeting about making access to scholarship information more open, he responded, "I am the chairman of the scholarship committee . . . whoever wishes to may write to me and their affairs will be considered."[25]

Waltenberg and his enemies all understood the importance of scholarships. Some Shambaa Lutherans suspected that he was limiting scholarships and sending weak students abroad so that he could delay the emergence of a generation of Africans capable of taking over church leadership. One wrote, "We only hear that the Church has opportunities for study, which are open. We do not know who will fill these places, or when. . . . It needs to be made known that it is by this path, of delaying people from filling opportunities for study, that it becomes possible to say that there are no people with the knowledge to do responsible work in this church. . . . How long will it be until the church gets African leaders?"[26] The most important break came over this question. Silas Shemdoe lost his job, and Olimpa Shauri lost the vice-presidency because Shemdoe had written, and Olimpa approved, a letter to the Americans asking about educational opportunities. Waltenberg could not tolerate being bypassed on this issue.

Waltenberg's personal control over scholarships and his assumption of lifetime office as bishop raised once again the issue, important within government also, of the separation of person and office — a prerequisite for achieving bureaucratic forms of action. The rebels complained that church rules gave control over scholarships to the education committee and not to the person of the bishop. Waltenberg kept control over scholarships because he personalized the office of bishop, making it into a role of undifferentiated religious authority — authority which had the potential to reach into every sphere of the community's life. As the rebels saw it, Waltenberg was not particularly well educated himself; his main qualification for leadership had initially been a racial one; and he used his personal authority to make his son principal of the Usambara Trade School, one son-in-law manager of the Vuga Press, and the other a teacher at Magamba secondary school.

Once again we can see the appeal of bureaucratic norms to a generation of Africans engaged in a democratic struggle against racial dominance. By asking for tests of technical competence, they were saying that careers should be open to anyone of talent, not simply to people with white skins. By asking for the separation of person and office, they were discounting the central qualification of influential persons in their generation — once again, white skin. The problem was that defining these democratic impulses in technocratic terms led, a few years later, to authoritarian control by the technocrats over the peasants.

10

Rain in Independent Tanzania:
A Drama Remembered
but Not Performed

In 1980 people spoke with what seemed like nostalgia about the days when you could be certain about rainmakers, when you could really know that they controlled the rain. The particular nostalgia I am remembering was rarely a longing for past prosperity. The time remembered was often the 1950s, and those years were recalled as difficult times, when compulsory tie ridges made farming difficult. The nostalgic memories focused on moments when all local women joined together in collective tribute-payment, certain that their chief controlled the rain, and that the women's obeisance would bring rain.[1]

A recurrent story told on many of the occasions when people spoke about rain described how, in earlier years, the women streamed into the chiefdom capital on the assigned day, then spent the day cultivating the famous chief's farm. As they walked home, hoes on their shoulders, they were drenched to the skin with wonderful rain, the chief's reward for their labors, given to them immediately. That is what they had lost by 1980: the possibility of a unified ritual, the open performance of a collective drama. They had lost a time when all women appeared on the assigned day to farm for the chief, or when every woman contributed a shilling to the chief's well-being. It was as though there was a moving ritual they could no longer carry out, a play remembered—the plot recalled vividly—but which, for reasons not altogether clear, they no longer chose to perform. What was missing was not so much trust in the old principles (although some people did question those) as the opportunity to act out the old way of doing things, to perform the ritual, or to read the script aloud.

In what people actually said about control over rain there were deep contradictions in 1980. The most interesting contradictions were not those between the discourse of one person and another—believers versus skeptics; the contradictions came within the discourse of single individuals. One old man, a devout Muslim, explained to me on a dry day, when the

245

rains ought to have come, that we were seeing God's will revealed. "He wants us to be taken aback. It is God's way," the old man said, "of revealing himself." In his opinion, the dry spell was the work of God, not the Kilindi. Three weeks later I happened to be visiting in the same village, in a modest house, its interior blackened from the smoke of a cooking fire, a house with bare thatch which could not have held out the rain if it had come. The same devout Muslim elder came visiting, asking a donation of a shilling from each man for the Kilindi rainmaker, who would then resolve everyone's difficulties by bringing the rain. How are we to understand the thought of a man who explained that rain came from God, but then collected shillings for the rainmaker? Was it a matter of saying one thing and doing another? That is too simple.

Then there was the official of the Chama cha Mapinduzi (CCM), a leader in the ruling political party, the successor to TANU. One day, in September 1979, he described to me a time of drought several years earlier, a time when this man had been a village chairman. The senior men of the village went to their Kilindi rainmaker to ask for his help. The chairman did not go along to the rainmaker, but he provided funds for tribute, drawn from the village treasury. And he made certain that the party's ward secretary, who would have approved but would not have wanted to be responsible, did not hear of these events. A month after the first conversation with him, the same ex-chairman explained to me that now, under the CCM, no one pays attention to rain charms or Kilindi. "You know," he said, "that the country belongs to CCM and the rain is God's." I asked him about the inconsistency of his position: how could he have given the old chief money from the village treasury if he believed that the rain was God's? He explained that the party was in sole control "because there has been a lot of rain. . . . But if the sun of famine were shining, people would trek off to the rainmaker. Although it is true that some people hold the whole idea in contempt."

This conversation was very strange but very characteristic. The ex-chairman knew that the party held political control, and that the rain was God's, but also knew that if drought came, people would take tribute once again to a rainmaker. One might think that the ex-chairman was a skeptic and at the same time a practical politician: he thought the rain belonged to God, but that the chairman must accept the views of a majority of his villagers, whatever his own thoughts. This is not the case. During the second discussion I asked him which is more effective, scientifically improved farming or rain medicines. His answer was clear: "It is rain medicine [which is efficacious]," he said. "If you do not use chemical fertilizer and do not weed properly you get half a crop. But if you lack rain you don't get anything at all." This man's understanding, we can see, is that the rain is God's, that men who control rain medicines are capable of preventing hunger, and that some people hold rain medicine in contempt.

A possible explanation of these contradictions focuses on my own role. Could it be that the men and women with whom I spoke knew that I, as a visitor from the United States, would doubt the efficacy of rain charms? Perhaps I would look down on them for accepting such things. This might have played a small role, but the contradictions were deeply rooted within local village life. One man from this same village pleaded with me to take back a message to those in authority: that some villagers held rain medicine in contempt, that it was difficult now to take the proper measures for making the rain, and that people were suffering hunger as a result. Couldn't I see to it that something was done to improve the situation? In this man's view the problem came from within the village, and I, as ethnographer, might be the channel towards its solution.

The contradictions were deeply rooted, not simple ones between spoken principle and accustomed action. It was not a matter of people saying one thing and doing another, but of contradictions within what people said, and further contradictions within what they did.

The moment of money-collecting was a revealing one, a practical test, not an event staged for my benefit. The respected elder entered the smoke-blackened room, which held (I think) eight men, and asked for a shilling from each one to pay the rainmaker. Half the men paid. A couple said they did not happen to have money, which was perhaps true, or perhaps a polite way of refusing. One man, himself a Kilindi but not known for rain, said, "If I want rain, I would just as soon take hold of a drinking-gourd myself," meaning that he would pour beer on the ground, with an invocation to his ancestors, rather than rely on the rainmaker. Another man, a famous healer about sixty years old, but not a Kilindi, refused to pay, saying, "You go and tell him [that I haven't paid and so he ought] to stop the rain from falling on my farm." This is an example of the "contempt" about which villagers complained when they said times had changed and rainmaking was a problem.

In March 1980, when the women set aside a day to farm for the widow of a major rainmaking chief, thirty women appeared. Two decades earlier, when the chief was still alive, hundreds of women would have come.

People noticed the change, and discussed it. Many regretted, as we have seen, that rainmakers were now "held in contempt." Some found it shocking that the widow of the chief had gone without voluntary labor for her banana grove in 1979, and without gifts of firewood. Others complained about changes in the rainmakers themselves, saying that they were just after money these days. One woman said, "The problem these days is that the Kilindi have multiplied. Every one of them buys rain medicines."

The unifying thread in 1979 and 1980 was a sense that times had changed, that the old principles no longer applied. One man told me that he was hardly surprised by the change in rain medicines; so much else had changed. He explained that cholera had never been a problem in the past, but was now a major threat; a new disease wiped out the chicken flocks; and prices were inflated to levels unimaginable in the past. If the entire character of the times has changed, he said, then it is clear that the rain and the sun ought to have changed also.

People understood that the great change in rain had come with the death of the old chief, well after independence, and after the government abolished chiefship. Through the sixties people paid tribute to the chief, and he made the rain. This did not cut off his subjects from the politics of TANU, which many of them joined. Local people took part in the new politics in other ways too. After the Arusha Declaration, one village asked to be made an *ujamaa* village. Women in several villages started cooperative farms under party leadership. But the women also farmed together in the banana groves of the retired chief. For as long as he was alive, they could act together, working on his farms and knowing when rain drenched them that it was his.

The old chief's death presented a problem. Who was to be the successor? In the nineteenth century the heirs might have fought it out with spears and arrows, or the chiefdom might have been sent a new man, son of the Simba Mwene at Vugha. In the 1920s it was the British who would have had the final say. Under the new conditions the process of selection was driven underground, and was therefore aborted, cut off before a clear successor emerged. People told stories about a minor Kilindi, inappropriate for the succession, who allegedly tried to use the confusion to his advantage. He came to the capital, it is said, and took the key to the house of rain charms. When he opened the door a harsh wind blew out at him from inside the house. He persevered and went inside to take the box of rain charms, but found himself incapable of lifting it. The box had become stuck to the floor, the story goes, because he was the wrong person, and so he left, to recede into the insignificance from which he came.

Many people said that there was one son of the old chief who had been favored by his father, and who would be able to control the rain. But the young man left Shambaai (perhaps because of the difficulty of his position as a potentially illegal rainmaker) to work hundreds of miles away in a supervisory job for an international firm. The old chief's favored widow remained in charge of the homestead and the rain charms, helped by a son who took a white-collar job nearer to home. The son at home took care never to make grandiose claims, and never to set himself up as a fully practicing rainmaker. The incomplete succession in this chiefdom was not necessarily repeated in the same form everywhere; a different pattern of succession would lead to a different pattern in the behavior of ordinary people.

Since the most credible heirs in this chiefdom refused to play a public role, the field was left to minor practitioners of the rainmaker's art. Local people speculated about which of the old chief's sons would ultimately emerge, but were in the meanwhile forced to request rainmaking from local Kilindi, men who might in the nineteenth century have become "Kilindi of the common hearth." Each minor rainmaker, as he sought an advantage over his rivals, tried to make it appear that he had the approval of the old chief's widow. In one village I visited, a non-Kilindi Muslim teacher claimed power over the rain, it was said. Locals reported also that he was working to win the favor of the old chief's widow, saying poisonous things about his Kilindi rival. No one knows the full truth about the convoluted hidden maneuvering in rivalries over rain.

After the death of the great colonial-period chief, villagers faced an altogether new problem in interpreting the relationship between politics and rain. The scale of relevant political action became smaller just at the time when the scale of knowledge about the weather became very much larger. With the chief now dead, and no new chief to take his place, villagers looked to a minor rainmaker who claimed to control the weather on their small hillside. Minor rainmakers were characteristic of this period because major ones, influential over a large area, were likely to attract the attention of the authorities. But when villagers tried to judge the effectiveness of their own minor rainmaker, they were forced to observe how well he improved the rainfall on his own hillside in comparison with the rains on adjacent hills. They saw some differences, because the rains do vary from hill to hill in Shambaai. But the villagers could not see as great a variation from one rainmaker to the next as they had seen when the great rainmaking chiefs were still alive, each one controlling the weather over a large part of Shambaai. In those days they expected the whole territory, with all its hillsides, to receive its rain from the chief. The villagers who looked to a single chief for rain came from all different parts of a large climatic region. Daudi Sozi, for example, had his court at Bumbuli, and he made rain for the large part of the mountains which received the heaviest monsoon moisture carried on winds from the southeast. Hassani Kinyashi of Mlalo served the area of *vuli* rains from the northeast. Daudi's rains were, according to any kind of observation, very different from Hassani's. Now, however, the villagers expected each new minor rainmaker to control the weather on a single hillside within the climatic region. This appeared much more difficult to achieve.

All this meant, too, that in the most recent period rituals of obeisance are much less satisfying than they had been, and are only rarely carried out on a large scale. There were occasions in the 1940s when thousands of women came to pay tribute to Hassani Kinyashi. The women all knew, when they went home, that the rain which fell on their farms was his. In the southeast, people sent bits of earth from all the different home hillsides to the court of Daudi Sozi. Women came from all the nearby villages to farm for him. On a somewhat smaller scale, all the villages of Mshihwi farmed for Mnkande Kimweri, and the sons of Kinyashi commanded allegiance and tribute at Vugha.

In most cases the death of a great rainmaker meant that the collective experience of paying tribute and receiving rain disappeared. The women and the men remembered the rich drama of walking home in the rain after farming for the chief; now they could not experience that drama, for the great chiefs had passed. Paying tribute at the empty court was not convincing, did not feel as though one was acting out that ancient drama. And paying tribute on one's own hillside seemed mean and insignificant, lacking in dignity, and not convincing as a demonstration of control over the clouds and the rain. It is no wonder that some people now held the rainmakers in contempt, as they had not in the days of the great chiefs. No wonder that some villagers called the hillside rainmakers by scathing names of ridicule. And no wonder that the healer in the smoke-blackened room said, when asked for a shilling of tribute, "You go and tell him [the rainmaker] to stop the rain from falling on my farm." If he can make the rain fall on everyone's farm but mine, he implied, then I will pay tribute. Otherwise, don't bother me about this pitiful imitation of a rainmaker. The healer would never have said that about the dead chief.

The changes of the 1970s provide an instructive model, though not a precise recapitulation, of what might have happened back in the German period, when the colonial authorities destroyed chiefship, and rain ideas appeared to be in decline. The Germans were far more brutal in their attack on chiefship than the independent Tanganyikans would be. The Germans hanged the Simba Mwene at Vugha, murdered Daudi Sozi's father Kibanga at Bumbuli, drove Hassani Kinyashi's father to flee across the border to "Mombasa" (the local term for the British zone), and reduced Kinyashi, the new Simba Mwene at Vugha, heir to the major rain charms, to a figure of ridicule, called a "pig" in his subjects' songs.

The destruction of the dignity and standing of the major Kilindi chiefs had not eliminated ideas about rain from people's heads; it made it impossible, however, for people to act out the ritual drama in which they worked on the chief's farms and then returned home drenched with rain. It is not surprising, seen in this light, that Kinyashi of Vugha, who had been despised by his subjects under the Germans, provoked "extraordinary demonstrations" at Mlola in 1925 when the short rains broke on the day the British brought him there to announce his restoration. The ritual drama could once again be performed.

The 1970s saw a much more gentle decline of chiefship than had occurred in the German period, but with one powerful influence on popular perception, of a kind which had not existed under the Germans. Just at the time, in the 1960s and 1970s, when the territory of a typical rainmaker became very small, ordinary people came to know about the weather over a much larger geographical area than ever before. This enormous expansion came with the rapid spread of radios in Shambaai. Radio transmission to the whole of Tanganyika had not existed before 1955. In the ten years between 1958 and 1968 the number of radios in the country increased tenfold, from over 50,000 to over 500,000. A survey conducted in four villages of Lushoto District in 1969–70 found that 82 percent of all men and 62 percent of all women listened to the radio some of the time. Many of these presumably heard it only during a visit to a village shop, or at the house of a neighbor.[2]

People who listened to the national weather report heard about conditions all across Tanzania and tried to integrate this new knowledge of weather with their knowledge of rainmakers. In 1980, for example, at a time when the rains were late in coming, a villager explained his understanding of the problem in the following terms:

> If this were a matter of Kilindi control over the rain, then there would be rain here, and "sun" [i.e. drought] in another section. But for the entire country, there is only sun. So it's a matter of climatic conditions. . . . If you listen to the radio, according to measurements by the experts there has been a shortage of rain everywhere — Lushoto, Mbeya [in the south of the country], everywhere. A man came home on leave from his work in Dodoma. The trees there are weak because of the drought.

Other radio-listening villagers spoke in very similar terms. As they saw it, a drought which covers the whole country cannot be caused by a single rainmaker, or even by a whole district full of Kilindi rainmakers.

The man who was quoted above used radio weather reports to make a critical assessment of the efficacy of rainmakers, but he did not categorically reject the idea that Kilindi control the rain. He explained further, "The Kilindi work by luck. They match their activities with the observable conditions showing that rain is coming. If rain falls, we say it is their doing. But if you ask me whether they have effective rain medicines, the answer is yes. It is becoming weaker now, because we don't bring them gifts of sheep." Once again we have the characteristic contradictions, but now the meaning of those contradictions ought to be clearer.

The radio-listener says that Kilindi do have effective rain medicines: "If you ask me whether they have effective rain medicines," he volunteers, "the answer is yes." The radio-listener explains, however, that droughts which we might have attributed to the Kilindi under other circumstances we now know are nation-wide, beyond the scope of any one rainmaker to control. The radio-listener understands that particular events which, at another time, he might have seen as evidence of Kilindi control, he now sees as natural occurrences. The power to control the rain exists, but its effective sphere is narrower than once thought. The reason for its decline, in his view, is "we don't bring them gifts of sheep." If local people paid tribute as they did in the old days, he says, then Kilindi rain medicines would be more effective. This is correct, although radio would still have had some effect. Nevertheless, if the old large-scale rain chiefs were still at work, acceptance of rainmaking powers would not have declined to the same extent. Villagers would still feel comfortable acting out the drama of tribute payment and its reward — being soaked through with the chief's rain. Today the context does not exist in which local people can pay their tribute to believable rainmakers.

Up to this point, all the explanations of change in the folk understanding of rain and drought, famine and prosperity, have revolved around the changing fate of intellectuals. The destruction of chiefship under the Germans, its revival under the British, its elimination in independent Tanzania, all played a crucial role in shaping the changing uses of healing the land and harming the land. The emergence of competing intellectuals — in particular of literate clerks who evolved into bureaucrats — led also to the emergence of alternative varieties of political language. Political ideas did not emerge mechanistically; the intellectuals created their own political ideas, drawing on the cultural materials at hand. The intellectuals created their own ways of explaining experience and the world in which they lived. Each intellectual role had its own history and its own inherited ideas. Every chief thought about the world around him, and created his own understanding anew, but at the same time every chief was forced to work with inherited ideas about chiefship in its relation to subjects and to the natural world. The brief discussion of radio here is a digression, an alternative form of historical explanation. In this case the change in fundamental ideas is linked to a change in technology. Intellectuals enter the story only tangentially. The heart of the story is about how information about the weather can be gathered quickly, and then broadcast widely. The mere fact that peasants hear about today's weather in many parts of the country at the same time leads them to reformulate their understanding of the natural world.

The change did not overturn accepted knowledge, but shifted its emphasis. Radio did not tell people anything, in relation to the weather, that they had not known before, but it gave them some kinds of knowledge in greater detail and with greater frequency. People knew in the nineteenth century that some famines spread much more widely than the boundaries of any one kingdom. These could not easily be explained as the work of a Kilindi, or of any other political leader. In the nineteenth century widespread famine may, in some cases, have been seen as caused by a strange monster from the ocean. But in others cases, a famine too wide for any one political leader was described as *mbui ya Muungu*, "the word of God," or "the action of God." Since knowledge of widespread climatic events was less common in 1880 than it was to be in 1980, it is quite possible that explanations of climate with reference to "the action of God" became more common over time. It seems to me that they became more common between 1968 and 1980, but my own observations on this particular issue are not sufficiently comparable to be certain.

The opposition between "the rain of the Kilindi" and "the rain of God," which was common in the spoken language of 1980, was a derivative usage, drawn from other terms with a primary use in the world of healing. These were "illnesses of humanity" as opposed to "illnesses of God." An "illness of humanity" (*utamu wa mntu*) is one caused by human action, especially by sorcery. It is the outcome of aggressive action by a bitter enemy, or the work of a medicine man demonstrating his dominance. Drought is, in a sense, an illness of humanity raised to a public level: it is the product of a rainmaker's demonstration of dominance. He shows that he is stronger and that political power, or tribute, should be his. The way to heal an illness of humanity is to employ a medicine man who is stronger than the sorcerer; the way to end a drought is to give the land to the strongest rainmaker.

An "illness of God" is one that just happens, with no human cause. The closest term in English for this sort of causation is *natural*. When a person suffers from an illness of God, the cure might be good food, or herbs, or rest, or it is possible that no cure exists. In the case of an illness of God, counter-sorcery will do no good. When a drought covers an area much larger than the domain of any one rainmaker, it is recognized as "an action of God" (*mbui ya Muungu*). Another way of talking about an illness of God is to say that it just happens, that it has no cause.

In the same way, people sometimes talk about a drought which is not thought to be caused by a Kilindi as *zuwa du,* "just drought," or literally "just the sun."

Illness of humanity is described here as primary and *drought of the Kilindi* as secondary, because *illness of humanity* is a term used in every household, nearly every day. The opposition between *illness of humanity* and *illness of God* is the most fundamental distinction that people make in diagnosing illness in the Shambaa language. Cognate terms exist in many Bantu languages (Feierman and Janzen forthcoming). The distinction between the two illness terms is part of the ancient core of therapeutic practice for much of sub-Saharan Africa. *Drought of the Kilindi* and *drought of God* are therefore derivative usages.

With the introduction of radio, people became increasingly aware of famines that were more widely distributed than the domain of any one rainmaker and were therefore "just drought," rather than the "drought of the Kilindi." People therefore borrowed the language of illness (a kind of discourse used for large-scale famine since the precolonial period) and talked increasingly about God's rain, and to a lesser extent about God's drought. The full impact of this was seen in the 1970s, a time when increasing numbers of people were reflecting on the nature of God within Islam and Christianity. In discussions of rain and drought, *God* is normally used with the same meaning as in illness, for events which "just happen," without a moral cause. But a minority of people have in mind a very personal God when they speak about God's rain. The only way to illustrate the range of variation is with a few quotations from everyday conversation, with a brief interpretation of each one.

1. "The rain is falling in all parts of the country. I heard it on the radio. It is an action of God." In this first quotation the rain is described as God's because it is falling over the whole of Tanzania, over too large an area to be controlled by any one rainmaker.

2. "The recent drought was God's; it struck every place." Once again, as in the first quotation, events that cover the whole country are, by definition, natural, they "just happen," or in more usual terms "they are God's."

3. "There is the rain of the Kilindi and the rain of God. In other lands the rain falls, but there are no Kilindi. But there is also the rain of the Kilindi." This statement is opaque in literal translation. The person is saying that the rain falls in places where there are no Kilindi, and therefore no rainmakers; the rain in those places must be called *the rain of God,* since no Kilindi take any initiative to make it fall. But then there are also the more familiar places with Kilindi rainmakers, and so we know that the *rain of the Kilindi* exists.

4. "It is the Kilindi who deny us rain. . . . God controls the rain, but he loves us. He cannot withhold it from us. The one who withholds it from us is the Kilindi." Here we have a shift in the meaning of *God*. In the other sentences, the word refers to an impersonal principle of causation, used for events that happen with no particular human or moral cause. In this sentence *God* is taken to be a loving being who cannot withhold the rain.

The examples could be multiplied, but the range of variation should by now be clear.

The parallel between rainmaking and healing is an instructive one. When people in Shambaai treat illness, they do not follow an invarying chain of reasoning from a physical sign—a pain in the chest, a cough, or a skin ulcer—to a named cause of illness and its therapy. People do not reach an unshakeable conclusion that it is an illness of God, or an illness of humanity. Instead, they work by trial and error. If a woman is coughing, and she is given a simple herb, and the cough goes away, then the illness must have been one of God, not of humanity. If the cough does not go away, then it is time to try a sorcery cure, and call the illness one of humanity. As time goes by, the process of trial and error, of defining and redefining the illness, continues. Illnesses that are acute and lead to dramatic decline or are chronically unresponsive to treatment are usually labeled *illnesses of humanity*.

Similarly with the weather. People hear on the radio that the "sun" is striking all regions of the country, and so the drought, beyond the borders of any one rainmaker, must be the work of God. If the drought then continues, if people feel desperately threatened, then they try to do what they can: they approach the local rainmaker for help. They care less, at this point, about tight logic in which they compare the precise territory of the rainmaker with the distribution of the drought, and more about trying every possible measure in the hope that something will work. They are like the relatives of a cancer victim in America, who decide to try all possible measures, even those which have not given positive results in clinical testing. Trying all possible measures in a difficult time is what the CCM party official was talking about when he said, "If the sun of famine shone, people would trek off to the rainmaker." People trekked off to the rainmakers in the mid-seventies, even though the famine affected the whole of Tanzania, and its known geography could not have matched the boundaries of any rainmaker in Shambaai. Even the great old chiefs would have looked puny. When people are driven to the rainmakers by crushing drought, they restore, for a period, the sense that collective ritual is possible. Great numbers of people now are willing to try every possible measure, and so they join together, once again performing the drama which seemed in other times to have disappeared from lived experience.

Even then, carrying tribute to the rainmaker and cultivating his banana grove are underground rituals, partly invisible. Political rituals, which occur in the open, are the rituals of independent Tanzania and its ruling party. These are outside the scope of the present book, although for a fully contextualized picture, the reader must imagine hundreds of village, ward, and district meetings taking place alongside the hidden and increasingly infrequent ceremonies in which ordinary people pay obeisance to the rainmakers.

In one minor detail, the language of party meetings exerts pressure to reshape the language of rain. From TANU's early days, the party described its job as one of *building* the country. The party song, sung by every schoolchild in the 1960s, announced that *TANU yajenga nchi,* "TANU builds the country." The word *-jenga* (Shambaa *-zenga*) entered popular political usage together with *-bomoa,* "to break down, especially as in breaking down a house." The two terms, *building up* and *breaking down,* defined a vision of politics somewhat different from healing and harming the land. The metaphors of healing the land (*-zifya shi*) and harming the land (*-bana shi*) carry implications of restoring health and of repairing the social fabric. A person who has been ill can be healed, in the meaning of *-zifya.* The word can also be used for repairing a social breach, ending a quarrel between relatives, or restoring harmony after close friends have offended one another. It describes a return to a desirable previous state, the restoration of the human body or the social fabric. *Kuzenga,* "to build," as in building a house, carries stronger implications of progressive movement, the construction of something which had not been there before. It is hard to know how significant this is in shaping people's historical vision, but observation of village meetings shows that *building* and *breaking down* have become common figures of speech in political discourse.

Up to this point ideas and actions have all been described from the viewpoint of an ordinary farmer, not from the viewpoint of a rainmaker. We have seen that the ordinary woman or man asks whether a particular instance of drought was caused by a Kilindi, or whether it just happened naturally, as caused by God. Ordinary folks decide whether to pay money and give labor to a rainmaker. They try hard to understand which of the many Kilindi is likely to be an effective rainmaker. Commoners listen to the weather report on the radio and try to find an explanation for the uniformity of weather conditions across the country, irrespective of the presence of rainmakers in one place or another.

The rainmakers themselves must also make sense of experience, and their work in this respect is triply hard. They must answer many of the same questions as ordinary people; they too listen to the radio. They have three added burdens. First, they know full well what they have and have not done as rainmakers and can make direct observations of the effectiveness of their own work. Secondly, they try to understand the meaning of their work in a way that does not violate their religious understanding of the world. Like many other local people, the rainmakers have converted to world religions, especially to Islam or to Lutheran Evangelical Christianity. Thirdly, they must meet two conflicting sets of needs and interests: the needs of their peasant neighbors, who rely on them for rainmaking and will not take no for an answer, and the interests of the party and government, which tend to see tribute collection and rainmaking as treasonous activities, challenges to governmental authority.

My direct knowledge of the world as seen from the point of view of the rainmaker is limited to two occasions, one in 1966 and the other in 1980. The information gained in these two moments informs the questions asked about other rainmakers met only briefly, or observed at a distance.

The first occasion (in 1966), coming as it did soon after the abolition of chiefship, showed that government pressure was important in shaping the rainmakers' response. The events occurred in an arid and isolated part of Shambaai. The *vuli* rains were late, and when I went outside my house one morning I saw two men on a path further up the hillside leading a bull of tribute to the village of the old chief, whom I have earlier called Mkoma Sala. When I asked what was happening, neighbors told me that the drought was the work of the chief's competitors, rainmakers who were envious of the loyalty they gave him. The envious competitors, according to this interpretation, were the ones holding up the rain.

The government's divisional executive officer saw things differently: he treated the drought as Mkoma Sala's challenge to his own authority. The executive officer, who was himself from Shambaai, understood that some local people would see the drought as Mkoma Sala's protest against the end of chiefship and as his demonstration that if people did not remain loyal, they risked drought and famine. The officer therefore arrested and jailed two of Mkoma Sala's sons, to show that TANU had covered over the land, and that the old chief was not powerful enough to challenge its authority.

Mkoma Sala responded by saying that he had given up making rain long ago, that he had converted to Christianity, and that the divisional officer had misunderstood his position entirely. The chief invited the local lay evangelist to hold a prayer meeting, where Christians would pray together for rain. The chief in this prayer meeting was in a position very similar to that of the outsider-rainmaker at a chief's court. When the outsider joins commoners in paying tribute, he demonstrates that he is subservient and that he is not the one holding back the rain.

I was invited to the prayer meeting. Perhaps it was because I was present on that day, collecting historical traditions, perhaps it was so that I could be a semiofficial witness. There were about fifteen of us, standing together in a circle, outdoors, at the edge of Mkoma Sala's village. Halfway through the prayers, a poisonous snake appeared just outside our circle. A number of people shouted a single word: *Sheitani, Sheitani*. This word is used in possession rituals for an illness-cause in a particular relationship to the person who is ill, but in local Christian doctrine it is the word meaning *Satan*. The snake was a sign of the presence of Satan; they were saying that it was Satan who had held back the rain. The people had found a way, within the context of a Christian prayer meeting, to refute the claim that Mkoma Sala was holding back the rain. They showed that while the drought was indeed a matter of *nguvu kwa nguvu*, "power against power," the struggle was not one of the chief against TANU; it was instead the power of Satan against the power of God.

Several days after the prayer meeting, Mkoma Sala's sons were released. The drought continued, and then the next farming season the rains were good again. The executive officer had shown that his power was irresistible. The old chief agreed, but it seemed likely that the next time the rains did not fall, people would bring tribute to Mkoma Sala once again, to convince him that the rains ought not to be held back.

In 1980, fourteen years after the snake appeared at the prayer meeting, I came out of the bank in Lushoto and saw a young man, whom I shall call Ng'wa Zumbe, whose father (by then dead) had been one of the supreme rainmakers of Shambaai. Ng'wa Zumbe was a very well-educated young man whom I had met casually many times before. This time he needed a ride and I had a car, so we rode together for the next couple of hours. I decided to risk boldness and said to him as we drove off from Lushoto that many people had told me (as in fact they had) that he was the heir to his father's rain charms. This question set him off on an extended reflection, for the whole of the ride, on his father's rain and on his own position. I was unable to take notes, but over the years I have worked hard learning to memorize bits of conversation — their texture, their sense, and some of their words, if not the precise dialogue verbatim. I did that now, and dictated my recollections into a tape recorder on the same day. I am putting quotation marks around his words to mark them off, but they are the words as remembered, not reported verbatim.

I was fascinated by the delicacy with which Ng'wa Zumbe spoke about his father's rain. "When we were children," he said, "we used to ask our father about his rain medicines. We would ask, do you really have rain medicines? How do they work? What is it all about? He used to say that if people know you have rain medicines, they pester you all the time. This one wants it to rain today, and that one doesn't. This person is upset about the rain and that one is happy. It leads to a lot of conflict. But mostly father used to avoid the question with his own children and go about his work. This leads me to think," Ng'wa Zumbe said, "that you will never actually see anyone who has rain medicines talking openly about them."

Ng'wa Zumbe was setting me a riddle. If no one who has rain medicines will talk about them openly, then how was I to take the fact that Ng'wa Zumbe did not discuss his own medicines? Perhaps this showed that he controlled his father's medicines, among the most powerful in Shambaai; and then perhaps he simply did not have them. Then later, Ng'wa Zumbe acknowledged that his father must have had special powers. "I distinctly remember times," he said, "when people would come bringing father sheep, and firewood, and money. They would come and present these things to father, and on their way home from bringing the gifts the rain would invariably pour down on them. Just from the fact that it happened so frequently — people bringing things and the rain pouring down on them, you would have to think that father had rain." It is very interesting that when Ng'wa Zumbe wanted to affirm his father's powers, he told the same narrative as commoners: a description of the ritual drama in which people come to pay tribute and go home dripping with the chief's rain. The overall effect of this part of Ng'wa Zumbe's narrative was to say that father doubted he had rain, but we can see that really he did, and now Ng'wa Zumbe doubted that he himself had rain, and you can draw any conclusion you want from that.

The question that most preoccupied Ng'wa Zumbe was how to explain control over rain without violating his understanding of the world as learned in school or through adherence to a world religion. His answer to this had several strands. He talked about a particularly grisly case of occult murder which had been reported on the radio, the point being that if the radio reports the occult, then it must be a legitimate part of our world. He also mentioned an article in *Drum* magazine about a reporter who visited a rainmaker in Kenya and challenged the rainmaker to make it rain hard enough for the reporter to be stuck in the mud on his way home. The rainmaker agreed and the reporter's car became mired.

The core of Ng'wa Zumbe's argument had to do with the rainmaker as merely an intermediary in bringing together the needs of people and the power of God. Ng'wa Zumbe's father would give away much of his tribute as religious donations. He never told anyone he was making these contributions, but felt obligated to do so because he recognized that his powers came from God. Ng'wa Zumbe's father, if challenged, could have said just what Mkoma Sala said in the 1966 prayer meeting: I have no powers to make the rain, I simply pray to God.

At another point during the conversation in the car, Ng'wa Zumbe talked about Islam, and about the Sharifian line of descent from the Prophet. "People accept," he said, "that just because of who the Sharifs are, they have greater power when they pray for something." Their prayers are accepted more readily than the prayers of ordinary people. Ng'wa Zumbe was saying that prayer to God might have been the source of his father's rain; the prayers of the old rainmaker were more likely to succeed than the prayers of other people because of his personal identity. Another man, a healer, made the same argument about Ng'wa Zumbe's father, in this case using the Swahili word *karama*, which is the capacity to pray to God for a need and to have the request acceded to immediately. Ng'wa Zumbe's father, according to the healer, had a special gift for bringing the rain through his prayers. Another way it was put, this time by a Christian man about sixty years old, was that "many people choose to rely on the rainmaker, and so his requests are answered when he prays. . . . God consents because of the trust which people place in the rainmaker." In this last version, it is not the person of the rainmaker which has special qualities or special powers; it is the trust of the multitude which is the source of that power. This is a relatively unusual position, the more common one being Ng'wa Zumbe's, that the rainmaker has personal qualities, personal powers, which make his prayers effective.

One common thread running through many of the accounts, whether they explain rainmaking as brought by prayer, or as brought by manipulating ritual objects, is that a special quality inheres in the rainmaker's person. If someone prays but is not the true rainmaker, or if someone performs the ritual but is not the true rainmaker, the rain will not fall. We saw this in the story about the minor Kilindi who came during a moment of confusion in succession, trying to enter the house of rain charms and to carry them off. When he opened the door, a harsh wind blew out at him from inside the house; when he tried to lift the box of rain objects, he found that it had become stuck to the floor. The implication of the story is that he could not take the rain charms because he was not meant to have them.

Ng'wa Zumbe directs our attention away from the parts of rainmaking which are parochial, which would sound unfamiliar, perhaps bizarre, to an American visitor, or to a Tanzanian bureaucrat, or to Ng'wa Zumbe's own colleagues at work—educated men and women in salaried employment. In what is both a defensive strategy (like Mkoma Sala's response to the divisional executive officer) and a way of making the world coherent for himself, Ng'wa Zumbe places the central emphasis in rainmaking on prayer to God and on God's rain. One effect of this is to direct attention away from any possible elements of conflict. In the past the core of rainmaking had always been competition between rainmakers, and the central goal had been to impose a single powerful chief over the whole land, to heal it, and to avoid a breakdown into "power against power": competition that damages the land. In the old way of doing things, people brought tribute to convince the rainmaker not to hold back their rain; they hoped he would be powerful enough to prevent anyone else from holding it back. We have seen many times over that Shambaa discourse about rain has conflict at its core. A significant effect of Ng'wa Zumbe's emphasis on harmonious prayer to God is to minimize the importance of those elements in the classic interpretation which point attention towards conflict between rainmakers and the state, or towards conflict among rainmakers. These are the elements which the authorities would see as politically dangerous.

Despite Ng'wa Zumbe's central emphasis on prayer and his movement towards a harmonization of rainmaking and contemporary world religion, one element of his interpretation is completely at odds with the core conceptions of the bureaucratic/democratic Tanzanian state. For Ng'wa Zumbe there is no separation between person and office. In fact office is irrelevant, because the office of chief had been abolished. Ng'wa Zumbe's father was a rainmaker, whether or not he was a chief, because he had unique personal powers. These had to do with his personality, but they came to him through a line of descent. Someone who is not the son of a great rainmaker cannot become one. The reader will remember the basis of TANU's rejection of chiefship, that it gave authority to a person "because of his birth from a particular father and mother" and that such a person "cannot be removed except by death." The skills of the rainmaker were not skills other men could learn, so that they could take up the job after schooling. If the wrong person opens the door leading to the rain charms, a harsh wind blows out from inside the house.

Even though most bureaucrats practice a world religion, merging rainmaking and a world religion does not make rainmaking acceptable in the world shaped by the bureaucrats. Rainmaking is unacceptable because it is a base of power independent of theirs, and also because it builds on a definition of the person which is very alien to the bureaucratic world. The reader might remember that Mulonda Haki, the great nationalist of the early 1950s, understood the character of this conflict. He said, "The chiefship which came down from Mbegha was not good, it was wrong, because it was government by a private individual . . . who has only to consult himself." Ng'wa Zumbe would agree that an individual makes the rain — but that individual's role grows out of his special personal powers.

The abolition of chiefship, the decline of the public drama of tribute payment, and the decline also of the drama of open chiefly competition, have meant that it is much easier for individuals to impose their private meanings on rainmaking, on the observed fertility of the land, and on rain itself. Individuals create their private understandings of the world in any event, at all times, but in the realm of rain, public rituals reimposed a shared experience. Now, without an accepted ritual, there is a bubbling up of new ideas, no one of them official. Political thinkers now disagree on basic issues. Mulonda Haki and Ng'wa Zumbe disagree on the right of a private individual to use his inherited personal traits in shaping public life. It has also become legitimate to express idiosyncratic ideas. One woman, for example, explained that the experts flew up into the sky and found that only two iron tanks of rain water remain. This, she said, is the source of the current problem with rain.

Despite the bubbling up of new interpretations and the emergence of individual variations, the discussion of rain has a cultural coherence. This is so because of the continuity of the old terms of discourse, but also for another reason, which we have seen: that the realm of culture beyond the usual limits of chiefship or politics provides a language for discussing rain and, more generally, for discussing the relationship between human agency and change. The expanding discussion about the rain of the Kilindi and the rain of God draws on the broader everyday categories for explaining illness — categories rooted in everyday life and not dependent on chiefship for their existence. Earlier debates on rain focused on a search for hierarchy, for control by the one dominant Kilindi rainmaker who would be strong enough to heal the land. Even though political dominance by a Kilindi is now impossible, people continue to discuss competition among the rainmakers. In addition, they have opened a new debate alongside the old one, this on whether the particular immediate experience of rain or sun, prosperity or poverty, is attributable to the Kilindi or attributable to God and therefore accidental, natural, occurring in a way which "just happens." The commoners draw on the language of illness; Kilindi draw on the language of commoners, for the Kilindi pray to God for rain and in this way work to recapture "the rain of God" which has escaped them.

We have seen at several points in this book that competition among chiefs to heal the land is merely a contingent expression, one narrow and specific form, of a more general cultural idea that organizes healing: that the power of medicines which can either heal or kill is used to bring life when a healer "owns" that which he is healing. The king brought his subjects plenty rather than famine if they made him the "owner" of the land; in ordinary people's sacrifice, the healer brought the rite to an effective, life-giving conclusion only when he became the "owner" for one night of the afflicted house.

In a similar way, the assessment of famine as either famine of God or of the Kilindi is a contingent expression — one among many — of the pervasive distinction between illnesses of God (afflictions which "just happen," not caused by human agency) and illnesses of humanity (brought about by destructive human intervention).

Even now that the authority of chiefs has declined, and debate over public well-being is not cast as often in terms of dynastic politics, the deeper cultural principle survives. In this case it is drawn from the treatment of illness.

Once again, the history of intellectuals is central. Chiefs have lost power, but local people still fill roles that are organizational, educative, directive, or expressive. The most numerous of local intellectuals are still the healers. Peasants still rely on them to treat most sicknesses. The government has neither suppressed nor supplanted *waghanga* (local healers) in everyday treatment. For this reason, among others, the central healers' categories, illnesses of God and of humanity, remain central in popular thought. In the realm of individual illnesses, these categories are in daily use in thousands of individual judgments. Some prominent healers treat entire communities when it appears that illnesses of humanity have become broadly distributed and destructive. These nonroyal healers administer oaths and medicines to remove sorcery from community life. Famine brought by the Kilindi is, then, only one form of public illness of humanity.

At the same time, intellectuals in the religious communities of Islam and Christianity have their own visions of how to achieve the public good — how to expand the sphere under God's dominion in order to reduce the scope of malevolent human action (which in local Islam is called *elimu ya dunia*, "worldly knowledge"). In local Christianity also, the choice is cast as one between true adherence to religion and the world of sorcery, the action of God and of humanity. In both cases, in Islam and in Christianity, the particular way religious visions are brought to bear on public life is shaped by the place of prominent Muslims and Christians in public life: Muslims are more frequently private traders, and Christians are more frequently government servants.

Christian and Muslim debates about the desired form of public order in independent Tanzania are outside the scope of this work, except insofar as they have shaped discussion of rain. It is important, however, to acknowledge them, and to understand that they are rooted in local understandings of misfortune as caused by God or by human action. The chiefs have lost their leading position as government-sponsored intellectuals, and discussions of rain are no longer sharply focused. But other intellectuals drawn from amongst the peasantry have risen to prominence. Peasant debates on survival, subsistence, and the public good continue.

Notes

List of Interviews

Bibliography

Index

Notes

Abbreviations

A.D.O.	Assistant District Officer
Bethel MS	Bethel Mission Archives
CMS	Church Missionary Society Archives
DAR	*District Annual Report*
D.C.	District Commissioner
D.O.	District Officer
DVR	*Divisional Annual Report*
i/c	in charge
NaoM	*Nachrichten aus der ostafrikanischen Mission*
P.C.	Provincial Commissioner
PVH	Pangani Valley History Project documents
TNA	Tanzania National Archives
UMCA	Universities' Mission to Central Africa
UNTC	United Nations Trusteeship Council

More complete information on the archives and serials consulted appears at the beginning of the bibliography. Interviews are cited by name and date and listed separately following these notes.

Chapter 1: Introduction

1   Dar es Salaam historians of the 1960s paid special attention to the creation of a national scale of political action, emphasizing the role of resistance. The classic early statement was Ranger's article, "Connexions between 'Primary Resistance' Movements and Modern Mass Nationalism in East and Central Africa" (1968). Isaria Kimambo showed the importance of precolonial history (Kimambo 1969). John Iliffe played a prominent role in the activities of the history department. He, like Ranger, wrote about resistance and about the origins of nationalism, but his orientation was quite different from Ranger's (Iliffe 1967). The continued emphasis on the Maji Maji Rebellion in the Dar es Salaam history department led to Gwassa's dissertation on the subject (1973). Lonsdale (1968) explored the local roots of nationalism in East Africa, in an article which remains influential today. His work on the nature of the state in Africa (1981) raises important questions on the

nature of the relationship between precolonial, colonial, and postcolonial states.

2   On the introduction of a new approach to history during those years, see John S. Saul (1972), and A. J. Temu and Bonaventure Swai (1981).

3   In the middle and late 1970s Dar es Salaam students wrote an important series of M.A. theses in economic history, documenting local transformations within the context of imperialism and capitalism. See, for example, Gershom Tumwesigye Mishambi (1978). On southern Shambaai, see the excellent work by Helen Mhando (1977). The general approach of the Dar es Salaam historians in the 1970s is given in M. H. Y. Kaniki (1979).

4   The major work on the transforming power of nineteenth-century trade is by Sheriff (1987). Cooper (1977) has written an important history of the coastal trade and of the character of slavery in this period. Cooper's continuing work is central for an understanding of the relationship between worldwide economic trends, the colonial state, and the evolution of local African society (see, for example, Cooper 1981, 1987).

5   The mechanism by which continuities in ritual are made to appear eternal while enduring through very different historical circumstances is described with unequaled subtlety in a now forgotten work by Henri Hubert and Marcel Mauss, "Étude sommaire de la représentation du temps dans la religion et la magie" (1929). They show that the rhythmed time of rites coexists with other time modes. The sense that rites impose a rhythm on the experience of time's passage is much more workable than the Lévi-Straussian conception of reversible time. It leaves the possibility of the irruption of a real event.

6   See Vacca (1982) and Adamson (1980:143). Gramsci does not use the word *expressive*, which I use in my own definition above, although he includes artists among the intellectuals, and it is difficult to see artistic creations as directive, organizational, or educative. All humans engage in expressive activities. The key to defining artists as intellectuals is in the social recognition of their activities.

7   See Gramsci (1971:6) on the peasantry's inability to elaborate its own intellectuals. See also Gramsci's "The Southern Question" (1957, esp. p. 43) for a discussion of intellectuals drawn from among the rural population. See also Mouffe (1979b:178) and Adamson (1980:146). David Arnold shows that Gramsci understood the ambiguities of the peasant situation, but that ultimately (in Gramsci's view) peasants, as subaltern groups, "are always subject to the authority of ruling groups, even when they rebel and rise up" (1984:164). Arnold, together with Ranajit Guha and a number of others, formed a subaltern studies group for South Asian studies which was inspired by Gramsci but went beyond Gramsci's position to argue that subaltern politics was an autonomous domain in the history of India. "It neither originated from elite politics nor did its existence depend on the latter" (Guha 1982a:4). The central point of Guha's position is "an important historical truth, that is *the failure of* the Indian bourgeoisie to speak for the nation"

(1982a:5). Guha's own analysis of peasant positions may be found in *Elementary Aspects of Peasant Insurgency in Colonial India* (1983).

8   See Femia (1975, 1981). See also Fiori (1970) and the contributions to Mouffe (1979a).

9   Quoted in Sheridan (1980:217). On hegemony, see Femia (1975:29) and Williams (1960:587). See also Anderson (1976–1977).

10   For an important recent review of peasant studies in Africa see Isaacman (1990). Definitions of the term are given by Mintz (1979:218), Wolf (1966: 3–4), Saul and Woods (1971:105), and Meillassoux (1973:82).

11   Bourdieu's *Outline of a Theory of Practice* does not work at disentangling the relationship between knowledge and power. The author states that the issue is central: "The constitutive power which is granted to ordinary language lies not in the language itself, but in the group which authorizes it and invests it with authority" (1977:21). This points towards a study of intellectuals, but the matter is dropped there. A more significant failing is the fact that the book does not mention the French — not once — even though the Kabyle lived under French rule during a period of armed struggle. If the sovereign holders of power remain completely invisible in an ethnography of practice, then it is of course impossible to trace the actual links between practice and power.

12   Scott writes: "Gramsci is, I believe, misled when he claims that the radicalism of subordinate classes is to be found more in their acts than in their beliefs. It is more nearly the reverse. The realm of behavior — particularly in power-laden situations — is precisely where dominated classes are most constrained. And it is at the level of beliefs and interpretations — where they can safely be ventured — that subordinate classes are least trammeled" (1985:322).

13   Crick (1982:295) writes about "informant variability," and explains that within a single society men and women, old and young, rich and poor, may have different bodies of knowledge. This is important, but the current argument attempts to go beyond this approach in several ways — in specifying streams of discourse which have their own coherence and which endure historically, and in systematically locating the bearers of the discourse within the wider structures of power and production.

14   See Berry (1985). The word *peasantry* in the description is my own; Berry explicitly rejects the term.

15   On discourse as spread across domains, Foucault's discussion of the unities of discourse in *The Archaeology of Knowledge* (1976) is very useful. I have not relied on him more substantially because of his insistence on a thoroughgoing decentering of the subject, which is at odds with the core position of this book, and which is at the heart of Foucault's understanding of discourse. Nevertheless Foucault's understanding of the web of relations that hold discourse at their core is enormously useful: "Discursive relations are not, as we can see, internal to discourse: they do not connect concepts or words with one another; they do not establish a deductive or rhetorical struc-

ture between propositions or sentences. Yet they are not relations exterior to discourse, relations that might limit it, or impose certain forms upon it, or force it, in certain circumstances, to state certain things. They are, in a sense, at the limit of discourse: they offer it objects of which it can speak, or rather (for this image of offering presupposes that objects are formed independently of discourse), they determine the group of relations that discourse must establish in order to speak of this or that object, in order to deal with them, name then, analyse them, classify them, explain them, etc. These relations characterize not the language (*langue*) used by discourse, nor the circumstances in which it is deployed, but discourse itself as a practice" (Foucault 1976:46).

16   According to Crummey, the positions taken in this literature were undermined by the continuation of revolts and dissident religious movements *after* national independence (1986:2).

17   See, for example, the newspaper *Mambo Leo.*

18   The terms are from Rude (1980). An argument that late colonial Andean peasants were not merely parochial and backward-looking is made by Stern (1987:13–14): "The peasants' aspirations and ideological commitments go beyond narrow obsessions with local land, subsistence guarantees, or autonomy (i.e., the desire simply to be left alone). Nor can we say that the peasants' material experience, social connections, and political understandings were largely bounded by the 'little worlds' of communities and haciendas. For the late colonial period, both directly and through intermediaries, peasants moved in social, economic, and ideological orbits that stretched considerably beyond their principal locales of residence and work. Mobilization to install a new Inca-led social order reflected not a simple yearning for local subsistence and autonomy, but an effort to forge a new macrolevel polity that blended more successfully local peasant needs and aspirations with supraregional political order. . . . The dream of an Inca-led resurgence . . . fired the imagination of more 'cosmopolitan' individuals, and made it possible for Andean peasants to envision a social order that allied them with nonpeasants and nonindigenous peoples under Inca auspices."

Chapter 2: Tribute and Dependency in Late Nineteenth-Century Shambaai

1   The accession rite was described in a series of oral accounts, including many by custodians of various parts of the rites, but also by other observers. Mbaruku Jambia (22 January 1968); Mdoe Loti (10 April 1967); Mbwana Mkanka Mghanga (24 January 1968); Mdoe Barua and Ng'wana Aia (18 April 1967); Mdoembazi Kilua (10 April 1967); Mdoe Loti (29 April 1967); Bakari Kilua (15 October 1966); Mdoe Loti (1 May 1967); Group testimony of court officials, organized by Kimweri Mputa Magogo (July 1968); Bakari Shekwaho (17 July 1967); Kimweri Mputa Magogo and Mbwana Mkanka Mghanga (19 May 1967); Mdoe Saudimwe (7 August 1967); Mwambashi [Mnango].

There are written accounts by Storch (1895a), Kaniki (1903), and Abdallah bin Hemedi 'lAjjemy (1962). See also LangHeinrich (1903), Paul Wohlrab (1918), and Karasek (1923–24).

2   *Simba* means "lion" in a number of languages, but not in the Shambaa language, in which it is *Shimba. Mwene* is simply an honorific greeting. The title was in use by the middle of the nineteenth century (Krapf 1964: part 2, 303). The parallel to *ng'wenye mzi* was suggested by Ruth Besha (1 November 1988).

3   *Ng'wana nyumba nkuu ni unde ja mpaa, nkagheekwa.* Literally, "The son of the great house is a portion of impala meat. You cannot add to it." If you bought beans at the market, you would conclude your discussion of price by asking the seller to give you a bit extra. Impala meat was cut into precise portions, so that it was impossible for the seller to add anything except an entire additional portion. In a similar way you cannot give anything more to the king. This was described to me as a precolonial proverb, and I am assuming that this is correct because impala meat was commonly sold in this way in the nineteenth century, but it would have been unusual after 1914.

4   There are numerous German-period descriptions of the rite of sacrifice, which was essentially the same as the rite I observed a number of times in the 1960s. The broad regional distribution of variants of the rite throughout northeastern Tanzania support the argument by informants that the rite existed in the years before the creation of the Shambaa kingdom (Ng'wang'washi n.d.). The accounts given to the German missionaries indicate that this was the case. See F. Riese (n.d.); Rösler (1906); K. Wohlrab (n.d.); P. Wohlrab (1915:25–26); Becker (1896).

5   See Feierman (1974: chap. 2); see also the version of the Mbegha myth in Abdallah bin Hemedi 'lAjjemy (1962). Abdallah was involved in the kingdom's politics between 1867 and 1873.

6   The generalization on bridewealth is based on participant observation of marriages in the 1960s, historical reconstructions of the bridewealth paid by all the senior men of the village of Ghalambo, as remembered in 1980–81, and some recorded accounts, including Dahlgrün (1903), LangHeinrich (1903), Dupre (n.d.:31–45), Karasek (1911:186–91), Karasek (1918–22:82–89), P. Wohlrab (1918), and Cory (1951: part 2).

7   Bethel MS, *Tagebuch Wuga* (4 June 1897).

8   For the history of relations with the Bondei, see Feierman (1974), and CMS, CA5/09–15, Rev. John James Erhardt, "Journal containing an account of my journey to Usambara & back, and of a three months' stay with the King of the Country Kimeri from the 9th of August to December 1853," entry for 26 August (see also 10 August). This was not an isolated incident. A year earlier the missionary explorer Krapf passed through another Bondei village where a peasant had shot three of Kimweri's soldiers while they were collecting tribute; see CMS, CA5/016, 177, "Journal describing Dr. Krapf's proceedings from the 10th of February to the 14th of April 1852," entry for 3 March.

9   *Central Africa*, 2 June 1884, 101.

10   See, for example, Batimayo Mbughuni (11 April 1967) and Singano Tundwi (8 February 1968).

11   Bethel MS, *Tagebuch Neu Bethel* (26 February 1894).

12   Semnguu Koplo (7 November 1967), reported that the term of the *walughojo* was four days. Ng'wana Aia (18 December 1967) reported the term as five days, which is the length of a market cycle. Ng'wana Aia was a hereditary court official, more directly involved in these affairs than Semnguu Koplo.

13   *NaoM* (November 1891): 173; (January 1895): 5–6. See also Bethel MS, *Tagebuch Hohenfriedeberg* (14 December 1895) and Bethel MS, *Tagebuch Neu Bethel* (23 November 1894).

14   See Karasek (1913:99, 103). The discussion of the Zigula raid is from CMS, CA5/09–15, Erhardt, "Journal containing an account of my journey to Usambara & back, and of a three months' stay with the King of the Country Kimeri from the 9th of August to December 1853," entry for 21 October.

15   See LangHeinrich (1921:310). For the same usage in an oral tradition of the 1960s, see Yonatani Abrahamu (15 November 1966).

16   On collection for need, see Bethel MS, *Tagebuch Hohenfriedeberg* (22 February 1895) and interviews with Kasimu Kimweri (1 February 1968); Mnkande Kimweri (2 December 1966); Mbwana Mkanka Mghanga (13 November 1967).

17   See Krapf (1964: part 2, 281, 304). For an example of a chief minister plotting against his own king, see Kwavi Senkunde (28 May 1968).

18   See LangHeinrich (1903:261). The missionaries of Neu Bethel observed a case in which a childless woman and her husband both agreed that the marriage should end, but the woman's father refused to accept this and therefore refused to accept her return. The woman fled to the chief's court. In the same period women fled to the mission station for many of the same reasons; see Bethel MS, *Tagebuch Neu Bethel* (13 October 1896). On pawning in famine, see P. Wohlrab (1918:169).

19   See the following interviews: Mbwana Mkanka Mghanga (13 November 1967); Mdoe Barua (14 November 1967). See also LangHeinrich (1903:255, 260); Karasek (1918–22:81).

20   See Storch (1895a), LangHeinrich (1903), and Wohlrab (1918). See also the following interviews: Mzimbii Paula (14 July 1967); Mbwana Mkanka Mghanga (13 November 1967); Semnguu Koplo (16 November 1967); Kofia Guha (July 1967); Shekwavi Shemkala (15 November 1967); Mdoe Barua (14 November 1967).

21   *Mpuna* was the word for a slave soldier; see LangHeinrich (1921:46). On the role of slave soldiers, see Semnguu Koplo (7 November 1967).

22   See the following interviews: Nkanieka Mdoe and Paulo (30 December 1966); Semnguu Koplo (29 May 1968, text 2).

23   See LangHeinrich (1903:264). See also Krapf, "Journal of a Journey to Usambara, July-December 1848," CMS, CA5/016–173 (10 August 1848); and "Journal describing Dr. Krapf's proceedings from the 10th of February to the 14th of April 1852," CMS, CA5/016–177 (15 March 1852). On Kimweri's wives,

see Burton (1872 2:227). For wives of the last kings, see Storch (1895a:312) and LangHeinrich (n.d.).

24 See the following interviews: Batimayo Mbughuni (11 April 1967). Mdoe Barua (14 November 1967). Mbwana Mkanka Mghanga (17 May 1967).

25 See the following interviews: Ng'wang'washi (12 October 1966); Mbwana Mkanka Mghanga (17 May 1967). See also Krapf (1860:396); Bethel MS, *Tagebuch Neu Bethel* (11 December 1895); *NaoM* (May 1892): 98, and Karasek (1911:162).

26 Mzaia Shekumkai (13 July 1967).

27 The usages are drawn mostly from the oral traditions, but are confirmed and in some cases added to on the basis of LangHeinrich's dictionary entries and illustrative sentences, collected between 1895 and 1906 (LangHeinrich 1921). See the entries for *duluma, gogolo, -kisanyiza, kombo, mkinda, mpuna, mshumba, mndele, mtung'wa, muntulima, nkole,* and *washi.* Dependent statuses are discussed in many places in the Bethel Mission archives, especially *Tagebuch Neu Bethel* (1894, 1895).

28 For an extended discussion of the heart of the court as wilderness, see Feierman (1972, chap. 6).

29 Shechonge Kishasha (28 June 1968); *NaoM* (January 1892): 10–11; LangHeinrich (1903:223). Mhina (n.d.) reports on the basis of oral traditions he collected at Bungu in 1974 that land was not sold in precolonial Shambaai. My informant Uchungi of Ghalambo agreed with this point. Nevertheless, it is clear that land near villages was bought and sold. Several very old informants at Vugha agreed on this point, including Ng'wana Aia, heir to the position of a major court official whose ancestors would have administered this law (18 December 1967). See also Salehe Ali (20 December 1967) and Semnguu Koplo (19 December 1967). These informants also provide circumstantial detail. It is quite possible that land was sold at Vugha, which was a high-density area, but not at the particular parts of Bungu or Ghalambo from which the informants came, since these were low-density areas. In any event, the collections of Shambaa law made in the German period are unequivocal on the fact that land was sold (P. Wohlrab 1918; Storch 1895a:318; LangHeinrich 1903:262).

30 Turn-of-the-century proverbs describe the man who farms for cows as completely self-denying — someone who has to live off wild berries rather than eat the same food as others (Johanssen and Döring 1914–15:139).

31 *NaoM* (February 1907): 28. For the more general sources on marriage, see Dahlgrün (1903), LangHeinrich (1903), Dupre (n.d.:31–45), Karasek (1911: 186–91), Karasek (1918–22:82–89), P. Wohlrab (1918), and Cory (1951: part 2).

32 Changes in the *kifu* group are difficult to document because it is the sort of intimate social institution that is not the subject of explicit traditions that describe its evolution. The documentary and the oral descriptions of nineteenth-century litigation are explicit on the role of the *kifu* group in paying indemnities. See especially LangHeinrich (1903:222, 224) and interviews with Ng'wana Aia (18 December 1967), Salehe Ali (20 December 1967), and Leo Hassani (August 1967). See also Storch (1896:43). In 1979 and 1980 I

systematically collected accounts of the dissolution of *kifu* among the ancestors of the older men of a single village; the interviews of August 1980
were conducted by a research assistant. The accounts include those of Bakari Shemzighua (13 November 1979), Hamisi Mkong'wa ni Fua (18 October 1970), Ismail Zayumba (23 August 1980), Kingazi Gia (25 August 1980),
and Omari Shekibula (5 March 1980). Other oral lineage histories revolving around *kifu* include those of Kazushwe (August 1967), and Juma Kaoneka
(23 May 1968). See also the autobiography of Lukas Sefu (1911:10) for an
account of the *kifu* group in crisis. Abdallah bin Hemedi 'lAjjemy, who
knew the Shambaa language and lived in Shambaai in the late 1860s and
early 1870s, defined *kifu* as "property of the house, property laid up in the
past by one person, and now the property of many." He wrote to explain
the demand by Kilindi that the king divide the *kifu* of their father (1962:
Sura 130).

33   Mbwana Mkanka Mghanga (13 November 1967). For the legal principle on
      incest, see LangHeinrich (1903:261).

34   See Storch (1895a); Karasek (1918–22:81–82); LangHeinrich (1903); and Wohl-
      rab (1918). See also the following interviews: Idi Kibarua (30 October 1967);
      Mbwana Mkanka Mghanga (13 November 1967).

35   For the rule that a man could not pawn his wife, see Wohlrab (1918:163).

36   On cooking-pot suicide, see Karasek (1911:190) and the interviews with Hatibu
      Hassani (24 April 1968) and Mdoe Msagati (5 December 1966). I collected
      reports of a number of actual cases in the early 1980s of the treatment of
      cooking-pot suicide.

37   See the following interviews: Mdoembazi Guga (29 November 1967); Mntangi
      Saidi and Mandia Nguzo (25 February 1968); and Jaha Mtoi (28 November
      1967). See also Storch (1895a:317).

38   Interview with Yonatani Abrahamu (15 November 1966).

39   Interview with Sheshe Mbea Vintu (July 1966).

40   Interview with Shemng'indo Mtunguja (August 1967).

41   For sources on the decline of *kifu*, see note 32 above.

42   In some cases the bridewealth feast was limited to the *kifu* group. On the
      larger group, see the references for note 4.

43   See Feierman (1974: chap. 1). The major agricultural population of the moun-
      tains has lived around the rim for many centuries. The lexical distinction
      between *nyika* and *shambaai* existed at the turn of the century, its meaning
      then the same as now; see *NaoM* (March 1904): 46. Many nineteenth-century
      sources describe parts of the farming pattern and of the residential pattern:
      Burton and Speke (1858:212–13, 216); Krapf (1964: part 2, 114, 119, 296);
      Holst (1893b); Baumann (1890:103–4); UMCA *Bluebook* (1867); Baumann
      (1891:173–74, 180–82); Johanssen (n.d.:54); and Karasek (1911:155).

44   For a somewhat garbled account of folk description of the seasons at the
      turn of the century, see Holst (1893a).

45   Manioc and sorghum were mentioned by Burton and Speke (1858:211) and
      listed in Steere's word list (1867). Buchwald mentioned that neither crop
      was grown in Shambaai (1897:85). Bananas and/or sugar cane in Shambaai

were described by Baumann (1890:104), Burton and Speke (1858:212–13), and the UMCA *Bluebook* (1867). Karasek's informants described bananas as the food of the ancestors (1911:176), and he mentions sugar cane (1913:116). See also Krapf, who also describes maize (1964: part 2, 114, 296). Maize is mentioned by Steere (1867), Buchwald (1897:83), Baumann (1891:181), and many others. The importance of maize can be judged from the number of specialized words in LangHeinrich's dictionary (1921: see the entries for *bulwa, bwanda, -fununuka, ludezu wa mbuzi, gombo, ghobwelo, ghodola, ghodolo, hangale, himpi, hofi, iko, kese, kibulu, mbega, mchukulu, mpule, mpuluzi, mpungwi, nkese,* and a great many others). For farming patterns in general, see also Holst (1893a, 1893b, 1893c), Dupre (n.d.), LangHeinrich (1913), and the other works already mentioned (Krapf, Burton and Speke, Karasek, Baumann) in references throughout their works. The Bethel MS *Tagebücher* are filled with descriptions of agriculture in the 1890s. See also the interview with Shechonge Kishasha (28 June 1968).

46   Traditions about three major furrows and their controlling lineages in three separate parts of Shambaai (the furrows of Mpambei, Hambaawe, and Shee), all confirm the picture of furrows under peasant control. Lihani Shemnkande (12 June 1967) described how his ancestors came to Gare for its irrigation furrow before Kilindi times. See also Chamhingo wa Mkumbara (25 December 1967), Nkanieka Mdoe (March 1967), and Semnguu Koplo (19 December 1967), as well as other accounts of Gare traditions. See also Karasek (1911:175; 1913:86), Holst (1893b:23), and *NaoM* (November–December 1898: 194).

47   Interview with Yesaia Shekifu (24 May 1967). For the definition of fraternal groups, and on their use of wealth in cases of famine and illness, see the final section of this chapter.

48   Bakari Kilua (October 1966). A great many villages of Shambaai which are still occupied today can be shown to have existed before 1850 on the basis of historical traditions, supplemented in a few cases by documentary evidence. The traditions do not have the intention of proving the antiquity of the villages; they simply mention events which happened in them. The following list is drawn only from the chiefdom of Vugha; similar lists could easily be made for other chiefdoms. The list includes the name of the village (in capital letters), the date for which we have probable evidence, and then a listing of the evidence. ZIAI, 1700: Makao Sangoda, Idi Kibarua, Selemani Shebawa — group testimony (10 May 1967); Idi Kibarua (30 October 1967). KIDUNDAI, 1750: Mbwana Mkanka Mghanga (7 May 1967); Shemaeze wa Kishewa (9 May 1967). KIHITU, 1750: Kimweri Mputa Magogo (24 March 1967); Makao Sangoda et al. (10 May 1967); Kasimu Kimweri (1 February 1968). KIGHUUNDE, 1820: Mhammadi Kika (20 April 1967); Mbwana Mkanka Mghanga (7 May 1967). MPONDE, 1790: Nkinda Kimweri (6 June 1967); Kimweri Kibanga (3 June 1967); Krapf (1964: part 2, 297). MKUMBAA, 1850: Mbwana Mkanka Mghanga (13 November 1967). MANKA, 1850: Abdallah bin Hemedi 'lAjjemy (1962: Sura 42); Waziri Nyeghee (1 July 1967). KISHEWA, 1750: Kimweri Mputa Magogo (3 April

1967); Ng'wana Aia (20 March 1967). MPANGAI, 1800: Mwokechao Gila (10 August 1967); Mbwana Mkanka Mghanga (13 November 1967). SHA-SHUI, 1750: Mdoembazi Guga (15 June 1967). MBUZII, 1850: Mhammadi Kika (20 April 1967). NKOONGO, 1850: Salehe Mwambashi (29 March 1967). MZIYASAA, 1800: Abdallah bin Hemedi 'lAjjemy (1962: Sura 31).

49   Interview with Jaha Mtoi (22 April 1967).

50   See Feierman (1974:78–80). For a full discussion of marriage patterns as they affected the neighborhood fabric, see Feierman (1972: chap. 3).

51   Alington (UMCA *Bluebook* [1867]). On the requirement that every house be occupied every night, see Dupre (n.d.:21) and Kwavi Senkunde (28 May 1968). On the population of Vugha, see Burton and Speke (1858:216). Later in the century, when it was smaller, LangHeinrich estimated its population as three thousand (1902).

52   Salehe Ali (20 December 1967).

53   See Erhardt, "Journal," CMS, CA5/09 (14 October 1853).

54   The 1870s and 1880s were not a peaceful time. In many parts of Shambaai, groups of brothers sent along armed guards with women when they went to the fields (Feierman 1974: chap. 7).

Chapter 3: Healing the Land and Harming the Land

1   For a listing of sources on the accession, see chapter 2, note 1. The rite of burial and accession was unlike any other Shambaa rite, for it was an initiation rite for the new king, but one in which there were no previous initiates to escort and inform the new king. The transmission of the rites was intentionally fragmented. No single individual saw the entire sequence of the rites. The king's representatives (the major courtiers) were burying the old king at the capital at the same time that the headman of Kihitu, with some members of the royal household, was installing the successor. The rites performed at a place called Tekwa, along the new king's path, were preserved by the Nango lineage of that village. When the new king came near Vugha, he was passed from one group of officials to another. One result of the fragmented transmission is that any one informant, whether ordinary subject at Vugha, king's representative, or the king himself, describes only one part of the rite. My own account is reconstructed from a number of detailed fragments, collected from each of the separate experts on his own part of the rite. No individual informant described the entire rite. An extended reconstruction can be found in Feierman (1972).

2   The timing of this event is not totally clear. It happened either at the very time the drum was beaten or in the preceding few days.

3   On strangers fleeing in 1853, see CMS, CA5/09, Erhardt, "Journal . . . of my journey to Usambara" (20 August 1853). On warfare during the mourning period, see Krapf (1863:300) and Abdallah bin Hemedi 'lAjjemy (1962: Suras 40, 69). On violence on the paths, see P. Wohlrab (1918:172); Karasek (1923–24:20); and Marko Kaniki (1903). See also the following interviews:

Mbaruku Jambia (22 January 1968) and Mbwana Mkanka Mghanga (24 January 1968). On the *mshangi*, see Mzee Shevumo (20 April 1968), and Mdoe Loti (n.d., text 4).

4   According to Mdoe Barua (26 January 1968), the point of the rite was that the people of Vugha should be startled to learn, after hearing the beating drum, that a new king had already been enthroned.

5   On measures to keep the rite hidden, see Karasek (1923–24:19–20). Oral traditions on this include Mdoe Barua (26 January 1968), Mbaruku Jambia (22 January 1968), and Ng'wana Aia (19 May 1967). The timing of the rites is very difficult to reconstruct, since two rites were going on simultaneously, much of the rite was intentionally kept secret, and each informant was expert in only that part of the rite which was his own responsibility. The fact that accession and burial took place at the same time was explained only by a few of the most privileged informants. The man who was clearest and most coherent in his description of the relationships between the separate actions was Ng'wana Aia (19 May 1967). He was keeper of ritual for the lineage of the hereditary chief minister. If there had been need for a rite in the 1960s, he would have been the closest to an overall coordinator of the total event. Others who discussed this issue were Mdoe Barua, in a joint discussion with Ng'wana Aia (18 April 1967), Mdoe Loti (10 April 1967, 29 April 1967), Mbaruku Jambia (22 January 1968), and Mbwana Mkanka Mghanga (7 May 1967). According to most descriptions of the burial, the drum called *Nenkondo* was beaten and slit to signal the completion of the burial; according to most descriptions of the accession, *Nenkondo* was beaten and slit to signal the arrival of the new king. Both descriptions make sense once it is understood that the new king arrived in Vugha on the same night as the burial. In addition, the death of the king was not publicly acknowledged until his successor had been installed.

6   Interview with Ali Shechonge (30 November 1967).

7   Interview with Mdoe Loti (10 April 1967, 29 April 1967). Mdoe Loti saw the installation of Kinyashi in 1895. It is also described in a fragmentary written account (Storch 1895a). On the events at Fune and Kihitu, see also Mbaruku Jambia (22 January 1968), Mdoe Barua and Ng'wana Aia (18 April 1967), and Mbwana Mkanka Mghanga (24 January 1968). See also Abdallah bin Hemedi 'lAjjemy (1962).

8   See the Bethel MS, *Tagebuch Neu Bethel* (15 May 1895) and "Heuschrecken und kein Ende" (*NaoM*, May 1895, 70–73).

9   See the following interviews: Bakari Shekwaho (17 July 1967), Mwejuma Ngoda (August 1967), Kimweri Mputa Magogo (1 December 1967), Saguti Shekiondo (30 July 1967), Mbwana Mkanka Mghanga (24 January 1968, and 7 May 1967), and Mdoe Barua and Ng'wana Aia (18 April 1967). See also Abdallah bin Hemedi 'lAjjemy (1962: Sura 48).

10   For the sources on this, see note 7.

11   See the interview with Mngano Mahimbo (5 November 1966) on the *fika* of the smiths.

12   All traditions about the political history of the nineteenth-century kingdom

are built on the armature of Kilindi descent. A few representative traditions include those recounted by Boaz Mjata (15 July 1967), Ng'wa Paula
s/o Ng'wa Kimungu (12 July 1967), Shedoekuu wa Baghai (12 March 1967),
Mdoembazi Guga (15 June 1967), Hassani Magogo (25 December 1967),
Kasimu Kimweri (1 February 1968), Kimweri Mputa Magogo (24 March
1967), and Jaha Mtoi (22 April 1967). See also Shekulwavu s/o Kinyashi (July
1968).

13   Male names of the Shekulwavu generation include Kimweri, Mtoi, She-
mlughu, Shemkai, Bughe, Ng'wa Mbegha, Ng'wa Paua, Kihiyo. Female
names of the Shekulwavu generation include Okimea, Omtoi, Oshimba,
Mamlughu, and Mamnkande. Male names of the Shebughe generation include Mnkande, Mbegha, Shekumkai, Mlughu, Ng'wa Mtoi, Shekimweri,
Hoza (husbands of Kilindi women only), and Shekumlughu. Female names
of the Shebughe generation include Makihiyo, Omlughu, Omkai, Ogao,
Okinyashi, and Omnkande.

14   Interviews with Kimweri Mputa Magogo (24 March 1967), Shebughe Kingazi Shemnkande (17 August 1966), and Waziri Nyeghee (1 July 1967).

15   The 1905 edition was listed as the work of Hubert alone, even though he
wrote the essay in collaboration with Marcel Mauss. I am quoting from the
1929 edition.

16   Shedoekuu wa Baghai, for example, argues that Kimweri ye Nyumbai healed
all the illnesses of the land because he had power over his sons, all of whom
respected him (21 March 1967). Other traditions demonstrating the point
include those recounted by Mdoembazi Guga (15 June 1967), and Kwavi
Senkunde (28 May 1968).

17   See the UMCA *Bluebook* (1868), letter from Alington, 23 June 1868.

18   Mandughu Chai (15 June 1968).

19   See the discussion of *nguvu* later in this chapter. Steere's dictionary of 1867
list the word as *nguzu* (1867:28, 81), but neither of his informants spoke
Shambaa as a mother tongue.

20   On the locusts in 1894, see the Bethel MS, *Tagebuch Neu Bethel* (22 January
1895). On the incident in 1908, see TNA, File on Majio (no number), Winzer
to Bezirksamtmann Wilhelmstal (20 October 1908).

21   Yeremia Kusaga (April 1967).

22   *Mafuniko*, "covering," is related to the verb *-funika*. Among the traditions
which mention Kibanga's nickname is that recounted by Zumbe Barua s/o
Makange (22 February 1968).

23   Mbaruku Jambia (22 January 1968).

24   Juma Kaoneka (March 1967).

25   On the poisoned arrow, see the interview with Nkanieka Mdoe and Paulo
(30 December 1966). On Kilindi women in *gao*, see Storch (1895a:311). On
Kilindi women taking men, see Mbwana Mkanka Mghanga (10 April 1968)
and Semnguu Koplo (29 May 1968). On Kilindi marriage and sexuality, see
Batimayo Mbughuni (11 April 1967), Yonatani Abrahamu (15 November
1966), and Mbwana Mkanka Mghanga and Kimweri Mputa Magogo (10
April 1968). On adultery as bringing the death penalty, see Salehe Mwa-

mbashi (29 March 1967). We shall see in the next chapter that the last autonomous king was himself executed by the Germans for administering the death penalty in just such a case.

26   Ng'wana Aia (24 May 1968).

27   The traditions are explicit about the implications of either centralization or decentralization of power for litigation, warfare, and tribute. In warfare, for example, the relevant test was whether a chief could say that he had been "insulted" by a foreign power. In a time of centralization, only the king could say that he had been insulted (-bewa). One tradition explains that in the days of Kimweri ye Nyumbai, his son Mshuza at Ubiri could not make war. "The only one who could make war against a foreign power was Kimweri, when he had been insulted. How could Mshuza go to fight against another land? What right did he have to say, 'I have been insulted (nabewa)'"? (Mdoembazi Guga 15 June 1967). All the traditions make the same distinction. A similar one exists for litigation: only the king in time of centralization, or an autonomous chief in decentralized times, has hukumu, the right to sentence a subject to death. The overall pattern is elucidated through reconstructions of patterns of action within many of the separate chiefdoms, based on sources as described in note 37 below. For an extended reconstruction of the configurations of royal descent, see Feierman (1972:148–208), and for the implications for litigation, warfare, and tribute, see Feierman (1972:307–63).

28   This is supported by the entire run of oral traditions, with other evidence concurring. The debates among Kilindi after Kimweri ye Nyumbai's death, for example, focused on the inheritance of his wives and cows and on what the relations were to be among his sons and grandsons (Abdallah bin Hemedi 'lAjjemy 1962: Suras 60–70). Even while Kimweri ye Nyumbai was still alive, he devoted much attention to the future relationship between his heir (his grandson Shekulwavu) and his sons. The descriptions of these discussions in a whole range of oral traditions are almost identical to Kimweri's speech at Vugha, as described in 1853 by Erhardt (CMS, CA5/09, "Journal . . . of my journey to Usambara," 19 September 1853).

29   The cycle was reconstructed on the basis of oral traditions transmitted at several levels. First, there were the oral traditions about royal affairs at Vugha. Second, I collected traditions among the major chiefly lines at each of a number of local chiefdoms: Gare, Ubiri, Mlalo, Mponde, Bumbuli, Shembekeza, Mkaie-Tamota, Mlungui, and others. In addition, at each of the separate chiefdoms I collected traditions wherever possible from among the descendants of Kilindi lines which had lost power when the dominant Kilindi took over, and also from representatives of pre-Kilindi local lines and of peasant lines which had intermarried with chiefs. Many of the traditions are listed in the footnotes to Feierman 1974:108–19. An extended analysis of the oscillating pattern is in Feierman 1972:148–208.

30   Many of the oral traditions say that there had been no Kilindi chiefs in the separate chiefdoms before the time of Kimweri ye Nyumbai (e.g., Kimweri Mputa Magogo [24 March 1967]). In many of the chiefdoms, however, it

is possible to trace earlier chiefly lines which had been supplanted by Kimweri ye Nyumbai's sons. The total pattern in one chiefdom, Gare-Ubiri,
is revealed by the comparative analysis of the traditions recounted by Athumani Mdoe (5 February 1968), Hassani Magogo (25 December 1967), Jaha
Mtoi (22 April 1967), Lihani Shemnkande (12 June 1967), Mdoe Zayumba
(8 June 1967), and Mpira Sanju (31 January 1968).

31   When Ng'wa Kimwungu of Shembekeza was suspected of murdering his
half-brother Mnkande, the royal heir, he was removed from his chiefdom
and sent off to take up a territory in Bondei, to the east (Ng'wa Paula s/o
Ng'wa Kimungu [12 July 1967]). When Mkanka Mghanga of Mponde killed
his mother's brother (whom he suspected of causing his mother's death),
he was removed and sent off to a more distant territory; see the interviews
with Abdallah Mweta (13 June and 15 June 1968); Kasimu Kimweri (1 February 1968); Mahimbo Kihedu (1 February 1968); and Mbwana Mkanka
Mghanga (13 November 1967).

32   The sources on Semboja at Gare include the traditions listed in note 30 and
also the tradition published by Karasek (1923–24:46–47).

33   Interview with Boaz Mjata (15 July 1967).

34   The following narrative on the events following Kimweri ye Nyumbai's death
is a summary of events described more fully in *The Shambaa Kingdom* (Feierman 1974).

35   Kimweri Mputa Magogo and Mbwana Mkanka Mghanga (19 May 1967).

36   Interviews with Mahimbo Kihedu (1 February 1968) and Mbwana Mkanka
Mghanga (10 April 1968).

37   The traditions are quite explicit on the oscillation, and on its implications
for litigation, warfare, and tribute; they include those recounted by Mdoe
Saudimwe (7 August 1967), Mdoe Barua and Ng'wana Aia (18 April 1967),
Mdoembazi Guga (15 June 1967), Shedoekuu wa Baghai (21 March 1967),
Kimweri Mputa Magogo (24 March 1967), Ng'wa Paula s/o Ng'wa Kimungu
(12 July 1967). In addition, the many separate traditions about litigation,
warfare, and tribute have embedded within them knowledge about the locus
of power at any particular time.

Chapter 4: Alternative Paths to Social Health
in the Precolonial Kingdom

1   Interviews with Zumbe Hassani Kinyashi (July 1968), Nasoro Maghembe
(July 1968), and Yosua Hermasi (July 1968).

2   Interviews with Athumani Mdoe (5 February 1968); Mwokechao s/o Gila
(10 August 1967).

3   Interviews with Mbogho s/o Mzao (9 February 1968, 19 July 1968), Saguti
Shekiondo (21 July 1967, 30 July 1967, 14 February 1968), Gottfried s/o
Salomon Shangali (7 February 1968), Hemedi Mbogho s/o Wa Kanali (6 Feb-
ruary 1968), Kiluwa Shemhina (9 February 1968), Mhammadi s/o Shekashiha

(8 February 1968), Sylvano Shekalaghe (27 July 1967), and Shemzighua Rupia (7 February 1968).

4   Juma Kaoneka (June 1967).

5   Interviews with Singano Tundwi (8 February 1968), Idi Kibarua (30 October 1967), and Makao Sangoda (10 May 1967).

6   Interviews with Chamhingo wa Mkumbara (25 December 1967), Nkanieka Mdoe (March 1967, text 2), Semnguu Koplo (19 December 1967). See also Karasek (1911:175; 1913:86); Holst (1893b:23); and *NaoM* (November–December 1898): 194.

7   On Wambagha locust medicines, see the interview with Mandughu Chai (15 June 1968), a descendant of the Wambagha who settled in Shambaai. See also Jaha Mtoi (28 November 1967), Kimweri Mputa Magogo, Mdoe Barua, and Ng'wana Aia (22 July 1968), Bethel MS, *Tagebuch Neu Bethel* (6 June 1894, 22 January 1895, 16 July 1895); *Tagebuch Hohenfriedeberg* (4 March 1895, 4 July 1895); *Tagebuch Wuga* (14 May 1898). See also *NaoM* (May 1895): 70–73; F. Gleiss (1898); and Karasek (1923–24:23).

8   One of the richest accounts is by Karasek, a planter who spoke Shambaa, lived with a Shambaa woman, and spent much time visiting with her relatives; see especially Karasek (1911:168–69, 190–97, 204; 1918–22:89; 1923–24:13, 33, 36). Missionaries reported many cases of illness and therapy. A limited sample of reports on cases and therapies includes the following: Hosbach (1911); K. Wohlrab (1929); Dale (1896); P. Wohlrab (1913); Riese (n.d.); Marko Mkufya (n.d.); *NaoM* (1902): 98–100; (1906): 40–44, 108–114; (1892): 73–74; (1894): 84–85, 87, 89, 122; (1899): 106–7; (1903): 99, 143; (1903): 189–91. See also Baumann (1891:141–2); Farler (1879:92); Bethel MS, *Tagebuch Neu Bethel* (10 March 1894); Dupre (n.d.); Döring (1900a); Steere (1867:11, 17–19); *Central Africa* (1892:196); Hosbach (1925); P. Wohlrab (1915); Burton (1872; 2:216); LangHeinrich (1903:231, 262; 1921: entries for *kulo, laghula, mageleta, malape, mandali, mashale, matabano, mazumba, mbu za kizongo, mubughi, mbulashi, mubuntu, mchanjo, mulamulo,* and many others); Krapf (1964; 2:63, 110, 116, 118, 121); and Johanssen (n.d.; 1:138). See also CMS, CA5/09, Erhardt, "Journal containing an account of my journey to Usambara & back . . . , 9th of August to December 1853," (1, 7–8, 21 September, 29 October, 14 November); CMS, CA5/016, "Journal Describing Dr. Krapf's proceedings from the 10th of February to the 14th of April 1852," (17 and 18 March).

9   See the sources in the preceding note. Karasek (1911:196) outlines the apprenticeship process. Two case studies, among others, are in Hosbach (1911), and P. Wohlrab (1913).

10   See the sources in note 8.

11   For sources on spirits entering Shambaai, see Feierman (1974:201–2). Karasek (1911) describes the significance of journeys of discovery. *NaoM* (1902): 99 discusses the perceptions of the dangerousness of introduced illnesses. Krapf and explorers describe the king's expectations of their own roles as healers, and also mention exotic healers at Vugha; see CMS, CA5/016, "Jour-

nal Describing Dr. Krapf's proceedings from the 10th of February to the 14th of April 1852" (17 and 18 March).

12   The sources in note 8 are rich in herbal treatments and natural explanations. For death explained by natural causes, see *NaoM* 1906:124. On natural causes and treatments, see also Marko Mkufya (n.d.), and K. Wohlrab (n.d.).

13   See Riese (n.d.) and Bethel MS, *Tagebuch Neu Bethel* (10 March 1894).

14   For a notable case in which a chief brought a patient to the missionaries, see *NaoM* (1899): 106–7. Krapf treated Kimweri ye Nyumbai, as described in CMS, CA5/016, "Journal describing Dr. Krapf's proceedings from the 10th of February to the 14th of April 1852," entry for 18 March.

15   Most of the proverbs cited in this paragraph are still in use. Evidence that this and the following proverbs were in use during the early colonial period is from Johanssen and Döring (1914–15:149).

16   See Döring (1900a:51). The proverb, as in the other cases, is from Johanssen and Döring (1914–15:149).

17   Shils wrote a number of works on intellectuals; see, for example, Shils (1972).

18   The interpretation of Weber's views on rationalization is based primarily on his 1978 work, *Economy and Society.*

19   For an extended discussion of this debate and of the literature, see Mudimbe (1985).

20   Interview with Juma Kaoneka (June 1967).

21   Shekulwavu, as Kimweri ye Nyumbai's chosen heir, would have received the main rain charm. The discussion of the body part is from Kimweri Mputa Magogo and Mbwana Mkanka Mghanga (19 May 1967).

22   Glassman (1988) gives a brilliant account of rituals of citizenship in nineteenth-century Pangani. The point about caravans is from page 138.

23   CMS, CA5/09, Rev. John James Erhardt, "Journal containing an account of my journey to Usambara & back . . . 9th of August to December 1853," entry for 1 September.

24   Abdallah bin Hemedi 'lAjjemy describes serving as Shekulwavu's interpreter from Swahili to Shambaa (1962: Sura 111). On Kimweri Maguvu's literacy, see J. P. Farler, "News from Magila," *Central Africa* 6 (June 1888): 82–85.

25   Interview with Mdoembazi Guga (29 November 1967).

26   Interview with Jaha Mtoi (28 November 1967).

27   Semboja did not altogether discourage this view, perhaps because of his weak position in dynastic politics. He openly acknowledged violating the ritual prohibition against farming during the mourning for his father, Kimweri ye Nyumbai; see Abdallah bin Hemedi 'lAjjemy (1962: Sura 73).

28   This remark come up frequently in the oral narratives. The quotation is from Theodore Isaka, the important nationalist of the 1950s (10 November 1967, text 2).

29   See, for example, Moore (1966:257).

30   Maukindo's story was told by her grandson, Saidi Shembago (8 October 1979). The story of the Vugha kidnappers is from Shechonge Kishasha, whose father was one of the rescuers (11 March 1967).

31   Interview with Salehe Mwambashi (29 March 1967).

32   There was some question about whether the Bondei soldiers of Kilindi chiefs
      would join the rebellion. Chanyeghea's messenger was concerned about this
      when he said to the Bondei plotters, "There are many of the Bondei who
      are of Kilindi blood [who intermarried with the Kilindi], who are accustomed
      to robbing people of poultry and goats. If they have orders from the Ki-
      lindi, Arrest your father, they go and do it without shame. . . . Will you
      be able to persuade them to join you in the business of the Kilindi?" (Feier-
      man 1974:161). At another time, a Kilindi asked the Bondei elders, "Which
      of the Kilindi has a Yao slave? Are not these highway robbers your own
      children?" (Abdallah bin Hemedi 'lAjjemy 1962: Sura 170; on Tumba's sol-
      diers, see Sura 181).

Chapter 5: Colonial Rule and the Fate of the Intellectuals

1   In this chapter, as in the twentieth-century chapters of this book, oral infor-
     mants are not named in the footnotes, except in those rare circumstances
     when the informant requested that he or she be cited by name. The politi-
     cal conflicts described still arouse passions. The research of 1979–80 was
     carried out under a grant which held, as an explicit condition, that indi-
     vidual informants not be cited as the sources of particular bits of informa-
     tion. A full list of interviews is given after the endnotes, without an indica-
     tion of the subject discussed in each interview.
2   See Rochus Schmidt (1892:175) on Semboja and Kibanga in 1890. See also
     UMCA, Box A1 VIII, Woodward to Child (20 February 1890). See the follow-
     ing: NaoM (March 1895): 39–42; (July 1895): 103; Bethel MS, Wohlrab, "Be-
     richt über die untersuchungsreise nach Wuga"; Rhodes House MSS, Afr. s.
     462, Report by R. W. Gordon, keeper of the German records.
3   See the Bethel MS, Tagebuch Hohenfriedeberg (2 January 1895); Tagebuch
     Wuga (February–April 1895); LangHeinrich to Bodelschwingh (7 January
     1895). See also NaoM (March 1895): 39–42; (May 1895): 66–67, 70–73; (July
     1895): 102–6).
4   This account is based largely on oral sources, but it is described also by Lieu-
     tenant Storch in NaoM (Sept. 1895): 138–40. See also Bethel MS, Tagebuch
     Neu Bethel (15 May 1895).
5   The events of the period are recorded in the Vugha station diary of the Bethel
     Mission. There is an excellent description in LangHeinrich (1902) and frag-
     ments in Gleiss (1928).
6   Lieutenant Storch, "Über das Strafverfahren gegen den Jumben Mputa von
     Wuga," Deutsches Kolonialblatt 6, no. 15 (August 1895): 379–80.
7   See Bethel MS, Tagebuch Wuga (June–September 1895), and TNA, G7004,
     Land, Wilhelmstal, 1895–1906.
8   F. LangHeinrich, "Vergangene Pracht," NaoM 16 (1902): 77.
9   Bethel MS, Tagebuch Wuga (16 July 1896, 24 January 1896, 20 February
     1896).
10   NaoM (1903): 15.

11   Baumann (1890:82, 107; 1891:180); P. Wohlrab (1915:29); Johanssen (n.d., vol. 1:49–93); *NaoM* (July 1898): 119–20; Bethel MS, *Tagebuch Hohenfriedeberg* (1895).
12   *NaoM* (June 1901): 100–101; (June 1902): 85; (December 1900): 213–17.
13   Bethel MS, *Tagebuch Wuga* (4 June 1897, 24 February 1896); *Tagebuch Hohenfriedeberg* (1894–95, especially 4 March 1895); *Tagebuch Neu Bethel* (22 January 1895, 23–24 February 1895). See also *NaoM* (June 1897): 96.
14   *NaoM* (July 1898): 118; (August 1897): 124–27. As late as September 1898, Mbugu were seen leading cows to Kinyashi at Vugha in the hope that he would bring rain. It seems the Mbugu did not decisively reject the possibility the Kilindi still controlled the rain, but rather considered that others might also have the power; see *NaoM* (November–December 1898): 194. Kinyashi's poverty at this time makes it unlikely that he was receiving great quantities of tribute from his Shambaa subjects.
15   Ernst Johanssen, "Der Riese Hundju," *NaoM* (November 1899): 203–4.
16   Bethel MS, *Tagebuch Neu Bethel* and *Tagebuch Wuga* (1899–1900).
17   See *NaoM* (July 1903): 100–06; (June 1904): 88. Bethel MS, *Tagebuch Neu Bethel* (23 September 1894, 7 and 13 October 1896, 26 March 1897, November and December 1909); *Tagebuch Hohenfriedeberg* (22 February and 11 March 1895).
18   Johanssen (n.d., vol. 1:223); *NaoM* (April 1899): 78; (June 1899): 106–11; P. Wohlrab (1915:44); Bethel MS, *Tagebuch Neu Bethel* (23 October 1899).
19   *Usambara-Post*, "Missionen und Arbeiterfrage" (29 August 1908); H. Dupre (n.d.:63); Iliffe (1979:153); *NaoM* (September 1905): 140; (October 1907): 174–75; (January 1912): 20–23; TNA, German Files, XI A3, Wilhelmstal. Bezirksamtmann Meyer to Trappists at Gare (18 June 1903).
20   *NoaM* (July–August 1916): 39.
21   For a listing of *akidas* in Wilhelmstal District, see Iliffe (1969:184). My own informants claimed that *akida* Tupa had been a slave of Kibanga, but I am not certain of the reliability of the account.
22   *NaoM* (September 1900): 166; (July 1902): 103; (October 1910): 206.
23   *NaoM* (April 1908): 54–63; (January 1909): 2–12.
24   *NaoM* (May 1911): 45–48.
25   *NaoM* (September 1905): 140; (June 1902): 91; (March 1907): 37–40; (January 1914): 3–5. See also LangHeinrich (n.d.:7–11); Paasche (1906:210, 214, 216, 220); *Usambara-Post*, "Einsendugen und Besprechungen wirtschaflichen Inhalts," 29 February 1908, and "Wilhelmstal," 28 October 1911; Bethel MS, *Tagebuch Wuga* (3 July 1897); Iliffe (1979:143); TNA, Wilhelmstal, 'Kronland (Generalia),' unnumbered file.
26   *NaoM* (May and September 1909).
27   Woodward (1913:105–8); P. Wohlrab (1915:76–77). On Lushoto's clerk, see the interview with Jaha Mtoi (28 November 1967).
28   *NaoM* (April 1908): 54–63; (January 1909): 2–12.
29   Indirect rule as a cult is described by Sir Philip Mitchell (1954). See also Iliffe (1979:319–20).
30   See Austen (1968:152). Sir Philip Mitchell describes the role of Grigg (1954:

104). For Cameron's violent prejudices against Grigg, see Margery Perham (1976:45).

31   See the Tanganyika *Provincial Annual Reports* (1935:103).

32   This is taken from a Confidential Print of 1925, as given by Austen (1968: 153).

33   For an excellent discussion of self-sufficiency, see McCarthy (1982). In 1948 District Commissioner Piggott, who governed the Shambaa kingdom in Lushoto District, complained that the people of his district were too rich and that if food imports were not restricted, local people would be able to purchase their food needs out of cash earnings — an unacceptable possibility. At Moa, on the ocean in Tanga District, fishermen with limited land were pressed to spend their time growing cassava instead of fishing so that they would remain self-sufficient — this in a province desperately short of protein; see TNA, 72/62/6/III, Lushoto *DAR* (1948). On Moa, see TNA, 4/411/IV/118, D.C. Tanga to P.C. Tanga (15 December 1943).

34   TNA, 4/411/IV, Tanga Province, Native Foodstuffs, 110–12; Chief Secretary to all Provincial Commissioners and District Commissioners (7 July 1943).

35   Rhodes House, MSS Afr. s. 462, "Proposal for Usambara District Native Administration," by W. S. G. Barnes.

36   The description of Kinyashi counting his money was given in oral accounts by a number of people around the court in Vugha.

37   "Education Policy in British Tropical Africa. Memorandum submitted to the Secretary of State for the Colonies by the Advisory Committee on Native Education in the British Tropical African Dependencies" (March 1925), Cmd. 2374, p. 4. See also A. R. Thompson (1968:15–32).

38   The district officer's comment is from TNA, Secretariat 11682, *Tanga Province Annual Report* (1928). The description of the threatening letter is from the reliable oral account given by Kinyashi's clerk.

39   TNA, 72/44/16, 103, David Mshumba to Chief Secretary Dar es Salaam (15 April 1952).

40   TNA, 72/44/11, "Native Affairs. General Associations and Tumaini la Usambaa." Selected documents of these associations are reproduced in University of Dar es Salaam, Department of History, Pangani Valley Historical Documents (PVH), "Local Government and Politics in Usambara."

41   The school population for 1912 is in *NaoM*, "Jahresbericht." (January 1913). The 1946 pupil total is in TNA, 304/711/1, 29, Provincial Education Officer Tanga and Northern Provinces to P.C. Tanga (7 October 1946).

42   TNA 72/62/6/III, 210, *Annual Report*, Korogwe Division (1947).

43   TNA, 72/43/3, 76–76A, Isaac Rashidy and Saguti Sabali, President and Secretary, Lushoto Local African Association, Lushoto, 11 June 1947, to D. C. Korogwe, "Maoni ya Chama juu ya mkutano wa Mombo," in Lushoto, Native Administration, Chief's Personal.

44   Ibid.

45   TNA, 4/6/2, 338, Extract from P. C.'s Safari Notes, 19/3/47–22/3/47.

46   TNA, 72/43/3, 10, Native Treasury Clerk Korogwe to Shebuge Magogo (November 1937).

47   For the meeting, see TNA, 4/6/2, 353, Mohamadi Mandia, Selemani Mbelwa, and others to D. C. Korogwe (10 June 1947).
48   TNA, 72/44/16, 2A, "Maulizo Mbele ya Bwana." For the date, see Mlughu Kiluwa and Mdoe Barua to D. C. Korogwe (2 August 1947), reproduced in PVH "Local Government and Politics in Usambara," document 30.
49   TNA, 72/44/16, 2A, "Maulizo Mbele ya Bwana."
50   TNA, 72/44/16, 12, Meeting at Kitala cha Mlugu, 15–16 (August 1947).
51   TNA, 72/44/11, 53, Umoja wa Wasambaa Tanga Mjini to Ramadhani K. Mwinyikheri (16 April 1948).
52   TNA, 72/44/16, 14, Saguti Sabali and Isaac Kilo to editor, Mambo Leo, "Uhusiano wa Wasambaa na Wakilindi" (6 June 1947).
53   TNA, 72/44/16, 14A, TAA Usambara Branch (23 August 1947).
54   The assessment of Shebughe's *kilema* as an issue is based on numerous informal conversations at Vugha. The coffee rules are discussed in TNA, *Lushoto District Book*.
55   For the most part this draws on oral accounts, especially those of Nkanieka Mdoe. I had general discussions about the period with Mnkande Kimweri, the chief in question.
56   TNA, 72/62/6, 94–95, *Annual Report Lushoto Division* (1941); 72/3/1A, 43, Hassani of Mlalo to D. O. i/c Lushoto (9 February 1942); 72/3/1A, 53, Mwamkali of Mtae to D. O., (received 26 February 1942); 72/3/1A, 56, Hassani Magogo Vuga to A. D. O. (4 March 1942); 72/62/6/II,140ff., *Annual Report Lushoto Division* (1942); TNA, 31207, "Native Chiefs: Lushoto District." For comparable chiefly censuses, see also Mhando (1977:42).
57   TNA, 72/62/1A/I, 71, R. D. Linton, Agricultural Officer Lushoto, to D. C. Korogwe (2 May 1942).
58   PVH, "Mlalo Rehabilitation Scheme," p. 56, Government Sociologist to P. C. Tanga (2 June 1946).
59   TNA, 72/62/6/III, 207B, Lushoto Division – Korogwe *DAR* (1946). This refers to Ali Mashina, another name for Ali Chankoa.
60   TNA, 31207. A. V. Hartnoll, P. C., Tanga, to Chief Secretary Dar es Salaam (19 June 1946 [ref. no. 487/40] and 19 August 1946).
61   PVH, "Mlalo Rehabilitation Scheme," p. 39, Director of Agricultural Production to Chief Secretary Dar es Salaam (6 February 1946).
62   PVH, "Mlalo Rehabilitation Scheme," p. 46, P. C. Tanga to Acting Administrative Secretary Secretariat (19 August 1946).
63   PVH, "Mlalo Rehabilitation Scheme," p. 59, D. O. i/c Lushoto District to P. C. Tanga (31 August 1946).
64   TNA Secretariat, 33049, "Postwar Reconstruction: Development of the Western Usambaras," vol iv, note by his Excellency the Governor on his visit to Mlalo, 31 December 1949.
65   PVH, "Mlalo Rehabilitation Scheme," p. 89, "Mlalo Rehabilitation Scheme Annual Report," 1947. TNA, 72/62/6/III, 209, *Lushoto Division Annual Report*, 1947.
66   Makao Makuu ya TANU ya Wilaya ya Lushoto (1975). Cited hereafter as

TANU na Wananchi Lushoto (1975). (For archival sources on this dispute see TNA, 4/6/2.)

67 T. L. M. Marealle, "Social Survey of the Mlalo and Mwangoi Areas, Lushoto District," TNA, Secretariat 16721.

68 TNA, 4/6/2, 353, Mohamadi Mandia, Selemani Mbelwa, and others to D. C. Korogwe (10 June 1947).

69 For the meeting of 4–5 June, see TNA, 72/43/3, 70, Shebuge Magogo Kimweri to D. C. Korogwe (6 June 1947); 72/44/16, 5, Mlugu Kiluwa and Mdoe Barua to D. C. Korogwe (2 August 1947). See also PVH, "Local Government and Politics in Usambara," p. 9, document written by Hassani Kinyasi of Mlalo and Salehe Mtoi of Gare. For the meeting of 23 June, see PVH, "Local Government," p. 12, Shebuge Magogo Kimweri to Daffa Kivo (23 June 1947), also found in TNA, 72/43/2, 79. See also TNA, 72/62/6/III, 209D, *Lushoto Division Annual Report* (1947).

70 PVH, "Local Government" p. 21, Mlughu Kiluwa and others to all subchiefs (17 August 1947).

71 For the disturbance of 25 July, see TNA, 72/44/16, 13, Mlugu Kiluwa, Kimweri Kibanga, Salimu Nkinda, and Batholomeyo Mbuguni for Ushirika wa Washambaa na Wakilindi to Wazumbe Wakuu Wote (16 August 1947); for the correspondence from both sides on the meeting of 4 August, see TNA, 72/44/16, 4, Shebuge Magogo to D. C. (received 3 August 1947); TNA, 72/44/16, 5, Mlugu Kiluwa and Mdoe Barua to D. C. Korogwe (2 August 1947); TNA, 72/44/16, 6, Yusufu Shewedi, Salehe Mwanyoka, Isak Hoza, Seleman Mbelwa, and Matayo Dada (sic.) to D. O. Lushoto (5 August 1947); TNA, 72/44/16, 7, Yusufu Shewedi and others to D. C. Korogwe (2 August 1947); TNA, 72/44/16, 8, A. D. O. Lushoto to D. C. Korogwe (6 August 1947); TNA, 72/44/16, 9A, Ramadhani Msumali to D. O. Lushoto (4 August 1947). See also PVH, "Local Government," p. 18, Hassani Magogo to D. O. i/c Lushoto (2 August 1947).

72 PVH, "Local Government" p. 20, Ushirika wa Wasambaa na Wakilindi, Minutes of a Meeting (15–16 August 1947).

73 For the goals of the TAA in Usambara in August 1947, see TNA, 304/A6/28, 4–6, Makusudi na Shabaha za Tanganyika African Association (Usambara Branch) (received by P. C. 28 August 1947). The TAA repudiated the local association in TNA 4/6/2, 385, Abdiel Shangali to African Association, Usambara Branch (11 November 1947), with copy to District Commissioner; Shebughe's abdication is mentioned in TNA, 72/62/6/III, 210B, *Annual Report*, Korogwe Division (1947).

74 TNA, 4/6/2, 414, D. Green, Secretary of the Usambara Association, to Chief Secretary, Dar es Salaam (19 December 1947); TNA, 4/6/2, 396, Kiluwa Shemweta, Barua Ng'wamaghembe, and Batimayo Mbuguni to Chief Secretary, Dar es Salaam (9 December 1947); TNA, 4/6/2, 400, Nkinda Kimweri, Omari Nkinda, and Shemngkwe [sic] Doekulu to the Chief Secretariat To The Native Affairs (sic), Dar es Salaam (12 December 1947).

Chapter 6: Royal Domination and Peasant Resistance, 1947–1957

1   TNA, 4/6/2, 425, Piggott to P. C. Tanga (24 February 1948). The oral informant quoted in this paragraph is not cited by name, nor are other oral informants quoted in this chapter, for reasons given in chapter 5, note 1.

2   The protesters sent their telegram to the Provincial Commissioner on 15 June;
arrests began several days later. See TNA, 72/43/3, 126A, Raia wa Usambaa
to P. C. Tanga (15 June 1948); TNA, 72/43/3, 128, D. Sozi to D. C. Lushoto
(21 June 1948); TNA, 72/43/3, Piggott to Mazumbe Wote (26 June 1948);
TNA 72/43/3, 131, Piggott to Mazumbe Wote (29 June 1948).

3   See TNA, 72/43/3, 139, Kimweri Mputa, Hotuba ya Siku Kuu (delivered
11 September 1948). Kimweri had been named chief on 23 June; TNA, 4/6/2,
474, K. M. Magogo [public speech?] (26 July 1948).

4   See TNA, 72/43/3, 157, Piggott to Kimweri Mputa Magogo; TNA 72/43/3,
158, D. C. Lushoto to Kimweri Mputa Magogo (11 February 1949); TNA,
72/43/3/II, 205, Kimweri Magogo to D. C. Lushoto (5 January 1950).

5   For a list of members of Kimweri's council in September 1948, see TNA,
4/6/2, 481, "Usambara Native Authority Council," D. C. Lushoto to P. C.
Tanga (3 September 1948). On Hassani Kinyashi and the Muslim Association, see TNA, 72/44/11, 45, Zumbe Hassani to D. C. Lushoto (19 March
1948). On Kimweri and the Shehe, see TNA, 72/62/6/III, 221, Lushoto *DAR*
(1949).

6   See TNA, 72/44/11, 63a, "Maoni ya Mkutano wa Kwanza wa Manaibu wa
Chama cha 'Tumaini la Ushambaa' uliofanyika Korogwe Tarehe 3 Julai 1948;
TNA, 72/44/11, 99, General Secretary [Sem Shemsanga, of Tumaini la Usha-
mbaa] to Wanachama wote (7 April 1952); TNA, 72/44/11, 100, Secretary
to the Usambara Native Authority to General Secretary Tumaini la Ushambaa (15 April 1952); TNA, 72/44/11, 102A, Tumaini la Usambaa, Minutes
za Mkutano Mkuu . . . 29.12.51. TNA, 72/44/11, 104, Sam Shemsanga to the
Members, Tumaini la Usambaa (7 June 1952); TNA, 72/44/11, 114, General
Secretary Ushambaa Union (23 August 1952); TNA 72/44/11, 121, General
Secretary, Tumaini la Usambaa, to D. O. i/c Usambara Scheme, Lushoto
(22 January 1953); TNA, 72/44/11, 126, General Secretary Tumaini la Ushambaa to D. O. i/c Usambara Scheme (8 February 1953); TNA, 72/44/11,
127, D. O. i/c Usambara Scheme (12 February 1953). On the association for
Muslim education, see TNA, 72/44/11, 158, Education Secretary, Provincial
Muslim Education Committee to D. C. Lushoto (18 August 1955). The same
connections are made clear in TNA, 72/44/11, 167a, Mkutano wa Tatu wa
Halmashauri ya Elim ya Islam Jimbo la Tanga Uliofanyika Vuga Usambara
Tarehe 26-3-55.

7   TNA, 72/44/8/VI, Native Affairs, General Complaints, 1948–53, 419, 421.

8   TNA, 72/62/6/III, 221, Lushoto *DAR* (1949). The price ratio in 1951 was
the same. In February of that year the agricultural officer estimated the
illegal trade as less than one-tenth of the total. This might well have been

an underestimate. He estimated in March that ten tons out of the total month's crop of fifty-four tons was sold illegally; see TNA, 72/3/2/II, 65 and 66, *Monthly Agricultural Reports, Lushoto District* (February–March 1951).

9 On the illegal maize trade, see TNA, 72/62/6/III, 238, Lushoto *DAR* (1953). The end of the monopoly is described in TNA, 72/62/6/IV, 21a, *Usambara Development Scheme Annual Report* (1955).

10 See TNA, 72/62/6/III, 234, Lushoto *DAR* (1952).

11 For cases in which legal tea houses were closed down for UCU or TANU activity, see TNA, 72/44/8/VIII, 10, D. C. Lushoto to Mlughu Ali Bereko (19 March 1955); TNA, 72/44/8/VIII, 11, Mlughu Ali Beleko to D. C. (20 March 1955); TNA, 72/44/8/VIII, 13, Ali Beleko to D. C. Lushoto (4 April 1955); and TNA, 72/44/8/VIII, 17, Ali Beleko to D. C. Lushoto (16 April 1955). See also *TANU na Wananchi Lushoto* (1975).

12 Mohammed Singano's arrest and conviction are described in TNA, 72/3/1A/I, 91, D. C. Korogwe to A. D. O. Lushoto (7 July 1942) and TNA, 72/3/1A/I, 93 A. D. O. Lushoto to D. C. Korogwe (8 August 1942). For his career as a rebel, see TNA, Secretariat 31207, 52A, Salehe Shauri, Mohamed Singano, Jaha Mtoi, Gotfride Shauri, Ernest Singano, and Salumu Guga to Magistrate, Dar es Salaam (July 1952); see also PVH, "Local Government and Politics," p. 73, Secretary Usambara Native Authority to Kimweri Magogo (14 May 1951:73). The career of Bumbuli's illegal cloth trader is drawn from an oral account as supplemented by TNA, 72/44/16, 50, Kimweri Magogo to D. C. Lushoto (9 September 1950), and PVH, "Local Government and Politics," p. 13, Hezekia Saul to D. O. i/c Lushoto (28 June 1947).

13 See TNA, 72/62/6/III, 225, Lushoto *DAR* 1950.

14 See TNA, 72/43/3/II, D. C. Lushoto to Director Gailey and Roberts (15 April 1953) and TNA, 72/43/2/II, 240, D. C. Lushoto to Regional Director British Council, Dar es Salaam (15 April 1953).

15 TNA, 72/62/6/III, 221, Lushoto *DAR* (1949).

16 On La Touche, see TNA, 72/62/6/III, 210C, *Annual Report Korogwe Division* (1947). Instructions to try *chama* members appear in TNA, 72/44/16, 28, D. C. Lushoto to Bakari Kimweri (20 May 1948). For an example of beating and lock-up, see TNA, 72/44/8/VI, 549, Isaka Hoza to D. C. Korogwe (5 October 1950) and TNA, 4/6/2, 568, Salehe Shauri to District Commissioner (28 January 1952).

17 The district borders of Wilhelmstal in 1920 were much larger than any British districts would be in later periods. The 1920 population estimate, however, listed populations by ethnic identification. The total of all Shambaa, Kilindi, and Wambugu was 69,000, with perhaps another 11,000 people listed under other ethnic labels within the borders of what was to become Korogwe District. The estimated population of that area in 1941 was 172,770, of whom 136,270 were listed as Shambaa. By 1946 the African population within those boundaries was 203,615. Population grew rapidly during the late 1940s and 1950s; see TNA, Secretariat 1733, *District Annual Report, Wilhemstal* (1920); 72/62/II, 1941, *District Annual Report, Korogwe*; 72/62/III, *Annual Report,*

Korogwe District (1946). The estimates are all approximate, but the general trend is clear.

18 See TNA, Secretariat 11682, *Annual Reports, Tanga Province* (1927, 1929).

19 The district and provincial annual reports all through the 1920s and 1930s confirm the picture that not many highland people worked on estates. The judgement on grazing is based on several sets of evidence. The cattle population increased between the 1920s and 1950s, and at the same time, as the following argument shows, farmers converted grazing land into farms for cash cropping. Among a set of about 160 domestic economic histories collected by the author near Bumbuli in 1979–80 were a number which referred to the 1920s. They show that cattle were central to Bumbuli's domestic economy at that time.

20 The 1936 figures are taken from Tanganyika, *Provincial Annual Reports*. The 1956 figure is from TNA, 72/62/6/IV, 32A, Lushoto *DVR* (1956). The judgment on the religion of coffee farmers is based on personal acquaintance with the largest postwar coffee farmers at Vugha, the most important coffee area at that time. This is supplemented by acquaintance with some of Bumbuli's prominent coffee farmers. The archival materials emphasize the fact that Christians were the coffee farmers of the interwar period. This was clearly not true in southern Shambaai after 1945, although Thompson (1984) observes that this was still true in Mlalo in the late 1970s.

21 Wartime purchases are documented in TNA, 72/3/1A.I, Lushoto, Agriculture, Increased Production by Natives; in 72/3/2/I, II, and III, Lushoto, Agriculture, and in *District Annual Reports*. Exports of tobacco, mostly from northern Shambaai, reached their high point at 170 tons in 1950: TNA, 72/62/6/III, 225, Lushoto *DAR* (1950). For the wattle boom of the early 1950s, see TNA, 72/US/29, 6 *Usambara Scheme October Report* (6 November 1950). Wattle exports reached their height in the middle 1950s. Local cultivators sold 3180 tons of wattle bark between October 1954 and June 1955: TNA, 72/62/6/IV, 21A, *Usambara Development Scheme Annual Report* (1955).

22 For the loss of plains land to estates, see TNA, 72/62/6/III, 209I, Lushoto *DVR* (1947). The shift of land from food crops or grazing to commercial crops is especially clear in the domestic economic histories collected in 1979–80 and is confirmed in the *District Annual Reports*. See, for example, TNA, 72/62/6/III, 225, Lushoto *DAR* (1950). The 1930s erosion rules are recorded in the District Book. By 1938 contour weed-lines were generally visible: TNA, 72/62/6, *Annual Report, Lushoto Division* (1938). The authorities demanded three times as many contour hedges in 1941 as previously, provoking peasant complaints about the amounts of land lost: TNA 72/62/6/II, *Annual Report, Lushoto Division* (1941). For cattle trampling hedges, see TNA, 72/3/2/II, Lushoto, *Agricultural Reports* (1943–54).

23 See TNA, 72/62/6/III, 224, Korogwe *Division Annual Report* (1950); TNA, 72/62/6/III, 225, Lushoto *DAR* (1950); TNA 72/62/6/III, 234, Lushoto *DAR* (1952).

24   For the judgment that one-third of taxpayers worked at sisal related jobs, see TNA, 72/62/6/IV, 225, Lushoto *DAR* (1952). On the emigration of Mlalo's young men, see TNA, 72/62/6/III, 211E, Lushoto DAR (1948). A similar picture is drawn in TNA, 16721, "Social Survey on the Mlalo and Mwanga Areas, Lushoto District: Report by T. L. M. Marealle" (22 April 1947).

25   See TNA, 72/3/1A/I, 24, Zumbe Daffa to A. D. O. Lushoto (6 January 1942).

26   See PVH, "Mlalo Rehabilitation Scheme," p. 12, Pasture Research Officer to P. C. Tanga, D. C. Korogwe, and D. O. Lushoto (n.d.).

27   See TNA, 72/44/16, 2A, "Maulizo Mbele ya Bwana" (ca. 1947).

28   PVH, "Mlalo Rehabilitation Scheme," p. 231, D. O. Lushoto (February 1951).

29   See Iliffe (1979: 450–51) on numbers of settlers; see Swainson (1980: chap. 3) on the general postwar economy; see Orde-Browne (1946) on the need to preserve self-sufficiency in the face of rural decline.

30   TNA, 4/6/2, 479, I. L. Robinson, Acting Provincial Commissioner, to The Secretary for African Affairs (28 August 1948). The meeting at Mlalo was held on 25 August.

31   TNA, Secretariat 33049/IV, 326, "Note by His Excellency the Governor on his visit to Mlalo," E. T. to Chief Secretary (31 December 1949).

32   PVH, "Mlalo Rehabilitation Scheme," 109.

33   PVH, "Mlalo Rehabilitation Scheme," 109–10.

34   TNA, 72/US/29, 4, W. Macmillan, D. C., *Usambara Scheme. 1950 Progress Report.*

35   PVH, "Mlalo Rehabilitation Scheme," 100: Minutes of a Meeting Held at Lushoto (23 November 1949).

36   PVH, "Mlalo Rehabilitation Scheme," 242: D. C. Lushoto (R. H. J. Thorne) and A. O. Lushoto to the Royal Commission.

37   TNA, 72/3/2/II, Lushoto, Agricultural Reports (1943–54).

38   TNA, 72/62/6/III, 225, Lushoto *DAR* (1950).

39   TNA, 72/US/29, 6, *Usambara Scheme October Report* (6 November 1950); TNA, 72/US/29, 9, [Usambara Scheme] *December Report* (3 January 1951).

40   TNA, 72/US/29, 3, *Usambara Scheme October Report* (1950).

41   TNA, Secretariat 33049/IV, 411, *Usambara Scheme Annual Report* (1951).

42   TNA, 72/US/29, 8, *Usambara Scheme Monthly Report,* November 1950. TNA, 72/62/6,III,225, *Lushoto District Annual Report,* 1950. The discussion between Hassani and his subjects is drawn from oral accounts. The archival sources are fully consistent with their interpretation.

43   TNA, 72/44/16, 63, Memorandum. Ujumbe wa watu 3354 waliotoka Usambara umewasilisha Kilimanjaro Union Office (23 April 1951). TNA, 72/44/16, 135, D. C. Lushoto to P. C. Tanga (26 September 1952).

44   TNA, 72/US/29, 11–12, *Usambara Scheme February Report* and *March Report;* TNA, 72/62/6/III, 224 Korogwe *Division Annual Report* (1950).

45   TNA, 4/6/2, 513, Kimweri Mputa Magogo to Kondrad Kiramba (7 April 1949).

46   TNA, 4/6/2. 437–8, "Raiya Zako wote wa Usambara to P.C. Tanga," 18 July 1950.

47 TNA, 72/44/16, 50, Kimweri Magogo to D. C. Lushoto (9 September 1950).

48 TNA, 72/44/16, Omari Lwambo, Bazo, Vugha (9 March 1951).

49 TNA, 304/A6/28, 7, letter to *Mambo Leo* (6 June 1947).

50 TNA, 4/6/2, 565, Letter with forged signatures to Mputa Magogo, no date, received 1951.

51 TNA, Secretariat 15928, 82A, confidential letter C.27 from W. Macmillan to P. C. Tanga (9 April 1951).

52 For an example of a P. C.'s concern that the TAA be controlled, see TNA, Secretariat, 15928, 58, P. C. Lindi to Chief Secretary Dar es Salaam, in response to a request for a general discussion of policy on the TAA (18 July 1948).

53 TNA, 72/44/16, 62a, Draft Usambara Citizen Union — Umoja wa Wenyeji wa Usambara, Misingi na Sheria (Bye-Laws); TNA, 72/44/16, 63, Memorandum, Ujumbe wa watu 3354 waliotoka Usambara umewasilisha Kilimanjaro Union Office (23 April 1951).

54 See TNA, 72/US/29, 14, *Usambara Scheme May Report* (1951); TNA, Secretariat 15928, 86, R. de Z. Hall, Member for Local Government, to P. C. Tanga (14 May 1951); TNA, 72/44/16, 68, A. Mbago to Simbamwene (18 May 1951).

55 TNA, Secretariat 33049, 415A, *Usambara Scheme Annual Report* (1952).

56 The documents on this incident are in TNA, 72/44/16, Lushoto, Native Affairs General, Usambara Native Associations (Chama undermining Native Authority), Including Anonymous Letters.

57 TNA, Secretariat 15928, sheet 136, p. 13, Petitions from Representatives of the Washambala. For the house-burning at Gare, see TNA, 72/3/2/II, 85, Agricultural Reports, monthly report (August 1952). The men charged with burning Hamisi Mwanyoka's house — Ayoub Nyero and his two sons — were all government workers. For the trial, see United Nations Trusteeship Council Document T/PET.2/170, Add.1, "Petition from the Representatives of the Washambala Concerning Tanganyika," Addendum of 17 January 1955.

58 TNA, 72/3/2/III, 33A, Department of Agriculture, *Annual Report* Tanga Province, Part I, (1955).

59 TNA, 304/A6,28, 101, Donaldson and Wood, advocates, to P. C. Tanga (26 September 1957).

60 Zem Shemsanga's career during these years is pieced together from a number of sources: see TNA, 4/6/2, 350, Mkutano wa Mazumbe wa Viti, Mombo (4–5 June 1947); TNA, 72/44/16, 131, S. Shemsanga to D. C. (19 September 1952); PVH, "Local Government and Politics," p. 32, Agenda, Tumaini la Ushambaa meeting of 7–8 January 1948; TNA, 72/62/6/IV, 12a, Lushoto *DVR* (1954); TNA, 72/43/3/II, 177, Sam Shemsanga to D. C. Lushoto (18 January 1951); TNA, 72/43/3, Hezekia Saul to D. C. Korogwe, Vuga, Bazo (16 July 1947). The TNA file 72/44/11, "Lushoto District: Native Affairs, General Association and Tumaini la Usambara," has many documents on Zem's activities.

61 Personal interview. J. J. Hozza (n.d. [1969]), relying in part on informants at Vugha, agrees that avoiding repression was a central goal of the UCU.

62 UNTC, T/COM.2/L.24, p. 3, Communication from Representatives of the Washambala Concerning Tanganyika (10 March 1955). See also TNA, 72/62/6/IV, 12A, Lushoto *DVR* (1954); TNA, 72/62/6, 13, Korogwe *DVR* (1954).
63 TNA, 72/62/6/II, 12A, Lushoto *DVR* (1954).
64 TNA, 72/3/2/III, 33A, Department of Agriculture, *Annual Report* Tanga Province, Part I, 1955.
65 TNA, 72/62/6/IV, 12A, Lushoto *DVR* (1954).
66 TNA, Secretariat 15928, 136, Petitions from Representatives of the Washambala.
67 TNA, 304/A6/28, 9, TANU Territorial headquarters [signature eaten by termites] (12 December 1955).
68 Theodore Isaka (2 May 1980).
69 TNA, 304/A6/28,74, E. Kisenge to D. C. Lushoto (22 February 1957).
70 TNA, 72/44/11, 207A, Mkutano No. 2, "Shambaa Citizens Union" (4 April 1956); TNA, 72/44/11, 214, Mkutano wa President Tanganyika Citizens' Union (26 August 1956); TNA, 72/44/11, 216 President Ushambaa Citizens' Union [Petro Njau] to Provincial Superintendent of Police (29 August 1956); TNA, 72/44/11, 217, Shambaa Citizens' Union Finance Committee (1 September 1956).
71 TNA, 72/3/2/IV, 77 *Usambara Scheme Annual Report* (1958); TNA, 72/62/6/IV, 41A, Lushoto *DVR* (1957).

Chapter 7: The Struggle over Erosion Control

1 The interpretation of the impact of *matuta* on different kinds of households is based on general knowledge of household processes derived from a study of productive resources and health-care payments in all the households of a village near Bumbuli in 1979–80. On the basis of this knowledge and of the general history of *matuta*, I formulated hypotheses on the impact of *matuta* at the household level, which I tested in interviews near Bumbuli, with women and men who had been vigorous adults at the time of the Usambara Scheme. The oral informants are not cited by name, for reasons given in chapter 5, note 1.
2 Patrick Fleuret, an extremely well-informed observer of the agriculture of Shambaai, argues that people terraced vegetable plots but rejected ridging on maize plots because the relative cash returns for terracing are much higher on the vegetable plots (Fleuret 1978:106). Fleuret does not cite data on cash returns. The explanation is complementary to my own.
3 Fleuret observed the same land loan system at a village near Lushoto. Subsistence land was still being lent rent-free near Bumbuli in December 1988. At that time, however, I was told by a well-informed local official at Mlalo that subsistence land there was commanding high rentals.
4 A friend said in December 1988 that, these days, the land owner would not allow a borrower to build *matuta*, for fear he or she would then claim owner-

ship to the land. A number of informants concur that owners permitted this in the 1950s. The friend explained the change by saying that borrowers of land were more trustworthy in the 1950s.

5   TNA, 33049/IV, 411, *Usambara Scheme Annual Report* (1951).

6   I interviewed a dozen people, women and men, some several times. All had been economically active during the 1950s. They were all people I had known for a number of years.

7   R. H. Tawney, *Land and Labor in China*, quoted in James C. Scott (1976).

8   For the judgment that one-third of taxpayers worked at sisal related jobs, see TNA, 72/62/6/III, 234, Lushoto *DAR* (1952). On the emigration of Mlalo's young men, see TNA, 72/62/6/III, 211E, Lushoto *DAR* (1948). A similar picture is drawn in TNA, Secretariat 16721 "Social Survey on the Mlalo and Mwanga Areas, Lushoto District: Report by T. L. M. Marealle" (22 April 1947).

9   TNA, 72/US/29, 9, *Usambara Scheme Monthly Report for December 1950* (3 January 1951).

10   D. O. Lushoto (R. H. Gower) to the Community Development Journal; see TNA, 269/5/III (February 1951:253–67), as reproduced in PVH "The Mlalo Rehabilitation Scheme, 1945–1953," 225–32.

11   According to an anonymous document of 1950, "The way to bring out people is this: let us destroy the *matuta*. . . . Many people will come out for this purpose, but [the planners] have another intention, to remove Sultan Kimweri." See PVH, "Local Government and Politics" p. 69, anonymous letter of 8 September 1950. The peasant understanding that Kimweri was the scheme's creator is mentioned in TNA, Secretariat 15298, 82A, W. Macmillan to P. C. Tanga (9 April 1951). The letters that accuse Kimweri of being an *akida* are numerous. For one example, see TNA, 72/44/16, 88, Mkutano wa Wasambaa Mlungui to Kimweri Magogo (n.d.), copy received by D. O., 27 October 1951.

12   In 1968 I asked 138 men at Vugha the names and life-patterns of all their children, including adult sons. Of the married sons, 21 percent (16 of 77) had settled far from Vugha.

13   See UNTC, T/PET.2/170/Add.1, p. 12, Petition from Representatives of the Washambala Concerning Tanganyika (17 January 1955).

14   See TNA, 72/62/6/III, 225, Lushoto *DAR* (1950); TNA, 72/62/6/III, 211K, Lushoto *DAR* (1948).

15   One of the peasant rebels of the early 1950s, who was interviewed in 1979, echoed a common accusation: "Kimweri wanted to sell the land of Shambaai, to send the Shambaa off to the land of the Zigula. . . . The Europeans gave Kimweri enough [money to do this]. They like the [mountain] climate here. But the Shambaa people are uncomfortable in the lowlands."

16   See TNA, 72/62/6/III, 211K, Lushoto *DAR* (1948); TNA, 72/62/6/III, 229, Lushoto *DVR* (1951); TNA, 72/62/6/IV, 13, Korogwe *DVR* (1954); see TNA, 72/62/6/III, 211K, Lushoto *DAR* (1948) for a report on ten estates taken over by the Native Authority. TNA, 72/62/6/III, 229, Lushoto *DVR* (1951) dis-

cusses Custodian of Enemy Property estates which were taken over by the Native Authority.

17   For resentment against uncultivated land, see for example, TNA, 72/62/6/IV, 21A *Usambara Development Scheme Annual Report* (1955); TNA, 72/62/6/III, 210, Korogwe *DVR* (1947); TNA, 72/62/6/III, 220, Korogwe *DVR* (1949); TNA, 72/62/6/III, 225, Lushoto *DAR* (1950). Ambangulu labor cards are discussed in TNA, 72/62/6/III, 224, Korogwe *DVR* (1950). On the attempt to exclude non-Shambaa, see TNA, 72/62/6/III, 225, Lushoto *DAR* (1950).

18   See *TANU na Wananchi Lushoto* 1975:5 and the interview with Theodore Isaka (2 May 1980).

19   TNA, 72/62/6/IV, 41A, Lushoto *DVR* (1957).

20   My own research on health-care decisions and health-care payment in about 160 households in 1979–80 showed that households were dependent on relatives for cash to help with health care, and that better-off men helped in this way with great regularity.

21   See UNTC, T/PET.2/196, p. 6, Petition from Representatives of the Washambala concerning Tanganyika (17 August 1955).

22   On Gomba Estate, see TNA, 72/62/6/IV, 33a, Korogwe *DAR* (1956). Kwalukonge Estate was expanding at the same time. The expansion of tea and sisal acreage is documented year by year in the *District Annual Reports:* TNA, 72/62/6/III and 72/62/6/IV. See also Mhando (1977:89–90, 120).

23   See Mhando (1977:58) and TNA, Secretariat 11682, 248–49, *Annual Report on Tanga Province* (1930).

24   TNA, 72/3/2/III, 1, Agricultural Officer, Tanga Province (West) to Regional Assistant Director of Agriculture, Arusha (11 January 1954).

25   TNA, 304/A3/2, 103, Tanga Province — Monthly Letter, Agriculture (December 1961).

26   TNA, 72/3/2/III, 2a, *Annual Report of Agriculture*, Lushoto District (1953).

27   TNA, 72/3/2/III, 5, Monthly Report, Agricultural Officer, Tanga Province (West) (January 1954). On estates uprooting coffee, see TNA, 72/62/6/III, 212C, Korogwe *DVR* (1948).

28   TNA, 72/62/6/IV, 41A, Lushoto *DVR* (1957).

29   TNA, 72/3/2/II, 104, *Lushoto Agricultural Reports*, Monthly Report, (September 1953).

30   In a collection of economic life histories which I made near Bumbuli, men who worked as laborers on sisal estates were unable to purchase land with their earnings. Fleuret (1978) found that the men who were able to use earnings for the purchase of farms worked near home. My own findings are the same.

31   On pollution, see TNA, 72/62/6/IV, 12A, Lushoto *DVR* (1954) and TNA, 72/62/6/IV, 33A, Korogwe *DVR* (1956). On the desire to remove plantation owners, see Mhando (1977:123). For the general history of the sisal labor force, see Tambila (1974) and Shivji (1986).

32   This case of the government manipulating TANU's local-level relationship with the unions is not discussed in Shivji's work (1986), which necessarily

focuses on the national level. See TNA, 72/62/6/IV, 42A, Korogwe *DVR* (1957); for the closing of TANU offices, see TNA, 304/A6/28, 70, D. O. Korogwe to Wazumbe Wakuu Wote (23 January 1957); TNA, 304/A6/28, 98, Provincial Superintendent of Police to Officer i/c Police Lushoto (13 August 1957); TNA, 304/A6/28, 132, TANU District Secretary Korogwe to P. C. Tanga (14 October 1959).

Chapter 8: Gender, Slavery, and Chiefship

1   In 1956 Ubiri, Gare, and Vugha supplied 70 percent of UCU membership, very much higher than their percentage of the population of Shambaai; see TNA, 72/44/11, 204B. The rain chief at Lushoto, who governed Ubiri, had been an active UCU supporter before taking office.
2   See TNA, 72/44/16, 63 and 72/44/11, 204B.
3   See UNTC, T/PET.2/170, Petition from the Representatives of the Washambala Concerning Tanganyika (31 August 1954).
4   Ibid.; See also UNTC, T/PET.2/170/Add.1, Petition from Representatives of the Washambala Concerning Tanganyika (17 January 1955);. UNTC, T/COM.2/L.24, Communications from Representatives of the Washambala Concerning Tanganyika (10 March 1955); UNTC, T/PET.2/196, Petition from the Representatives of the Washambala Concerning Tanganyika (17 August 1955); UNTC, T/PET.2/196/Add.1, Petition from Representatives of the Washambala Concerning Tanganyika (4 October 1955); and UNTC, T/PET.2/196/Add.2, Petition from Representative of the Washambala Concerning Tanganyika (30 January 1956).
5   TNA, 4/6/2, 503, Usambara Union, Mombo, to Victor Collins, MP; Received at the Provincial Commissioner's office, 22 February 1949.
6   TNA, 304/A6/29, 2–4, Mkutano No. 2, Shambaa Citizens Union (4 April 1956).
7   TNA, 72/44/11, 205, Meeting of 4 April 1956.
8   Njau's views can be found in the minutes of UCU meetings. On the Council of Chiefs, see Iliffe (1979:494).
9   This continuity is also noted by Hozza (n.d.:20).
10   Emphasis my own. TNA, 72/44/11, 214B, Poster: Maazimio ya Umoja wa Raia Ushambaa Yaliokubaliwa na Serikali, received at the District Office, Lushoto (3 September 1956).
11   TNA, 72/44/11, 214, Minutes, Mkutano wa President Tanganyika Citizens' Union (26 August 1956).
12   TNA, 72/44/11, 214B, Poster: Maazimio ya Umoja wa Raia Ushambaa Yaliokubaliwa na Serikali, received at the District Office, Lushoto (3 September 1956).
13   In addition to the impact of Nyerere's speeches, the language of TANU entered Shambaai through newspapers, especially *Mwafrika*, which was read by a number of peasant rebels, according to their own accounts.
14   See TNA, 72/44/8/VIII, 22, Daniel Nehemia Ndago to D. C. Korogwe

(2 May 1955). This account of precolonial society is, of course, not entirely accurate.

15   TNA, 72/43/3, 76–76A, Isaac Rashidy and Saguti Sabali to D. C. Korogwe (11 June 1947).

16   UNTC, T/PET.2/170, Petition from the Representatives of the Washambala Concerning Tanganyika (31 August 1954).

17   This is the consistent message of the history texts used in Tanganyika's schools during this period. For a list of texts in school libraries, see Tanganyika, Department of Education (ca. 1953) and Tanganyika, Department of Education (1955).

18   TNA, 304/A6/29, 2–4, Mkutano No. 2, "Shambaa Citizens Union" (4 April 1956).

19   See the *Green Paper*, reproduced in *TANU na Wananchi Lushoto* (1975).

20   Ibid., 16–18.

21   TNA, 72/US/29, 3, *Usambara Scheme Monthly Reports*, (October 1950).

22   TNA, 304/711/1, 29, Provincial Education Officer to Provincial Commissioner Tanga (7 October 1946).

23   TNA, 72/44/11, 214B, Poster: Maazimio ya Umoja wa Raia Ushambaa Yaliokubaliwa na Serikali, received at the District Office, Lushoto (3 September 1956).

24   *Mwafrika*, 14 November 1959.

25   TNA, 72/44/8,VIII, 175, Bakari Sanju, Hasani Mtangi and Alli Singano to Chief Secretary, Dar es Salaam (6 May 1957).

26   Geiger 1987. For the date of the visit to Shambaai, see TNA, 304/A6/28, 9, TANU Territorial Headquarters, signature eaten by termites (12 December 1955).

Chapter 9: Chiefs and Bureaucrats

1   See *Who's Who in East Africa, 1963–1964* and *Who's Who in East Africa, 1965–1966* (1966). Those who stayed in their home districts might be underrepresented in this count because the survey appears to have favored individuals with the highest educational qualifications, and because the 1950s activities of the individuals surveyed are not always clearly stated.

2   See Bienen (1970:52–53) on the effects of requiring civil servants to remain outside politics.

3   *Tanganyika Standard*, 15 May 1957. The quotation is from the newspaper's summary, and not verbatim from Twining's remarks.

4   For an example of scorekeeping on TANU, see Tanganyika, *Parliamentary Debates (Hansard)* (16 February 1963:338ff).

5   Tanganyika, *Parliamentary Debates (Hansard)*, 16 February 1963.

6   Tanganyika, *Parliamentary Debates (Hansard)*, 10 December 1962.

7   Misingi ya Demokrasi," from *Sauti ya TANU*, No. 47, as reprinted in Barongo 1966:220–23.

8   Ibid.

9   *Sauti ya TANU*, No. 48, "Aina za Serikali," 224–227, reprinted in Barongo (1966).
10 Ibid.
11 The speaker was Rashidi Kawawa; see Tanganyika, *Parliamentary Debates*, National Assembly, Official Report (Dar es Salaam: Government Printer, 16 February 1963), 339.
12 "Hotuba ya Rais" (10 December 1962:2–10), in Tanganyika, *Parliamentary Debates*, National Assembly (Dar es Salaam: Government Printer).
13 *Tanganyika Standard*, 10 December 1962.
14 The quotation is from Martin (1976:57–58), who gives the clearest account of this case. Tanga Region files show that local chiefs were concerned with this question; see TNA, 481/L5/4, Future Position of Chiefs (Minutes of Meeting) (17 July 1962). For a debate on whether chiefs deserved compensation, see Tanganyika. *Parliamentary Debates*, National Assembly, Official Report (Dar es Salaam: Government Printer, 16 February 1963).
15 TNA, 304/A6/28, 218, Administrative Secretary Tanga Region to D. C. Same (25 July 1962). See also TNA, 304/A6/28, 235, for a list of prohibited associations, including the Muscat-Oman Arabs Association, the Umoja wa Wambughu, and fourteen others (D. C. Same, public letter [9 August 1962]), Vyama Viliyopigwa Marufuku Wilaya ya Same [Pare]).
16 The most important sources for the end of chiefship in Shambaai, aside from the oral ones, are Makao Makuu ya TANU ya Wilaya ya Lushoto (n.d. [1975]), which includes a copy of the *Green Paper*, and issues of *Mwafrika* for 14 November 1959, 16 January 1959, 3 April 1960, 8 October 1960, 3 December 1960, and 17 December 1960.
17 Much of my understanding of the role of cooperatives comes from the unpublished research of Kenneth Curtis. For a convenient summary, see John S. Saul (1973). On cooperatives in politics, see G. Andrew Maguire (1969). For a useful corrective to Saul, see Andrew Coulson (1982:60–69, 98–99).
18 Issa Shivji (1986) describes these workers as semiproletarian.
19 *Mwafrika*, 21 May 1960.
20 The evolution of the party is described in Bienen (1970). The permission for Tanga Region civil servants to join TANU is given in TNA, 304/A6/28/II, 326, Permanent Secretary for Administration to All Administrative Secretaries (14 July 1964).
21 For a description of the survey by one of the makers, see Gordon M. Wilson (1966). The survey's results were also analyzed by McGowan and Bolland (1971). The survey was the basis of three volumes of *Who's Who in East Africa*, published by Marco Surveys beginning in 1964.
22 The best account of this event is an unpublished paper by M. H. Y. Kaniki (n.d.). A rich collection of the documents, including minutes of most important meetings, was collected and duplicated as part of the Pangani Valley Historical Research Project (PVH), Department of History, University of Dar es Salaam, under the title, "The Lutheran Church in Usambara" (173 pages, n.d.).

23   Waltenberg wrote a long autobiographical letter to all Church members in 1962. PVH, "The Lutheran Church in Usambara," pp. 133ff.
24   The date given by Waltenberg does not agree with Kaniki's date; see PVH, "Lutheran Church in Usambara," p. 126, Church President (H. Waltenberg) on 70th Anniversary of U.D.L.C., "Halleluya" (27 August 1961).
25   PVH, "Lutheran Church in Usambara," p. 103, Minutes of SALTU General Meeting (10 May 1961).
26   Letter from S. A. Sheiza to Church President, 18 March 1961, in PVH "The Lutheran Church in Usambara," 98.

Chapter 10: Rain in Independent Tanzania

1   The detailed knowledge of the way people used language in 1979–80 is derived from repeated visits to a single village, which will go unnamed because of the sensitivity of the information. Many people within the village were interviewed individually about their general understanding of the relationship between chiefship and rain and about their interpretation of the climatic conditions they were experiencing at crucial points during the year. The research data also include individual conversations in other parts of Shambaai during 1979–80. The village study provided information about the range of individual variation in the use of language on these issues. The data are likely to be representative for the whole of Shambaai, with the exception of the places (of which the author knows only one) where succession to the position of a great rainmaker has been direct and is widely accepted. In that place, there is likely to be less evidence of change in ideas since the 1960s.
2   For a nationwide account of the growth of radio and newspapers, see G. L. Mytton (1976). Figures on radio ownership are in vol. 2:68, 272; the growth of radio broadcasting is described in vol. 2:171–78. The survey of radio listeners in Lushoto is reported in Judith Molloy (1971:148).

List of Interviews

The 506 interviews on the following list were all conducted by the author. With the exception of three early interviews conducted in English, occasional lapses by Shambaa-speakers into Swahili, and thirteen texts in the Mbugu language, all the interviews were conducted in Shambaa with no interpreter. Many of the Shambaa traditions were tape recorded and then transcribed by the author in Shambaa. The rest were recorded verbatim in Shambaa by the author in an improvised shorthand, and then transcribed in Shambaa by him. The Mbugu traditions were conducted by the author in Mbugu (with occasional lapses into Shambaa), then transcribed by a research assistant in Mbugu, and translated by the assistant into Shambaa. Copies of the majority of the texts have been deposited in the East Africana Collection of the University of Dar es Salaam, available for use by anyone who reads Shambaa. Neither sociological survey data collected by the author nor additional interviews conducted by a research assistant are listed below in the roster of interviews. Places are in parentheses. S/o, d/o, and m/o are used for son of, daughter of, and mother of, respectively.

1–2. Abdala Mweta, Rangwi, 13 June 1968; 15 June 1968.
   3. Abdalla Hamisi, December 1979.
   4. Abdalla Musa, 10 January 1980.
5–6. Abdalla Uchungi, November 28, 1979; 11 April 1980.
   7. Abdallah Kighenda, 24 December 1988.
   8. Abedi Hassani Chambegha Shekulwavu, 26 December 1988.
   9. Abedi s/o Ng'wa Kimungu, Ng'wangoi (Mlalo), July 1968.
10–12. Agasa Kihiyo, 6 November 1979; 10 January 1980; December 1988.
  13. Ali Chankoa s/o Zumbe Chankoa (Mlalo), December 1967.
  14. Ali Mashina s/o Kimweri (Dule, Mlalo), n.d. [July 1968?].
  15. Ali Mntangi, 7 February 1980.
  16. Ali Msangazi, 23 January 1980.
17–19. Ali Mzonge, 8 November 1979; 28 December 1979; 10 March 1980.
  20. Ali Sabago (Funta), 20 February 1968.
  21. Ali Saidi Kupaza, 31 December 1979.
22–25. Ali Shechonge, Bazo (Vugha), 11 March 1967; 30 November 1967; 6 October 1979; 23 April 1980.
  26. Amina Muitango, 6 November 1979.
  27. Amina Ramadhani, 16 January 1980.
  28. Amina Salehe, 18 January 1980.
  29. Amiri Hemedi Msangazi, 22 December 1979.
30–31. Amiri Mngazija, 1 November 1979; 11 January 1980.

32–34. Andrea Singano, 10 October 1979; 6 November 1979; 4 January 1980.
   35. Antony Sheiza, 21 September 1979.
   36. Asha Juma Mshihii, 6 February 1980.
   37. Asha Omari Kingazi, 4 February 1980.
   38. Asha Saidi Hemedi Msangazi, 3 January 1980.
   39. Asia Hauseni Sheuwawa, 17 January 1980.
   40. Asia Leo (Mshihwi), May 1967.
   41. Asumani Abdallah, August 1967.
   42. Asumani Kaoneka, Kumbamtoni (Vugha), 17 April 1968.
   43. Asumani Msagati, Mahezangulu, August 1967.
44–45. Asumani Saidi, 31 December 1979; 18 April 1980.
   46. Asumani Shemdoa, 23 January 1980.
   47. Athumani Mdoe (Mlalo), 5 February 1968.
   48. Athumani Mlongesanga, 5 January 1980; 30 March 1980; 11 April 1980.
   49. Augustino Tindikai, 7 January 1980.
   50. Avuniwa, Kisiwani (Mshihwi), 11 July 1966.
   51. Ayubu Nyeo, Kianga (Gare), 31 January 1968.
   52. Bakari Kilua (Mshihwi), 15 October 1966, n.d., October 1966.
   53. Bakari Kimeri (Dule, Mlalo), July 1968.
   54. Bakari Mshihii, 6 February 1980.
   55. Bakari Shekwaho (Tekwa), 17 July 1967.
56–57. Bakari Shemzighwa, 19 September 1979; 13 November 1979.
   58. Bakari Tupa, 14 February 1980.
   59. Bakari Uchungi, 28 November 1979.
   60. Barua s/o Makange s/o Magogo (Ngulu, Muungui), 22 February 1968.
   61. Batimayo Mbughuni, Kwa Mongo, 11 April 1967.
62–63. Blandina Phanueli, 28 March 1980; 24 December 1988.
   64. Boaz Mjata, Shembekeza, 15 July 1967.
   65. Chamhingo wa Mkumbara, Mazinde, 25 December 1967.
   66. Charles Amiri, 4 February 1980.
67–69. Chempome, Kwe Mkonde (Vugha), 20 April 1968; 22 April 1968; 1 May 1968.
70–72. Costa Singano, 2 October 1979; 1 November 1979; 28 March 1980.
   73. Daniel Magogo (Bethel bei Bielefeld), November 1965.
   74. Edward Maghembe, 24 May 1966.
   75. Eliza Joel, n.d. 1980.
   76. Elizabeti Michael, 21 January 1980.
   77. Emilia Yona, 15 February 1980.
   78. Fatuma Hemedi, 18 January 1980.
   79. Fatuma Ramadhani, 6 February 1980.
   80. Francis Amiri, 4 February 1980.
   81. Fimwoni Ali (Mshihwi), June 1966.
   82. Frank Msumari, 1980.
   83. Frank Salehe, 2 January 1980.
   84. Ghoda ja Kae (Mayo, Bumbuli), 12 July 1967.
   85. Gottfried s/o Salomon Shangali (Ngwelo, Mlola), 7 February 1968.

86. Habiba Abdalla, 17 January 1980.
87. Hadija Ramadhani, 18 January 1980.
88. Hadija Ramadhani Nyangasa, 21 December 1979.
89. Haimasi Kipingu (Mgwashi), 2 August 1967.
90. Halija Hamisi, 15 October 1979.
91. Halima Saidi, 21 January 1980.
92–94. Hamisi Abedi, 13 November 1979; 29 November 1979; 25 December 1988.
95–98. Hamisi Mkong'wa ni Fua, 14 September 1979; 15 October 1979; 2 January 1980; 14 March 1980.
99. Hamisi Ng'wa Nyoka (Gare), 5 April 1967.
100. Hamisi Omari Shekibula, 4 February 1980.
101. Hassani Abdalla Mhammedi, 11 April 1980.
102. Hassani Cha Murungwana (Mshihwi), August 1966.
103. Hassani Kinyashi (Mlalo), July 1968.
104. Hassani Magogo, Mkumbara, Mazinde, 25 December 1967.
105. Hassani Mzonge, 6 February 1980.
106–8. Hassani Shechonge (Vugha), 11 April 1968; 18 April 1968; 23 April 1968.
109. Hassani Shekidee, February 1980.
110–18. Hatibu Hassani (Bazo, Vugha), 26 October 1967; 6 November 1967; 30 November 1967; 18 March 1968; 3 April 1968; 10 April 1968; 20 April 1968; 24 April 1968; 25 May 1968.
119. Hauseni Alimasi, 7 February 1980.
120. Hauseni Uchungi, 29 November 1979.
121. Heinrich Shedili (Bumbuli), July 1967.
122. Hemedi Mbogho s/o Wa Kanali, Tuliza Moyo (Mlalo), 6 February 1968.
123–25. Hemedi Mbughuni (Bazo), 20 March 1967; 11 April 1968; 24 May 1968.
126. Hemedi Mntangi, 15 November 1979.
127–28. Hemedi Msangazi, 18 November 1979; 25 December 1988.
129. Herman Kimweri (Mshihwi), July 1966.
130. Hokelai Hassani, 21 January 1980.
131. Ibrahimu Mbilu, 15 October 1979.
132. Ibrahimu Uchungi, 28 November 1979.
133–34. Idi Hamisi, 2 January 1980, 20 March 1980.
135. Idi Hemedi, 22 December 1979.
136. Idi Kibarua, 30 October 1967.
137. Idi (Mshihwi), July 1966.
138. Isai (Bumbuli), 31 October 1979.
139–40. Isaka Mdamanyi, May 1980; 29 June 1988.
141. Ishika Kibabu (Kitanga Zigha), 19 June 1968.
142. Ishika Kumoso (Hemandari), 10 June 1968.
143–45. Ismail Zayumba, 2 October 1979; 16 October 1979; 4 January 1980.
146–48. Jaha Mtoi (Ubii), 22 April 1967; 3 June 1967; 28 November 1967.
149. Jani Kunguu (Mahezanguu), n.d. [1967?].
150–51. Jawa Samahoza (Mkumbara, Mazinde), 25 December 1967; 23 February 1968.

152. Joseph Hassani (Mshihwi), November 1966.
153. Joshua Mtunguja, 28 June 1988.
154. Joyisi Peta, 15 November 1979.
155. Juma Hamisi, 15 October 1979.
156–58. Juma Kaoneka (Bazo, Vugha), March 1967; June 1967; 28 January 1968; 23 May 1968; 6 October 1979.
159. Juma Shekumkai (Handei, Mlalo), July 1968.
160–61. Kam Kamwe, 14 September 1979; 28 September 1979.
162. Kasimu Kimweri (Bagha), 1 February 1968.
163–66. Kazushwe (Mayo), n.d. 1967, August 1967, 30 December 1979, 9 May 1980.
167. Kibanga Daudi, 8 May 1980.
168. Kibibi Shemng'indo, 10 October 1979; 1 November 1979.
169. Kiluwa Shemhina, Viti, Shume, 9 February 1968.
170. Kimwea wa Kihingo Kikuu, 17 June 1967.
171. Kimweri Kibanga (Mponde), 3 June 1967.
172–74. [Zumbe] Kimweri Mputa Magogo (Mombo Mlembule), 24 March 1967; 3 April 1967; 1 December 1967.
175. Kimweri Mputa Magogo and Mbwana Mkanka Mghanga (Mombo Mlembule), 19 May 1967.
176. Kimweri Mputa Magogo, Mdoe Barua, and Ng'wana Aia (Vugha), 22 July 1968.
177. Kimweri wa Kaghambe (Mshihwi), July 1966.
178. Kingazi Gia, 24 December 1979.
179. Kofia Guha (Mayo, Bumbuli), July 1967.
180. Kupe s/o Kerefu s/o Ng'wa Mbiu s/o Gwando (Ngwelo, Mlola), 7 February 1968.
181. Kwavi Senkunde (Mgwagwai, Soni), 28 May 1968.
182–93. Leo Hassani, n.d. [ca. July 1966]; August 1966, November 1966, 2 January 1967; 3 January 1967; 3 March 1967; May 1967; June 1967; August 1967; 18 October 1979; 20 January 1980; 3 May 1980.
194. Leo Hassani and Neemani, September 1966.
195. Lihani Shemnkande (Handei, Gare), 12 June 1967.
196. Mahimbo Kihedu (Bagha), 1 February 1968.
197. Majiza Ramadhani Gia, 6 March 1980.
198. Makao Sangoda (Ziai), 10 May 1967.
199. Makihiyo m/o Heliet, 8 April 1980.
200. Makimweri Rajabu, n.d. [ca. 1980].
201. Mambazi Msa Mngazija, 10 January 1980.
202. Mamdoe Juma Mshihii, 15 February 1980.
203. Mamdoe Saidi, 6 February 1980.
204. Mamlughu d/o Shebughe Hinda, 17 January 1980.
205–6. Mamlughu Ufumbo, 11 March 1980, 17 March 1980.
207. Mandia Ntuue (Mayo), 23 July 1967.
208. Mandughu Chai, 15 June 1968.

209. Mangeda Saidi Shembago, 26 December 1988.
210. Mangoda Mzalia, 25 January 1980.
211. Manyeo Abrahamu Mlongesanga, 18 January 1980.
212. Maria Augustino, 7 January 1980.
213. Maria Christopha, 11 January 1980.
214. Maria Joseph, 18 January 1980.
215. Mariamu Bakari Omari, 8 February 1980.
216. Mariamu Christopha, 6 November 1979.
217. Mariamu Salehe Gia, 6 February 1980.
218–24. Martin Msumari, 20 September 1979; 20 October 1979; 1 November 1979; 20 March 1980; 23 December 1988; 24 December 1988; 25 December 1988.
225. Masaidi Mbegha, 21 November 1979.
226. Mashuki s/o Shemoka (Bazo), July 1968.
227. Matalene Wilson, 2 November 1979.
228. Matia Masago, n.d. [ca. 1980].
229. Mavoa Shambo (Kitanga Zigha), 19 June 1968.
230–31. Mbaruku Jambia (Kienge), 8 November 1967, 22 January 1968.
232. Mbilu wa Mshihwi, June 1966.
233–34. Mbogho s/o Mzao (Ng'wangoi, Mlalo), 9 February 1968; 19 July 1968.
235. Mbura Kidala (Mtumbi), 19 June 1968.
236–41. Mbwana Mkanka Mghanga (Mshwai, Vugha), 7 May 1967; 17 May 1967; 21 May 1967; 13 November 1967; 24 January 1968; 10 April 1968.
242. Mbwana Saidi Kaniki, 27 December 1979.
243. Mcharo Mizighi (Mpanda), 12 June 1968.
244–51. Mdoe Barua (Vugha), 12 March 1967; 15 March 1967; 14 November 1967; 7 December 1967; 26 January 1968; 9 April 1968; 9 May 1968; 24 May 1968.
252. Mdoe Barua and Ng'wana Aia, 18 April 1967.
253–64. Mdoe Loti (Lunguza), n.d.; 10 April 1967; 29 April 1967; 1 May 1967; 12 May 1967; 27 May 1967; 13 June 1967; 26 June 1967; July 1967; 7 November 1967; 2 April 1968; 18 April 1968.
265. Mdoe Mlongesanga, 5 January 1980.
266. Mdoe Msagati (Mshihwi), 5 December 1966.
267. Mdoe Saudimwe (Wena), 7 August 1967.
268. Mdoe Zayumba (Kizaa, Gare), 8 June 1967.
269–70. Mdoembazi Guga (Kwe Tango, Gare), 15 June 1967; 29 November 1967.
271. Mdoembazi Kilua (Vugha), 10 April 1967.
272. Melina Ismail, 4 February 1980.
273. Mgunda Ng'wamba (Bumbuli), 24 July 1967.
274. Mhammadi Kika (Kighuunde Kwa Ng'wenda, Soni), 20 April 1967.
275. Mhammadi Kupaza, 21 December 1979.
276. Mhammadi Mngazija, 10 January 1980.
277. Mhammadi Mshaka Ngoto (Tufyai, Mayo), 7 August 1967.
278. Mhammadi s/o Shekashiha (Mlalo), 8 February 1968.

279–80. Mhammedi Rajabu (Bumbuli), 1 April 1980; 24 April 1980.
281–85. Mhammedi Uchungi, 19 September 1979; 28 November 1979; 24 January 1980; March 1980; 24 December 1988.
   286. Michael Besha and Martin Kaniki, 22 May 1966.
   287. Mika s/o Kimweri s/o Shatu (Mshihwi), 13 July 1966.
   288. Mikaeli Juma, 24 December 1979.
   289. Mngano Mahimbo (Lola wa Mshihwi), 5 November 1966.
290–94. Mnkande Kimweri (Mshihwi), 13 September 1966; September 1966; 16 November 1966; 2 December 1966; 26 December 1966.
   295. Mntangi s/o Saidi, (Manka), and Zumbe Mandia s/o Nguzo (Tamota, Bungu), 25 February 1968.
   296. Mpira Sanju, (Kianga, Gare), 31 January 1968.
   297. Mshaka Ngoto (He Mkonde, Vugha), 15 November 1967.
298–99. Muimi Nkonde, 21 January 1980; 25 January 1980.
   300. Muitango Abrahamu, 17 January 1980.
   301. Muivano Augustino, 26 December 1988.
   302. Musa Salimu, 14 March 1980.
   303. Mussa Ngeleza (Mshihwi), July 1966.
   304. Mwambashi, (Msongoo), 31 July 1967.
   305. Mwanaidi Zuberi, 20 March 1980.
   306. Mwejuma Ngoda, August 1967.
   307. Mweri Kitojo (Kifinyu Mpanda), 12 June 1968.
   308. Mwokechao s/o Gila (Mgwashi), 10 August 1967.
   309. Mzaia Shekumkai (Ghalambo), 13 July 1967.
   310. Mzimbii s/o Mpemba, July 1968.
   311. Mzimbii Paula (Mayo, Bumbuli), 14 July 1967.
   312. Nasoro Maghembe (Mlalo), July 1968.
   313. Neemani s/o Mleka Ng'ombe, n.d. [1968?].
314–7. Neemani (Mshihwi), July 1966; September 1966; 9 October 1966; 3 December 1966.
   318. Ng'wa Kika bini Kika (Mshihwi), 29 November 1966.
   319. Ng'wa Mnkande, Nkongoi, (Mgwashi), 3 August 1967.
   320. Ng'wa Nyeo (Handei, Mlalo), July 1968.
   321. Ng'wa Paula (Mayo), August 1967.
   322. Ng'wa Paula s/o Ng'wa Kimungu (Mayo), 12 July 1967.
323–29. Ng'wana Aia (Vugha), 20 March 1967; 1 April 1967; 19 May 1967; 6 November 1967; 7 December 1967; 18 December 1967; 24 May 1968.
330–39. Ng'wang'washi [Kimea Abdalla], Kwe Mbaazi, August 1966; 18 September 1966; 6 October 1966; 12 October 1966; October 1966; October 1966; November 1966, text 1; November 1966, text 2; 1 December 1966; 8 January 1967.
340–42. Nkanieka Mdoe (Mshihwi), January 1967; March 1967, text 1; March 1967, text 2.
   343. Nkanieka Mdoe with Paulo (Mshihwi), 30 December 1966.
   344. Nkinda Kimweri (Mponde), 6 June 1967.

345. Nkondo, Kwe Mkonde (Vugha), 22 April 1968.
346. Noah wa Shefuno, 11 July 1966.
347. Nuru Asumani Nyangasa, 8 February 1980.
348. Nyaki Sempombe, Kinko, 21 June 1968.
349. Omari Bakari, 31 March 1980.
350. Omari Hauseni, 31 December 1979.
351. Omari Kaniki, 4 October 1979.
352-53. Omari Shekibula, 23 January 1980; 5 March 1980.
354. Pauli Kimela (Mshihwi), 16 June 1966.
355. Paulina Francis, 6 November 1979.
356. Phanueli Machungi, 16 October 1979.
357. Phanueli Mweta, 11 January 1980.
358. Philimoni Shemghambie, 2 November 1979.
359. Piazisi Vitalesi, 11 January 1980.
360. Rahel Yona, 18 January 1980.
361. Rajabu Juma n.d. [ca. 1979].
362. Ramadhani Gia, 4 February 1980.
363. Ramadhani Hauseni Mlughu, 31 December 1979.
364. Ramadhani Hemedi Msangazi, 3 January 1979.
365. Ramadhani Juma, 29 March 1980.
366. Ramadhani Musa, 29 November 1979, 18 April 1980.
367. Ramadhani Mwavu, 22 January 1980.
368. Ramazani s/o Ng'wa Butu, s/o Ng'wamkai, n.d. [ca. 1967].
369. Rashidi Beleko (Vugha), 30 November 1967.
370. Rashidi Kaniki, 5 January 1980.
371. Rashidi Karata, 22 December 1979.
372. Rashidi Mjata, 18 December 1979.
373. Rashidi Sefu Salomo, 22 January 1980.
374. Rashidi Shemmea (Gare, Tongoi), 19 February 1968.
375. Rere Komba (Fwizai, Rangwi), 15 June 1968.
376. Richard Msumari, 23 December 1988.
377-79. Saguti Shekiondo (Wena), 21 July 1967; 30 July 1967; 14 February 1968.
380-82. Saidi Hamisi, 15 October 1979; 2 December 1979; 20 March 1980.
383. Saidi Kaniki, 28 December 1979.
384-89. Saidi Shembago, 8 October 1979; 2 November 1979; 27 November 1979; 24 December 1979; 7 March 1980; 3 April 1980.
390-92. Salehe Ali (Ha Shaghi, Vugha), 11 November 1967; 20 December 1967; 8 April 1968.
393. Salehe Gila, 26 December 1988.
394. Salehe Kajiru (Gare), 19 February 1968.
395-96. Salehe Kangajaka, 22 October 1979; 12 November 1979.
397. Salehe Kiluwasha, 20 March 1980.
398. Salehe Mbaruku (Bughai), 11 June 1968.
399. Salehe Mwambashi (Nkolongo), 29 March 1967.
400. Samweli Shemnkande, 8 February 1980.
401. Sefu Salomo, 22 January 1980.

402-4. Selemani Sheiza, 6 November 1979; 7 November 1979; 4 February 1980.
405-10. Semnguu Koplo (Kilole, Vugha), 7 November 1967; 16 November 1967; 27 November 1967; 19 December 1967; 3 April 1968; 29 May 1968.
411. Senmpeho (Bumba, Mshihwi), 27 December 1966.
412-6. Shebughe Kingazi Shemnkande (Mshihwi), 15 June 1966; August 1966; 17 August 1966; September 1966, text 1; September 1966, text 2.
417-19. Shechonge Kishasha (Bazo, Vugha), 11 March 1967; 29 May 1968; 28 June 1968.
420-21. Shedangilo wa Ngwilu, 3 June 1968; July 1968.
422. Shedoekuu wa Baghai (Vugha), 21 March 1967.
423. Shekulwavu s/o Kinyashi (Mlalo), July 1968.
424-25. Shekulwavu Sabuni, 5 October 1979; 28 March 1980.
426-27. Shekwavi Shemkala (Kibaazi, Vugha), March 1967; 15 November 1967.
428-30. Shemaeze wa Kishewa, 4 April 1968; 9 May 1967; 25 May 1968.
431-33. Shemakoko Kubo, 5 January 1980; 20 March 1980; 11 April 1980.
434. Shemgaa, 19 December 1979.
435-37. Shemghambie Machungi, 2 October 1979; 16 October 1979; 3 January 1980.
438-41. Shemjata, 19 October 1979; 20 March 1980; 9 April 1980; 18 April 1980.
442. Shemng'indo Mtunguja (Mayo), August 1967.
443. Shemueta Gimbika (Mshihwi), August 1966.
444. Shemweta s/o Shembilu (Mgwashi), 2 August 1967.
445. Shemzighua (Mkumbara, Mazinde), 25 December 1967.
446. Shemzighua Rupia (Kivumo), 7 February 1968.
447. Shengovi Hoza (Ubii), June 1967.
448-49. Sheshe Mbea Vintu (Mshihwi), July 1966; 6 September 1966.
450. Shevumo (Kibaazi), 20 April 1968.
451. Simoni Kaoneka (Mayo), July 1967.
452. Singano Tundwi (Ng'wangoi, Mlalo), 8 February 1968.
453. Singo Kumoso, Kijelwa, 11 June 1968.
454. Singo s/o Shambo (Kitanga Zigha), 19 June 1968.
455-56. Stefano Kingazi, 27 November 1979; 24 December 1979.
457. Stella Rashidi, 21 January 1980.
458. Steven Andrea, 4 January 1980.
459-60. Sylvano Shekalaghe (Tekwa), 27 July 1967; 2 August 1967.
461. Tamilwai Asumani, 5 January 1980.
462-63. Theodore Isaka (Vugha), 10 November 1967; 2 May 1980.
464-66. Uchungi Mbilu, 20 September 1979; 28 November 1979; 29 November 1979.
467. Umali Kuchenji (Mshihwi), July 1966.
468. Visenti wa Mshihwi, October 1966.
469. Waziri Kingazi Gia, 27 December 1979.
470. Waziri Nyeghee, Vuruni Kilwani, 1 July 1967.
471. William Christopha, 11 January 1980.
472. William Saidi Karata, 21 January 1980.

473. Yafeti Shedaffa, 15 November 1979.

474. Yeremia Kusaga (Dochi, Lushoto), April 1967.

475. Yeremia Muati, n.d.

476. Yesaia Shekifu, Ngulwi (Lushoto), 24 May 1967.

477–78. Yohana Hassani Mzalia, 4 November 1979; 22 January 1980.

479. Yohana Hoza (Vugha), May 1967.

480–91. Yonatani Abrahamu (Mshihwi), June 1966; July 1966; July 1966; 20 July 1966; September 1966, text 1; September 1966, text 2; September 1966, text 3; September 1966, text 4; 8 October 1966; 15 November 1966; 25 November 1966; 5 December 1966.

492. Yosua Hermasi (Mlalo), July 1968.

493. Yulia Musa, December 1988.

494. Yusufu Hauseni, 22 October 1979.

495–96. Zacharia Machungi, 1 November 1979; 4 January 1980.

497. Zacharia s/o Shekighenda (Tekwa), 2 August 1967.

498. Zahabu s/o Mrindoko (Kitanga), 19 June 1968.

499. Zaharia Sefu Hamisi, 14 March 1980.

500. Zaina Bakari Mzalia, 21 January 1980.

501–2. Zaina Msa Mngazija, 3 January 1980; 20 March 1980.

503. Zaina Rajabu Kupaza, 21 December 1979.

504–6. Zuberi Singano, 15 October 1979; 2 January 1980; 27 December 1988.

Bibliography

Archives Consulted

Bethel Mission, Bethel bei Bielefeld.
Church Missionary Society Archives, microfilm collection, Memorial Library, University of Wisconsin, Madison.
Rhodes House, Oxford.
Tanzania National Archives, Dar es Salaam.
United Society for the Propagation of the Gospel, archives of the Universities' Mission to Central Africa, London.
University of Dar es Salaam, Department of History. Pangani Valley History Project documents.
University of Dar es Salaam Library. East Africana Collection.

Serials Consulted

Central Africa: A Monthly Record of the Universities' Mission.
Nachrichten aus der ostafrikanischen Mission.
Mwafrika.
Tanganyika, *Parliamentary Debates.*
Tanganyika, *Provincial Annual Reports.*
Tanganyika Standard.
United Nations Trusteeship Council Documents.
Universities' Mission to Central Africa, *Bluebooks.*
Usambara-Post: Zeitung für die Nordbezirke Tanga, Pangani, Wilhelmstal.

Books, Articles, and Manuscripts

Abdallah bin Hemedi 'lAjjemy. 1962. *Habari za Wakilindi*. Ed. J. W. T. Allen and William Kimweri bin Mbago. Nairobi: East African Literature Bureau.
Abdallah bin Hemedi 'lAjjemy. 1963. *The Kilindi*. Trans. J. W. T. Allen and William Kimweri bin Mbago. Nairobi: East African Literature Bureau.
Adamson, Walter L. 1980. *Hegemony and Revolution: A Study of Antonio Gramsci's Political and Cultural Theory*. Berkeley and Los Angeles: University of California Press.
Allen, G. M., and A. Loveridge, 1927. "Mammals from the Uluguru and Usambara Mountains." *Proceedings of the Boston Society of Natural History* 38: 413–41.

Anderson, David. 1984. "Depression, Dust Bowl, Demography, and Drought: The Colonial State and Soil Conservation in East Africa During the 1930s." *African Affairs* 83:321–43.

Anderson, Perry. 1976–77. "The Antinomies of Antonio Gramsci." *New Left Review*, 100.

Anonymous. 1939. "Salt Production among the Wasambaa." *Tanganyika Notes and Records* no. 8:102–3.

Arnold, David. 1984. "Gramsci and Peasant Subalternity in India." *Journal of Peasant Studies* 11 (July): 155–77.

Asad, Talal. 1973. *Anthropology and the Colonial Encounter.* London: Ithaca Press.

Asad, Talal. 1979. "Anthropology and the Analysis of Ideology." *Man,* n.s. 14, no. 4:607–28.

Attems, Manfred. 1967. *Bauernbetriebe in tropischen Höhenlagen Ostafrikas.* (IFO Institut für Wirtschaftsforschung, Afrika Studien, Nr. 25.) Munich: Weltforum Verlag.

Attems, Manfred. 1968. "Permanent Cropping in the Usambara Mountains," in *Smallholder Farming and Smallholder Development in Tanzania,* ed. Hans Ruthenberg. Munich: Weltforum Verlag, 138–74.

Austen, Ralph. 1968. *Northwest Tanzania under German and British Rule.* New Haven and London: Yale University Press.

Baker, E. C. 1934. *Report on Social and Economic Conditions in the Tanga Province.* Dar es Salaam: Government Printer.

Barongo, E. B. M. 1966. *Mkiki Mkiki wa Siasa Tanganyika.* Dar es Salaam: East African Literature Bureau.

Bates, J. Darrell, 1950. "Democracy among the Pare." *Corona* 2:53–6.

Baumann, Oscar. 1889a. "Usambara." *Dr. A. Petermanns Mitteilungen aus Justus Perthes Geographischer Anstalt,* 25:41–47.

Baumann, Oscar 1889b. "Karte von Usambara." *Dr. A. Petermanns Mitteilungen aus Justus Perthes Geographischer Anstalt,* 25:257–61.

Baumann, Oscar. 1890. *In Deutsch-Ostafrika während des Aufstandes.* Wien und Olmutz: Eduard Holzel.

Baumann, Oscar. 1891. *Usambara und seine Nachbargebiete.* Berlin: Dietrich Reimer.

Baumann, Oscar, and Hans Meyer. 1888. "Dr. Hans Meyer's Usambara-Expedition." *Mittheilungen von Forschungsreisenden und Gelehrten aus den Deutschen Schutzgebieten* 1:199–205.

Becker. 1896. "Das Hauptopferfest der Waschambaa." *Nachrichten aus der ostafrikanischen Mission* 10:177–81.

Becker, Dr. A. 1911. *Aus Deutsch-Ostafrikas Sturm und Drangperiode.* Halle: Otto Hendel Verlag.

Behr, H. von. 1891. *Kriegsbilder aus dem Araberaufstand in Deutsch-Ostafrika.* Leipzig: Brockhaus.

Beidelman, T. O. 1964. "Correspondence: Shambala." *Tanganyika Notes and Records* 62:106–08.

Beinart, William. 1984. "Soil Erosion, Conservationism, and Ideas about Development: A Southern African Exploration, 1900–1960." *Journal of Southern African Studies* 11:52–83.

Beinart, William, and Colin Bundy. 1987. *Hidden Struggles in Rural South Africa*. London: James Currey; Berkeley and Los Angeles: University of California Press.

Bellville, Alfred. 1875–1876. "Journey to the Universities' Mission Station of Magila on the Borders of the Usambara Country." *Proceedings of the Royal Geographical Society* 20: 74–78.

Bennett, George. 1962. "An Outline History of TANU." *Makerere Journal* no. 7: 15–32.

Bennigsen, Rudolf von. 1897a. "Bericht des Finanzdirektors v. Bennigsen über seine Reise nach Westusambara und dem Pare Gebirge." *Deutsches Kolonialblatt* 8, no. 16 (15 August): 486–89.

Bennigsen, Rudolf von. 1897b. "Die Versuchsstation Kwai in Hochusambara und das Pare-Gebirge." *Der Tropenpflanzer* 1:286–87.

Berntsen, John. 1979. "Pastoralism, Raiding, and Prophets: Maasailand in the Nineteenth Century." Ph.D. Diss., University of Wisconsin, Madison.

Berry, Sara. 1985. *Fathers Work for their Sons: Accumulation, Mobility and Class Formation in an Extended Yoruba Community*. Berkeley, Los Angeles, and London: University of California Press.

Bethel Mission. 1930. *Ushimolezi: Schambala Lesebuch*. Vuga (Tanzania): Vuga Press.

Bienen, Henry. 1970. *Tanzania: Party Transformation and Economic Development*. Expanded ed. Princeton, N.J.: Princeton University Press.

Bloch, Maurice. 1977. "The Past and the Present in the Present." *Man* (n.s.) 12: 278–92.

Bloch, Maurice. 1986. *From Blessing to Violence: History and Ideology in the Circumcision Ritual of the Merina of Madagascar*. Cambridge: Cambridge University Press.

Böhler, H. 1901. "Ost-Usambara; Denkschrift zur Karte von Usambara." *Mittheilungen von Forschungsreisenden und Gelehrten aus den Deutschen Schutzgebieten* 14:40–61.

Bolton, Dianne. 1978. "Unionization and Employer Strategy: The Tanganyikan Sisal Industry, 1958–1964," in *African Labor History*, ed. Peter Gutkind, Robin Cohen, and Jean Copans. Beverly Hills: Sage Publications 175–204.

Boteler, Capt. Thomas. 1835. *Narrative of a Voyage of Discovery to Africa and Arabia performed in His Majesty's Ships Leven and Barracouta from 1821 to 1826 under the Command of Capt. F. W. Owen*. 2 vols. London: Richard Bentley.

Bourdieu, Pierre. 1977. *Outline of a Theory of Practice*. Trans. Richard Nice. Cambridge Studies in Social Anthropology, vol. 16. Cambridge: Cambridge University Press.

Braudel, Fernand. 1980. *On History*. Trans. Sarah Matthews. Chicago: University of Chicago Press.

Buchwald, Johannes. 1896. "Beitrag zur Gliederung der Vegetation von West-Usambara." *Mittheilungen von Forschungsreisenden und Gelehrten aus den Deutschen Schutzgebieten* 9:213–33.

Buchwald, Johannes. 1897. "Westusambara, die Vegetation und der wirtschaftliche Werth des Landes." *Der Tropenpflanzer* 1:58–60, 82–85, 105–8.

Burton, Richard F. 1872. *Zanzibar: City, Island, and Coast.* 2 vols. London: Tinsley Brothers.

Burton, Richard F., and J. H. Speke. 1858. "A Coasting Voyage to the Pangani River; Visit to Sultan Kimwere; and Progress of the Expedition into the Interior." *Journal of the Royal Geographical Society* 28:188–226.

Busse, Walter. 1901. "Reisebericht der Expedition nach den deutsch-ostafrikanischen Steppen." *Der Tropenpflanzer.* 5:20–32, 105–17, 299–317.

Cameron, Donald C. 1939. *My Tanganyika Service, and Some Nigeria.* London: G. Allen and Unwin.

Caulk, Richard. 1986. "'Black snake, white snake': Bahta Hagos and his revolt against Italian overrule in Eritrea, 1894," in Crummey (1986:293–309).

Cell, John, ed. 1976. *By Kenya Possessed: The Correspondence of Norman Leys and J.H. Oldham, 1918–1926.* Chicago: University of Chicago Press.

Charbonnier, G. 1969. *Conversations with Claude Lévi-Strauss.* London: Jonathon Cape.

Chidzero, B. 1961. *Tanganyika and International Trusteeship.* London: Oxford University Press.

Christen, Kommunal Sekretär. 1907. "Notizen über einige Eingeborenen-Kulturen." *Der Pflanzer* 3 (5 July 1907): 138–41.

Clanchy, M. T. 1979. *From Memory to Written Record: England 1066–1307.* Cambridge, Mass.: Harvard University Press.

Cliffe, Lionel. 1970. "Traditional Ujamaa and Modern Producer Co-operatives in Tanzania," in *Cooperatives and Rural Development in East Africa,* ed. C. G. Widstrand. New York: Africana Publishing, 39–60.

Cliffe, Lionel. 1972. "Nationalism and the Reaction to Enforced Agricultural Improvement in Tanganyika during the Colonial Period," in *Socialism in Tanzania,* vol. 1, ed. Lionel Cliffe and John Saul. Nairobi: East African Publishing House, 17–24.

Cliffe, Lionel, William L. Luttrell, and John E. Moore. 1969. "Socialist Transformation in Rural Tanzania—A Strategy for the Western Usambaras." Rural Development Paper No. 6, Rural Development Research Committee, University College Dar es Salaam.

Cole, J. S. R. and W. N. Denison. 1964. *Tanganyika: The Development of its Laws and Constitution.* London: Stevens.

Comaroff, Jean. 1985. *Body of Power, Spirit of Resistance: The Culture and History of a South African People.* Chicago and London: University of Chicago Press.

Comaroff, John L. and Jean Comaroff. 1987. "The Madman and the Migrant: Work and Labor in the Historical Consciousness of a South African People." *American Ethnologist* 14, no. 2:191–209.

Cooper, Frederick. 1977. *Plantation Slavery on the East Coast of Africa*. New Haven and London: Yale University Press.

Cooper, Frederick. 1981. "Africa and the World Economy." *African Studies Review* 24:1–86.

Cooper, Frederick. 1987. *On the African Waterfront: Urban Disorder and the Transformation of Work in Colonial Mombasa*. New Haven and London: Yale University Press.

Copland, B. D. 1933–34. "A Note on the Origin of the Mbugu with a Text." *Zeitschrift für Eingeborenen Sprachen* 24:241–45.

Copland, B. D. 1957. "Note on the Officials of the Kilindi Kingdom and the First rulers." *Journal of the East African Swahili Committee* no. 27:64–65.

Cory, Hans. 1947–48. "Jando." *Journal of the Royal Anthropological Institute*, in two parts as follows: 1947, part 1, 77:159–68; 1948, part 2, 78:81–94.

Cory, Hans. 1951. "Sambaa Law and Custom." Typescript, revised and edited by E. B. Dobson. Copy in the Cory Collection, University of Dar es Salaam.

Cory, Hans. 1956. *African Figurines: their Ceremonial Use in Puberty Rites in Tanganyika*. London: Faber.

Cory, Hans. 1962a. "The Sambaa Initiation Rite for Boys." *Tanganyika Notes and Records* nos. 58–59:2–7.

Cory, Hans. 1962b. "Tambiko (Fika)." *Tanganyika Notes and Records* nos. 58–59:274–82.

Coulson, Andrew. 1982. *Tanzania: A Political Economy*. Oxford: Clarendon Press.

Crick, Malcolm. 1982. "Anthropology of Knowledge." *Annual Review of Anthropology* 11:287–313.

Crummey, Donald, ed. 1986. *Banditry, Rebellion and Social Protest in Africa*. London and Portsmouth, N.H.: James Currey Heinemann.

Curtis, Kenneth. 1984. "Trade in Colonial Tanganyika: The Underdevelopment of an African Commercial Petite-Bourgeoisie." M.A. thesis, University of Wisconsin, Madison.

Dahlgrün, H. 1903. "Heiratsgebräuche der Schambaa." *Mitteilungen aus den deutschen Schutzgebieten* 16:219–30.

Dale, Godfrey. 1896. *An account of the principal customs and habits of the natives inhabiting the Bondei country*. London: Harrison and Sons. Also published as an article in the *Journal of the Anthropological Institute* 25 (1896): 181–239.

Dammann, Ernst. 1937–38. "Bonde-Erzählungen." *Zeitschrift für Eingeborenen-Sprachen* 28:299–318.

Dammann, Ernst. 1938. "Bonde-Märchen." *Afrikanische Studien* (part 3 of Mitteilungen des Seminars für Orientalischen Sprachen) 1938:1–16.

Dammann, Ernst. 1968. "Sprachliche Bemühungen von Betheler Missionaren um das Schambala." *Ostafrikanischen Studien*. Nürnberger Wirtschafts- and Sozialgeographische Arbeiten, vol. 8. Nuremberg: Friedrich-Alexander-Universität, 301–08.

Dar es Salaam, University, Department of History. n.d. Pangani Valley Historical Documents. "Agriculture and Politics in Meru-Arusha."

Dar es Salaam, University, Department of History. n.d. Pangani Valley Historical Documents. "Local Government and Politics in Usambara."

Dar es Salaam, University, Department of History. n.d. Pangani Valley Historical Documents. "The Lutheran Church in Usambara."

Dar es Salaam, University, Department of History. n.d. Pangani Valley Historical Documents. "Mbiru."

Dar es Salaam, University, Department of History. n.d. Pangani Valley Historical Documents. "The Mlalo Rehabilitation Scheme, 1945–1953."

Dar es Salaam, University, Department of History. n.d. Pangani Valley Historical Documents. "The Pangani-Tanga Region: Land Tenure and General Description."

Dar es Salaam, University, Department of History. n.d. Pangani Valley Historical Documents. "Pare District, 1928–1954."

Des Forges, Alison L. 1986. "'The drum is greater than the shout': the 1912 rebellion in northern Rwanda," in Crummey (1986:311–31).

Dobson, E. B. 1940. "Land Tenure of the Wasambaa." *Tanganyika Notes and Records* no. 10:1–27.

Dobson, E. B. 1954. "Comparative Land Tenure of Ten Tanganyika Tribes." *Journal of African Administration* 6, no. 2:80–91.

Döring, P. 1900a. *Lehrlingsjahre eines jungen Missionars in Deutsch-Ostafrika.* Berlin: Martin Warneck.

Döring, P. 1900b. *Hohenfriedeberg: eine Missionsstation in Usambara.* Berlin: Martin Warneck.

Döring, P. 1901. *Morgendämmerung in Deutsch-Ostafrika.* Berlin: Martin Warneck.

Döring, P. 1948. "Unter seinen Flügeln." Typescript in the Bethel Mission archives.

Dryden, Stanley. 1968. *Local Administration in Tanzania.* Nairobi: East African Publishing House.

Dundas, Sir Charles. 1955. *African Crossroads.* London: Macmillan.

Dupre, H. n.d. "Land und Volk in Usambara." Manuscript at the Bethel Mission archives.

Durkheim, E., and M. Mauss. 1963. *Primitive Classification.* Trans. and ed. Rodney Needham. London: Cohen & West.

East African Statistical Department. 1958. *Tanganyika Population Census, August 1957.* Nairobi.

Edelman, Murray. 1977. *Political Language: Words That Succeed and Policies That Fail.* New York: Academic Press.

Egger, Kurt, and Bernhard Glaeser. 1975. *Politische Ökologie der Usambara-Berge in Tanzania.* Bensheim: Kübel Stiftung.

Eichinger, A. 1911. "Über Weidedüngungsversuche in Westusambara." *Der Pflanzer* 7:698–707.

Eick, Landwirth. 1896. "Bericht über meine Reise in Kwai- und Masumbailand (Usambara) vom 12. bis 16. März 1896." *Mittheilungen von Forschungsreisenden und Gelehrten aus den Deutschen Schutzgebieten* 9:184–88.

Ekemode, G. O. 1968a. "Arab Influence in the 19th-Century Usambara." *African Historian* [Journal of the Historical Society, University of Ife] 2:14–20.

Ekemode, G. O. 1968b. "Kimweri the Great." *Tarikh* 2, no. 3:41–51.

El Zein, Abdul Hamid M. 1974. *The Sacred Meadows*. Evanston, Ill.: Northwestern University Press.

Engler, A. 1894. *Über die Gliederung Vegetation von Usambara und der angrenzenden Gebiete*. Physikalische Abhandlungen, Abhandlung 1. Berlin: Abhandlungen der Königlichen Akademie der Wissenschaften zu Berlin.

Erhardt, W. F. 1892. "Bemerkungen zu meinem Itinerar vom 22. Juni bis 4. Juli 1891 auf der Route Kwale-Mlalo." *Mittheilungen von Forschungsreisenden und Gelehrten aus den Deutschen Schutzgebieten* 5:206–10.

Fabian, Johannes. 1983. *Time and the Other: How Anthropology Makes its Object*. New York: Columbia University Press.

Farler, J. P. 1878. *The Work of Christ in Central Africa: a Letter to the Rev. H.P. Liddon*. London: Rivington's.

Farler, J. P. 1879. "The Usambara Country in East Africa." *Proceedings of the Royal Geographical Society* n.s. 1:81–97.

Farler, J. P. 1882. "Native Routes in East Africa from Pangani to the Masai Country and the Victoria Nyanza." *Proceedings of the Royal Geographical Society* n.s. 4:730–42, 776.

Farler, J. P. 1885. Letters to the editor, *The Times* (London), 16 October and 13 November.

Farler, J. P. 1889. "England and Germany in East Africa." *The Fortnightly Review*, n.s. 45:157–65.

Farriss, Nancy M. 1987. "Remembering the Future, Anticipating the Past: History, Time, and Cosmology among the Maya of Yucatan." *Comparative Studies in Society and History* 29:566–93.

Feierman, Steven. 1968. "The Shambaa," in *Tanzania before 1900*, ed. Andrew Roberts. Nairobi: East African Publishing House, 1–15.

Feierman, Steven. 1972. "Concepts of Sovereignty among the Shambaa and their relation to Political Action." Ph.D. diss., Oxford University.

Feierman, Steven. 1974. *The Shambaa Kingdom: A History*. Madison, Wis.: University of Wisconsin Press.

Feierman, Steven. 1986. "Popular Control Over the Institutions of Health: A Historical Study," in *The Professionalisation of African Medicine*, ed. Murray Last and Gordon Chavunduka. Manchester: Manchester University Press, in association with the International African Institute, 205–220.

Feierman, Steven, and John M. Janzen. Forthcoming. *The Social Basis of Health and Healing in Africa*. Berkeley and Los Angeles: University of California Press.

Femia, Joseph. 1975. "Hegemony and Consciousness in the Thought of Antonio Gramsci." *Political Studies* 23:28–48.

Femia, Joseph. 1981. *Gramsci's Political Thought: Hegemony, Consciousness, and the Revolutionary Process*. Oxford: Oxford University Press.

Fields, Karen E. 1985. *Revival and Rebellion in Colonial Central Africa*. Princeton: Princeton University Press.

Fiori, Giuseppe. 1970. *Antonio Gramsci: Life of a Revolutionary*. London: NLB.

Fleuret, Patrick C. 1978. "Farm and Market: A Study of Society and Agriculture in Tanzania." Ph.D. diss., University of California, Santa Barbara.

Fleuret, Patrick C., and Anne K. Fleuret. 1978. "Fuelwood Use in a Peasant Community: A Tanzanian Case Study." *The Journal of Developing Areas* 12: 315–22.

Foucault, Michel. 1976. *The Archaeology of Knowledge*. Trans. A. M. Sheridan Smith. New York: Harper Colophon.

Friedland, William. 1969. *Vuta Kamba: the Development of Trade Unions in Tanganyika*. Stanford, Calif.: Hoover Institution Press.

Geiger, Susan. 1982. "Umoja wa Wanawake wa Tanzania and the Needs of the Rural Poor." *African Studies Review* 25:45–65.

Geiger, Susan. 1987. "Women in Nationalist Struggle: TANU Activists in Dar es Salaam." *International Journal of African Historical Studies* 20:1–26.

Giblin, James. 1986. "Famine, Authority, and the Impact of Foreign Capital in Handeni District, Tanzania, 1840–1940." Ph.D. diss., University of Wisconsin, Madison.

Giddens, Anthony. 1979. *Central Problems in Social Theory: Action, Structure and Contradiction in Social Analysis*. Berkeley and Los Angeles: University of California Press.

Glaeser, Bernhard, ed. 1980. *Factors Affecting Land Use and Food Production*. Sozialwissenschaftliche Studien zu Internationalen Problemen, vol. 55. Saarbrücken, Fort Lauderdale: Verlag Breitenbach.

Glaeser, Bernhard. 1984. *Ecodevelopment in Tanzania*. Berlin, New York, Amsterdam: Mouton.

Glassman, Jonathon Philip. 1988. "Social Rebellion and Swahili Culture: The Response to German Conquest of the Northern Mrima, 1888–1890." Ph.D. diss., University of Wisconsin, Madison.

Gleiss, Franz. 1898. "Magili, der Herr der Heuschrecken." *Nachrichten aus der ostafrikanischen Mission* 12:128–30.

Gleiss, Franz. 1908. *Schambala-Sprachführer*. Tanga (Deutsch-Ostafrika): Kommunal Druckerei.

Gleiss, Franz. 1926. *An Meinen Hirten!* Bethel bei Bielefeld: Bethel Mission.

Gleiss, Franz. 1928. *Vor den Toren von Wuga*. Bethel bei Bielefeld: Verlag der Schriftenniederlage der Anstalt Bethel.

Glickman, Harvey. 1972. "Traditional Pluralism and Democratic Processes in Mainland Tanzania," in *Socialism in Tanzania*, vol. 1, *Politics*, ed. Lionel Cliffe and John S. Saul. Nairobi: East African Publishing House, 127–44.

Goodman, Morris. 1971. "The Strange Case of Mbugu," in *Pidginization & Creolization of Languages*, ed. Dell Hymes. Cambridge: Cambridge University Press.

Goody, Jack. 1977. *The Domestication of the Savage Mind*. Cambridge: Cambridge University Press.

Goody, Jack. 1986. *The Logic of Writing and the Organization of Society*. Cambridge: Cambridge University Press.

Goody, Jack. 1987. *The Interface Between the Written and the Oral*. Cambridge: Cambridge University Press.

Goody, Jack, Michael Cole, and Sylvia Scribner. 1977. "Writing and Formal Operations: A Case Study Among the Vai." *Africa* 47:289–304.

Goody, Jack, and Ian Watt. 1968. "The Consequences of Literacy," in *Literacy in Traditional Societies*, ed. Jack Goody. Cambridge: Cambridge University Press.

Graham, James D. 1976. "Indirect Rule: The Establishment of 'Chiefs' and 'Tribes' in Cameron's Tanganyika." *Tanzania Notes and Records* 77–78:1–9.

Gramsci, Antonio. 1957. *The Modern Prince and other writings*. New York: International Publishers.

Gramsci, Antonio. 1971. *Selections from the Prison Notebooks*. Ed. and trans. Quintin Hoare and Geoffrey Nowell Smith. New York: International Publishers.

Great Britain. "Education Policy in British Tropical Africa. Memorandum submitted to the Secretary of State for the Colonies by the Advisory Committee on Native Education in the British Tropical African Dependencies." March 1925. Cmd. 2374.

Green, E. C. 1963. "The Wambugu of Usambara." *Tanganyika Notes and Records* no. 61:175–89.

Guha, Ranajit. 1982a. "On Some Aspects of the Historiography of Colonial India," in Ranajit Guha (ed.) (1982b). *Subaltern Studies I: Writings on South Asian History and Society*. Delhi: Oxford University Press.

Guha, Ranajit, ed. 1982b. *Subaltern Studies I: Writings on South Asian History and Society*. Delhi: Oxford University Press.

Guha, Ranajit. 1983. *Elementary Aspects of Peasant Insurgency in Colonial India*. Delhi: Oxford University Press.

Guillain, Charles. 1856. *Documents sur l'Histoire, la Géographie et le Commerce de l'Afrique Orientale*. 3 volumes. Paris: Arthus Bertrand.

Guth, W. 1939. "Der Bodengott der Asu." *Africa* 12:450–59.

Gwassa, Gilbert. 1973. "The Outbreak and Development of the Maji Maji War, 1905–1907." Ph.D. diss., University of Dar es Salaam.

Haberlandt, M. 1900. "Dr. Oskar Baumann, ein Nachruf (mit Bild)." *Abhandlungen der K.K. Geographischen Gesellschaft in Wien* 2:1–20.

Halbwachs, Maurice. 1980. *The Collective Memory*. Trans. F. Ditter and V. Ditter. New York: Harper Colophon.

Heanley, R. M. 1909. *A Memoir of Edward Steere*. London: UMCA.

Heijnen, J. D. 1974. *National Policy, Foreign Aid and Rural Development: A Case Study of LIDEP's Vegetable Component in Lushoto District (Tanzania)*. Bulletin, Sociale Geografie Ontwikkelingslanden, serie 2, no. 3. Utrecht: Geographical Institute, University of Utrecht.

Heussler, Robert. 1971. *British Tanganyika: An Essay and Documents on District Administration*. Durham, N.C.: Duke University Press.

Hinsch, Richard. 1904. "Nochmals die Besiedlungsfrage in Westusambara." *Der Tropenpflanzer* 8:251–53.

Hobsbawm, E. J. 1973. "Peasants and Politics." *Journal of Peasant Studies* 1, no. 1:3–22.

Hobsbawm, E. J., and Terence Ranger. 1983. *The Invention of Tradition*. Cambridge: Cambridge University Press.

Holst, Carl. 1893a. "Der Landbau der Eingeborenen von Usambara." *Deutsche Kolonialzeitung* 6:113–14, 128–30.

Holst, Carl. 1893b. "Die Kulturen der Waschambaa." *Deutsche Kolonialzeitung* 6:23–24.

Holst, Carl. 1893c. "Zur Klimakunde von Hochusambara." *Mitteilungen aus den Deutschen Schutzgebieten* 6:93–102.

Höhnel, L. 1894. *Discovery of Lakes Rudolf and Stefanie*. Trans. Nancy Bell. 2 vols. London: Longmans Green.

Horton, Robin. 1967. "African Traditional Thought and Western Science." *Africa* 37:50–71, 155–87.

Horton, Robin. 1971. "African Conversion." *Africa* 41:85–108.

Horton, Robin. 1975. "On the Rationality of Conversion." *Africa* 45:219–35, 373–99.

Hosbach, W. 1911. "Eine Geistergeschichte." *Nachrichten aus der ostafrikanischen Mission* (25): 209–13.

Hosbach, W. 1925. *Abraham Kilua, der schwarze Vikar von Neu-Bethel*. 2d ed. Bethel bei Bielefeld: Bethel Mission.

Hountoundji, P. 1977. *Sur la Philosophie Africaine*. Paris: Maspero.

Hoza, Yohana. n.d. "Sheuta: Dini ya Kishambala, au Miviko ya Kishambala." Manuscript.

Hozza, J. J. n.d. [1969] "The Hoza Rebellion and After: A Study in Innovation." Political Science Dissertation [B.A.], University of Dar es Salaam.

Hubert, H., and M. Mauss. 1929. "Étude sommaire de la représentation du temps dans la religion et la magie," Pp. 189–229 in H. Hubert and M. Mauss, Mélanges d'histoire des religions. Paris: Librairie Félix Alcan, 189–229.

Iliffe, John. 1967. "The organization of the Maji Maji rebellion." *Journal of African History* 8, no. 3:485–512.

Iliffe, John. 1969. *Tanganyika under German Rule, 1905–1912*. Cambridge: Cambridge University Press.

Iliffe, John. 1979. *A Modern History of Tanganyika*. Cambridge: Cambridge University Press.

Isaacman, Allen. 1990. "Peasants and Rural Social Protest in Africa." *African Studies Review* 29 (fall 1990).

Isaacman, Allen, in collaboration with Barbara Isaacman. 1976. *The Tradition of Resistance in Mozambique: the Zambesi Valley, 1850–1921*. Berkeley and London: University of California Press.

Isaacman, Allen, and Barbara Isaacman. 1977. "Resistance and Collaboration in Southern and Central Africa, c.1850–1920." *International Journal of African Historical Studies* 10, no. 1:31–62.

Isaacman, Allen, Michael Stephen, Yussuf Adam, Maria Joao Homen, Eugenio Macamo, and Augustinho Pililao. 1980. "'Cotton is the Mother of Poverty': Peasant Resistance to Enforced Cotton Production in Mozambique, 1938–1961." *International Journal of African Historical Studies* 13, no. 4:581–615.

Janzen, John M. 1982. *Lemba 1650–1930: A Drum of Affliction in Africa and the New World*. New York: Garland.

Johanssen, Ernst. n.d. Führung und Erfahrung in 40 jährigem Missionsdienst. Vols. 1 and 2. Bethel bei Bielefeld: Verlagshandlung der Anstalt Bethel.

Johanssen, Ernst. 1899. "Der Riese Hundju." *Nachrichten aus der ostafrikanischen Mission* 13: 203–4.

Johanssen, Ernst, and Döring, Paul. 1914–1915. "Das Leben der Schambala, beleuchtet durch ihre Sprichwörter." *Zeitschrift für Kolonialsprachen* 5:137–50, 190–226, 306–18.

Johnston, H. H. 1886. *The Kilima-Njaro Expedition*. London: Kegan Paul Trench.

Johnston, Keith. 1879. "Notes of a Trip from Zanzibar to Usambara, in February and March 1879." *Proceedings of the Royal Geographical Society* n.s. 1:545–64, 616.

Kaerger, Dr. Karl. 1892. *Tangaland und die Kolonisation Deutsch-Ostafrikas*. Berlin: Herman Walther.

Kähler-Meyer, E. 1962. "Studien zur tonalen Struktur der Bantusprachen." *Afrika und Uebersee* 46:1–42.

Kallenberg, Friedrich. 1892. *Auf dem Kriegspfad gegen die Massai*. Munich: Beck.

Kaniki, M. H. Y. (ed.). 1979. *Tanzania under Colonial Rule*. London: Longman.

Kaniki, M. H. Y. n.d. "What Was Behind the Usambara-Digo Lutheran Church (U.D.L.C.) Conflict, 1961–1963." Duplicated. University of Dar es Salaam.

Kaniki, Marko. 1903. "Bestattung der grossem Kilindi." *Nachrichten aus der ostafrikanischen Mission* 17:190–91.

Karasek, A. 1908. "Tabakspfeifen und Rauchen bei den Waschambaa." *Globus*, 2:285–287.

Karasek, A. 1911–24. "Beiträge zur Kenntnis der Waschambaa." Ed. August Eichhorn, for *Baessler-Archiv*, as follows: 1911, part 1, 1:155–222; 1913, part 2, 3:69–131; 1918–22, part 3, 7:56–98. 1923–24, part 4, 8:1–53.

Kersten, Otto. 1869. *Baron Carl Claus von der Decken's Reisen in Ost-Afrika in den Jahren 1859 bis 1861*. Vol. 1. Leipzig und Heidelberg: E. F. Winter'sche Verlagshandlung.

Kimambo, Isaria N. 1969. *A Political History of the Pare of Tanzania, c. 1500–1900*. Nairobi: East African Publishing House.

Kimambo, Isaria N. 1971. *Mbiru: Popular Protest in Colonial Tanzania*. Historical Association of Tanzania, Paper No. 9. Nairobi: East African Publishing House.

Kimambo, Isaria N. Forthcoming. *Capital Penetration in the Pare District of Northeastern Tanzania, 1860–1960*. London: James Currey.

Kirk, John. 1873. "Visit to the Coast of Somali-land." *Proceedings of the Royal Geographical Society* 17:340–41.

Koch, Robert. 1953. "Report on West Usambara from the Point of View of Health (5/8/1898)." *Tanganyika Notes and Records* no. 2:67–71.

Kocher, James Edward. 1976. "A Micro-Economic Analysis of the Determinants of Human Fertility in Rural Northeastern Tanzania." Ph.D. diss., Michigan State University.

Koritschoner, Hans. 1936. "Details of a Native Medical Treatment." *Tanganyika Notes and Records* no. 2:67–71.

Krapf, Johann Ludwig. 1860. *Travels, Researches, and Missionary Labours, during an Eighteen Years' Residence in Eastern Africa.* London: Trübner and Co. A translated and abridged version of Krapf 1964.

Krapf, Johann Ludwig. 1863. An excerpt from Krapf's journal in the *United Methodist Free Churches Magazine*, 6:300.

Krapf, Johann Ludwig 1964. *Reisen in Ostafrika.* Stuttgart: Brockhaus. A reprint of the edition of 1858.

Kurtze, Dr. Bruno. 1913. *Die Deutsch-Ostafrikanische Gesellschaft.* Jena: Gustav Fischer.

Lackner, Helen. 1973. "Social Anthropology and Indirect Rule. The Colonial Administration and Anthropology in Eastern Nigeria: 1920–1940," in Asad (1973: 293–309).

LangHeinrich, F. n.d. "Wie ich Missionar wurde." Typescript in the Bethel Mission archives.

LangHeinrich, F. 1902. "Vergangene Pracht." *Nachrichten aus der ostafrikanischen Mission* 16:73–78.

LangHeinrich, F. 1903. "Die Waschambala," in *Rechtsverhältnisse von eingeborenen Völkern in Afrika und Ozeanien*, ed. S. R. Steinmetz. Berlin: Verlag von Julius Springer, 218–267.

LangHeinrich, F. 1913. "Die Entwickelung des Verkehrs in Westusambara." *Nachrichten aus der ostafrikanischen Mission* 27:7–12.

LangHeinrich, F. 1921. *Schambala-Wörterbuch.* ("Abhandlungen des Hamburgischen Kolonialinstituts," Band 43.) Hamburg: L. Friedrichsen.

Latham, R. G. 1862. *Comparative Philology.* London: Walton and Maberly.

Leach, E. R. 1954. *Political Systems of Highland Burma: A Study of Kachin Social Structure.* London: G. Bell and Sons.

Lemenye, Justin. 1953. *Maisha ya Sameni Ole Kivasis, yaani Justin Lemenye*, ed. H. A. Fosbrooke. Nairobi: East African Literature Bureau.

Lerner, Gerda. 1986. *The Creation of Patriarchy.* New York and Oxford: Oxford University Press.

Lévi-Strauss, Claude. 1966. *The Savage Mind.* Chicago: University of Chicago Press. Translated from the French, *La Pensée Sauvage*, Paris: Plon. 1962.

Liebert. 1897. "Bericht über die Inspektionsreise des Kaiserlichen Gouverneurs." 8(1 June 1897): 313–19.

Lonsdale, John. 1968. "Some Origins of Nationalism in East Africa." *Journal of African History* 9:119–46.

Lonsdale, John. 1981. "States and Social Processes in Africa: A Historiographical Survey." *African Studies Review* 24:139–225.

Lonsdale, John. 1986. "Kikuyu Political Thought and the Ideologies of Mau Mau." Paper for the Institute of Commonwealth Studies Seminar, University of London, 16 January 1986.

McCarthy, D. M. P. 1982. *Colonial Bureaucracy and Creating Underdevelopment: Tanganyika, 1919–1940.* Ames: Iowa State University Press.

McGowan, Patrick J., and Patrick Bolland. 1971. *The Political and Social Elite of Tanzania: An Analysis of Social Background Factors.* Eastern African Studies, vol. 3. New York: Syracuse University, Program of Eastern African Studies, Maxwell School of Citizenship and Public Affairs.

Maguire, G. Andrew. 1969. *Toward "Uhuru" in Tanzania.* Cambridge: Cambridge University Press.

Makao Makuu ya TANU ya Wilaya ya Lushoto. n.d. [1975]. *TANU na Wananchi Lushoto.* Soni [Lushoto]: The Vuga Press.

Malinowski, Bronislaw. 1929. "Practical Anthropology." *Africa* 2:22–38.

Malinowski, Bronislaw. 1930. "The Rationalization of Anthropology and Administration." *Africa* 3:405–430.

Marks, Shula. 1986. "Class, Ideology and the Bambatha Rebellion," in Crummey 1986:351–72.

Martin, Robert. 1976. *Personal Freedom and the Law in Tanzania: A Study of Socialist State Administration.* Nairobi: Oxford University Press.

Mason, H. 1952. "Progress in Pare." *Corona* 4:212–19.

Matango, Reuben R. 1979. "The Role of Agencies for Rural Development in Tanzania: A Case Study of the Lushoto Integrated Development Project," in *African Socialism in Practice*, ed. Andrew Coulson. Nottingham: Spokesman, 158–72.

Meeussen, A. E. 1955. "Tonunterschiede als Reflexe von Quantitätsunterschieden im Schambala," in *Afrikanistische Studien*, ed. J. Lukas, Berlin: Akademie Verlag, 154–56.

Meillassoux, Claude. 1973. "The Social Organisation of the Peasantry: The Economic Basis of Kinship." *Journal of Peasant Studies* 1, no. 1:81–90.

Meillassoux, Claude. 1975. *Femmes, greniers et capitaux.* Paris: F. Maspero.

Meinhof, Carl. 1904–06. "Linguistische Studien in Ostafrika." *Afrikanische Studien* (part 3 of Mitteilungen des Seminars für Orientalischen Sprachen); part 2, 1904:217–236; part 8, 1906:278–84; part 10, 1906:294–323.

Meyer, Hans. 1900. *Der Kilimanjaro: Reisen und Studien.* Berlin: Dietrich Reimer.

Meyer, Hans. 1909. *Das Deutsche Kolonialreich.* Vol. 1. Leipzig und Wien: Verlag des Bibliographischen Instituts.

Meyer, Hans, and Oskar Baumann. 1888. "Dr. Hans Meyer's Usambara Expedition." *Mitteilungen aus den Deutschen Schutzgebieten* 1:200–205.

Mhando, Helen P. 1977. "Capitalist Penetration and the Growth of Peasant Agriculture in Korogwe District, 1920–1975." M.A. thesis, University of Dar es Salaam.

Mhina, A. K. n.d. "Agricultural Change in Korogwe District–Bungu Division. Study Case. From Precolonial Period to 1974." [Undergraduate] Dissertation, Department of History. University of Dar es Salaam.

Mihalyi, Louis. 1969. "The Usambara Highlands: A Geographical Study of the Changes during the German Period, 1885–1914." Ph.D. diss., University of California, Los Angeles.

Milne, G. 1937. "Soil Type and Soil Management in Relation to Plantation Agriculture in East Usambara." *The East African Agricultural Journal* 3 (July): 7–20.

Milne, G. 1944. "Soils in Relation to the Native Population in West Usambara." *Geography* 29:107–13.

Mintz, Sidney W. 1974. *Caribbean Transformations*, Chicago: Aldine.

Mintz, Sidney W. 1979. "Slavery and the Rise of Peasantries." *Historical Reflections* 6, no. 1:213–53.

Mishambi, G. 1978. "Peasantry Under Capitalism: A Case Study of the West Lake Region Tanzania." M.A. thesis in history, University of Dar es Salaam.

Mitchell, Philip. 1930. "The Anthropologist and the Practical Man: A Reply and A Question." *Africa* 3:217–23.

Mitchell, Sir Philip. 1954. *African Afterthoughts*. London: Hutchinson.

Mnkondo, I. H. 1968. "Politics in Usambara." Political Science diss. [B.A.], University College Dar es Salaam.

Molloy, Judith. 1970. "Some Aspects of the Implementation of 'Ujamaa' in Lushoto District." Seminar Paper, University of Dar es Salaam, 27 August.

Molloy, Judith. 1971. "Political Communication in Lushoto District, Tanzania." Ph.D. diss., University of Kent at Canterbury.

Moore, Barrington. 1966. *Social Origins of Dictatorship and Democracy: Lord and Peasant in the Making of the Modern World*. Boston: Beacon Press.

Moore, John E. 1971. "Tanzania's Overcrowded Land of Bananas." *The Geographical Magazine*. 43:624–29.

Moreau, R. E. 1939–42. "Bird-Nomenclature in an East African Area." *Bulletin of the School of Oriental and African Studies* 10:998–1006.

Moreau, R. E. 1940–41. "Bird Names used in Coastal North-Eastern Tanganyika Territory." *Tanganyika Notes and Records* 10:47–72; no. 11:47–60.

Moreau, R. E. 1941. "Suicide by 'Breaking the Cooking Pot.'" *Tanganyika Notes and Records* no. 12:49–50.

Mouffe, Chantal. 1979a. *Gramsci and Marxist Theory*. London: Routledge & Kegan Paul.

Mouffe, Chantal. 1979b. "Hegemony and Ideology in Gramsci," in *Gramsci and Marxist Theory*, ed. Chantal Mouffe. London: Routledge & Kegan Paul, 168–204.

Mudimbe, V. 1985. "African Gnosis, Philosophy and the Order of Knowledge: An Introduction." *African Studies Review* 28:149–233.

Mueller, Susanne. 1981. "The Historical Origins of Tanzania's Ruling Class." *Canadian Journal of African Studies* 15:459–97.

Müller, F. F. 1959. *Deutschland – Zanzibar – Ostafrika: Geschichte einer deutschen Kolonialeroberung.: 1884–1890*. Berlin: Rütten & Loening.

Mwakyosa, D. A. 1947. "The Rule of Witch-Craft among the Wasambaa." *Makerere* 1:121–23.

Myres, J. L. 1929. "The Science of Man in the Service of the State." *Journal of the Royal Anthropological Institute of Great Britain and Ireland* 59:19–52.

Mytton, G. L. 1976. "The Role of the Mass Media in Nation-Building in Tanzania." Ph.D. diss., Faculty of Economic and Social Studies, Manchester University.

Needham, Rodney. 1972. *Belief, Language, and Experience*. Oxford: Basil Blackwell.

Needham, Rodney. 1975. "Polythetic Classification: Convergences and Consequences." *Man* n.s. 10:349–69.

Neubaur, Paul. 1902. "Die Besiedlungsfähigkeit von Westusambara." *Der Tropen-pflanzer* 6:496–513.

New, Charles. 1873. *Life, Wanderings, and Labours in Eastern Africa.* London: Hodder and Stoughton.

New, Charles. 1875. "Journey from the Pangani, via Wadigo, to Mombasa." *Proceedings of the Royal Geographical Society* 19:317–23.

Nyerere, Julius K. 1960. "Tanganyika Today: the Nationalist View." *International Affairs* 36, no. 1 (January): 43–47.

Nyerere, Julius K. 1967. *Freedom and Unity; Uhuru na Umoja: A Selection of Writings and Speeches, 1952–1965.* London: Oxford University Press.

O'Barr, Jean. 1975–76. "Pare Women: A Case of Political Involvement." *Rural Africana* no. 29:121–34.

Orde-Browne, Major G. St. J. 1946. *Labour Conditions in East Africa.* Colonial Office. Colonial No. 193. London.

Ortner, Sherry. 1984. "Theory in Anthropology Since the Sixties." *Comparative Studies in Society and History* 26 no. 1:126–66.

Owen, W. F. W. 1833. *Narrative of Voyages to Explore the Shores of Africa, Arabia, and Madagascar.* Ed. Heaton Bowstead Robinson. London: Richard Bentley.

Paasche, Hermann. 1906. *Deutsch-Ostafrika.* Berlin: C. A. Schwetschke und Sohn.

Packard, Randall M. 1981. *Chiefship and Cosmology: An Historical Study of Political Competition.* Bloomington: Indiana University Press.

Parkin, David. 1982. "Introduction," pp. xi-li in *Semantic Anthropology*, ed. David Parkin. A.S.A. Monograph 22. London and New York: Academic Press.

Parkin, David. 1984. "Political Language." *Annual Review of Anthropology* 13: 345–65.

Parsons, Talcott. 1963. "On the Concept of Political Power." *Proceedings of the American Philosophical Society* 107:232–62.

Peel, J. D. Y. 1983. *Ijeshas and Nigerians: The Incorporation of a Yoruba Kingdom, 1890s–1970s.* Cambridge: Cambridge University Press.

Perham, Margery. 1976. *East African Journey.* London: Faber and Faber.

Peters, Karl. 1895. *Das Deutsch-Ostafrikanische Schutzgebiet.* Munich: R. Oldenbourg.

Prain, R. L. 1956, "The Stabilization of Labour in the Rhodesian Copper Belt." *African Affairs* 55 (October): 305–12.

Pratt, Cranford. 1978. *The Critical Phase in Tanzania, 1945–1968: Nyerere and the Emergence of a Socialist Strategy.* Nairobi: Oxford University Press.

Przeworski, Adam. 1980. "Material Bases of Consent: Economics and Politics in a Hegemonic System." *Political Power and Social Theory* 1:21–66.

Ranger, Terence. 1968. "Connexions between 'Primary Resistance' Movements and Modern Mass Nationalism in East and Central Africa." Parts 1, 2. *Journal of African History* 9, no. 3:437–53; 9, no. 4:631–41.

Ranger, Terence. 1983. "The Invention of Tradition in Colonial Africa," in Hobsbawm and Ranger (1983:211–62).

Ranger, Terence. 1985. *Peasant Consciousness and Guerrilla War in Zimbabwe: A Comparative Study.* London: James Currey; Los Angeles and Berkeley: University of California Press.

Riese, F. n.d. "Die Opfer der Schambala." Manuscript at the Bethel Mission archives, Bethel bei Bielefeld.

Riese, F. 1911. *Etwas über die Mysterien der Schambala*. Bethel bei Bielefeld: Bethel Mission.

Rodney, Walter. 1972. *How Europe Underdeveloped Africa*. London and Dar es Salaam: Bogle-L'Ouverture Publications and Tanzania Publishing House.

Rodney, Walter. 1983. "Migrant Labour and the Colonial Economy," in Rodney, Tambila, and Sago (1983:4–28).

Rodney, Walter, Kapepwa Tambila, and Laurent Sago. 1983. *Migrant Labour in Tanzania during the Colonial Period: Case Studies of Recruitment and Conditions of Labour in the Sisal Industry*. Arbeiten aus dem Institut für Afrika-Kunde No. 45. Hamburg: Institut für Afrika-Kunde.

Roehl, Karl. 1911. *Versuch einer systematischen Grammatik der Schambalasprache*. ("Abhandlungen des Hamburgischen Kolonialinstituts," Band 2.) Hamburg: L. Friedrichsen.

Rösler. 1906. "Die Furcht im Leben des Schambala." *Nachrichten aus der Ostafrikanischen Mission* 20:107–14, 121–26, 139–44.

Rösler, Frau Missionar O., and Franz Gleiss. 1912. *Schambala-Grammatik*. ("Archiv für das Studium deutscher Kolonialsprachen," Band 13.) Berlin: Georg Reimer.

Rogers, Susan Geiger. 1972. "The Search for Political Focus on Kilimanjaro: A History of Chagga Politics, 1916–1952, with Special Reference to the Cooperative Movement and Indirect Rule." Ph.D. diss., University of Dar es Salaam.

Rude, George. 1980. *Ideology and Popular Protest*. London: Lawrence and Wishart.

Sahlins, Marshall. 1981. *Historical Metaphors and Mythical Realities: Structure in the Early History of the Sandwich Islands Kingdom*. Association for Social Anthropology in Oceania Special Publications No. 1. Ann Arbor, Michigan: University of Michigan Press.

Sahlins, Marshall. 1985. *Islands of History*. Chicago and London: University of Chicago Press.

Samassa, Paul. 1909. *Die Besiedlung Deutsch-Ostafrikas*. Leipzig: Verlag Deutsche Zukunft.

Sangai, G. R. Williams. 1963. *Dictionary of Native Plant Names in the Bondei, Shambaa, and Zigua Languages with their English and Botanical Equivalents*. Nairobi: East African Herbarium.

Saul, John S. 1972. "Nationalism, Socialism, and Tanzanian History," pp. 65–75 in *Socialism in Tanzania*, ed. Lionel Cliffe and John S. Saul. Vol. 1, *Politics*. Nairobi: East African Publishing House, 65–75.

Saul, John S. 1973. "Marketing Co-operatives in a Developing Country: The Tanzanian Case," in *Socialism in Tanzania*, ed. Lionel Cliffe and John S. Saul. Vol. 2, *Policies*. Nairobi and Dar es Salaam: East African Publishing House, 141–52.

Saul, John S., and Roger Woods. 1971. "African Peasantries," pp. 103–114 in *Peasants and Peasant Societies: Selected Readings*, ed. Teodor Shanin. Harmondsworth, Middlesex: Penguin, 103–14.

Saussure, Ferdinand de. 1966. *Course in General Linguistics.* New York: McGraw-Hill.

Schmidt, Rochus. 1892. *Geschichte des Araberaufstandes in Ost-Afrika.* Frankfurt a. Oder: Trowitzsch.

Schönmeier, Hermann W. 1977. *Agriculture in Conflict — The Shambaa Case.* Bensheim: Kübel Foundation.

Scott, James C. 1976. *The Moral Economy of the Peasant.* New Haven and London: Yale University Press.

Scott, James C. 1985. *Weapons of the Weak: Everyday Forms of Peasant Resistance.* New Haven and London: Yale University Press.

Sefu, Lukas. 1911. *Lukas Sefu: ein schwarzer Prediger der Gnade.* Compiled by Franz Gleiss from the letters and writings of Lukas Sefu. Bethel bei Bielefeld: Verlag der Evangelischen Missionsgesellschaft für Deutsch-Ostafrika.

Seidel, A. 1895a. "Beiträge zur Kenntnis der Schambalasprache in Usambara." *Zeitschrift für afrikanische und oceanische Sprachen* 1:34–82, 105–117.

Seidel, A. 1895b. *Handbuch der Schambalasprache in Usambara.* Dresden-Leipzig: A. Köhler.

Seidel, A. 1896. "Eine Erzählung der Wa-Schambala." *Zeitschrift für afrikanische und oceanische Sprachen* 2:145–49.

Sheridan, Alan. 1980. *Michel Foucault: The Will to Truth.* London and New York: Tavistock.

Sheriff, Abdul. 1987. *Slaves, Spices & Ivory in Zanzibar: Integration of an East African Commercial Empire into the World Economy, 1770–1873.* London: James Currey; Nairobi: Heinemann; Dar es Salaam: Tanzania Publishing House; Athens: Ohio University Press.

Shils, Edward. 1968. "Intellectuals." *International Encyclopedia of the Social Sciences,* vol. 7, 399–415. New York: Macmillan.

Shils, Edward. 1972. *The Intellectuals and the Powers and Other Essays.* Chicago and London: University of Chicago Press.

Shivji, Issa. 1980. "Rodney and Radicalism of the Hill, 1966–1974." *Maji Maji* no. 43:29–39.

Shivji, Issa. 1986. *Law, State and the Working Class in Tanzania.* London, Portsmouth, N.H.: Heinemann; Dar es Salaam: Tanzania Publishing House.

Steere, E. 1867. *Collections for a Handbook of the Shambala Language.* Zanzibar: Central African Mission Press.

Stern, Steve J. 1987. "New Approaches to the Study of Peasant Rebellion and Consciousness: Implications of the Andean Experience," in his *Resistance, Rebellion, and Consciousness in the Andean Peasant World, 18th to 20th Centuries.* Madison, Wis.: University of Wisconsin Press.

Stock, Brian. 1983. *The Implications of Literacy.* Princeton: Princeton University Press.

Storch, E. 1895a. "Sitten, Gebräuche und Rechtspflege bei den Bewohnern Usambara und Pares." *Mitteilungen aus den Deutschen Schutzgebieten* 8:310–31.

Storch, E. 1895b. "Ueber das Strafverfahren gegen des Jumben Mputa von Wuga und über die Einsetzung des Jumben Kipanga von Handei in Wuga." *Nachrichten aus der ostafrikanischen Mission* 9:139–40.

Storch, E. 1896. "Die Wakilindi und Waschambaa." *Nachrichten aus der ost-afrikanischen Mission* 10:22–28.

Swainson, Nicola. 1980. *The Development of Corporate Capitalism in Kenya, 1918–1977.* London: Heinemann.

Sykes, Colonel. 1853. "Notes on the Possessions of the Imaun of Muskat, on the Climate and Productions of Zanzibar, and on the Prospects of African Discovery from Mombas." *Journal of the Royal Geographical Society.* 23:101–19.

TANU na Wananchi Lushoto. 1975. See Makao Makuu ya TANU ya Wilaya ya Lushoto (1975).

Tambila, Anse. 1974. "A History of the Tanga Sisal Labour Force: 1936–64." M.A. diss. in history, University of Dar es Salaam.

Tanganyika. Department of Education. ca. 1953. *Provisional Syllabus of Instruction for Middle Schools.* Dar es Salaam: Government Printer.

Tanganyika. Department of Education. 1955. *Provisional Syllabus of Instruction for Secondary Schools. 1955.* Dar es Salaam: Government Printer.

Taylor, J. Clagett. 1963. *The Political Development of Tanganyika.* Stanford and London: Stanford University Press.

Taussig, Michael. 1980. *The Devil and Commodity Fetishism in South America.* Chapel Hill: University of North Carolina Press.

Temu, A. J. and Bonaventure Swai. 1981. "The Intellectual and the State in Postcolonial Africa: The Tanzanian Case." *Social Praxis* 8:3–4, 25–52.

Thompson, A. R. 1968. "Ideas Underlying British Colonial Education Policy in Tanganyika," in *Tanzania: Revolution by Education,* ed. Idrian Resnick. Nairobi: Longmans, 15–32.

Thompson, Graham. 1984. "The Merchants and Merchandise of Religious Change: The New Orthodoxies of Religious Belief and Economic Behaviour amongst the Shambala People of Mlalo, North East Tanzania." Ph.D. diss., Clare Hall College, Cambridge.

Thornton, Richard. 1865. "Notes on a Journey to Kilima-ndjaro made in the Company of the Baron von der Decken." *Journal of the Royal Geographical Society* 35:15–21.

Throup, David W. 1988. *Economic and Social Origins of Mau Mau.* London: James Currey; Nairobi: Heinemann; Athens: Ohio University Press.

Thurnwald, Richard. 1935. *Black and White in East Africa.* London: G. Routledge and Sons.

Vacca, Giuseppe. 1982. "Intellectuals and the Marxist Theory of the State," in *Approaches to Gramsci,* ed. Anne Showstack Sassoon. London: Writers and Readers, 37–69.

Vickers-Haviland, L. A. W. 1938. "The Making of an African Historical Film." *Tanganyika Notes and Records* no. 6:82–86.

Vosseler. 1904–06. "Die Wanderheuschrecken in Usambara im Jahre 1903/1904." *Berichte über Land- und Forstwirtschaft* 2:291–374.

Warburg, O. 1894. "Die Kulturpflanzen Usambaras." *Mittheilungen von Forschungsreisenden und Gelehrten aus den Deutschen Schutzgebieten* 7:131–99.

Ward, Gertrude. 1898. *The Life of Charles Alan Smythies.* Ed. Francis Russell. London: UMCA.

Weber, Max. 1964. *The Theory of Social and Economic Organization*. Translated by A. M. Henderson and Talcott Parsons. Glencoe, Ill.: The Free Press of Glencoe.

Weber, Max. 1978. *Economy and Society: An Outline of Interpretive Sociology*. Ed. Guenther Roth and Claus Wittich. Berkeley, Los Angeles, and London: University of California Press.

Werner, Alice. 1933. *Myths and Legends of the Bantu*. London: Harrap.

Who's Who in East Africa, 1963–1964. 1964. Nairobi: Marco Surveys, Ltd.

Who's Who in East Africa, 1965–1966. 1966. Nairobi: Marco Publishers (Africa).

Who's Who in East Africa, 1967–1968. 1968. Nairobi: Marco Publishers (Africa).

Williams, Gwyn. 1960. "The Concept of Egemonia in the Thought of Antonio Gramsci." *Journal of the History of Ideas* 21:586–99.

Williams, Raymond. 1977. *Marxism and Literature*. Oxford: Oxford University Press.

Wilson, George Herbert. 1936. *The History of the Universities Mission to Central Africa*. London: UMCA.

Wilson, Gordon M. 1966. "The African Elite," in *The Transformation of East Africa*, ed. Stanley Diamond and Fred G. Burke. New York and London: Basic Books.

Winans, Edgar V. 1962. *Shambala: The Constitution of a Traditional State*. London: Routledge & Kegan Paul.

Winans, Edgar V. 1964. "The Shambala Family" in *The Family Estate in Africa*, ed. Robert F. Gray and P. H. Gulliver. London: Routledge & Kegan Paul., 35–61.

Wohlrab, Karl. n.d. "Die Religion der Schambala und die christliche Missionspredigt." Manuscript at the Bethel Mission archives.

Wohlrab, Karl. 1929. *Die christliche Missionspredigt unter den Schambala*. Tübingen: Buchdruckerei der Tübinger Studentenhilfe.

Wohlrab, Paul. 1913. "Ein Neuer Dämonen-Kultus in Usambara." *Nachrichten aus der ostafrikanischen Mission* 27:186–89.

Wohlrab, Paul. 1915. *Usambara: Werden und Wachsen einer heidenchristlichen Gemeinde in Deutsch-Ostafrika*. Bethel bei Bielefeld: Verlagshandlung der Anstalt Bethel bei Bielefeld.

Wohlrab, Paul. 1918. "Das Recht der Schambala." *Archiv für Anthropologie* 44:160–81.

Wohltmann, F. 1898. *Deutsch-Ostafrika*. Schöneberg-Berlin: F. Telge.

Wohltmann, F. 1902. "Die Aussichten des Kaffeebaues in den Usambara-Bergen." *Der Tropenpflanzer* 6:612–16.

Wolf, Eric. 1966. *Peasants*. Englewood Cliffs, N.J.: Prentice-Hall.

Woodward, H. W. 1913. "Islam in Korogwe Archdeaconry." *Central Africa* 31: 105–108.

Woodward, H. W. 1925. "Bondei Folktales." *Folk-Lore* 36:178–85, 263–78, 366–86.

Young, Roland, and Henry Fosbrooke. 1960. *Land and Politics among the Luguru of Tanganyika*. London: Routledge & Kegan Paul.

Index

www.ingramcontent.com/pod-product-compliance
Lightning Source LLC
Chambersburg PA
CBHW020603270326
41927CB00005B/154